Neither Palaces Nor Prisons

Constitutions of Order Among the Nuer

Wal Duany

Published by
South Sudanese Friends International, Inc.   www.southsudanfriends.org

Cover photo courtesy of Julia Aker Duany

The original draft of *Neither Palaces Nor Prisons* was submitted by Wal Duany to the Faculty of the Graduate School in partial fulfillment of the requirements for the degree Doctor of Philosophy in the Joint Ph.D., Program of the Department of Political Science and School of Public and Environmental Affairs, Indiana University, Bloomington, Indiana, June 1992.

ISBN-13:978-1479152759
ISBN-10:1479152757
Neither Palaces Nor Prisons is available on kindle.amazon.com

What Future for our Little Ones?

They see light where the river gleaming,
rings sluggishly and
winds through hill, plain, and desert.
The mind of the little ones;
what they see,
so their thoughts will be.

This land, is she the source of time?
This river, the source of Life
which has placed them awake upon it breasts?

Who can see the green earth anymore?
Who could imagine her fields in the sunshine,
unworn by the hoe?
Who now thinks as they thought:
the ones who then roamed this land:
her vigorous warrior sons.

Julia Aker Duany

Contents

List of Illustrations

Preface

This book is about the constitution of order among the Nuer as an acephalous, self-governing society. It speaks also for many acephalous societies in Africa and elsewhere in the world. The motivation for writing this book is my desire to better understand the institutions of an acephalous polity and how they work.

Democracy in America by Alexis de Tocqueville is a classic study of a self-governing society. Tocqueville's writings are a strong influence on my own work, and on the work of many scholars throughout the world. One of them, Barbara Allen (*Tocqueville, covenant, and the democratic revolution: harmonizing earth with heaven*, Lexington Books, 2005), wrote:

"Readers today who have known fascism and totalitarianism may now admit the unwelcome truth that equality can exist without political liberty, while ignoring other equally sobering conclusions: 'democracy' reduced to corporate capitalism hardly translates into liberation; religious belief may so greatly influence social structure and political culture as to make liberal democracy and a people's self-determination incongruous goals; voluntary associations may reflect nothing but selfishness taken to the level of 'collective individualism'; and a jurisprudence of rights without a jurisprudence of obligation cannot sustain meaningful expressions of liberty for individuals or cultures. These are not the statements of a political partisan. After the general idea of virtue, there was, Tocqueville said, no higher principle than right; it was 'the *spirit of religion* and the *spirit of liberty*' that combined to make self-government a reality in America."

I have personally experienced the sobering conclusions Allen enumerates. In the Republic of Sudan during 1977 – 1983, then President Ja'far Mohammed Nimeiri embarked upon rule that imposed Islamic program of democratic centralism. Nimeiri's rule was one party rule that imposed Islamic Sharia. When the South protested, leaders were arrested and detained for months without charge. I was one of them. I opposed declaring Islam as the national religion and also opposed the arbitrary and unconstitutional division of the Southern Sudan into smaller regions. After my release from detention, my life was insecure and there was no prospect for useful activities or any prospect of a better future for my children, my wife, and the people of Southern Sudan.

Bob McCandliss, Director of USAID in Juba (1976 – 1984) had followed very closely developments in the country. I contacted him and said I would like to continue my Ph.D. program, which I suspended nine years earlier to serve the people of the Sudan in government after the first civil war. Since I did not have anything useful to do, I was ready to return to my studies. Bob connected me with Vincent Ostrom at Indiana University, Bloomington, Indiana. I received a letter from Dr. Ostrom inviting me to join the Workshop in Political Theory and Policy Analysis. Vincent Ostrom's invitation gave a perfect opportunity to commence a joint Ph.D. program in the Department of Political Science and in the School of Public and Environmental Affairs.

The process of completing my studies has taken longer than I imagined. During the last decade, my central focus has been the reconceptualization of the constitution of order among the Nuer people. I was and am still in the center of the struggle for democratic self-governance in the Southern Sudan. The rise of centralized, Islamic government in Sudan is the reason democratic self-governance has entered into the popular consciousness of many Southerners, especially among the acephalous societies. These societies cannot easily be molded into patterns of autocephalous governance, which is what the centralized government in the Northern Sudan has been trying to do.

Meanwhile in not unrelated activities, the subject of democratic self-governance has taken on a much more prominent role in academic and, I would say acephalous, intellectual discourse, as scholars independently around the world, and especially in Africa, acknowledge, and struggle, to understand the different choices of structures that different societies have made, and are making, in fashioning their way of life. This book is therefore, a part of a larger body of studies that have been carried out in Nigeria, Senegal, Liberia, Kenya, Mali, and Somalia. Gaining deeper understandings of these African societies is the very objectives of these studies.

Therefore, the opportunity for me to step back from what was happening in Sudan and into the Workshop in Political Theory and Policy Analysis under the eminent guidance of Vincent and Elinor Ostrom has been a stimulating, high-powered, and thoroughly practical academic endeavor. The experience had the benefit of bringing me into connection with an impressive array of scholars from different countries, studying different aspects of human societies which are related to constitutions of order and stability.

Since the inception of the Republic of Sudan as an independent country, the Nuer as an acephalous polity, as well as other acephalous groups in Sudan and Africa generally, have been perceived as irrelevant and "backward". This attitude was and is still well established, because, in the opinion of most observers, the Nuer society lacks institutions. What many observers have failed to recognize is that existing social arrangements constitute forms of social capital which need first to be understood, before further development might take place. The survival of Nuer society is evidence that it is not without order. It is obvious that individual persons are highly vulnerable in meeting the requirements of life and have a low chance of survival unless they can draw on the capabilities of others. Such capabilities depend very much on how the society is ordered.

Vincent Ostrom (*The Meaning of Democracy and the Vulnerability of Democracies: A Response to Tocqueville's Challenge*, 1997) argued that reliance on a single center of Supreme Authority in egalitarian societies runs a strong risk of creating a culture of dominance, a polity in which individuals are reduced to servitude and subject to the command and control of those exercising the rulership prerogatives. The Nuer as an acephalous society is constituted on self-organizing and self-governing capabilities, rather than relying on a culture of dominance, or as Vincent Ostrom puts it, the formalization of "machine politics", "boss rule", or "majority tyranny." In other words, the Nuer possess a *spirit of liberty*, and do not look to the State to rule over them.

The Nuer combine their views of God, law, and relationships in a way that creates a covenantal concept of life. As *Kuoth* (God) has given them rules of life, so they are to make agreements with one another and develop orderly ways of life that show commitment to each other's well being. The key idea for the constitution of order among the Nuer comes from a covenantal theology which has strong parallels to the covenantal theology of the Israelites. The covenantal theology was applied to the constitution, not only of civil society, but also to the exercise of governmental authority in the sense of making laws, determining the proper application of laws, and enforcing laws.

The underlying concept of the Nuer covenant is *Nguot*, which means to cut. Therefore, the Nuer "cut a covenant" or cut an agreement between people. People negotiate and compromise to reach an agreement, but the formulating element of the right to an agreement (commitment) is essential to establishing the relationship. The covenant foundations of the Nuer religious traditions are the conceptual foundations of Nuer polycentric arrangement of governance. A polycentric arrangement and an acephalous order in particular, is more than institutional arrangements as defined by inter-governmental relations (e.g., structures of federalism). To understand these arrangements, is therefore necessary to think outside of many of the basic constructs of western political theory. For example, the idea of a covenant or covenantal society (and acephalous societies are mostly covenantal societies) opposes any notion of absolute authority, thus challenging contemporary views of sovereignty and dominion associated with conventional theories of state.

The acephalous idea is grounded in a presupposition of human moral equality. Because human beings are fallible, however, human conflict is a fact of existence. In an acephalous society, this reality calls for shared authority and modalities of deliberation and choice. In researching the connections between covenantal thinking and democratic / acephalous practices, the oral sources of acephalous societies (e.g., the Nuer Oral Tradional Texts I have collected) constitute an important window into the ways that the *spirit of religion* and the *spirit of liberty* combine to make self-government a reality.

I now pass on to my readers what I have examined for the last decade about the history and future of democratic self-governance of the Nuer as an acephalous society.

The Scope of this Inquiry

Historical Period and Areas

Constitutional arrangements of peoples may change over time. Adaptation to change is a process that continues, since people must respond to change in their physical, social, political, and even spiritual environments. The process of adaptation to change has always fascinated me. Perhaps this is because I grew up during the latter half of the twentieth century, a time of rapid, radical change for my people, the Nuer of the Sudan region of Africa. Many of the changes I experienced were set in motion before I was born. Nevertheless, as a youth and now as an elder of my people, I accept the fact that my life is different from that of my father and grandfathers.

Change has transformed the rules governing the lives of the Nuer. Some changes the Nuer adopted by choice, in response to the opportunities and challenges of the modern era. Other changes were forced upon them. Despite adaptation to change on varying levels in the society, I believe that there still is a coherent, constitutional order that applies to all Nuer regions. Local changes are variants of more general patterns of order.

The time frame for this study is 1850 to 1990. This is the time of Nuer migration from Nuer lands west of the Nile River to lands east of the Nile in the area that is now Southern Sudan (Jal, G. 1987). This study is a synthesis of library research, archival resources, and data collected firsthand by means of interviews. The study area is the Southern Clay Plains of the Sudan. This study presents observations concerning the Nuer peoples of this region, including the Ethiopian Nuer. I have used historical as well as contemporary data.

The Nuer Oral Traditional Texts

This study relies mostly upon the Nuer Oral Traditional Texts (NOTT) and secondary sources previously published. The Nuer Oral Traditional Texts are a collection of interviews, songs, and stories that I recorded from the Nuer peoples, both east and west of the Nile, during fieldwork undertaken in 1989.

In the summer of 1989, I traveled to the Sudan. For more than three months, I visited many places, including sites in Khartoum, Khartoum North, Omdurman, Wad Medani, Kosti, Renk, Hasahesa, and many villages where the Nuer could be located and tape-recorded in interviews. Unfortunately, at that time I could not get to the major towns in the Nuer land of Southern Sudan, due to warfare in the area. However, many of those people had been forced out of their villages and now resided in the areas that I visited.

I interviewed community leaders of specific villages, from both east and west of the Nile and within each area. Questions concerned the role of age-set groups, the Nuer conception of their universe, family genealogies, marriages, cattle and cattle exchanges, the governing of villages and cattle camps, organization of cattle camp life, and conflict and conflict resolution. I also tape-recorded interviews with "specialists," persons who are regarded as authoritative resources because they are knowledgeable about custom and history. Specialists are able to provide detail, for example, on how Nuer village residents resolved disputes arising from cattle damaging a neighbor's crops, or how they approached conflicts related to the sharing of the grazing lands during the dry season. I also tape-recorded, translated, and transcribed accounts told to me about the history of Nuer relations with their acephalous neighbors.

Other key sources are found in archives, especially the Central Record Office (CRO), Khartoum, which carries considerable data about the Anglo-Egyptian policy on the Nuer from 1898 to the early 1950s. Others are the Public Record Office (PRO) and the Sudan Archives (SAD) at the Oriental Library, University of Durham, England. Each archive contains important documents on various Nuer groups.

Acknowledgments

This book was born of many long hours of thoughtful discussions and nourished by many cherished relationships. I owe a debt of gratitude to many people, but first of all, to my family. I am indebted to my wife, who for the last eleven years has been without a husband for an average of eight months each year. Then there are my children, Duany, Nyagon, Kueth, Nok, and Bil, and my nephew Ger, whose basketball games and graduation commencements I missed. My wife and children have remained ever supportive and willing to lend me confidence when my own was on the wane.

I also am indebted to my colleagues and friends at the Workshop in Political Theory and Policy Analysis at Indiana University who encouraged me to trust my instincts and ideas. This includes the graduate students who work each day to understand constitution of order in human societies as key to harmony and progress in disparate communities. Above all, I am indebted to my teacher, colleague, and friend Vincent Ostrom. Professor Ostrom has given to me more than I can ever acknowledge in words. He has been the primary source of energy and inspiration behind this book. The book itself would not have been possible without the generous support of the Workshop in Political Theory and Policy Analysis. My sincere thanks to Professors Elinor Ostrom and Vincent Ostrom for their continuous support to allow me the use of the facilities of Indiana University. The comfortable working conditions at the Workshop have made the completion of this book possible.

My greatest debt in writing is to Isabel Hogue of South Sudanese Friends International. Virtually everything I write is first read by Isabel, and every idea in this book has been shaped by our discussions. When Novalis said, "It is certain any conviction gains infinitely the moment another soul will believe in it," he could have been talking about my reliance on Isabel's advice, opinions, and her gift of catching little but important details. Special thanks to Jerry Hogue for his cooperation with his wife Isabel in this project, without his support it would have taken me much longer to complete this study.

Over the last few years, as this book has taken shape, I have been moving back and forth between academic endeavors and the People-to-People Peace Process in the Sudan. Both I enjoy greatly. My ability to maintain this peripatetic lifestyle has depended on the support of a wide range of people and institutions, including Christian churches both in Africa and the United States that supported my travel to and from Africa. Special thanks are due to William O. Lowrey (known in Nuer as *Dhurbil or Mabil*) for his role in the mobilization of many Christians and Muslims to work together to end the war in the Sudan. I also wish to acknowledge with thanks the support I received for peace and reconciliation from my colleagues and friends at the South Sudan Liberation Movement in Nairobi, Kenya: Gabriel Yoal Dok, William Kuol Chol, Mary Nyacin Chol, Evalyne Maluza Lugunza, Abbey Makungu, Simon Hoth Duol, Andrew Kuong Ruai, Gabriel Gai Riam, Michael Thiec Nyuon, Galia Galou Riak, and Simon Yuer Dang. I thank Timothy Taban Juc, Kueth Duol Kueth, Samuel Thabac Duany, and late sister Nyabar Reath Kok for their dedication and support for peace with justice in the war zone in Akobo Region, Southern Sudan.

My affiliation with the Indiana University has been loose, but none the less very rewarding. As both a teaching and research institution, Indiana University is ideally suited for my research in African civilization, African ways of life, and, in particular, my study of the constitutional order and development among the Nuer of Southern Sudan as a case to understand the place of indigenous institutions in the modern world. I would like to express my gratitude to many friends and colleagues in the Workshop in Political Theory and policy Analysis for many hours of discussions on these topics. I owe special debts to Patty Lezotte, Gayle Higgins, Ray Eliason, and Carlson Lee for their help in the process of shaping this book.

Finally, this book is dedicated to my parents: Duany Wunbiel and Nyabiu Deang, who taught me each day of their lives the meaning of justice in human relationships; that it is the source of freedom and infinite joy.

Chapter 1 - Acephalous Societies and Problems of Order

Not so with the Nuer. . . . their institutions are invisible. Every now and then a regulatory idea surfaces and marshals activity, then sinks out of sight, while another becomes visible in its effect upon movements of cattle and people. If they can be said to have anything corresponding to political institutions, these have absolutely no physical form, no architecture of palaces or prisons, no embodiment in piles of stones. . .

—Mary Douglas

      This book is about Constitutions of Order among the Nuer as an acephalous society. The basic concepts of how one creates order in different groups are important to understand in general-and to build upon in efforts to reconstitute peace and order in a society. The traditional Nuer political system has no single recognized chief to run it and no exclusive judiciary to control it. Rather, persons are divided among political units without any single administrative hierarchy of officials and without any single person to direct all of the common affairs of the society. Although the Nuer lack the machinery of centralized government, this does not lead to mere anarchy and indiscriminate violence. There are regulative ideas at work-being acted upon-which are constitutive of a way of life. Though this book is about the Nuer of Southern Sudan, it speaks to many peoples and governments in Africa. Constitutions are living relationships and documents that reflect the changing contexts of enduring relationships. Constitutions emerge from and inform shared understanding of a shared way of life. Constitutions are the fundamental rules of any institution that exercises governmental powers (rule-making, rule-application and rule-enforcement, and conflict resolution), including but not limited to the nation-state, village communities, water users, family, pasture and woodstock governance groups, as well as cooperatives, religious and ritual organizations and many others that have constitutions in this sense. Constitutions need not be written, nor need be approved by some overlapping governments to be effective.

This book is also an effort to elaborate on how Nuer of Southern Sudan maintain and cope with rules violations without a head or single source of authority. Understanding of the ideas in which a people have recourse in their local environment, the language they use, and how they marshal activities is important in constituting a self-governance order. How Nuer in their local communities organized themselves as largely autonomous "local government" units, the way power was used to make and implement collective decisions, enforce rules and resolve conflicts can provide knowledge to other communities in some parts of Sudan and Africa.

Many questions emerge in the case of "Sudan." Here are three: What is the basis of shared understandings? How much of a "shared life" must be shared? and What institutions contribute to the strength of shared understanding?

First, what is the basis of shared understandings? The shared understandings of a people are based partly on their shared cosmology and partly on similar experiences. The choices people make in constituting their societies and the principles they used are not uniform. The primordial identities of Sudanese's peoples are highly segmented, with family, clan, religious, and regional fractures one of the characterizing features of the social fabric. Affiliations based on these various schisms have led to a patchwork of allegiances rather than a unifying commitment to a common greater good. In the absence of agreement based on covenantal thinking, there never has really been a sound basis around which to construct a legitimate political system in Sudan. The country went from being administered (from Cairo) as an Ottoman territory to being a British colony and then to independence without ever fully resolving the nature of co-existence between differing political and cultural groups. Without a consensus over the fundamental aspects of the political system, legitimacy has been elusive, and the country descended into the bloody violence of civil wars that further undermined confidence in the system and claimed the lives of over 2,000,000 Sudanese.

The four regions of Sudan differed in their public philosophy, view of liberty and freedom of action, understanding of relationship between civil and ecclesiastical authority, and orientation to political order. Within regions different periods of settlements, languages, and religions resulted in institutional variation. Yet each of the regions also shared the common experience of internal political crises that led to a more definitive articulation of culture and politics in increasingly explicit institutional decisions. In all the regions, these internal adjustments often maintained the distinctiveness of localities in what amounted to associational forms of confederacy. Similarly, the distinct biophysical, cultural, and political environments also influenced and shaped the political institutions. Part of this environment included the framework set by the British colonial orders. These differences need to be taken into serious account when putting together an acceptable constitution.

Instead of building shared understanding or consensus, what was established was a constitution which posits a territorial nationalism in which birth automatically confers citizenship. No attempts were made to understand the meaning of citizenship among the Fur of western Sudan, Beja of eastern Sudan, and the Nuer of Southern Sudan. Also the term nationalism did not reflect feelings or sentiments of all Sudanese. Sudan is a plural society in nature as indicated above. The Northern Sudanese political culture was originally, and is still today, defined by Arab-Islamic elites who assumed that the wider society would absorb their cultural values and religious symbols. With independence, they promoted a country that seeks to homogenize in language (Arabic) and religion (Islam) and to be intrinsically linked to Islamic civilization (Lesch, 1998). General Ibrahim Aboud (1958-1964) Arabized administrative and educational systems in the South and expelled foreign Christian missionaries. Northern political parties which were based in Islamic religious movements promoted a homogenizing drive in the mid-1960s as did Ja'far Nimeiri (1969-1985, when he instituted Islamic penal, commercial, and tax codes in 1983. Prime Minister Al Sadiq al-Mahdi (1986-1989) sought to retain Islamic laws, while exempting non-Muslims in the South. The current president Omer al-Beshir, who seized power on June 30, 1989, argues that he is fighting for Sudan's Arab-Islamic existence: "We believe that what we now apply in Sudan is God's will." The tragic consequences of the homogenization drive are elaborated in this study.

Integration based on shared understanding of covenantal and federal principles can preserve the internal diversity of a whole system formed by the willing consent of parties who retain their capacities for constitutional and collective choice. The Comprehensive Peace Agreement of 9 January, 2004 (between Sudan People Liberation Movement and National Congress

Party) and the Interim National Constitution which embedded the bill of rights that defined national, regional, and state institutions were clear expressions of a federal government that is compatible with the Nuer institutional arrangements. Government by consent whether ecclesiastical or civil, requires limits on all authority, including a majority with the votes necessary to enforce its will. Federal designs were premised on this fact, as well as the idea that shared belief and shared authority promote self-imposed limits. From a federal standpoint, the values of local, even individual freedom of action, and community cohesiveness should not be viewed as contradictory aims.

The second question is how much of a "shared life" must be shared? A brief background, for readers who are not familiar with Sudan will be helpful. The British employed indirect rule in the Sudan. That system deliberately kept the northern and southern Sudan separate and preserved the distinctiveness of each region. The colonial administration in the southern Sudan also preserved the Nuer federation and autonomy (Evans Pritchard, 1940). The covenantal theology remained authoritative in the Nuerland where the British administration allowed distinct religious bodies (Church Mission Society, Catholic Church, Africa Inland Mission, and American Presbyterian Church) and local communities to respond institutionally to regional problems as well as internecine disputes.

The Covenantal principles guiding the Nuer institutional development provided a shared basis for interethnic (con)federation or commonwealth in the southern Sudan. In this way, federal principles bequeathed the rationale and practical means for uniting different ethnic groups and politics for common purposes without negating established boundaries, identities, or their existing forms of moral and political authority. Therefore, deliberative processes had to be designed and to evolve in order to transform the inevitable conflicts of a diverse people into productive sources of innovation.

Here then, is the institutional capital that provides the basis of shared understanding. Where it exists at the community level it enables people to resolve problems. Institutional capital denotes the set of rules that members of a community share in common, such as are recognized in de facto village governments, township councils (or group of villages' council), customary land tenure systems, and organizations such as cooperatives. Community members use these rules to channel their behavior, monitor conduct, and resolve conflicts. In other words, communities use these institutions to govern themselves, more effectively more rapidly, and at lower cost than if they have to rely on outsiders to provide these services. Nuer like many other peoples frequently, although certainly not always, consider their shared set of local rules to be better adapted to their circumstances, and local methods of conflict resolution more equitable than rules imposed by centralized governments.

The third question is what institutions contribute to the strength of shared understanding? In his *Democracy in America,* Alexis de Tocqueville enumerated the institutions that maintained self-government. Religion topped his list, immediately followed by the family. The lessons learned in families, like the guidance of religious teachings, encouraged voluntarism and enhanced public life. In Nuerland, family taught self-control and reciprocal regard as basic to self-government. Established family law is also part of wider political order and contributes to the strength of understanding among the people involved. The Nuer marriage covenants joined disparate individuals and their associations to promote broad accord or crosscutting alliance, preventing persistent differences from destroying commitments to the long term arrangements necessary for productive undertakings.

In the Sudan, intermarriage between Muslims and non-Muslims is not common. The non-Muslim who marries a Muslim is required to renounce his or her faith and embrace Islamic faith. Conversion of a Muslim to Christianity is punishable by death and is therefore not encouraged. Endogenous marriage among the Muslims and special customs set them apart and invokes a sense of unique worth. This thinking of Arab-Islamic elites as being special people dates back to the Turkiyya and Mahdiyaa periods in the nineteenth century, when Muslim traders and slavers coupled economic dominance in the South with the assumption that their own culture was superior to that of the Southern peoples. Religion, language, and race unified the people in the Northern Sudan but also separated them from the people in the Southern Sudan. The two regions have developed rival histories and incompatible genealogical myths. Thus, marriage and religion do not positively contribute to the strength of common understanding necessary to maintain the Sudan as a united country.

Despite the Islamic radical orientation and teachings there is no impasse in the basic teachings of Christianity and the basic Islamic teachings. It is the view in this book that the existence of ethnic "markers" is not sufficient in itself to denote political differences. A deliberate effort must be made to create or enhance cultural and social bonds by deepening networks of communication and consciously fostering shared values.

This point of view of Constitutions - the conception of constitutional choice calls the conception of "nation-state" into question. The conception of constitutional choice is how a people put together a system of governance. Constitutional choice is a process by which communities, through contestation and negotiations solve their daily problems make fundamental rules to address their governance dilemmas.

The Nuer as a stateless society have rejected concentration of political authority in the state. Their covenant idea in politics opposes any notion of absolute authority, thus challenging contemporary views of sovereignty and conventional theories of the state. There are many centers of power within the Nuer society. The existence of multiple and diffused sources of political authority permitted individuals in acephalous society to fully participate directly in the management of the affairs of their local communities. They have learned how to work together and to be self-governing within the framework of family, village, and cattle camps institutions. Their associated forms of government helped maintain liberty and freedom of action by encouraging individual initiative and discouraging the concentration of government power, thereby diffusing practical knowledge and extending the basis of wealth across disparate individuals and regions.

This book begins with a discussion of the question: how do people achieve order in human societies? Chapter 1 is devoted to a discussion of how a polycentric system of governance has allowed the Nuer for centuries to utilize their human capacities and material resources for organizing their patterns of life.

Chapter 2 describes the environmental conditions that provide the setting and the structure of opportunities in which the Nuer have sustained themselves successfully by relying on animal and crop production. It reviews historical settlement patterns, early contacts with the Mediterranean World and the Middle East, and the impact of these contacts on Nuer religious beliefs and political institutions of governance. It also provides the reader with some ideas of the challenges of the events of the twentieth century on the pastoral economy and their indigenous capacities.

Chapter 3 explores the Nuer conceptualization of their universe, where the conception of *kuoth* (God) as the source of creation is fundamental to the understanding of the institutional arrangements among the Nuer. On the basis of the belief in God and the concept of law, the Nuer develop their system of order which recognizes multiple agents with limited jurisdiction that can be called upon to resolve conflicts and take leadership when the need arises. Political processes involve diverse intermediaries whose task is to resolve conflicts or breaches of covenant where someone has offended against what is presumed to be right.

Chapter 4 explains how the Nuer build a system of rule and rule-ordered relationships through the medium of marriage, and also show how these relationships are maintained and perpetuated from one generation to another. Nuer family taught self-control and reciprocal regard basic to self-governance. Family and neighbors were the wellspring of civil society and local liberty and freedom of action ensured a renewal of civic affections with each generation.

Chapter 5 discusses how defense as a means of procuring security is organized among the Nuer as a headless society. The Nuer have learned to defend themselves by organizing militia. An examination of how armed citizens are organized along segmentary lines will elucidate the way regulative ideas have guided the coordination of activities for the common defense and security.

Chapter 6 describes in detail how Nuer as an acephalous system of order understand and manage disputes in all levels of their society. An insight of how they resolve conflicts is a key to understanding how they govern themselves.

Chapter 7 has two important problems to discuss: the first problem Nuer encountered during the British administration and the intrusion of the British Empire, through its exercise of hegemony over the Egyptian-Sudanese protectorate, resulted in the imposition of subject status upon the Nuer. Also the British rule gave rise to institutions alien to the Nuer. The British rule, even when accompanied by a commitment to indirect rule, was disruptive because law is conceived apart from covenantal commitment. The concept of covenant and covenantal way of life are so integrally related that to have the one without the other would be destructive of Nuer society. The British colonial office realized, however, the lack of knowledge was at the core of some of the problems they faced in their relationships with differently ordered societies. The British government, in an attempt to understand the Nuer, commissioned Edward Evans-Pritchard to study the institutional life among the Nuer. In spite of that effort, lack of knowledge has again and again been a constant source of conflict and misunderstanding between auto-cephalous and acephalous societies.

The second problem to discuss in Chapter 7 is the organization of the government of Sudan as an independent country. With independence, the organization of the government was highly centralized and predatory. The leaders who inherited governmental authority from the British colonial power promoted a country (Sudan) that seeks to homogenize in language (Arabic) and religion (Islam) and intrinsically linked to Islamic civilization. The cove-nant idea in politics of acephalous societies opposes any notion of absolute authority, thus challenging contemporary views of sovereignty and dominion associated with conventional theories of state. Also other groups do not want to be assimilated into Islamic civilization. The country descended into the bloody violence of civil wars that undermined confidence in the system and claimed the lives of over 2,000,000 Sudanese. Both periods of British rule and Islamic dominance in Sudan posed numerous threats to the Nuer as well as a range of potential opportunities. I have examined these problems in the book.

Chapter 8 examines briefly the Nuer experience during the first civil war. It also discusses the nature and magnitude of the violence, plunder, death and the misery these visited upon majority of Sudanese in the second civil war. The chapter also examines the role of key actors both within the government of Sudan and the Sudan People Liberation Movement and its military wing: the Sudan People Liberation Army.

Chapter 9 is the concluding chapter of the book. In this chapter, I re-turn to the issue of how does the Nuer indigenous culture demonstrate its viability in the face of British imperialism, Islamic dominance, Socialist transformation, and civil wars? And what does this imply for the future? De-spite the absence of a clear center of authority and ruling bureaucracy, a pro-cess of governance goes on. There are regulative ideas at work-being acted upon-which are constitutive of a way of life. Chapter 9 first considers how the Nuer maintain their autonomy as an acephalous community. Understand-ing how Nuer organized their relationships with one another will provide an insight to their indigenous development to continue as a society despite foreign disruptions; and how they build their relationships with neighboring Mitotic peoples. Second, Chapter 9 discusses how Christian and Muslim Arabs relate to one another in the Sudan. Third, it discusses Occidental influences on the African ways of life. I reminded the Sudanese people that the 2005 Comprehensive Peace Agreement (CPA) and Interim National Constitution (INC) which embedded the bill of rights is a result of a continuing struggle of the Sudanese people for democracy and self-governance which has been interrupted and hijacked by military and parties who missed used our gallant armed forces to promote their selfish interest. The Comprehensive Peace Agreement and Interim National Constitution will be meaningless without watchful concern about the breaches of covenants or agreements and enduring efforts to renew and reestablish covenantal relationships whenever breaches occur.

Achieving Order in Human Society

How do people achieve order in human societies? References in anthropological literature acknowledge two types of order. One is the tradition of state-governed societies; the other is that of stateless societies. These types of order are sometimes referred to as autocephalous and acephalous, meaning societies with heads and societies without heads.

State-governed societies, or societies with heads, are something generally well understood in Western societies. This understanding is voiced in *Leviathan,* the classic argument by Thomas Hobbes (1588-1679) for the necessity of submission to a sovereign and his will (his law) in order to achieve beneficial social order. Presumably, order and unity of law can be achieved through a unity of power whereby one man, or one body of men, gives coherence to the structure of law in a society. A major paradox arises, however, in such a system. When a single, autonomous head is the source of law, it is also above the law, and cannot be held accountable to the law by fellow human beings. Such systems have considerable difficulty coping with despotism on the part of their rulers.

Acephalous societies, on the other hand, while less understood, represent systems where despotism is less likely to arise. This difference is reason enough to strive for a better understanding of both the ways that acephalous societies are organized and the basic difficulties that may arise in their constitution of order.

Acephalous societies tend to be deeply ingrained in tradition. They work well so long as the central organizing principles of traditional ways can be maintained. Members of these societies, therefore, are required to develop an awareness of patterns of order, as well as an understanding of how to modify their organizational structures in response to changing conditions in the world around them. Problems may arise in accommodating to change, because essential tradition may be severely weakened, if not destroyed, by change. This does not imply that deeply ingrained tradition will be quickly forgotten. Among the Nuer of the Sudan region of Africa, the acephalous society survives as a distinct type of human social order.

The concept of acephalous order is not foreign to the Anglo-American mind. Scholars and observers have argued that acephalous societies exist, or have existed, in Western Europe and the United States. In his influential "The State as a Conceptual Variable" (1968), John Peter Nettle (1926-1968) argues that Britain is a "stateless" society because its governing authority is a system of institutions, rather than a single, sovereign entity. In his analysis of federal systems, Vincent Ostrom argues that the United States prior to World War II could be conceived as a "stateless" society. His argument is found in *The Political Theory of a Compound Republic: Designing the American Experiment* (1987) and in *The Meaning of American Federalism: Constituting a Self-Governing Society* (1991). Ostrom also suggests that Switzerland is a stateless society. A contrast between social orders is drawn by Alexis de Tocqueville in his two studies, *Democracy in America* ([1835, 1840] 1945) and *The Old Régime and the French Revolution* ([1856] 1955). The first pertains to a self-governing society, and the second to a society governed from the center. Regardless of the patterns of order, however, for purposes of international political relations, the community of nations nominally regards all social systems as state-governed.

Although the Nuer institutions have sustained themselves over many generations, among outsiders there has been a great temptation to ignore their viability. Neither colonial governments, nor post-colonial governments, nor the Liberation Movement with its Marxist-Leninist concepts have understood or respected the acephalous social ordering among the Nuer peoples of East Africa. Much of the policy experimentation during the last ninety years has treated the Nuer and similar societies as though they were irrelevant and "backward."[1] This attitude was and is well established, because in the opinion of most observers the Nuer society lacks institutions. What these governments, social engineers, and observers have failed to recognize is that social arrangements might instead be viewed as forms of social capital, which first need to be understood in order to appreciate how problems of further development can be addressed (Coleman, 1988).

Colonial powers sought to use a system of indirect rule and govern through local chiefs, though the Nuer had no chief, as such.[2] It is reasonable to suggest that if there had been an appropriate understanding of how people like the Nuer governed themselves, other governance structures might better have met the requirements of facilitating economic, social, and political development without having to superimpose an imperial system of control.[3] Eventually, the colonial powers came to understand that their own lack of knowledge was at the core of some of the problems they faced in their relationships with differently ordered societies. For example, the civil secretary of the British Colonial Office, in urging the appointment of Edward Evans-Pritchard to study institutional life among the Nuer, said: "There can be no doubt that our troubles with the Nuer have been intensified by our lack of knowledge of the social structure of this people and the relative status of the various kinds of chiefs and *Majors*" (McMichael, 1929, see chapter notes).[4] This lack of knowledge has again and again been the source of conflict and misunderstanding between autocephalous and acephalous systems of order.

All social orders are embedded in the shared understandings of a people and not just in their public institutions and visible structures of government, but how, as Mary Douglas asserts (see head note), their "regulatory idea(s) surface and marshal activities" remains to be determined. The ideas to which a people have recourse, the language they use, and the way they marshal activities create the fundamental foundation upon which their continuing existence and development are built. A policy is always conceptualized in relation to some "regulatory idea." The subsequent marshaling of activity consonant with such an idea is collective action. This is why Railcar Cabral urged that it was necessary to go back to the source in building a movement for national liberation in Africa when he said:

> Culture is simultaneously the fruit of a people's history and a
> determinant of history, by the positive or negative influence

which it exerts on the evolution of relationships between man and his environment, among men or groups of men within a society, as well as among different societies. Ignorance of this fact may explain the failure of several attempts at foreign domination—as well as the failure of some international liberation movements (Cabral, 1970).

For constructive patterns of change to occur among the Nuer and other peoples in Southern Sudan, it is necessary to go back to the cultural source and assess how regulatory ideas are generated and what processes are used in marshaling activities consonant with those ideas.

What to Unravel?

Understanding the foundations of an acephalous political order is a particular problem in political science due to traditional presuppositions, whether held consciously or unconsciously. A tradition in much of political science is to look for a single center of supreme authority and unravel the structure of relationships that reach from the center out to the aggregate structures of the larger society. This tradition presupposes a theory of sovereignty, which is then used as the basic organizing principle. One relies upon presupposed concepts of state, bureaucracy, and market in societies. In a sense, one looks for capitols, palaces, parliament buildings, courthouses, and prisons. Such a research procedure cannot be expected to work very well in an acephalous society. How then can one proceed?

To understand how the Nuer people govern themselves, it is important to see how their regulatory ideas marshal activities, to draw again on Mary Douglas's statement of the problem. We proceed by unraveling the context in which regulatory or governing ideas emerge, become linked to, and then bring together or order effective human action. Activities themselves usually imply efforts to accomplish something—to achieve certain results. Activities use regulatory ideas in a context where present means are being ordered to achieve some future apparent good.[5] Thus, there are circumstances where people develop and use regulatory ideas to marshal activities, and in so doing constitute a system of order that becomes a way of life.

This process of unraveling the context in which regulatory ideas marshal activities and of understanding how activities yield an orderly way of life among the Nuer people first requires a brief elaboration of essential features, principles, and arrangements. An extended analysis unfolds in this book.

Features of Environment

The environmental conditions in sub-Saharan Africa provide the setting and the structure of opportunities in which the Nuer people sustain themselves, live their lives, and communicate and work with one another. Nuerland is subject to extreme but highly regular fluctuations of climate. Rainfall varies in intensity and duration in the area. Changes of the seasons are largely determined by the direction of the wind. When the north wind (from the Sahara Desert) blows over the region, a dry season lasts for three to five months. Although the humidity is quite high, the expected rainfall at this time of the year is often less than 1.2 inches. Winds from the south create a rainy season that lasts for five to eight months, with August being the wettest month. The rainy season is the coolest period of the year. The average daily temperature varies seasonally between 68 to 81 degrees Fahrenheit.

Thus, adaptation to environmental change is a fundamental element entering into the way that the Nuer people govern their lives; the mediating factor being the cooperation enjoined by having common interests in cattle and livelihood in a variable environment. Nuer territorial organization is adjusted to fit the needs of living under both migratory and sedentary conditions. These environmental limitations and opportunities need to be taken into consideration in attempting to understand Nuer patterns of acephalous ordering.

Ordering Principles of Nuer Society

A condition of equality is of great importance in the emergence of acephalous ordering. Among the Nuer, the governing ideas that make freedom of action a virtue are derivative from the concept of equality. Individual differences are recognized in endowments, skills, and resources, but these differences are compatible with the broader, historical presumptions of equality that the Nuer have used to constitute within their society a proper way of ordering their relationships with one another.

The development and use of a common language among the Nuer reflect a long history of opportunities to communicate with one another in the various exigencies that bring people together and assign meaning to the world in which they live. Regulative ideas as evolved from history and expressed in language marshal activities because they depend upon a shared community of understanding. There is, then, a general system of expository ideas that shapes the intellectual world in which the Nuer people live. We will consider the realm of ideas that the Nuer use to understand the world in which they live, to perceive themselves, and to relate to one another and to the different peoples with which they may have contact.

Nuer individuals think of themselves as equals in the sense that they are not members of a caste society. This presumption of equality is based upon the religious belief that all Nuer people (*nei dial*) are derived from a common parentage. In Nuer tradition, human beings are *gaat kuoth*, children of God. God created Lic who was the father of Holnyang. Holnyang brought forth two sons: Ghaak and Gee. These sons, however, were born to different mothers. The two maternal lines imply division of the compound family of Holnyang into two segments. The principle of segmentation or federation, a constant feature of contemporary Nuer society, is perceived as grounded in the division of Holnyang's family. All Nuer clans claim to have either Ghaak or Gee as their common ancestor.[6]

Children of common ancestry are presumed to regard themselves in much the same way, even though specific values in particular times and places may differ. Generational and sexual differences are acknowledged, of course, but it is this attribute of common ancestry that above all enables individuals to understand one another as equals.

Equality is related to the Nuer concept of accountability. As people decide to hold others responsible for their actions, as they allow the same principle to extend universally, they create a particular kind of moral environment for each other. That is, they expect each other to be held equally accountable. Their commitment to a system of reciprocal accountability gives them incentives to work out the fuller exegesis of their system of regulatory principles. Within this moral environment, members of the Nuer society are fitted to reason out fair solutions to problems without appealing to a common head.

The reasoning process provides opportunities for open discussions (and at times bitter arguments) under the shade of a tree in an effort to understand one another and to generate ideas and regulatory mechanisms. The Nuer appreciate the value of open discussions that permit them to arrive at better understandings of who they are and how they can live productively together. As a people, the Nuer want to know the nature of the order in their universe to better fashion their understanding of themselves and the world in which they live.

In an acephalous order, the processes of governance are built by processes of conflict and conflict resolution, and made much clearer by focusing on these processes. Therefore, contestations or argumentations are common at various levels of Nuer society. To outsiders unfamiliar with Nuer political culture, such argumentations might give the appearance of a lack of lawful order. However, maintenance of an open decision process is the very essence of the processes of governance in Nuer villages and cattle camps. Every member of the village or cattle camp, including women, can air his or her views. The purpose underlying this openness is to meet the needs each member has to understand what he or she is facing within the context of a particular situation. Deliberation is a process of learning from what others have to say, of elucidating the nature of conflicts, and of deciding how the Nuer might order their relationships with one another to address the problems they have in common. This is both a way of building an understanding and a way to fulfill the will of their Creator.

Although the Nuer speak a common language, claim a single religious heritage, and celebrate a shared past, the glue of nationhood for them is to be found in an individual's freedom of action. Freedom of action and reciprocal accountability are the essential ingredients for the working order of an acephalous society. The Nuer individual believes God has given human beings life and a capacity to think and to act in ways that are consistent with one's own free choice. The individual respects the exercise of the same freedom of action by others.

When individuals choose to combine to form a village or cattle camp, they become kin who use their freedom of action to resolve their differences. Among the Nuer, some individuals are "ordained" to exercise priestly and mediating roles that carry unequal authority.[7] Those positions are exercised, however, as a public trust accountable to other members with whom they share the bond of mutual trust in covenantal relationships. The prerogatives of position among the Nuer are not to be considered as instruments of power to exercise dominance over others. Rather, they are the means to resolve conflicts that arise among members of an acephalous society.

Nuer Institutional Arrangements

Beyond basic ordering principles that apply to the constitution of Nuer society, we would expect the architectural patterns of Nuer institutional arrangements to specify the rules and relationships that apply to particular aspects of life in Nuer society. Each of these arrangements may in itself have the characteristic features of a governance structure. These arrangements have to do with marriage, kin, transgenerational continuities, family, village and cattle camp life, security, and conflict and processes of conflict resolution.

Marriage facilitates the establishment of family for the purposes of human reproduction, food production, and the establishment of the security necessary to maintain a family life. The family may be regarded as the basic unit of the kinship structures. This means that for every person, the relationships of kinship ties (or the affinity of any person) are all connections that are traced through his or her parents, siblings, spouse, or children (Radcliffe-Brown, 1951). These connections present a complex set of norms, usages, and patterns of behavior between kindred.

Kin relations among the Nuer are defined in terms of rights and duties. Where there is a duty, there also is a rule that a person should behave in a certain way. A duty may be positive, prescribing actions to be performed, or negative, forbidding certain acts. The duties of A to B are frequently considered in terms of the "right" of B. Reference to duties or rights is also a way of referring to social relations and the rules of behavior connected therewith (Radcliffe-Brown, 1951). Thus, the principle of social structure among the Nuer is one by which the solidarity and unity of the family (whether nuclear or polygynous) is used to order and define a more extended system of relationships. For example, a relationship to a particular person, along with its accompanying rights and duties, also becomes a relationship to that person's sibling-group as a social unit.

Transgenerational continuities create a natural architectural pattern. Within the family, there is a division of generations. Father and mother form one generation, their children another. As a result, an individual recognizes among all of his or her kin a positional relationship based upon rank in the generational order. By observing the different behaviors individuals exhibit toward persons of different generations, we can discover general principles.

The normal relation between Nuer parents and their children is described by Radcliffe-Brown as one of superordination and subordination. This is a result of the fact that, at a young age, children are dependent upon their parents. Parents provide for their children, care for them, and exercise control and authority over them. Any relationship of subordination, if it is to succeed, requires that the person in the subordinate position should maintain an attitude of respect towards the superordinate. The rule that children should not only love but also obey their parents is common to human societies, and it clearly is existent among the Nuer. There is, therefore, a relation of social inequality between proximate (i.e., preceding or following) Nuer generations. This is commonly generalized so that a person is subordinate to and owes respect to his relatives of the first ascending generation—that of his parents. The relation between the two generations is usually generalized to extend beyond the range of kinship.[8]

The relation between persons of two proximate generations is important for the constitution of order among the Nuer people. In an acephalous society, an essential feature in the orderly social life is some considerable measure of conformity to established usage or accepted patterns of conduct. Conformity can only be maintained if the rules have some measure of authority behind them. The continuity of the social order depends upon the passing on, from one generation to the next, the body of inherited tradition, knowledge and skill, manners and morals, religion, and taste. Among the Nuer, the largest share in the control and education of the young falls to the parents and other relatives of the parents' generation. It is their authority that is, or ought to be, effective.

In weaving together the threads of marriage, kin, and transgenerational continuities, the strong fabric of the family as an institution emerges. Family institutions, then, may be viewed as key to understanding the governance of relationships among individuals in the Nuer society. It is through marriage that systems of family relationships are formed, generational continuities are maintained, and crosscutting alliances including the establishment of voluntary associations are developed. Seeing the Nuer individual in the context of his or her family institutions helps to explain how the recognized, regulative ideas hold people together, order activities, and help in constituting an acephalous way of life.

Villages and cattle camps, along with their associated local communities, are the effective residential units. Both village and cattle camp life are governed and ordered by shared commitments to regulative ideas. Although ties of kinship and marriage link individuals across the Nuer society, individuals are not necessarily relegated to corporate localized communities on the basis of kin or lineage. The Nuer are free to reside anywhere they please. This freedom is possible because of the presumption of equality with reference to rules. Individuals are not penalized for living outside their place of birth, and continue to maintain their genealogical ties regardless of where they reside.

Lineage relationships, therefore, generally do not come into play in the day-to-day life of a residential unit. For instance, though a village may be closely identified with a specific lineage, and though members of that lineage live in that village, the majority of the village members usually are not of that specific lineage. The significance of lineage relationships emerges at specific occasions such as sacrifices, distribution of bridewealth cattle, and mortuary ceremonies. These are the occasions for making, reestablishing, or reinforcing covenants and covenantal commitments.

Villages are constituted to promote the security of property and the economic welfare of their members. In constituting a village, individuals are able to provide themselves with goods and services that would otherwise be difficult, if not impossible, for one family to secure on its own. The common interests in the village require that an individual take into account the interests of others when considering an action. Taking into account the interests of others presumes that the village members will hold together, resolve their affairs in accordance with recognized regulatory ideas, and back up their activities by sets of institutions that are well understood.

Cattle camps are units of governance outside villages. They are necessary because water and grazing are unavailable near most villages during the dry seasons. Villagers and their animals move to cattle camp sites along rivers and streams where both water and grazing are available. Each year, a family decides anew where to camp. Members of different genealogical groups often camp together. Residents of a particular cattle camp may not even be members of a common village. In the cattle camps, people agree to govern themselves. Such agreements, based on the presumption of equality, are enforceable by the elders of the camps, who share the responsibility for resolving conflict in the use of common-pool resources.

The common-pool resources—grazing lands, water, and fishing reserves—are group property. Members of a given lineage have rights to use these resources. The sharing of the use of common-pool resources poses the need for organization and regulating patterns of use. For example, the grass in grazing fields is subject to depletion or subtractability. At certain thresholds of supply, the use of grass by one person's cattle subtracts in part from its use or enjoyment by others.[9] Therefore, the leaders of a segment or lineage of a region must guard against overpopulation of the camp in order to protect the resources associated with that cattle camp. If the leaders fail to regulate the patterns for use at any one dry season, overgrazing will place demands upon the resource that exceeds its capacity. Obviously, ordering the uses of goods and services requires coordination of the demand and supply of goods and services. This poses a problem in an acephalous society, where there is no single person to bring about coherence in the camp. Yet there are identifiable mechanisms that the leaders of a segment or lineage of a region can fall back on to regulate the use of the resources, and thus maintain reasonable living standards for the users.

Security poses another problem for the acephalous society. The Nuer society, like most societies, must at some point confront the challenge of defending itself against aggression from outsiders. This kind of broad-based challenge may indeed require coordinated efforts for the society as a whole, that is, central authorities of some sort may be needed. Other strategies, however, may be possible. The Nuer have learned to defend themselves by organizing militias since the traditional military hierarchy is incompatible with acephalous ordering segmentary militias, or bodies of armed citizens organize along segmentary lines, constitute a feasible way to organize for the common defense of the Nuer society, A later examination of how segmentary militias are organized against external aggression will elucidate the way regulative ideas have guided the coordination of activities for the common defense and security.

Conflicts and processes of conflict resolution affect day-to-day relations among the Nuer. Indeed, conflict occurs in all human societies and must be resolved. Conflict is not necessarily bad. It is through healthy conflict that the Nuer people can maintain solidarity among segments and build processes of conflict resolution. Adults in conflict situations are considered equals who use their freedom to seek resolutions that are consistent with the requirements of harmonious relationships among persons in the society. The various ways of handling conflict among the Nuer need to be understood. It is important to grasp the fact that there is an underlying current established in institutions of Nuer community that enables the natural processes of negotiation to flow toward facilitating the processing of disputes in the effort to achieve conflict resolution.

Conclusion

Looking back over the time frame for this study (1850 to 2004), it is apparent that the course of human events has undermined the traditional Nuer social order. As this analysis progresses, it is therefore important to consider: (1) the possibility of radical social transitions associated with British imperialism; (2) the effects of the post-British political order established with reference to the Republic of Sudan; and (3) what these transformations may imply for the future.

Chapter 2 - The Physical and Biological Worlds of the Nuer

Introduction

This chapter describes the major physical and biological features of Nuerland, which provide the opportunities for, and limitations on, the capabilities of the Nuer to sustain themselves successfully by relying on animal and crop production. Many aspects of this physical environment must be taken as fixed. Other aspects impose high costs on those who might use this terrain as a home. Human organizational arrangements must in some way be fitted to these aspects of the natural world.

We first will describe briefly the environmental and historical settlement patterns. Second, we will examine the early contacts of the Nile Basin peoples (in which the Nuer are a part) with the Mediterranean World and the Middle East, and the historical impact of these contacts on Nuer religious beliefs and political institutions of governance. Third, we will discuss how the Nuer adapted their ways of life to the variable rainfall patterns. Fourth, we will attempt to explain the challenges of the events of the twentieth century on the Nuer pastoral economy and their traditional, indigenous technical knowledge.

Environmental and Historical Settlement Patterns

We know through Nuer oral traditions and secondary sources that for a long time the Nuer have formed a distinct part of Nilotic peoples (McLaughlin, 1967; Ehret, 1982; Ogot, 1967). In many ways, the distinctive features which characterize the modern Nuer society were functions of centuries-long processes of modification and transformation. For this study, it is neither necessary nor possible to establish a common origin of all the diverse groups (e.g., the Dinka-Nuer language group; the Luo speaking group; and the Padhola group) that mingled in the formative years of history to form the Nilotic peoples. Through historical linguistics, we can assume these groups were at some point in time together because they share common basic words, but it is meaningless to worry about the time-depth of their differentiation to specific speech communities. What is important is that much of the Upper Nile Basin had long been settled by related Nilotic-speaking peoples, who, though varying in social structure and political organizations, shared considerably in material assets (cattle), culture, social values, and religious ideas.[10]

The occupation of the Upper Nile Basin by Nilotic speaking pastoralists, their differentiation from each other, their movements, and their economic and political activities have taken place against the background of a progressive drying out of the region over millennia. Both long-term and short-term pulsations in the climate of northern Africa have been influential in the adoption of pastoralism as a way of life and the dispersal of pastoralist peoples throughout the Rift Valley or Nile Basin (Johnson 1994).[11] Pastoralism is a mode of production where livestock make up 50 percent or more of the economic portfolio of a small herder (Niamir 1999). The Nuer and other Nilotic peoples have a long history of alternating between pastoralism and cultivation in response to environmental and even political changes (Adams, W.Y. 1977).[12]

Because the general trend of desiccation has been punctuated by a succession of wetter and drier periods, the general movements of pastoralists have been neither unilinear nor unidirectional. Territory which was abandoned during one phase may have been reoccupied in a later phase. In any historical period there have been shifts in the availability of water, vegetation, and flood-free land, all of which have affected patterns of human settlement. The linguistic evidence suggests that there has been a considerable overlaying of peoples and languages, rather than a succession of population displacements. In this respect the most recent movements of Western Nilotic societies (e.g., Dinka, Nuer, Anyuak, and Shillluk) to the present homeland in Upper Nile must be recognized as modern representations of a far older pattern (Gowlett, 1988; Ehret, 1974; 1982; David, 1982; Johnson, 1986).

The Nilotic peoples, according to Bethwell A. Ogot (1967), usually refer to themselves as *Jonam*, a word of Luo origin meaning "people of lakes and rivers." It would appear that from ancient times the river valleys and lake areas have played a significant role in determining transhumant routes. Thus, the Nuer have adapted to their environment by developing a transhumant way of life (i.e., characterized by the seasonal movement of livestock between highland and lowland pastures, either under the care of herders or in company with the owners). Other factors which must have regulated the early Nilotic way of life were the climate and natural surroundings necessitating the changing of places of habitation seasonally and periodically, and the stretches of land that were not, and still are not, suitable for extensive cultivation.

The Nuerland is divided into five ecological zones. The zoning is influenced by differences in water regime. These are: 1) the Nile and other permanent water surfaces such as Lake No or Lake Ambadi; 2) permanent swamps of *papyrus* and related vegetation along the Nile, which remain flooded all year; 3) the flood plain (the Nuer *tuoch*), which is inundated from the rivers for a period of four to six months every year; 4) intermediate land areas, where flooding from the rivers is not likely, but which, because of the impeded drainage of the rain water, nevertheless become flooded for several months every year. The intermediate land is crossed by numerous watercourses that remain flooded for much longer periods and more closely resemble the flood plain; and 5) distinctly higher areas, either within or beyond the flood plain, described in the report of the Jonglei Investigation Team as "highland."[13] Highlands normally escape flooding from the river and have sufficiently permeable soils to drain quite quickly after rains (Barbour, 1961). Within this swampy land and rivers there are a number of ridges or highlands subject to different patterns of rainfall and river flooding. One Nuer elder composed a song about the Nuer area of settlement, saying, "The swampy land and rivers are our home. Thy entrance was unknown to the world. God did show the world thy gate."[14]

The Sudan Nilotic population is distributed among six general areas: First are the Shilluk and northern Dinka ridges that are located on either side of the White Nile below Lake No. This is in the central rain-land zones of Sudan, with mainly clay soils of relatively good fertility, but with cultivation limited by rainfall of 440-750 millimeters (17-30 inches) annually.

Second, the eastern Nuer areas are located beside the Sobat River near Nasir, up to the borders of Ethiopia. The eastern Nuerland is flanked on the west by the vast Macar swamps, a region that might provide plentiful grazing. Many people from Jikany Eastern Nuer as well as Lou Nuer prefer to move to the upper reaches of the Sobat and Baro Rivers. There is not only adequate pasture for their herds in this region, but also exceptionally good fishing and an opportunity to raise a rich crop of maize on the fertile silt left by the flood water during the dry season.

The third region is the highland from Akobo, west of Zeraf Valley and up to Duk and Duk Ridge. This is known as the Central Nuer Region. However, the whole area of Zeraf Valley, Lou Nuer, and Jikany Doar (i.e., Jikany Eastern) is referred to generally as "Eastern Nuer," in contrast to "Western Nuer," the region west of the Nile. Western Nuer is known to the Nuer who live east of it simply as *kui kiir* (over the Nile). This is widely believed to be the original homeland of the Nuer.

Fourth, the highland of the Western Nuer Region is divided into two geographical areas: (1) the area lying north of the Bahr el Ghazal river and partly west of it, and (2) the region south of that river. The difference in the terrain is not great. People north of the river rely on the Bahr el Ghazal itself or the rivers that flow into it. Those to the south rely almost entirely on the pastures provided by the natural and seasonal irrigation of the Bahr el Jebel River or by the floodwaters of rivers coming in from the southwest.

Fifth, the southern area includes the Nyuong, Dor, Dok, Haak (Aak), and Jagei Nuer communities. The permanent settlements and cultivation areas of these people are on a ridge of sandy ground that runs parallel to the Bahr el Jebel River. There they graze their cattle in the dry season along the edges of the river or along inland water systems referred to locally as the Bilnyang system. This system is partly dependent on overflow water from the Nile and partly on water derived from a different catchment area. Hence, in years when the Nile provides inadequate grazing or is inaccessible owing to heavy flooding, the Bilnyang system offers an alternative.

Sixth, north of the southern area peoples are the Jikany Cieng (Western Jikany) whose country lies in the triangle formed by the intersection of Bahr el Jebel and the Bahr el Ghazal. Although some of the Jikany move to grazing grounds across the rivers during the dry months of the year, nearly all the Leek and Bul Nuer live on the left bank of the Bahr el Ghazal. Thus, all the Nuer live in the flood region which covers most of the area now administratively called Bahr el-Ghazal and Upper Nile in the Sudan (see Figure 2.1: showing map of the Sudan). The flood region includes the area inhabited by the Nuer who are Ethiopian citizens. As already noted above, the area is subjected to extreme variability of seasonal flooding and drought. This situation limits its use for cultivation in the rainy season. A mixed local economy is thus what one would expect under these conditions. One finds in the region a heavy emphasis on cattle husbandry.

The varieties of grazing grounds found in the Nuerland provide pastoralists with grazing throughout the dry season, but this requires constant movement to take advantage of the irregular availability of water and the life cycles of different grasses. The most valued grasses are those found in the seasonally river-flooded grasslands, the Nuer *tuoch*, which are exposed late in the dry season as the floodwaters recede. All pastoral communities within the Nile Basin, therefore, try to ensure access to grazing land or *tuoch* wherever their wet season village may be.

Pastoralism in Africa encompasses a very wide range of production systems, ranging from sedentary populations who use extensive communal lands such as the Shona in southern Zimbabwe (Scoones 1998); to semi-transhumants who are sedentary for only parts of the year such as the Nuer of Southern Sudan; to full transhumants such as the northern Mauritanian pastoralists (Zeindane 1999) and Namibian pastoralists (Behnke 1999). The transhumant pastoralists are a rather large and significant minority of the world population (see Niamir-Fuller 1999). They constitute an estimated 16 percent of the population of the Sahelian Zone (Bonfiglioli and Watson, 1992). In Southern Sudan, and in a few countries such as Somalia and Mauritania, they are the majority of the people. Mobile pastoralists almost invariably have established symbiotic socio-economic relationships with less mobile populations.

According to Nuer political theory of fission and fusion, which is based on both historical and recent experience, political groups spread over larger territory as they increase in size, segmenting as they grow. Segments move away from the parent body as they become larger, claiming their own pastures and dry season cattle camps to satisfy their expanding needs and autonomy. These new settlements in turn attract later settlers, the latest of whom are often relegated to marginal areas not dominated by the earlier settlers. The newcomers tend to move off in search of better sites once their own numbers increase to the point where they are capable of surviving on their own. These movements are most usually organized around religious leaders or custodians who thus become the nuclei around which Nuer groups form and re-form (Evans-Pritchard 1940; Douglas 1986; Johnson 1990).[15] Among the Nuer, prophets traditionally have been the teachers of the way of life. Douglas Johnson observes:

People were attracted to the prophets by their generosity and fairness; those around them took note of everything they did and said and consulted them on many matters; though consulted the prophets were not always listened to, and it was frequently only after their deaths that people realized the full force of the truth of their words (Johnson 1994). A prophet's message, according to Douglas Johnson (ibid), is not delivered fully formed, though it may be remembered as such. It is developed and elucidated through dialogue, debate, and the analysis of events.

Outside Contact, Pastoral Mobility, and the System of Order

The acephalous system of order among the Nilotic peoples should be placed in the context of historical events leading to greater ideas of equality of social conditions accompanied by a belief that all people share essential qualities that reveal their equal moral worth. Nuer indigenous institutions of knowledge in particular reflect the self-organizing and self-governing aspects of indigenous communities leading toward a more covenantal or federal association that involves consent-based arrangements at all levels of social organization. Pastoral mobility and the need to accommodate the interests of others serve to enforce this acephalous system of order.

Two factors have influenced the development of the early Nilotic peoples: outside contact and pastoral economy. The early contacts with the outside world provide part of the historical context for this discussion. As a consequence of such contacts, the concept of freedom of action (a new political ideal) evolved and was confirmed by changes in the language to reflect equal political rights. Pastoralists valued and recognized that reciprocity is one of the ways in which interdependence among individuals and groups is established and maintained. In this view of equality, individual right enabled and obliged collective action. Thus, the following accounts of the transhumant Nilotic pastoralists' early contacts with the Mediterranean World are given in order to consider their impact on religious mores, social values, and patterns of political organization.

Early Contacts with Mediterranean World and the Middle East

The peoples who later were to inhabit the area of the Nile River Valley and the Great Lakes Region had contact with the peoples of the Mediterranean World and Middle East. The inhabitants of what is now the Northern Sudan were the primary point of contact, but also there was contact through trade activities along the East Coast of Africa (Kjeshus 1977; Weiner, et al., 2000). These early contacts produced influences which still are visible today. These influences include pastoralism (cattle herding), to believe in only one true God, and the acephalous systems of governance.

In ancient times, the name given to the country along the Upper Nile was Kush, a name also found in the Bible. Kush, or *Kash* in another vocalization, was the Old Egyptian name for the land immediately south of Egypt, the northern part of the country we now call Sudan. In the Bible, the name is mentioned in Isaiah 18; Ezekiel 29:9; Zephaniah 2:12 and Psalm 68:31. In Ezekiel 29:9, in a prophecy against Egypt, the exact location of Kush is described: Because you said, "the Nile is mine, I made it, therefore, I am against you and against your streams, and I will make the land of Egypt a ruin and a desolate waste from Migol to Aswan, as far as the border of Cush" (Wiener, Roland, Anderson, and Wheeler 2000). Migol is in the north of Egypt and Aswan is the southernmost town, beyond which the borders of Kush lay. A broader meaning of Kush sometimes used in the Bible encompasses the areas south of Egypt, including all of the modern Sudan and neighboring countries within the Rift Valley or Upper Nile Basin.[16]

This kingdom of Kush developed into the Meroitic Empire, which existed roughly between 700 B.C. and A.D. 300. Characteristic of this kingdom was its unique blend of indigenous African and Egyptian elements. Its capital was at Napata, near present-day Karima, and later moved to Meroe. The town of Meroe is some miles northeast of present-day Khartoum. Many archaeological remains from Meroitic times, such as temples and pyramids, are still visible in Sudan today.[17] The language of the Meroitic people has not yet been classified or understood. Although the Meroitic letters have been deciphered and attributed corresponding sound values, only 20-30 words are understood. Whether Meroitic language is a relative to Nubian languages, or to Hamitic languages (such as Beja), or to Nilotic languages (such as Dinka, Nuer, and Shilluk) is a matter of pure speculation.

The Meroitic Empire collapsed around A.D. 300 due to a general weakening of the internal political structures. There also were wars with the neighboring Christian kingdom of Axum to the southeast (Abyssinia/Ethiopia), and with the Nubians to the west (modern Kordofan and Dar

Fur), both of whom were attracted by the fertile Nile Valley and its wealth. The Blemmyes (ancestors of the Beja peoples) who inhabited the eastern hills of Sudan had also become strong. As they moved into the northern part of the Nile Valley, they pushed the Meroitic power south into the central Sudan.

Alwa was one of three Christian kingdoms that emerged from the collapse of the Meroitic Empire. Soba, the capital of Alwa, was located on the Blue Nile, upstream from present-day Khartoum. Alwa was a subsistence economy; cattle raising and trade were the most important sources of income. Roland Werner, William Anderson, and Andrew Wheeler (2000) explain that there was a quarter in Soba for the Muslim traders. This presence shows the importance of foreign trade to the local economy. Gold and salt were some of the popular communities traded. Alwa probably had open access to the Red Sea, and this would have meant that some cultural mingling would have reached Alwa without first filtering through peoples to the north. Archaeological finds indicate that Alwa had trade connections with the Middle East, South Arabia, India, and China, and most probably also with the countries of northern and western Africa, and also with Dongola, Egypt, and Ethiopia.

From the sixth century A.D. to the fifteenth century A.D., the Christian kingdoms of the Upper Nile region were known as Nubian. They prospered for centuries until dissolved by Arab intrusion. The effect of the mass immigration of Arab nomads into Nubia is described by Arab historian Ibn Khaldun (A.D. 1333-1405). Khaldun describes the events that led to the dissolution of the central power in Dongola (the capital of Nubia) in the fourteenth century, and the passing of power to the Arab intruders. He especially mentioned as a cause the intermarriage between Nubians and Arabs, which resulted in the Nubians adopting Arab "tribal" systems. Thus, the Arab came to occupy the country to the south of Egypt and made it a place of pillage and disorder to this day.[18] Nevertheless, the cultural and religious influences of the early peoples may still be seen among the present-day inhabitants of the Upper Nile Valley and the Great Lakes Region.

Rules, Pastoral Mobility, and Acephalous System of Order

Through institutional analysis we learn how institutional change can effect custom, habits, and, eventually, the culture of a people. We also learn of the limitations placed on institutional development by history and culture.

History, belief, culture and circumstance determine the meaning and effectiveness of particular rules of behavior and society's evolving governing framework. Acephalous societies, as opposed to autocephalous societies, are stateless.[19] They do not have the overwhelming single rulers or paramount rulers to impose rule enforcement. At the same time these societies exhibit order in the sense that conduct within them conforms to elementary goals of social coexistence. In the shaping of this conduct rules play important role in creating and maintaining order within any of these societies through use of rules of conduct made by the people themselves: kinship, alliance system, and promotion of common interests.

Rules are vital part of an acephalous system of order, and their effectiveness depends upon the carrying out of order-maintaining functions of making these rules, communication, administering, interpreting, enforcing, legitimizing, adapting and protecting them. In an acephalous society, rules do not emanate from a central rule-making authority, but arise from the people themselves who come together to govern their relationships with one another. Their established practices are confirmed by moral and religious beliefs communicated through the power of words. The power of words is vested only in a few: the prophets.

Greater economic mobility in and out of pastoral communities has also contributed to a greater diversity in needs, expectations, and power relationships. The needs, expectations, and power relationships have been important ingredients in determining how transhumant pastoralists relate to one another and to non-pastoralists. These factors also determine the contents of the traditional indigenous intellectual and cultural heritage of the Nilotic pastoralist population. The Nilotic peoples have depended upon this reservoir of traditional indigenous knowledge to develop new and innovative solutions and activities. Federation and open discussions have been some of the innovations in resolving problems of natural resource use. Further to these experiences, the Nilotic pastoralists, like other pastoralist groups share a sense of moral community.

The moral community of the Nilotic people involves, as Godfrey Lienhardt has observed, "a willingness to share, give, loan, and accept compensation for wrongs" (Lienhardt 1975). The moral community can be maintained only by an adherence to the values of good neighborliness, and by the willingness to accept mediation of disputes within the community itself. The challenge of the nineteenth century for many Nilotic societies, especially the Nuer, was to define who was included in the moral community and who remained outside it. The definition had to be flexible (Johnson 1994). Institutions were designed to allow for adaptation because some current understanding can likely be wrong, and biophysical and social systems change.

Building social capital in the context of local capacity building for resource management has received reasonable attention from the pastoralists (Ostrom, E. 1992). It is argued that without social capital, there will be less collective discipline to engage in and respect communal decisions. Social capital can include religious mores and values, social norms, traditional indigenous knowledge, perceived duties and responsibilities related to kinship bonds, and conflict resolution mechanisms. Customary leadership is one of the mechanisms through which social capital and collective discipline are made enforceable. It is considered legitimate for these customary leadership groups to resort to force to correct what they perceive as a violation of accepted behavior. Thus, order here depends upon a fundamental or constitutional principle, stated or implied, which single out certain groups as the sole bodies competent to discharge these political functions.

Adaptation to Variable Rainfall Patterns

The traditional Nuer wisdom guiding the application of rules about modes of ordering the Nuer society and its natural resources has emphasized acephalous systems of governance and communal ownership by clan and lineage with use rights to households and individuals. Nuer individuals, by identifying the problem commonly faced by the community of understanding and acknowledging the recognition of the nature of the goods (among other factors), have had the potential to address the problems at hand of joint action. In this section, I will consider traditional arrangements to use scarce natural resources and adaptive mechanisms to cope with the variability of climate in the region. Such coping mechanisms will include patterns of village life and encampment during the dry season.

Natural Resource Systems in Traditional Nuer Society

The Nuer perceive that natural resources are shared by the community of users.[20] The list of shared resources and facilities is both long and diverse.

It includes sandy ridges or highland, *tuoch* or grazing grounds, hunting fields, fishing reserves, rivers, pools, *khors*, and other bodies of water. Each of these resources can have a fixed location, such as grazing grounds or fishing reserves. The commons can either be renewable, such as grazing grounds and water pools, or not. The nature of these natural resources is such that individuals cannot easily divide them into pieces in order to avoid sharing the use of such resources with others in the community. In addition, resource units extracted by one person cannot be extracted by any others (Ostrom, E. 1990).

Resource systems are best thought of as stock variables that are capable, under favorable conditions, of producing a maximum quantity of a flow without harming the stock or the resource system itself. Resource units are what individuals use from resource systems. Resource units are typified, for example, by the tons of fodder consumed by animals from a grazing grounds and the quantity of aquatic resource used each year. The difference between the resource as a stock and the harvest of resource use units as a flow is useful in connection with renewable resources, where it is possible to define a replenishment rate. As long as the average rate of withdrawal does not exceed the average rate of replenishment, a renewable resource is sustained over time.

Grazing-Resource Tenure among the Nuer

Nuer are predominantly cattle-raising people, but also grow some cereals. Cattle are the Nuer's dearest possession, and they will risk their lives to defend their cattle or to increase their herds. Most of their social activities concern cattle, especially during the dry season. Their attitudes towards their neighbors are influenced by their interest in cattle and their desire to expand their herds and control pastures. An increase in cattle density, as Raymond Kelly (1985) explains, to the point where grazing shortages occur stimulates territorial appropriation, which in turn reduces cattle density to a level where grazing is adequate at least temporarily. Territorial expansion may thus be construed as a negative feedback mechanism, and maximum cattle density as the reference value that initiates compensatory adjustment. The regulatory sequence outlined above, however, is unrelated to the maintenance of the crucial variables within the biologically or ecologically defined ranges of viability that are essential to the persistence of the system as constituted.

Among the Nuer, cattle are used for many life purposes. They are used as compensation for life and limb. The union of marriage is brought about by payment of cattle, and every phase of the process is marked by the transfer or slaughter of cattle for ritual purposes. The success of bridewealth exchange and bloodwealth negotiations depends entirely on the wide-scale acceptance of cattle as a medium of exchange and for judicial reckoning. Nuerland was, and still is, owned by lineages and clans in communal systems. The management of lands, water, fish reserves was entrusted to indigenous leaders, while the right of use was held by the whole communities.

Property Rights

Nuer cosmology gives prominence to individual right to own property. The belief in individual right to own property is considered by the Nuer as the basis for the principle of being in the right in a case. Dungda, my thing/dungdu, your thing, and dungdan, our thing/dungdien, their thing, are concepts organizing the way persons act toward one another in an acephalous system of order. Harold Demsetz gives a working definition of property rights:

> Property rights are an instrument of society and derive their significance from the fact that they help a man form expectations which he can reasonably hold in his dealings with others. These expectations find expression in the laws, customs, and mores of a society. An owner of property rights possesses the consent of fellowmen to allow him to act in particular ways. An owner expects the community to prevent others from interfering with his actions, provided that these actions are not prohibited in the specifications of his rights (1967: 347).

Demsetz is discussing personal property rights, but this definition can be expanded to include group property rights as well. Among the Nuer, property rights give the holders of such rights certain presuppositions as to the actions of others. They also give others presuppositions as to the actions of the right holders. These presuppositions help persons devise strategies when they are interacting with respect to the resources over which the rights are defined. The specific form of the rights does proscribe certain actions and enhance other actions.

It is through the system of property rights that a mechanism of rightdoing and wrongdoing can be determined by both the law users and the law enforcers. It is the right of the right-holders to restrict others from claiming benefit to a resource over which the individuals have clearly defined property rights. Being in the right depends upon the recognition of the right possessed by another.

Land tenure, grazing rights, and rights in water are held by those who are recognized as descendants of the original occupiers of the area. This is particularly true of Nuer east of the Nile, for such rights are held by descendants of the original colonizers. An understanding of land tenure requires an analysis of the lineal structure of Nuer society.[21] Land tenure here means the holding of, and rights to, the ridges and sandy outcrops which the Nuer occupy during the rainy season (Howell 1954). Nuer build their permanent villages on these highlands. Households have their cattle-byres, cultivate a specific piece of land, and carry out various forms of land use for pastures and fishing. Certain communities have definite rights to distinct areas by right of traditional conquest that is clearly recognized by all Nuer. This right is enforceable as a rule by the Nuer. There are, however, different property rights depending on the type of resource, such as *tuoch* land, pools and lagoons, fishing reserves, and rights to drinking water. Because the Nuer society is segmented into household, lineages, clans, and wider society, the right of access to natural resources overlaps. The village, for example, owns the land around the village, pools, and lagoons. A lineage owns the *tuoch* lands. The use of water of River Nile, River Sobat, and major lakes is jointly controlled by the Nuer people as a whole. Thus, the rights of individuals, villagers, members of lineage groups, and the Nuer people overlap.

Individuals can also hold some rights in resources as a private property. They hold rights to use and to transfer to heirs such resources as farmland, livestock, wells, and pools. The technology that renders these resources productive, including byres, granaries, plows, and hand tools, are also held as private property. The general rule in regard to land is that all cultivated land, including well water and pools surrounded by cultivated land, has a proprietor, and that claims to these resources can be publicly affirmed, disputed, and enforced.

Patterns of Village Life as Coping Mechanism

Seasonal and lunar changes provide a Nuer individual with the physical environment around which he organized his life. The characteristic backward and forward movements from villages to camps is the Nuer's response to the climatic variation between seasons of rain and drought. In the Southern Sudan, the *ruon* (year) has two major seasons, *tot* (wet) and *mai* (dry). The rainy season, which extends from about the middle of March to the middle of September, roughly corresponds to the beginning of the rains, although it does not cover the whole season of rainfall (see Figures 2.1 and 2.2). Rain may fall at the end of September and into early October, and the land remains flooded in the months that belong to the dry season half of the year. Dry season commences at the decline of the rains and covers the period roughly from about the middle of September to the middle of March.

A Nuer village is organized on the basis of segmentary lineage systems in which there is a *diel* (dominant clan) to furnish a *mar* (kinship) framework on which political aggregations are built. The smallest political and territorial body is made up of a *cieng* (village). Each village is composed of homesteads consisting of a *luak* (byre) and *duel* (houses). Each homestead may contain a simple family group or a polygynous household. The household is often referred to by the Nuer as *gol*, a word meaning "hearth." The *cieng* is further divided into *dhor* (hamlets), which consist of a group of homesteads, and the gardens and grazing land surrounding it. A hamlet is generally occupied by close kinsmen—often brothers—and their households. This kind of group is considered a joint family.

Joint families or lineages provide the conceptual framework of the village structure. A village comprises a local community, linked by common residence and by a network of kinship and affinal ties. Members cooperate in many activities including provision for collective defense and regulating the use of common-property resources.

The most important activities centered in village life include cultivation, marriages, and the rite of *gar* to establish age-set groups. The need to supplement their insufficient milk diet with plant food prevents Nuer from being entirely transhumant. Sorghum, maize, bean, and pumpkin production is, therefore, important for survival. Research in the region has shown that the greater part of the Nuer diet comes from the grain crops they grow (The Equatorial Nile Project 1954: map E 12).

Lawful marriage is a village activity for two of reasons. First, marriage is a process that requires the presence of the bride and the groom's families and kin. The participation of such a large group of persons is to develop ways of insuring commitments to the long-term arrangements necessary for productive undertakings. The rainy season facilitates the participation of family in the processes of marriage negotiations, since the permanent village residence of each member of the extended families involved in any given marriage is known by everyone. Family members must be notified and be present at a certain date for the negotiations and distribution of bridewealth cattle. Because kin do not necessarily camp together during the dry season, it is difficult, if not impossible, to conduct marriages during this time of the year. The large numbers of people involved in negotiating the marriage agreements need food, accommodations, and drinks. It is the village that has the resources to meet such expenses for marriage, and there are more houses available for accommodation in villages than in cattle camp. Because of these reasons and others, marriages usually take place in the village between mid-July and mid-December when there is plenty of food. Second, conducting marriage contracts involves discussions of issues regarding building marriage alliances and common problems likely to confront the related individuals entering into such an alliance.

The age-set initiation is another key social activity taking place in Nuer villages. The formation of a new age-set system is accomplished through the ritual of *gar* (cuts) or initiation. The gar consists of cutting six marks across the forehead. The operation is performed by a man known as *gaar* (marker) who is skilled at the task. *Gaar* uses a small sharp knife for the cicatrization. Initiation into age-sets has three major objectives. The first is to create each age-set and then to train young men in the rules of conduct governing the relationships between initiates and non-initiates on the one hand, and between the members of different age-sets on the other. The second is to make initiates unafraid of the spear or blood, to accustom them to bearing pain, and to commission them to defend their herds, villages, and cattle camps. The third is to observe other communal rules, such as those rules on common-pool resource use and grazing land access, and the formation of new sets of decision-makers.

The Nuer Traditional Judicial System

The Nuer judicial system is composed of different levels and groups involved in processes of conflict resolution. Among the Nuer as an acephalous order, there is no central mechanism for conflict resolution. This means that each decision-making unit mediates conflict within its jurisdiction. This suggests that conflicts are resolved in different ways in different contexts.

The judicial system in Nuer villages, hamlets, and clans, and on the various levels of segmentation in the lineage system among the Nuer, depends upon the action of autonomous individuals who pursue their interests in ways that grant reciprocal respect for the autonomy of others. Disputants argue their case before elders and witnesses. Decisions are made based on the principle of who is in the right in the case. Decisions of the elders on one level can be appealed by going to the next level of segmentation in a lineage system. However, there are identifiable ways that can be considered as a common judicial system that operates among the people and across the land. These ways include process of mediation and contestation in the process of conflict resolution.

Conflict resolution among the Nuer was, and still is, through mediation. Mediation in the Nuer context is an adaptive and responsive process; in fact, it is altogether a rather loose process that captures considerable diversity. The forms of mediation reflect both the Nuer political structure in which it occurs and the nature of the conflict. Mediation is also used to resolve conflicts between the Nuer and Dinka, and between the Nuer and other groups.[22]

The openness of the Nuer society in which contestation is the norm makes development of different forms or cooperation possible. Getting to the negotiating table itself is extremely important, since it is only through interaction, dialogue, and debate that understanding can develop. It is within the dialogue process that the parties to a conflict are able to delineate and compare the actual differences in their positions. The differences, in many cases, do not prove to be so very different.

In order to promote their common interest in maintaining a village, residents have established standards of conduct. These standards are enforceable as rules of law by and for individuals who voluntarily covenant with one another to form governing structures. Officials (such as elders, lineage leaders, custodians, and age-set leaders) who are entrusted with rule enforcement are expected to discharge their responsibilities according to the concept of legal equality.

All villages and cattle camps maintain a regular police-like force. This *ngueni* (police force) is a component of the traditional *ream cieng* (home guards). The home guards are established to maintain lawful relationships within a village or a cattle camp and to protect against external aggression. Members of the home guards or militia are trained by their parents, peers, and age-set members to understand lawful relationships. They also are trained by their elders in how to use weapons. The decision taken by either the assembly of villagers or the camp residents authorizes the council of officials to use the police force in order to maintain order in the jurisdiction involved.

The Nuer Pastoral Institutions

Nuer *luak* (cattle byre) is the basic pastoral institution that is associated with the family. Each family must have a *luak* to keep cattle during the rainy season for protection from the swarms of mosquitoes and other insects which breed in standing water. The *luak* is where decisions are taken regarding movement to grazing grounds, land rights, water, and acquisition and distribution of cattle in marriage. The Nuer family is also referred to as a *luak* (household). A number of *luak* congregate into a *dhor* or hamlet.

As a pastoral institution, the *luak* is the guardian of two key traditional indigenous resources: *riek kuoth* and *gol*. These resources serve as the link between the material and spiritual realms, and between all life forms.

Riek kuoth is a sacred *nyiot* (a pole or "tree"). On the *ngapni* (hooks or branches) of the *riek* pole are hung special spears, small sacred gifts, and other items. Libation, the in form of milk, beer, or water is poured under the *riek* pole. Pouring libation is an act of thanksgiving to God for the welfare of the *luak* (household). It also is asking for forgiveness of wrongs committed. The *riek* pole as a uniquely Nuer institution symbolizes *kot liec*, where the Nuer were supposed to have emerged. The pole is an important symbol of common religion and culture. It is, therefore, a national symbol.

Gol is another pastoral institution of general significance among the Nuer. *Gol* means a joint family. It is a special hearth, a circular structure made of mud located in the center of the *luak*. Dried cattle dung is burned there, creating smoke that will protect animals from mosquitoes and insects. *Gol* is located in the permanent village *luak*; it is also in the *geau* (windscreen) in the cattle camp during the dry season. The structure of *gol* in the cattle camp is not exactly in the same form as it is in the *luak*, but the function is the same.

The *riek* pole is placed next to the *gol* hearth. Together, *gol* and *riek* constitute the center of the household of the Nuer people. It is around this sacred circle that men of the village sit for council and decision-making.

Cattle Camp and Environmental Governance

The cattle camp has emerged as the major way in which Nuer pastoralists historically have managed their common pool resources during the dry months. The Nuer cattle camp also is an adaptive mechanism for the production of livestock. The cattle camps function as important units of governance in Nuer society.

A cattle camp is formed by individuals who share the common interest of seeing that their family members and animals obtain a sufficient supply of water, grass, and fish to meet their needs. Herding cattle jointly is of potential advantage to all households, and the scarcity of grazing pastures during the dry season requires cooperation among disparate persons. The need for orderly access to water and fish also makes it necessary for persons to develop arrangements for mutual benefit. Without regard for others, it would be difficult, if not impossible, for anyone to take advantage of the grazing and water resources, because these resources cannot be easily divided. Uncoordinated attempts to use them could certainly generate conflict and destruction.

An intermediate cattle camp formed by households of a village in the early dry season, and in which members of neighboring villages participate, is known as *wec jiom*. Young men and girls move cattle to these nearby grazing grounds after the old grass has been burned and when green grass is coming up. This mobility is the first phase of the dry season movement. *Wec jiom* are usually established around mid-November through December each year, after the intermediate grazing is exhausted and the pools in the village have either dried up or are nearly dry. In the new grazing ground, cattle graze on marsh plants that abound in swampy depressions. Each section of the village may have different *wec jiom*, depending upon the capacity of the grazing grounds, availability of water, and size of the village. Smaller villages may camp together. People who camp in *wec jiom* are mostly kin and members of the same village.

Wec jiom also serves as an accommodation of some generational conflict. The young people are eager leave village maintenance work to older people and to take the cattle out to the camp as soon as the rain stops, even though grazing grounds and water still are available within the village. Building and repairs generally take place early in the dry season when there is plenty of straw for thatching and enough millet to provide beer for those who assist in the work. Young people are required also to help in these activities. Also, a second crop of *paan* (sorghum) has yet to be harvested. Cattle are usually retained nearby to eat the sorghum stocks after harvest. *Wec jiom* meets the desire of the young to leave the village, but keeps them near enough to help with village work.

Wec mai is the dry season settlement. Unlike *wec jiom*, it usually is a mixture of people of different villages, different lineages, or clans. In most cases, large camps are situated along the rivers, such as Sobat, Gile, or Pibor. Lakes, pools, and depressions which are deep and large enough to hold water through the dry season months also serve as camp sites.

Seasonal migration patterns in Nuerland vary according to the physical and biological conditions of each locality. Where villages may be located near their dry season grazing grounds, such as among the Gaawar Nuer, residents do not have to camp far from their village. Others, like the Lou Nuer, have to move their cattle a long distance almost every season. Variation of grazing and natural endowments calls for a high degree of flexibility and adaptation among users of natural resources.

Principles Behind Transhumance

The dry season movement from the permanent Nuer villages to cattle camp sites, where water and grazing are expected to last throughout the dry season months, is an annual event. However, the extent of such movements varies from one region to another. Organizing principles of individual right, as well as the realities of individual need, come into play.

Primarily, the transhumance of the Nuer is based upon need. The need for mobility in each season takes into account the best use of the natural resources. The herds from the different villages are moved from one grazing field to another, as there is the constant need to find water for humans and animals. Mobility is needed is to prevent overgrazing and the consequent spoiling of pastures. Existing pastures are not exhausted at each move. In comparison to the rainy season, the dry season is a time of scarcity among the Nuer. Securing food makes the mobility of a household a necessity.

These movements are not, however, limitless. Resource claims and boundaries limit mobility. Such regular movements of people may be understood by focusing on the principles of individual right behind the movements of clans such as Lou Nuer, Jikany Eastern Nuer, and the Zeraf valley communities. Figures 2.2, 2.3, and 2.4 show the movements of different communities during the dry season. The principles that underlie the dry season movements include: how rights overlap, how rights vary depending on the season, and how rights are negotiated. Because there are rarely acute shortages of grazing both in the intermediate lands and *tuoch* lands, the boundaries between regions or regional segments generally are not closely guarded.

In certain circumstances, however, protection of boundaries becomes essential. Their violation may then cause conflicts that result in violence and bloodshed. Sometimes there is an unusual shortage both of grass and water, and people who have normally allowed the intrusion of outsiders less favorably provided than themselves will then turn upon the outsiders and demand their withdrawal. Epidemic of some contagious disease, such as rinderpest or contagious bovine pleuro-pneumonia, makes exclusion of others necessary. Fear of the spread of disease compels cattle owners to guard their boundaries more closely. Bringing contaminated cattle into an area recognized as the exclusive right of other segments, where outsiders are only allowed on sufferance, is a particularly serious infringement of grazing rights and leads to hostilities unless outsiders promptly withdraw. Although fights have not been infrequent and boundary disputes are a common cause of blood-feuds, disputes of this nature are often settled peacefully by the council of elders, age-sets, and custodians.

Governing the Tuoch land

The functions of the Nuer pastoral economy are much more complex than simply maximizing the sustainable yield of cattle on certain grazing ground. The most important reason for this complexity is the variable and uncertain rainfall in the region. Not only must access to the grazing land be controlled, but also the risks of uncertainty of rainfall and drought must be managed if there is to be long term, sustainable use of the common-pool resource.

Access to *tuoch* land in most cases depends on some sort of relationship with others among the users of the grazing ground. Such relationships may be organized through marriage alliance and age-set arrangements. Marriage alliances and age-set arrangements facilitate access to resource sharing between clans and lineages in Nuer society. As John R. Commons (1950) wrote, "an institution is collective action in control, liberation, and expansion of individual action." They generates trust and confidence between disparate people so that they can carry out mutually beneficial relationships among themselves. Covenanting or making mutual agreements between groups to share use of a common-pool resource is another way to deal with foreigners who want to benefit from the use of common-pool resources.

The right of where a household may move to establish its cattle camp depends upon the season. Among the Nuer, no household follows exactly the same patterns of movement nor uses the same grazing areas in successive years. Subject to the seasonal limitation, a household has a wide choice of where to go. A family can go to any place either far from their village or near. The choices of dry season pasture are determined by proximity to water, by availability of food for human consumption, and by negotiations of access.

Negotiations in reference to access to *tuoch* land among individuals and groups are essential steps in the establishment of a cooperative arrangement between groups. The necessity of negotiated access to land-use applies, for example, to Lou Nuer who do not have a river that supplies them with water for humans and their animals in the dry season. The Lou have to negotiate with their neighbors. During the dry season, most Lou move to the Jikany Eastern Nuer area for access to grazing fields, but some move to Dinkaland, Murleland, and Anyuakland. Hence the situation enforces patterns of both transhumant and sedentary use over space and time.

A corollary of such patterns is interdependence. Both the less transhumant Jikany Eastern Nuer and more transhumant Lou Nuer had therefore to acquire relatively high levels of knowledge about their relationships to others who share the common resources. Such communication was only possible with active participation of those involved. The existence of institutional arrangements in which diverse types of collective actors can engage in an open contestation and in finding ways of accommodating complementary interests has been a blessing to the Nuer.

Land-use conflicts between Nuer segments are solved by recognized officials known as *kuar muon* (earth custodian) and *wud ghok* (cattle custodian). The conflict-resolution efforts of these religiously motivated third parties do more than merely offer a negotiating mechanism, a method of communication, or any other such purely procedural assistance. Rather, by introducing the authority of religion into the negotiating equation, they enable the parties to concede lands, assets, or claims to that authority itself, rather than to their antagonists. Concessions previously regarded as intolerable or as evidence of a lack of fortitude become politically acceptable when they are presented as acts of deference to religious teachings and religious personnel.

By reducing the vulnerability of disputants on each side to accusations of weakness, the range of politically feasible negotiating positions is expanded, more options for solution become available, and the chances of reaching a settlement are increased accordingly. Hence, the degree to which the religious authority evoked had an internal political validity for the disputants determines the degree of deference that either side may be willing to show to the other. Religiously based conflict resolution has been able to ameliorate an objective circumstance of conflict. It is not limited to operation within unchanging constraints. As already mentioned, religion is only one of the sources of third party authority; most notably, the council of elders and age-set leaders usually fulfill that function within a segment.

The use of natural resources shared by two or more federations is regulated by the peoples involved. In decades past, the Nuer as self-organizing and self-governing people instituted arrangements for a cycle of conferences to deal with constitutional matters. Elders and chiefs across clan lines met every five years at Fan-gak in the Central Nuer Region to see that basic constitutional arrangements kept pace with their changing environment and to address new challenges to the Nuer way of life. After the Sudan became independent, such conferences were discouraged by the representatives of the central government. The conferences were viewed as arrangements for usurping governmental functions. The last conference of elders, chiefs, and officials at Fan-gak was in 1963. There were and still are, however, multiple agents with limited authority to resolve conflicts arising between the groups using a resource held in common. The authority of such traditional leaders has largely been reduced by central government agents.

Changes in Transhumance Patterns

The political developments of the twentieth century in Nuerland have modified the traditional pastoral systems. The massive, seasonal movement of people with their cattle to grazing lands has declined for a variety of reasons. Economically, the profitability of agricultural activities has resulted in a decline in the frequency and distance of livestock mobility. This decline, to large extent, is due to encroachment by farmers and agro-pastoralists onto the traditional grazing grounds, reducing the size of available pastures in the village vicinity, and blocking the transhumance routes of herders. Encroachment also has reduced the radii of available grazing ground surrounding the cattle camps.

Politically, the Anglo-Egyptian Condominium conquest and subsequent imposition of colonial rule initiated a whole series of changes within pastoral societies in the Sudan. The Nuer (and other mobile Nilotic pastoralists such as the Karamajong in Uganda) offered fierce resistance to colonial rule. The sedentarization of the African pastoralists, whether forced or optional, has resulted in overgrazing and, consequently, land degradation in the semi-arid zones. A continental-scale rinderpest epidemic also brought about a decline in the level of pastoralism.

Ecologically, year-round grazing around the village is difficult, if not impossible to support without some source of water. In areas where water is readily accessible, continuous cattle grazing around settlement eventually will result in reduced vegetation cover and diversity and in soil degradation. Experience has also shown that lower grazing pressure in distant pastures results in an invasion of unpalatable plants (Galaty, 1988; Warren and Rajasekaran, 1993; Niamir, 1997). Sedentarization of pastoralists also results in a loss of traditional knowledge and a loss of controls on range, use leading less efficient management of the arid resources (Jacob, 1980; Farah, 1993).

Socially, changes in transhumance have had an adverse effect upon the Nuer way of life. Changes in mobility patterns, constraints imposed by a reduction in territory, decreasing herd sizes, and increasing population have all resulted in a lowering of the standard of living of the average herder. British Colonialism (in spite of the negative aspects) brought veterinary services, education, and access to markets both regionally and internationally (Duany, W, 1992), but these benefits were quickly negated as the Government of Sudan centralized control over political and economic activities.

Centralization under the institution of the state has led to weakening of traditional leadership among the southern peoples and fragmentation of authority. The customary leadership has been relegated to deal only with minor conflicts, and customary leaders are under heavy control by agents of central government. Land owned by the lineage has been taken by the nation-state under the pretense that the land was not being put into productive use by the community. Such lands are now used for government-owned farms, national wildlife parks, and forest reserves. Thus, the complex interplay of the apparatus of central government, the Nuer people among all different segmentary levels, and of rules both formal and informal, represents a downward spiral, contributing to the degradation not only of the pastoral land, but also to the decline of traditional technical knowledge. Until a strong system of nested institutions is put in place, the fatal threat to both pastoral ecosystems and traditional indigenous knowledge will remain.

Conclusion

The Nuer and other pastoral Nilotic peoples in the Nile River Basin have developed several strategies to adapt to the normal constraints of shortages of water during the dry season. These include complex cycles of transhumance to exploit several scattered production areas or *tuoch* lands with two major means: cattle herding and agriculture. Nuer use the sandy ridges to plant crops during the rainy season. Grain provides a reasonable (two-thirds) proportion of the Nuer caloric intake over the course of a year and is the most important single item in the diet in this respect. However, the size of the harvest is quite variable from year to year because of unreliable rainfall. Thus, the Nuer cannot completely depend upon grain. The diet must be supplemented with fish, meat, and dairy products.

Mobility of Nuer pastoralists during the dry season to cattle camps has been possible at any one point in time because groups have access rights and ownership claims to large land area. Each claim is mediated by the internal institutional arrangements, norms of reciprocity, and formal and informal regulations (Duany, W. 1999; Niamir-Fuller 1999). Access to a wider potential grazing land is facilitated by networks of relationships, marriage alliances, other interests, and force of arms. The herder's ability to respond to the high variability in ecosystem productivity is largely met through rules and covenants governed by negotiations and mediation between different peoples. Force has been a portent weapon used to expand pastures and other economic interests such as cattle or, as a last resort, when negotiations fail.

The Nuer ecosystems were relatively viable in the nineteenth century despite severe drought episodes (Johnson and Anderson, 1988; Niamir-Fuller 1999). A number of factors explain this situation, including low population, land-tenure security vested in customary communal institutions, governance of natural resources by traditional institutions, and the use of traditional indigenous improvement techniques. However, the Nilotic peoples were not—and still are not—homogenous. Nor are they always peaceful. Competition between Dinka and Nuer for use of natural resources and economic gain, for example, has shaped the dynamic evolution of Nilotic societies. However, what scholars and people involved in development need to understand is the array of economic, political, ecological, and social institutions that have allowed pastoral production systems to remain resilient to this time.

The resilience of pastoral ecosystems has been dependent upon traditional indigenous knowledge. The Nuer and other Nilotic pastoralists have built trust and reciprocal relationships among themselves, sharing the traditional technical knowledge of their environment. The Nilotic combine the spirit of religion and freedom of action in a manner that encourages the development of religious mores, customs, and indigenous institutions that operate according to principles of democratic self-governance. These people share a sense of moral community. They have created methods to adhere to the values of good neighborliness and willingness to accept mediation of disputes within the community itself. Such traditions that encourage a unity of purpose among transhumant pastoralists must be encouraged. It must not be destroyed. The nation-states within the River Nile Basin pose a deadly threat, not only to pastoral ecosystems, but also to the traditional indigenous knowledge that maintains the local ecology .

FIGURE 2.1   MAP OF THE SUDAN WITH PROVINCIAL TOWNS

FIGURE 2.2:   MAP OF THE VILLAGES AND DRY SEASON CAMPS OF LOU NUER
SECTIONS

Map of the Villages and
Dry Season Camps of Lou Nuer Sections

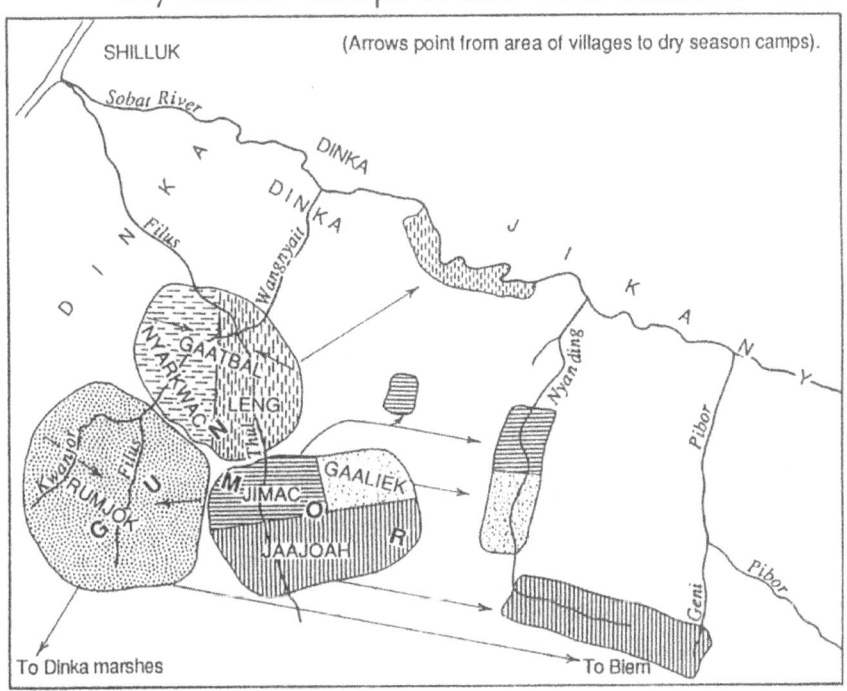

Source: Evans-Pritchard (1940a: 56).

FIGURE 2.3   MAP OF THE VILLAGES AND DRY SEASON CATTLE CAMPS OF THE
     EASTERN JIKANY NUER SECTIONS

Map of the Villages and
Dry Season Cattle Camps of
the Eastern Jikany Nuer Sections

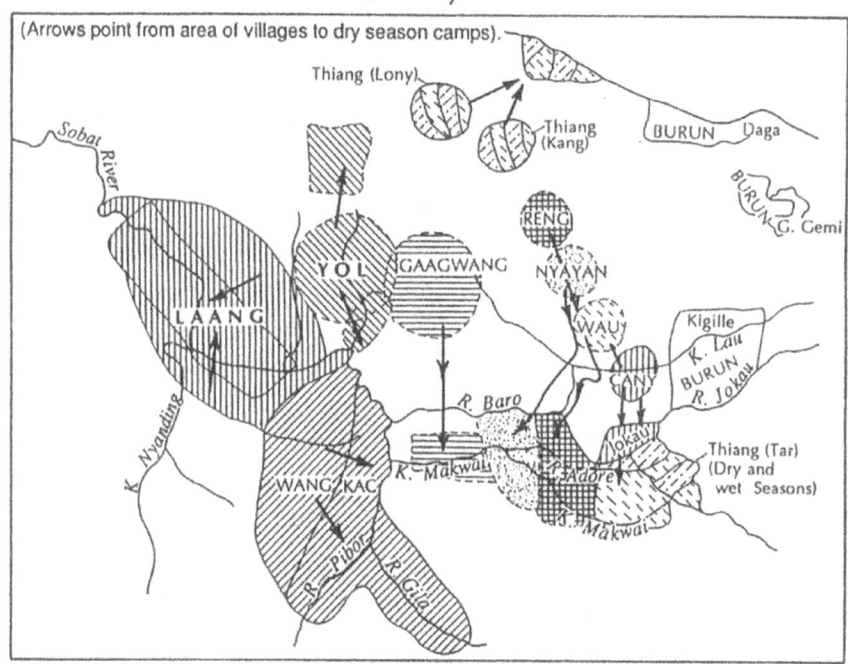

Source: C. L. Armstrong & Evans-Pritchard (1940).

FIGURE 2.4   MAP SHOWING THE DIRECTION OF MOVEMENTS IN THE DRY SEASON OF
THE ZERAF COMMUNITIES.

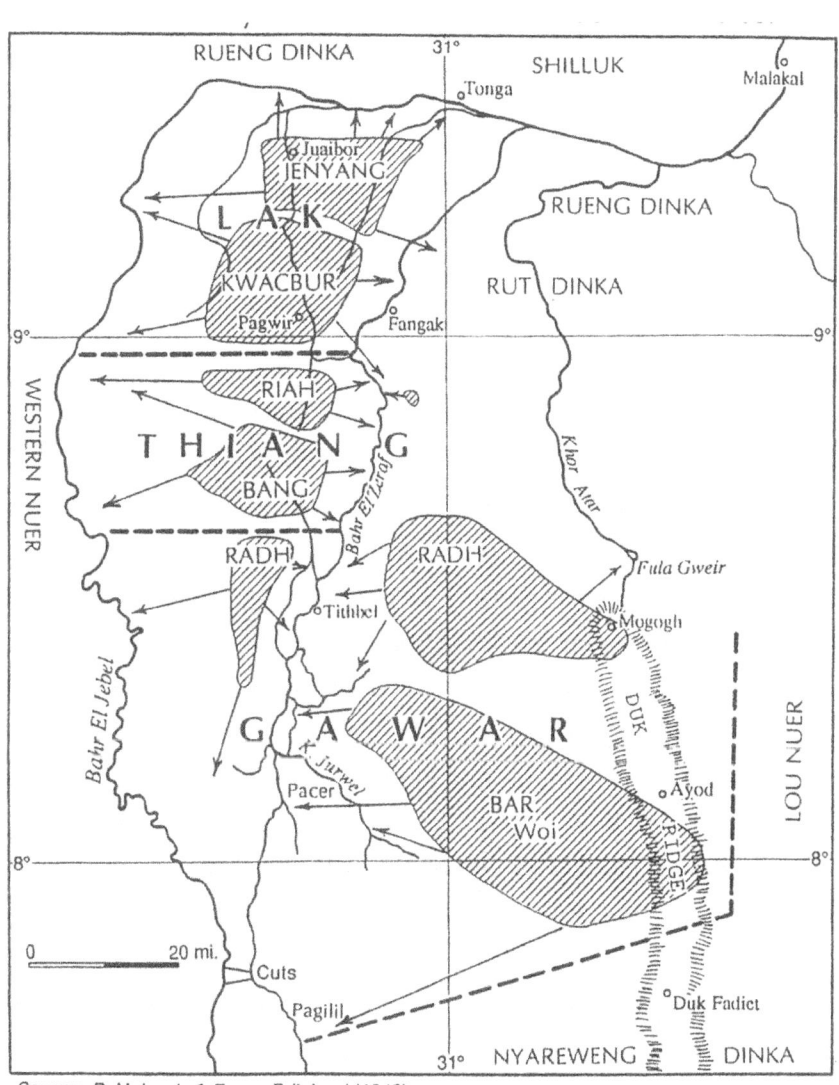

Source: B. H. Lewis & Evans-Pritchard (1940).

Chapter 3 - Nuer Conceptions and Nuer Law

Introduction

What are the essential elements that constitute a people and their ways of life? They are revealed in the ways a people think about themselves and in the ways they order their relationships with each other and with the larger world.

The shared understandings of a particular people are based partly on basic conceptions of universal order and partly on similar experiences of the past.[23] These understandings are made explicit when adults teach their young children the basic elements of their culture. In an environment where contact with other peoples is relatively infrequent, the way a people conceive and explain their constitutional arrangement is dominant. In an environment where contact with other peoples is frequent, however, the basic elements are susceptible to challenge.

The choices, therefore, that different peoples make in ordering their societies and organizing principles are not uniform. Despite evident differences in social ordering, scholars have tended to perceive that there is only one way to order human societies: the hierarchical structure of organizing authority relationships.[24] Acceptance of this presupposition is primarily due to a limited understanding of the ways that diverse human societies, operating in different cultural environments, realize their potential.

In reality, some societies have developed non-hierarchical arrangements for organizing authority relationships. Oral historical accounts suggest that the Nuer people have existed for a very long time in relative harmony without a common head or source of ultimate authority. Nuer society is grounded in concepts of covenantal relationships. Mutual agreements are created to resolve daily problems consistently, with equality and fairness, and without reference to mediating authorities. The individual Nuer does not see this arrangement as chaotic or primitive, but rather as equal, fair, and free.

Nuer Conceptions of Their Universe and Themselves

In this chapter, we will show how Nuer cosmology influences the way the Nuer people organize their institutions and their authority relation-

ships. Then, we will explain how this framework supports Nuer understandings of "being in the right" and remedies for wrongdoing. Finally, we will
explain how adaptation to the British concept of law has corrupted the traditional Nuer way of life.

Conceptions of the Creator and His Will

Understanding the Nuer conception of God (*Kuoth*) as the source of
creation is fundamental to understanding institutional arrangements among
the Nuer. As we will show, the existence of the humanity and the institutions
of marriage and family are all understood in terms of the Nuer idea of creation (*cak*) and the will of *Kuoth*.

The Creator

Used as a noun, *cak* means the creation, that is, all created things. As
a verb "to create," it signifies the act of creating. Because there can be no
creating of something from nothing, there is presumed to be an ultimate
source of creation, that is, a transcendent order or a God (*Kuoth*). The Nuer
concept of *cak* can also be used to refer to the imaginative constructions of
men: thinking of a name to give to a child, inventing a tale, working out a
system of rules, or composing a poem. *Cak* may be used in the same figura-
tive sense as when we say that an actor creates a part. The word, therefore,
means creation by thought or imagination, as in "God created the universe."
It also has the sense of "God thought of the universe" or "God imagined the
universe" (Douglas 1980, 96B97; Evans-Pritchard 1956, 4-5).

The Nuer believe that things are as they are because *Kuoth* has
willed it. *Kuoth* made the heavens, the earth, the waters on the earth, and all
living things. He ordained marriage for man and woman. He gave ritual
powers to some men and not to others. This inequality of powers was established in order to provide a means to order relationships between individuals
related to one another through a segmental family structure (an authority
structure, which also is viewed as a divine creation). Everything in nature, in
culture, in society, and in human existence is as it is because *Kuoth* willed it
so. The Nuer thinks of *Kuoth* as the giver and sustainer of life, and also as the
one who brings death.[25]

The Nuer *Kuoth* is conceptualized as neither a thing of wood or stone nor an anthropomorphic being, but rather as a spiritual entity. The Nuer do not act towards Him as though He were a man. If *Kuoth* is to be spoken about or to, He is given some human attributes. He is the Father of men and women, their Creator and their Protector. *Kuoth* is believed to be in the sky, but He is not the same as the sky. He is just especially in the sky in the same way as human beings are especially on the earth. *Kuoth* has no real physical location and no spatial boundaries. In addition, *Kuoth* is a creative spirit, ubiquitous and invisible. He sees and hears all that happens. *Kuoth* has emotion. He can be angry and He can love.[26]

While *Kuoth* is felt to be far away in the sky, He is also felt to be near in the sense that He can be communicated with through prayers and sacrifice. The conception of *Kuoth* as a protector is further elucidated in the frequent use of the word *rom* in prayers. This term refers to the care and protection that parents give to a child, especially a helpless infant. Another concept often used in prayers, *luek*, literally means to advise, or to guide. *Kuoth* is asked to *luek e naath*, to guide people. Evidence of His guidance confirms His presence. Also, a certain kind of contact with *Kuoth* is maintained through adherence to the social order that He has instituted.

The Creator's Will—Marriage and Family

The commitment of the people to adhere to *luek Kuoth*, or God's laws, suggests that human beings have an obligation to create social arrangements that will provide *ciaang*, or orderly living, in order that the will of the Creator may be fulfilled. The *Ciaang naath* is the customary practice of Nuer. *Naath* literally means "the people" and has an ethnocentric overtone. They are "the" people of the area. At base, these social arrangements consist of a man and a woman uniting in marriage. Domestic relations are what constitute life, or *ciaang* in the family (*cieng*). Marriage and the birth of children give rise to authority relationships, such as between husband and wife, parents and children, and between older and younger brothers. Rules (*nguot*) and customary practices govern household organization and relationships within the family.

Because the family is a key feature in the governance of Nuer society, established family law is also part of the larger political order. A wife must obey her husband. A man must respect his wife and his wife's kin.

Children must honor their parents and their parent's age-mates. Younger siblings must respect older siblings, but are not under their authority, since all siblings have equal standing before their father. If an individual fails to observe the rules (*nguot*), he not only loses the support of his kin but, it is also believed, the favor of his ancestors and of *Kuoth*. Retribution, in one form or another, is bound to come sooner or later.

The domestic group, the household, may break up through the death of the father, but the rightful or lawful family (the group of husband, wife, and children born of the wife) endures. The Nuer regulation by which a widow remains married to a dead husband gives the family institution stability and durability. The personnel of the household may undergo many changes, but the rightful family is fixed by the payment of bridewealth, which determines who is the rightful or lawful father of any children born of the wife, whether that man be alive or dead. Thus, the institutional structure family survives even the dispersal of its members.[27]

The position of father is lawfully predominant in Nuer society. Children trace their descent through their lawful father, even if he did not beget them. They belong to his clan and are entitled to enjoy the rights of that group. From the lawful father the children inherit. His herd is their birthright and any cattle that would have been due to him, were he still living, belong to his lawful children as his heirs. Whatever social or ritual status he may have had, they also inherit.

The Nuer think of a son in a lawful family as being dependent upon his father. A son has no property rights independent of his father's rights. He does not own cattle in the family herd, which belongs to his father. He has disposal of the cattle only through the permission of his father or through his standing as his father's heir.

The feelings of respect and affection of a son to his father are directed towards the man who actually is his physiological and lawful father. The mutual dependence between father and son tends to promote harmony between them. It is usually the son who cares for his aged father. For the Nuer male, begetting sons is a form of security for the future. A father raises his son, and in the future receives assistance from him.

The authority of a father is not, however, absolute. For instance, when a son quarrels with his father, a degree of external interference is allowable. It usually is minimal, but, depending upon on the nature of the conflict, may be significant. Conflict between father and son over mismanagement of property (cattle) by the father could very well involve close kin. Because of kin solidarity, relatives are concerned with each other's economic welfare and security. The acceptance of external interference implies that the authority of the father in the household is limited. Indeed, a father cannot kill his son with impunity. All family members stand equal before their Creator, regardless of status. Nevertheless, family disputes are usually contained within the household and resolved speedily to prevent interference and polarization of family members and kin.

The function of the lawful father may extend beyond a man's lifetime. If a man should die, then his nephew or brother may marry a woman and beget children in his name. Therefore, when a man marries in the name of his paternal uncle or of his brother who is dead, the son he begets is his father's brother's son or his own brother's son. The newborn son belongs to a different family, and potentially to a different *gol* or household, than that of the man who has begotten him. The legal personality of this son is not, therefore, merged with that of his genitor but rather with that of his dead father, whose status he assumes and whose property rights he inherits. *Mar* (kinship) relationships continue to be maintained, however, between the household of the genitor and the son's family.

Mar (kinship) relationships, including both agnatic (through an individual's male descent line) and cognatic (through any or all of an individual's acknowledged relatives) kin, provide the stable framework of kinship structures. These structures—family associations of one kind or another—have independent existence as non-hierarchical arrangements for organizing authority relationships. They anchor each individual to some group.[28] If a person breaks away from one group, sooner or later that person will attach himself or herself to another group and become part of its structure. There is an implication that the development of a group is viewed primarily as a process of mutual agreement among individuals. This in turn implies that the Nuer constitution of order is an artifact made by people to achieve important tasks and things of value for themselves.

Though bound to a framework of kinship structures, the individual Nuer thinks of himself or herself as having equal standing with others in constituting long-term patterns of order. Since God, or *Kuoth*, creates all Nuer people, all are *gaat Kuoth*, or sons of God, and stand equal before Him. And since God has given *ran*, or each person, life and the ability to think for himself or herself, each can do certain things to advance his or her own interests and to glorify *Kuoth*. Each person is valued as an individual and treated with consideration, sympathy, and respect. The Nuer conception of order emphasizes that the individual exists, but also that each individual is involved in the wider society. In other words, while individual persons are seen as viable agents in the maintenance of the social order, they also are subject to the interconnections that exist among members of a community and the consequences of their actions on the community.

Conceptions of "Being in the Right"

The presumption of equality before their Creator is what gives individuals equal standing in the establishment of patterns of order. The way the Nuer people think of their lives is reflected in the way they have organized their social relationships. A non-hierarchical order is regarded as intrinsic.

Because all people are children of God, "love thy neighbor as thyself" implies that neighbors are one's equals, and thus entitled to a fellow feeling of brotherhood. Orderly relationships in the wider community are achieved by extending the love of God's children to other social relationships outside the family. Since these relationships develop from the love of God and adherence to His laws, they remain harmonious under conditions of mutual respect. So long as each individual seriously takes into account the interests of others, destructive conflicts between individuals can be avoided.

So long as individuals follow the principle of "being in the right" (that is, conducting themselves according to the accepted code of behavior), they will pay respect to existing social rules and authority relationships. Failing to do this is considered wrong, incurs punishment from kin and from *Kuoth*, and reduces the honor and prestige of the family in the society.

An individual may know that he or she is in the right by the support he or she receives from kin. An individual's kin are involved, therefore, in the establishment of a new family. Marriage is believed to be ordained by *Kuoth* for the purpose of supporting the multiplication of humanity. A family is viewed as a means by which new social tissues are formed. It is considered a duty of a family to the Creator to raise and care for children. Loving and caring within the family constitute acting in accordance with the divine will of *Kuoth*. Love and care include the training of children. The goal of character building in Nuer society is to teach "being in the right." Human love to-wards one's parents is considered to be acquired by learning. Obedience is owed by children to parents (and by wives to their husbands), but only if the parents (or the husband) have in turn fulfilled their duty of care.

This principle of "being in the right" is the root of all virtues (Douglas 1980). Nuer tradition teaches that whoever is in the right is always doing *cuong* (right), but whoever is not in the right is always in the wrong and offends elders, religious leaders, equals, and his juniors.

As Mary Douglas (ibid.) observes, all relationships in Nuer society revolve around the practice of being in the right. To justify non-hierarchical relationships on a basis of "being in the right" has fundamental implications in a society of equals. Being in the right with others relies on the competence of individuals to maintain the integrity of non-hierarchical arrangements. Thus, authority relationships are generalized beyond family relationships.

The role of mediators is an example of how non-hierarchical authority is derived from "being in the right." Tensions within the structure of authority relationships are inevitable, particularly in cases where persons in conflict cannot meet to negotiate. In order to resolve conflicts among members, third party intervention by a mediator is required. Mediation by a third party works only if the people involved believe in the effectiveness of the system.

The Nuer believe that *Kuoth* endows mediators, as members of the priestly lineages, with the ability to cause harm to befall those who obstruct the process of dispute resolution. Mediators are believed to be authorized by God to coerce, curse, and to ban from His territory those individuals who are destructive of civil peace. In addition to their capacity to coerce, curse, or ban, mediators are well versed in Nuer traditional law. Due to the popular belief that their powers can cause harm to come to individuals, their knowledge of the law, their individual powers, and their skill at persuasion, the mediators are able to facilitate conflict resolution and maintain law and order. More will be said about mediators (spokesmen and custodians) later in this chapter.

Conceptions of Law

The Nuer, like other human societies, order their relationships by using rules. Rules reflect the norms people use to decide which actions should be forbidden and which should be permitted or required. Forbidding or imposing limits on some possible actions allows individuals to achieve predictability and still exercise considerable freedom of action. A shared set of rules orders behavior in daily life and supports the stable relationships that generate productive interdependence.

Rules are not, however, self-formulating. The task of making rules, enforcing rules, and altering rules is a key function of governance. In an acephalous society, the authority to create rules lies with the individuals who use covenanting as a method of formulating specific rules. A common understanding of the rules is an important prerequisite to an effective rule of law. Also, people must share a common interpretation of knowable rules if the rules are to be effective in ordering their behavior.

The absence of a single source of common authority to make rules poses a fundamental problem among the Nuer: how to create rules that apply equally to all members in a segmented structure of authority relationships. Because *Kuoth* has given all Nuer a set of general principles, individuals use these as a guide when making specific rules that are applicable among smaller communities. Actions consistent with the principle of doing right are permitted. Wrong actions are not allowed. Thus, specific, recognized rules exist that guide decisions people make in resolving a given dispute. This can be observed in the structure of the legal system, where *nguot* and *cuong* are recognized.

Nguot: The Legal Foundation of Covenantal Relationship

A substantial consensus concerning the rules that govern individuals is vital to establishing harmonious relationships among members of a community. People must understand what is allowed and what is forbidden if interdependence is to be meaningful and acceptable. People must perceive conduct as compatible with custom. For the Nuer, the spirit underlying the conception of proper conduct is clearly linked with their cosmology. This link is the Nuer concept of *nguot*.

The word *nguot* means "to cut." Used as it is here, *nguot* means to cut a covenant, to cut an agreement, or to establish a code of behavior for the transaction of tasks valued among individuals.[29] It is used to describe covenantal relationships made among individuals. *Nguot* suggests that an inviolable bond exists. The result of *nguot* is a commitment to an established relationship in connection with other people. People negotiate and compromise to reach an agreement, but it is the formalizing element of the *nguot* commitment that is essential to establishing the relationship. People involved in making a *nguot* commitment verbally declare the nature of the bond or agreement being made. In many cases, symbolic action accompanies the verbal commitment. These actions include the offering of sacrifice, such as the dividing of animals in performing the ritual for incest purification (*yang ruali*),[30] or the killing of an ox signifying an agreement about bridewealth (*nguot kuen*).

The binding character of a covenantal commitment is reflected in the terminology of "cutting."[31] As a *nguot* relationship is established, animals are "cut" in ritual ceremony. The most obvious example of this procedure is the shedding of blood in animal sacrifice. The rubbing of ashes on the back of the ox to be sacrificed is an act of substituting the life of a beast for the life of a human being. It is a clear identification of the one making the sacrifice with the animal victim. Depending on the type of *nguot* commitment being initiated, the meat of the animal may be cut into pieces and divided for consumption. The meaning of the division of animal meat at the point of the *nguot* commitment is fundamental to the integrity of the covenant. The division symbolizes a "pledge to the death" at the point of the *nguot* commitment. The dismembered animals represent the curse that the *nguot* maker calls down on himself should he violate the commitment he has made. By his transgression, he would call down upon himself the curses of the covenant or the rule. This would be the punishment prescribed by the covenant mediator, who oversees the process of establishing a covenant and renewing a covenant. The covenant mediator is believed to be designated for this role by *Kuoth* or God. The mediator serves as His representative and as His agent in the execution of justice. Thus, the man who violates the covenant might expect the dismemberment of his own body.

Once the *nguot* relationship has been established between individuals or groups, *nothing less than the shedding of blood may relieve the obligations incurred in the event of violation of the nguot commitment.* Changing a *nguot* commitment requires mutual agreement. It is in this life and death context of establishing covenantal relationships that the Nuer concept of *nguot* is to be understood.

Blood is significant in this context because it represents life.[32] Life is in the blood, and so the shedding of blood represents a judgment on life. When a breach of the bond is committed, the individual who has been wronged or unjustly deprived of his rights will be justified in fighting to enforce his rights. Community intervention may make fighting unnecessary by addressing the wrong and renewing the covenant. Sacrificing cattle that belong to the wrong doer is a method commonly used by Nuer to punish wrongdoing and to reestablish a covenantal relationship.

Cuong: The Rule of Proper Conduct in Community

The concept of *cuong* is derived from the idea of *nguot*. *Cuong* can mean "upright," for example, in reference to the upright supports of byres (*cuong cie-ke thier luak*). It is also used figuratively to mean "firmly established," as in the phrase *be gole cuong e pic*, or "may his hearth stand" (Evans-Pritchard 1956). It is most commonly employed, however, to mean "being in the right" in both a forensic and a moral sense.

Discussion in law cases is for the purpose of determining which party in the case has the *cuong*, or the right—or who has the most right. In any argument about conduct, the issue is always whether or not a person has conformed to the accepted norms of social life. If he has, then he has *cuong*. He has right on his side. The individual who has *cuong* is seen as doing that which morally ought to be done, that which is conformable with the *nguot* commitment, that which is conformable with good social order, or that which is in tune with the universal order. If a person has *cuong*, he has observed the rules of proper conduct in community life.

This concept of *cuong* relates directly to an individual's behavior towards his Creator. It also relates to the Creator in a more indirect way, in that He is regarded by the Nuer as the founder and guardian of human morality. This does not suggest that God immediately and directly sanctions persons for their wrongdoing. Rather, the Nuer believe that sooner or later and in one way or another "good will follow right conduct" and "ill will follow *duer*, wrong conduct." If a man keeps himself in the right, that is, if he does not break rules or wrong others, and if he fulfills his obligations to spiritual beings and to his kindred, he will avoid serious misfortunes or punishment. Evans-Pritchard observes that the Nuer (who he says are a quarrelsome people) avoid, in so far as they can restrain themselves, giving gratuitous offense because of the fear of God (Douglas 1980). The thought of God's heavy handed intervention encourages compliance with the rules of right conduct. Mary Douglas observes:

> If a man were to refuse to pay up in the social transactions, the whole system would collapse like a pack of cards. It is no small political achievement that any Nuer to whom a cow is owed can go and collect his debt in a camp of strangers with all the immunities of law, *because he was in the right* [emphasis added]. The pressure of cattle debts being strong, the wish to evade payment must be strong also. The possibility of fighting it out when one has had the misfortune to kill another must be more attractive than paying over full forty head of cattle (1980, 106).

Social debts, however, tend to be paid within geographical and social limits. These payments are seen as creating communities that recognize their own distinct identity and that are able to ally with neighbors to defend their rights against more distant foes. The moral influence to end strife and to negotiate a truce when balanced segments confront each other depends more on the inequality in transactions between God and the individual human being than it does on the equality in transactions between humans.

Cuong conceived of as justice and righteousness helps maintain a social order among Nuer people. The conception of the universal character of divine righteousness implies a uniform connection from God to human beings, and from person to person. Any violation of the rights of an individual is seen as an affront to divine will. This sense of *cuong* as justice and righteousness is a regulative principle. It is consistent with the argument that the non-hierarchical order among the Nuer emphasizes equality, autonomy, and individual responsibility.

Another way to understand *cuong* is to study trouble cases. The actual experience of the Nuer under the various *nguot* commitments reflects the continuity, rather than the discontinuity, of covenant relationships. John R. Commons' (1959) concept of working rules of going concerns emphasizes the important role played by concerned officials in establishing the law on a dispute by dispute basis. Commons' work suggests the trouble case methodology as the appropriate method for learning what actions are consistent with *cuong*. Karl N. Llewellyn and E. Adamson Hoebel (1941) argue that trouble cases—"instances of hitch, dispute, grievance, trouble"—reveal more accurately the reality of law in a culture than does the study of idealized, normative patterns of everyday behavior.

One ought by no means to ignore normative patterns or the practice of everyday behavior occurring within the constraints of the working rules. Both of these perceived "right ways" and normal ways of doing things interplay with locally sanctioned rules of law. But if regularities in human conduct are to be explained by reference to rules, then trouble cases are the way to see rules in action at the boundary points between licit and illicit action. In the end, trouble cases are the way to find out whether or not a stated norm is applied in practice, and if it is, how?

Recent trouble cases arising among the Nuer reveal which rules the elders used in attempting to assess the conduct of disputants or violators. The cases confirm that there is a standard application of who is in the right, or who is more nearly right, in particular cases.[33] However, the cases also show that the decision about who is in the right, or who is more nearly right, is, in practice, affected by structural distance in genealogical terms. This implies that a similar act can be evaluated differently according to the actors' social distance.

Conceptions of the Mediator

How do the Nuer enforce the law on those members of the society who deviate from the accepted norms? Because there is no paramount ruler, there is no single person or group of persons who has the power to enforce rules on everyone else.

The problem is that if rules cannot be enforced, some people will take advantage of others. The proper application of the rules both by users (*duek*) and enforcers (*kuar*) requires some impartial standard of judgment in order to maintain lawful relationships in the society. Persons are expected to make normative judgments by applying recognized criteria in distinguishing right from wrong.

The belief in equality among the Nuer supports the idea that each person is his own governor, meaning that he is accountable for his own actions to his fellowmen and to God, who is thought of as the guardian of morality. Associating human rules with transcendental power provides a possibility of orderly relationships among people. However, conceptualizing God as the guardian of the moral order poses some problems to man, because there are the things of above associated with the spirit, and the things of below associated with human life.

The Nuer believe that the divide is bridged: God intervenes in human affairs. The Spirit in the heavens descends to earth in natural ways, such as rain or lightning. The Spirit also works through individual persons to influence human affairs on earth. *Through an individual agent, a potential link is established between God and human society.* This idea is the basis upon which emperors of other cultures have presumed to be vicars of God, for example, Ivan IV (The Terrible) of Russia. For the Nuer, however, the power "to make a leader" or "to make a priest" is latent within the community. For the actual priesthood to emerge, a "form-giving intervention" is required.

This intervention is believed to have occurred when priestly powers were given to certain lineages—such as Jimem, Gatleak, and Jikul—in order to permit them to mediate effectively between individuals in conflict.[34] Members of the priestly lineages are known as *kuar*, custodians or "enforcers" of God's laws, while other lineages are *duek* or "users" of the laws. Members of the priestly lineages are scattered among communities in the Nuer society to provide mediating services.[35] It follows, then, that the office of mediator (or *kuar*, the custodian or enforcer of God's laws) is hereditary. The genealogical arrangement assures that an individual's participation as either a user or an enforcer of the law is accepted with the blessings of his forefathers.

Two other important principles are associated with the role of mediator and with the *nguot* commitment. One sanctions the removal of an individual Nuer from his or her position of privilege. The other sanctions the incorporation of strangers into Nuer society.

While the role of mediator is hereditary, *kuar* (custodians or enforcers of God's law) can forfeit their status (Dung, interview, 1989; Bum, interview, 1989). This principle of removal is grounded in the nature of the Nuer conception of God. *Kuoth* can love, but He can also become angry and withdraw favor or protection. A mediator is viable only because other Nuer have respect for him as the holder of the office. Therefore, the holder must behave in such a manner as to earn this respect. Users of the law, secure in the belief that God will do likewise, can withhold respect from a mediator who abuses his office. The mediator's curse will no longer be feared. The principle of removal from mediator status does not alter the genealogical position of the person concerned.

Through incorporation into existing lineages, a person of any origin can become Nuer in the fullest sense.[36] This implies that Nuer society is made up of collections of people of different origins.[37] Incorporation into Nuer society is accomplished through rituals of adoption—a *nguot* commitment. Through adoption, a person's status is changed from that of a foreigner to that of a family member in full standing, sharing equal rights and privileges with his or her adoptive parents. From that point onward, all children born to the adoptee become heir to all the rights and privileges enjoyed by the adoptee's lineage. The adoptee's line now stands as legitimate heir to the genealogical benefits accorded to the original line, whether priestly or not.

Spokesmanship

The Nuer recognize that the role of mediators—persons with special personal abilities to articulate problems and make normative judgments about who is or is not in the right—is important to the maintenance of their political order. Spokesmanship is seen as a quality vested in an exceptional mediator (*kuar*), a God-fearing person who is able to maintain or restore the *nguot* relationships between individuals.

One possessing the quality of spokesmanship (*ruic naath*) does not impose himself or enforce settlement of disputes by his personal prerogatives, but instead reveals the law to individuals and groups. He speaks to the people, but he cannot order them. Howell observes:

> There is no verb in the Nuer language meaning "to order," and the imperative is not used with any sense of authority behind it. To get another man to perform some task in his behalf, the Nuer must first draw attention to some special relationship between them, whether it is real or fictitious. It is an appeal to the mutual obligations inherent in kinship and is expressed in kinship terms. "*Gat mar*," or "O kinsman," is the preface to any request which might otherwise take the form of an order. By this I do not mean that the imperative is never used, but it is used only to persons with whom the speaker has an actual and constant relationship, and usually only when the speaker is a senior kinsman. When telling a

foreman woodcutter, for example, to order his men to cut down certain trees, the District Commissioner, allowed greater license than others, will use the imperative, but the foreman will pass the order on in more euphemistic terms and include himself in the effort to be made. This is merely an example of the exceptional independence of character of the Nuer and their refusal to admit superiority or domination (1954, 27B36).

A Nuer household is believed to be able to govern itself without outside interference. To protect rights threatened by other householders, households rely on the assistance of other kin. This implies self-help arrangements (Barkun 1968; Douglas 1986). The operation of the elementary principle of self-help usually produces great disparities of wealth and power. In the event of a free-for-all, there is a possibility that the strongest party will prevail, regardless of whether or not it was in the right. Among the Nuer, however, the strongest does not win for three reasons. First, wealth in the form of cattle, goats, and sheep is distributed fairly evenly among households. Cattle are given in bridewealth by each family in accordance with their means and are received by each family in accordance with the number of their daughters of marriageable age. (See Goody and Tambiah 1973 concerning the "leveling function" of bridewealth.) Second, there is no accumulation of power. Individual liberties have not been limited so as to allow power to accumulate with a single person or a body of men for the sake of the "good" order. Third, feuding resolves disputes and allows mutual adjustments between groups. Conflict, by creating regular patterns of alliance formation, serves as a functional substitute for a central government. It is, therefore, in conflict situations, rather than in everyday situations, that higher levels of organization become visible.

It is also in conflict situations that we see how regulative ideas are acted upon for marshaling activities in the society, even at higher levels of organization, where there is no single source of authority. The spokesman is a key figure in resolving a conflict situation and restoring the *nguot* relationship between individuals. Nevertheless, the spokesman does not influence the resolution of the situation because he is regarded as the authority over the parties. Rather, his words are heeded because he discerns the *nguot*.[38]

The Nuer believe, therefore, that as individuals they are capable of molding their own social context within the Nuer conception of order. They do not respond well to edict from a single source of authority. The conception of spokesmanship is germane to the challenges the Nuer face in modern Sudan's political environment for two reasons. First, the Nuer perceive the diminishing of the equality of members in a group as corrupting. Second, a spokesman must be able to maintain the unity of the group by the consent of its members. These insights open the possibility of developing an alternative system of political leadership. This possibility is all-important, because as the means of governance are worked out in twenty-first century Africa, it will be seen that the imposition of rule by one man or one body of men stifle the ancient, acephalous human societies from adapting to change. Indeed, the bloodshed and corruption of twentieth century Africa is testament to the need for alternatives. The challenge of Nuer governance will be maintaining the integrity of the *nguot* (covenant) relationships—and of the mediating services—which form the basis upon which to build constructive patterns of change

Custodians

The representation of the divinity in Nuer society is fragmented and distributed among members of several lineages, scattered through many villages, who function as mediating agents. Each of these persons can make decisions or judgments without reference to another center of authority. In order to maintain an ordered life, the Nuer rely heavily on multiple agencies (individuals) with special abilities to perform important functions on behalf of the entire community. Collectively, as we have seen, these individuals are known as *kuar*, the custodians or enforcers of God's law. Individually, they are known by their area of specialized function, which may, or may not, be priestly in nature.

These specialized abilities are confined to people of certain clans. As with the priestly clans, only a few people within the clan actually practice the regulatory activities, even though, theoretically, the ability is inherent in all members.[39] *Guan buthni* is the key spokesman of a lineage as a corporation of segments. He helps in the resolution of conflict within the lineage and is responsible for customs governing rearrangement of the social structure. *Guan buthni* conducts mortuary ceremonies, some of which are peculiar to the cause of death. For example, *colwic* ceremony is a memorial service of a person who was killed by lightning. *Kuar tang* (custodian for defense) plans offensive and defensive warfare. *Guan thoi* (water custodian) has the ability to assure the safety of water when members of a community fish or cross a body of water. The Nuer people can expect that when he assists, they will catch more fish. *Kuar yiika* (custodian for family affairs) mediates arguments on death and injuries, such as those which might occur to an abducted female, whether she is unmarried or married. These specialized spokesmen or custodians can be identified by the objects most often used in their regulatory activities, or by some natural element associated with their ability, as shown in the Table of Key Political Functionaries.

The Nuer recognize two major types of mediating tasks that must be performed in order to sustain their society. One is mediating between disputing parties. The other task is subduing the earth. In Nuer thought, humans have a unique responsibility to "subdue the earth." This subduing involves realizing all the potential within creation that might offer glory to the Creator.[40]

There are consequently two types of priests in Nuer society. The first is the *kuar muon*, the earth custodian or enforcer of God's laws regarding the earth. The second is *wud ghok*, the cattle custodian or enforcer of God's laws regarding cattle. Again, the representation of divinity, which is the role of these custodians, is exercised by diverse individuals scattered among Nuer communities.

Kuar muon (earth custodian) has priestly power derived from a divinity referred to as *Kuoth rieng*, the divinity of the flesh. The *kuar muon's* responsibilities are to control the earth and its productivity, and to promote the peace of God and the welfare of those who live on and by the earth (Jackson 1923; Schilde 1947; Evans-Pritchard 1956; Howell 1954). The earth custodians, as the enforcers of God's laws, mediate between disputants in conflicts concerning rights in shared land, grazing areas, or water.

They also are called in cases of homicide (Dung, interview, 1989; Evans-Pritchard 1940; Jackson 1923, 89). Homicide implies that the soil has been polluted with blood, which may explain why the earth custodian is an indispensable participant in the rituals of atonement and reconciliation. His ability to curse and to ban, which threatens any person obstructing the rightful course of a *kuar muon's* peacemaking duties, is believed to have divine origins. The earth custodian's powers are hereditary.

An earth custodian and a cattle custodian do not have extensive kin ties with other lineages the particular region where they reside. Neither the earth custodian's lineage, nor the cattle custodian's lineage would have been among the original settlers (*diel*) of the region. Rather, custodians live scattered among the *diel* of the various regions of Nuerland. As members of neutral lineages, earth custodian and cattle custodian are therefore able to mediate disputes between the dominant lineages of the region.

The *wud ghok*, or cattle custodian (enforcer of God's laws regarding affairs of cattle), belongs to one of a number of lineages believed to have special abilities to cure cattle diseases. Conversely, a *wud ghok's* curse can adversely affect the health of a man's herd.

The cattle custodian is also responsible for regulating the social processes of the age-set system. He is responsible for opening and closing the initiation periods, thereby, creating distinct age-sets. Age-set membership ranks people in order of seniority, equality, and juniority.
Age-set rank allows an individual, wherever he or she may be, to know what other persons he or she must treat with formal respect, and from what other men and women he or she should receive this respect. For this to be possible there must be a clear line drawn between successive sets. The cattle custodian's role in defining age-sets derives from the fact that initiation into an age-set system alters the relationship of young men to their cattle. For example, initiated young men are forbidden to milk cows. The defense of cattle from outside predation by animals or humans is another important connection between the cattle custodian and the age-set system.

The *wud ghok's* priestly powers, his economic and military importance, and his hereditary prestige together afford him the opportunity of acquiring the greater political status of *ruic naath* (spokesman). Nevertheless, the abilities of the cattle custodian are thought to be more limited than those of the earth custodian. What is important is that in both cases, the abilities are derived from the same principle: a hereditary and inherent virtue that is implicit in all men of priestly lineages. The virtue is active in some, but strong only in few. It is manifest in the deeds and, above all, in the words of the priestly positions (Johnson 1980).

Conceptions of Minimal Government

The traditional Nuer political system has no single recognized chief to run it and no exclusive judiciary to control it. Persons are divided among political units without any single administrative hierarchy of officials and without any single person to direct all of the common affairs of the society. Although the Nuer lack the machinery of centralized government, this does not lead to mere anarchy and indiscriminate violence. There are forms to maintain lawful order.

The Nuer depend upon common understandings and rules that enable each person to relate to others in productive ways. The operation of the society depends upon the capability of individuals to form stable expectations about the behavior of other members by knowing the rules of the community. Many scholars have assumed that the Nuer, because they do not have a centralized government, have no rules to govern themselves. But this assumption is incorrect. They do have rules.

The rules of the Nuer are built on the foundation of language. Yet, if words are to work in promoting social harmony in an acephalous system, then some arrangements must exist for formulating them, determining their application, and enforcing relationships in accordance with working rules (Commons 1959). These are the arrangements that are identified with governmental institutions in the broadest sense.

Among the Nuer, the members of a single *gol* (homestead) always recognize the authority of their senior member. If the *gol* is perceived as a self-governing unit and if the authority of the senior member is considered sufficient to establish rule ordered relationships, then it is clear that the family institution is, both in theory and practice, capable of ruling itself. It logically follows that the idea of minimal government may be consonant with the Nuer way of life, where there are multiple decision structures without a single person monopolizing the prerogatives of governance.

The Nuer give support to the concept of minimal government in two ways. First, there are rules and a common understanding of these rules. Persons are conscious of the existence of rules as rules. For example, no one questions that to kill is an offense. Second, certain persons function as leaders because they are respected as such. Leaders are elder members of the community. People will listen to what they say because of their age and wisdom. Others are respected as leaders because they have recognized priestly powers that are not shared by all members of the community. Only these men can perform certain ceremonies for the community. By performing ceremonies or acting out rituals, they effect decisions in relation to the persons involved.

In matters of governance, the autonomy of the individual has profound influence on the design of institutions in an acephalous society. Among the Nuer, there is no integrated bureaucratic structure to handle public issues. Individuals, family institutions, and voluntary associations are, therefore, left to regulate their own local affairs. This arrangement permits individuals to work with other members of the society to resolve their problems, instead of waiting for or depending upon an external authority to take action.

Nuer Law

To understand how the Nuer have mediated conflict over time, it is necessary to know what sets of rules concerning wrongdoing have applied in different historical periods. We will first define what is meant by the Nuer concept of *duer* and then explain how the Nuer originally provided for remedies, enforced obligations, and punished wrong doers. Finally, we will examine the effect of the imposition of British concept of law on the Nuer way of life.

Duer: A Code of Rules for Punishing Wrongdoing

Although *Kuoth* is asked to guide people (*luek e naath*), and a *nguot* commitment provides rules (*luek*) for ordering conduct, the Nuer accept that human beings can make wrong decisions that lead to wrongdoing. In order to maintain or restore lawful relationships when an individual's behavior deviates from the acceptable, a way must be found to stop unacceptable behavior and to bring it into conformity with accepted patterns of conduct.

The word *duer* means "a fault." The verb *duir* means "to be at fault." Like similar words in other languages (for instance, English, Arabic, and Swahili), *duir* has both the sense of missing a mark aimed at (as in throwing a spear) and of a dereliction (as in a fault that is characteristic of retribution). Any failure to conform to the accepted codes of behavior towards a member of one's family, kin, age-set, a guest, and so forth, is a fault that may bring about evil consequences. The evil consequences may come as the result of either a curse that is voiced or a silent curse generated by anger and resentment. The misfortunes that follow are regarded as coming ultimately from God, who supports the cause of the man who has the *cuong* (the right in the matter), and punishes the person who is at fault.

There are two punishments for *duer*, which reflect the type of fault committed. Repercussions from a religious fault, such as the breach of an interdiction or the neglect of some spirit, may be avoided by expressions of remorse and a sacrifice. The Nuer believe that sacrifice without remorse is meaningless. Repercussions stemming from a wrongdoing of a political nature can be avoided by the payment of reparations. The fact that the consequences of a *duer* can be stayed by contrition and compensation indicates that the results of wrongdoing are not perceived to be automatic (Evans-Pritchard 1956). There is a moral, an uncertainty, and an alterable element involved in the situation.

This is made clear by another circumstance. In estimating the number of cattle to be paid in compensation for the misfortune that has occurred, the earth custodian takes intent into account. The Nuer distinguish *duer* and *guac*. The concept of *duer* normally implies that the fault committed was deliberate, though this is not always the case. *Guac* means a mistake, an unintentional error. It implies that the action was incorrect but inadvertent, and that a person may ask to be excused. The fact that the action was not deliberate, to some extent, alters the circumstances. This is evident in cases where damage and compensation are involved. The manner of discussions and the amount of compensation depend on whether or not the slaying is premeditated or accidental. The difference in the weapon used is also a qualification. The Nuer consider the use of a fighting spear as an indication of intention.

The Creator is thought to take intent into account in breaches of moral law. However, in the Nuer scheme of things, individuals have to accept the consequences of their actions, whether they are deliberate or not. Certain acts are always a fault.

The Way of Mediating Conflict

As the discussion on mediators shows, maintenance of acephalous order is the function of multiple agents with limited jurisdiction in resolving conflict. Without these agents, the individual's freedom to regulate his own affairs would degenerate to anarchy. When a Nuer feels insulted or wronged, he does not take advice or seek arbitration, he prepares to fight. Threats may yield counter-threats. Hostility easily escalates to destructive fighting that breaches the covenant or the peace of the community. Anarchy does not result, since the openness of Nuer decision processes affords recourse to multiple agents who seek to do justice and maintain the peace of the community by finding means to resolve conflict when parties to a dispute cannot settle it peacefully themselves.

The Nuer way of mediating conflict is through a neutral mediator with the capacity to sanction. This is a necessary feature of an effective dispute resolution mechanism. Among the Nuer, the way is available through *kuar muon* (an earth custodian). *Kuar muons* live scattered among the Nuer. Each has the capacity to sanction because he is a member of a lineage with the power to punish or to ban from the territory the individuals who are obstructing efforts to settle disputes.

Disputes are argued before *ad hoc* assemblies of the acknowledged leaders of the kin groups involved. Conflict resolution involves compensation through the payment of cattle. The rate of compensation, as well as the time it will take to be paid, depends on the local availability of cattle. The settlement agreements are reached and compensation enforced according to the willingness of the kin groups involved. This willingness is often affected by the closeness of the kin relationship between the groups, the existence of other contemporaneous disputes between the groups, and the threats of physical retaliation made by the victim's group against the lineage of the wrongdoer.

A judicious use of the threat of banning or cursing enables an earth custodian to get groups to meet and to agree to a settlement. In addition to the power of his threat to curse or ban, the earth custodian's power of persuasion and his knowledge of traditional law are important factors in the settlement of disputes (Howell 1954; Barkun 1968).

As some offenses against a person—homicide, adultery, and incest—also involve spiritual "sin" (*duer*), which must be removed before a case can be completely settled, the earth custodian's other important duty is to perform the necessary rituals of spiritual cleansing. Thus, the settlement of many cases involves both the negotiation of reparations and spiritual atonement. It is necessary to emphasize that acts of spiritual atonement are necessary to any permanent settlement of conflict.

Sacrificing cattle is required to prevent the occurrence of a misfortune or sin, to appease an angry spirit, or to curtail or to get rid of a misfortune that has already occurred, as in times of plague. On all these occasions, the Nuer believe God intervenes, or may intervene, for better or (more often) for worse in the affairs of human beings. His intervention is always dangerous.

To accomplish atonement for the breach of a covenant, a cow must be sacrificed. A cow is important to the Nuer who, in fact, consider it nearly equivalent to the life of a human being. Thus, the payment for life-taking is made through bloodwealth cattle. The institution of restitution in bloodwealth cattle for the taking of human life has its counterpart in the institution of establishing the kinship bonds in bridewealth cattle for the creating of life in succeeding generations.

There is no single source of ultimate authority among the Nuer. The *kuar muons* (earth custodians) constitute multiple agents with limited jurisdiction, who are effective in resolving conflicts among the people. These agents are important for the maintenance of the equality and autonomy of individuals and for the renewal of covenantal relationships.

The Complementarity in Segmented Structures

In addition to the function of multiple agents, there is a sense of complementarity that facilitates order in a segmented structure of authority relationships. The Nuer acephalous structure is made up of many units that are formally independent of each other. Still, they take each other into account through the processes of cooperation, competition, conflict, and conflict resolution.[41]

The essential ingredient that makes it possible for these independent, segmented units to resolve their conflicting interests is kinship links. Although members of a single, polygynous household eventually become separated through the course of growing up and marriage, the relationship between the members as persons of common origin remains unchanged.

Though the related persons become members of other households, they maintain exchange relationships with the members of their household of origin.

Kinship links mean that Nuer segmented groups are held together as coherent communities of interest through taking account of the interests of others. All of their affairs are managed through their joint acceptance of the regulative ideas that marshal activities in the society. These regulative ideas, when they are acted upon, may be considered to form the constitution of the community and to embody the common understanding. Consequently, despite having interests that may conflict with others, a Nuer segment perceives that it is better off by taking into consideration the interests of other segments and by resolving disputes through negotiation and compromise.

The common understanding is the concurrence of the people of the community. It is not the will of a single superior. This may be seen through the way that rivalry and contestation play out among the segments. Naturally, people who live adjacent to each other have more in common to quarrel about than those who live away from each other. Competition over scarce resources such as land, grazing grounds, water, and fishing reserves may lead to fighting.

When rivalry is expressed in fighting, there are common understandings among communities of limits that bound the fighting. For example, the nearness or distance of relationships between the persons in conflict influences the choice of weapons used. Only clubs and sticks can be used to fight close kin. People who are closely related or who live in close proximity are not permitted to use spears against one another. A homicide resulting from a fight with a spear is considered wrong, because it can lead to the disruption of the economy and security of an entire community. When fighting with distant persons in the defense of the integrity of the community, the use of spears is permitted.

Thus, the complementarity in segmented structures of authority relationships implies varying degrees of communities of relationships. The shared interests of adjacent segments facilitate maintenance of a larger constitutional order among the Nuer.

The Formalization and Corruption of the Nuer Law

The British Imperial authorities recognized that Nuer society was rule ordered, but they were unaware of many of the institutional arrangements that helped maintain Nuer society. The imperial authority accepted the Nuer customary law of *duer* (the concepts of being "at fault") for use in the new British-style courts that they introduced into the areas under their control. If the new courts were to adjudicate on the basis of *duer*, it therefore had to be written down.

The *duer*, or the rule for punishing wrongdoing, was codified at the insistence of the British authorities. Obviously, administrators who were not familiar with the concepts of *cuong*, *duer*, and the underlying shared understandings in the community could not carry out their responsibilities without the written code. In their case, the purpose of written codes was to "...enable administrators and chiefs...to discuss common interests, and ensure some consistency in administrative policy" (Howell 1954). These written codes can be found in Howell's *A Manual of Nuer Law*, which was put together in 1954. The written codes are known by many Western scholars as penal law. Among the Nuer, they are known as *nguot Fan-gak*, or laws made in the town of Fan-gak.

Nguot Fan-gak is a list of mandates from the colonial administrators (including native chiefs). It includes penalties for specific offenses. *Nguot Fan-gak* constitutes a single standard of behavior, and is used by officials and chiefs as a code of law. In short, *duer* became a collection of predefined behavioral rules that exact obedience to the accepted patterns of behavior in the community. It is used as a basis to evaluate people's behavior and to punish those who fail to follow the correct form.

Duer, by definition, is failure to conform to the accepted codes of behavior. *Duer* therefore refers only to penal law. The model of proper conduct implied in *duer* can be identified with the principles of *cuong*, or being in the right. This classification shows that *duer* is, in fact, more of a supportive legal code than a challenge to the traditional ways of right behavior. The punishments applied only to those who had acted in ways that did not conform to accepted patterns of behavior. Thus, when *duer* appeared in written form, the change was not to destroy the traditional system of governance but, rather, to strengthen it.

The Consequences of a Written Nuer Law

The Nuer traditional rules of *cuong* and *duer* are complementary in their work of maintaining social order. However, the creation of the written codes brought about some important conflicts between the two. For example, the British courts replaced the traditional Nuer method of punishing wrong-doers (by requiring that they compensate their victims) with a system that exacted punishment on the perpetrator (Makec 1988).

With the establishment of the British-style court system came the appointment of chiefs. This change also conflicted with the Nuer scheme of things. First of all, before the creation of the chiefs' court, the various components of the village assembly (that is, the village council of elders, the religious leaders, and the age-set groups) played significant roles in the administration of justice. The creation of chiefs' court drastically curtailed the ability of these bodies to play their traditional judicial roles. Second, the British practice of physical confinement as a method of punishment was contrary to the Nuer principle of compensation. The Nuer punished deviations by requiring payment of cattle (money) from the wrongdoer and his kin to repair the damage.

The Nuer could not wholly accept the practice of physical confinement of the wrongdoer. It seriously undercut their sense of justice and the all-important bonds of covenantal relationships. It also meant a demand for jail facilities and the machinery for monitoring this type of punishment. The Nuer chose not to develop such facilities and penal institutions. They instead relied upon banishment, rather than imprisonment. They believed confinement would result in suffering, would generate bitterness on the part of supporters of the victim, and would undermine the harmony in the society.

The Nuer correctly perceived in *nguot Fan-gak* a substantial break with the individualism of the traditional law. Nuer customary law has an emphasis on property, freedom of covenanting, and limitations on liability for harm caused by *guac* or accident. It has a strong attitude toward fault or sin and many other basic postulates of the Nuer conceptions of creation (*cak*) and the will of *Kuoth*. Conversely, the introduction of Western-style codes have initiated a turn toward collectivism in the law with an emphasis on state and social property; the regulation of individual contractual freedom in the interest of society; the expansion of liability for harm caused by *guac* or accidental activity; a utilitarian rather than a moral attitude toward wrong doing; and many other new basic postulates.

The Nuer also challenged the application of *nguot Fan-gak* in the chiefs' court, because the courts were not concerned with the spiritual aspects of life. They maintained that it is the spiritual aspect of a person that maintains proper behavior. The Nuer believe that is the mind that guides men's behavior. The force that prevents men from committing crimes is the fellow feeling of brotherhood, that is, of covenantal relationships. If the doing of justice and righteousness were not developed in men, Nuer cosmology presumes, then men will disregard moral judgment. As a result, a lack of spirituality is thought to lower one's moral fiber and will power to resist evil temptations. The Nuer argue that every religious law and ritual is not an isolated pattern of behavior; rather, religion contributes in some way to shaping an individual's actions. They believe that no written law and no amount of punishment will prevent people from deviating from the accepted pattern of conduct unless the spirit of respect for the spirituality of each person is inculcated in the hearts and minds of all.

The Nuer realize that a person can make unintended errors as well as deliberate ones. This implies both ignorance and the potential to learn. This implies that with greater moral understanding, men and women can avoid having greater external restrictions imposed on them and become responsible to do right as they act in relation to one another. Constituting order in society requires the development of a fear of God and a sense of shame for being a wrongdoer (Reth 1989). A social order solely based on penal law and punishment has no moral foundation to build on. When people know the grounds on which to conduct disputations, they will use the written law to further their self-interests at the cost of others. Mutual trust among people is an important ingredient for self governance. To the Nuer, conflict resolution is grounded more on a conscience of doing right, repentance for doing wrong, and renewing covenantal relationships in a spirit of reconciliation and compromise.

Written law is inflexible. Once a government proclaims a law, then the government must follow it strictly to build credibility. In reality, human society is too complicated to be ruled by unalterable law. As already noted above, the Nuer, in dealing with one another, take into serious account the intention of the perpetrator and other relevant factors concerning his or her behavior. The existence of written codes, disjoined from appropriate processes of governance in ongoing communities of relationships, imposed Western conceptions upon the Nuer sense of justice. Inevitably, the fixed nature of the written code restricted the flexibility of inquiry. It also altered moral reflection about how to reestablish binding relationships with appropriate affective ties, respect, friendship, brotherhood, and affection. Finally, the ultimate authority of the written code downgraded the mediating prerogative of custodians or enforcers of God's laws, who seek to sustain the bonds of covenantal relationships.

For the British rulers who had to reorganize the governing of Nuerland within the Sudan, the concept of *cuong* became difficult to realize in a large and extensive political setting (Howell 1954). This is because there is a lack of purely objective criteria for the conception of *cuong*. The need to unify laws in order to govern the many autonomous units of Nuer society was paramount in the drive to use written law to order an acephalous society under alien rule. Also, the challenge of unifying laws was in accordance with the British principle of indirect rule.

The conference of Nuer chiefs held at Fan-gak in 1948 was called by the colonial authorities to evaluate the drafted rules. These chiefs were hand-picked by the British authorities and so were more obliged to accept what had already been decided. For example, the chiefs thought that the threat of physical confinement would be an important additional tool in achieving *cuong*. The Nuer were expected to adapt and to adjust to the new ways of doing things.

Adopting the written *duer* as Nuer law had several consequences for the constitution of order among the Nuer. First, the *nguot Fan-gak*, as it is locally known, was accompanied by a secularization of the Nuer system of governance. Persons with priestly powers were removed from the governance system and replaced with secular leadership. The British regarded the *kuar muon* and *wud ghok* as *kujur* (magicians). Because the lineages of the custodians were scattered among the Nuer, and thus constituted a minority in their areas of residence, the British appointed as chiefs those men who were perceived as *gat wec*, or original settlers of the area. These were the secular leaders belonging to the dominant lineages. The assumption of the imperial authorities was that since prophets and priests were of foreign origin, they must be usurping power from the local citizens. Men in traditional leadership positions and ordinary people opposed this change, but the colonial government prevailed.

A second consequence of adopting the written *duer* as Nuer law, resulted from the incentive to acquire wealth and power that the new system offered to the individuals designated as *gat tut*, or head man of an area. The head man sought to acquire a warrant, or license, from the government, since possession of a warrant enabled the recipient to become a member of the native court. Court membership under the new system was viewed as a rich prize. It was a quick avenue to wealth and power. This incentive is largely the reason for the extraordinary demand for warrants among the Nuer lineages.

The British presumption was that the person appointed as chief must have a warrant in order to validate his authority over his people. The scramble for warrants led to the appointment of many chiefs. In the process, the "ungodly" were exalted. This shift led to other changes in Nuer society beyond the evolution of both law and political organization as a system of governance. Ultimately, it led to a basic transformation of the social life. Leaders were seen as having two separate roles, one functioning in an alien administrative structure and the other in Nuer society. While the administrative structure was very much a part of Nuer life, it was never fully absorbed into Nuer society. Governance became increasingly separate from religious life.

Conclusion

The system of Nuer governance was shaped by the conceptions the Nuer hold about themselves, their universe, their relationships with each other, and their relationships with other people who may come into contact with them. These cosmological conceptions shaped the structure of the institutions that are essential to understanding how Nuer society was constituted as a way of life.

The Nuer perceive themselves as *gaat Kuoth*, or children of a common Creator, and therefore are inherently equal. The role of individuals within the social and religious system is an active one—of doing right and of being responsible for one's actions. The Nuer have clear ideas about what it is to be in the right. Because they share the same conception of God and God's law, and the same ideas of what could go wrong and how to set it right, they have the possibility of building covenantal relationships.

Covenantal relationships are grounded in the conception of *nguot* as a code of behavior. Persons entering into a *nguot* commitment contend with one another over the terms and conditions of an agreement as meeting the conditions for being in the right. Discussion enables the parties to understand the nature of the bonds being made with one another. Symbolic action, such as rituals and sacrifices, accompany the verbal commitment. The division of the meat of the sacrificial oxen symbolizes a "pledge to the death" to keep the *nguot* commitment. The dismembered animals represent the curse that the *nguot* maker calls down on himself if he should violate the commitments that have been made.

Covenantal relationships are, however, also subject to being breached. The Nuer, like other human beings, commit wrongs even though they strive to do what is right. Their moral code continually places them in ambiguous and conflicting situations. They should fight to defend their rights, but they must not shed human blood. This is an example of the moral constraints within which they continually must act. Their daily lives are filled with circumstances that might lead them to breach their covenants.

There is, then, the matter of reestablishing covenantal relationships. God provides a guide to right living—that is, the right way. The Nuer seek to be faithful to God and God's law. That faith is manifested in a commitment to living in a right way with one another. The remedy for doing wrong, or for breaching covenantal relationships, requires repentance, acknowledgment of wrongdoing, a search for reconciliation, and the renewal of the covenant, which again is ritually sealed with blood.

The Nuer understand that the violation of covenantal relationships is dangerous because it opens ways for the intervention of *Kuoth* (God) into man's affairs. The adverse consequences of a violation of covenantal relationships might be avoided by expressions of remorse and an animal sacrifice in order to reestablish covenantal relationships. Repercussions stemming from wrongdoing of a political nature might be avoided by payment of reparations. A fault of inadvertence might not have such serious consequences as a deliberate wrong, but might nevertheless entail grave consequences.

Before British rule and despite the absence of a clear center of authority and ruling bureaucracy, there was a process of governance among the Nuer. There were regulative ideas at work—and being acted upon—which were constitutive of a way of life. The spiritual permeated the cultural and social. Individuals could call on numerous persons possessing priestly (spiritual) powers to mediate sets of covenantal relationships—to tie the spiritual to the mundane (worldly) in the building and renewing of covenantal relationships.

The core ideas, then, are a covenantal cosmology, covenantal relationships, a watchful concern about the breaching of covenants, and an enduring effort to renew and reestablish covenantal relationships whenever breaches occur. This type of society is viable as a self-organizing, self-governing society. British imperial rule, even when accompanied by commitment to indirect rule, was disruptive of the social order. This is because under that system, law is not conceived of as a covenantal commitment, and law does not function to guard against breaching covenantal relationships or to aid in renewing and reestablishing those relationships whenever breaches occur. The concept of covenant and a covenantal way of life are so integrally related to one another that to have the one without the other would be destructive of Nuer society.

TABLE 3.1   TABLE OF KEY POLITICAL FUNCTIONARIES

Title[42]	Translation	Principal Functions
Guan buthni	Head of the lineage	Leads bridewealth negotiations Conducts mortuary and colwic ceremonies Settles blood-feuds Incorporates foreigners Initiates age-set Severs kin ties to allow intermarriage or cohabitation Authorizes the building of new byres Acts as master of ceremony in division of inheritance and property Acts as spokesman of the lineage as a corporation of segments
Kuar muon	Earth Custodian	Controls the earth (mud/muds *mun/muon*; tree *gen*) and its productivity Gives the slayer sanctuary Negotiates disputes about homicide, adultery, and incest Performs sacrifice to enable normal social relations to be resumed Rehabilitates the slayer Administers oaths

Wud ghok	Cattle Custodian	Guards the well-being of the cattle
		  a. prevents cattle disease
		  b. treats sick cattle
		  c. increases the fertility of the cattle
		  d. resolves disputes concerning pasturage
		  e. regulates the movements of cattle
		Regulates the age-set system
		  a. decides when a new age-set should commence and close
		  b. performs sacrifices to open and close periods of initiation
		  c. names the age-set

Kuar tang	Custodian for Defense	Controls tactical organization consisting of age-sets (*Guan tang, Ngol)* Decides strategies in war Advises on the safety of warriors in war
Guan thoi	Water Custodian	Blesses the water Ensures that there is an abundance of fish Ensures that people will be successful in catching fish Facilitates the crossing of crocodile infested waterways Determines when to fish the fish reserves
Kuar yiika	Custodian on Family Affairs	Responsible for resolving special problems of death that occur under unusual circumstances. If a man abducts a girl or a man runs away with another man's wife and the woman or girl dies during this period, it is the *kuar yiika* who is called to determine how to resolve this problem in an equitable fashion.

Chapter 4 - Marriage, Kin, and Transgenerational Continuities

Introduction

In the acephalous society of the Nuer, family institutions are key parts of governance arrangements among individuals in the society. The family is one of the major institutional arrangements used by the Nuer to (1) resolve conflicts among individuals, (2) punish those who do not behave according to the generally accepted rules, and (3) develop ways of insuring commitments to the long-term arrangements necessary for productive undertakings. In the process of family formation, kinship and cross-cutting alliances are formed.

The institutions surrounding the negotiation of a marriage union have been described in the published works on the Nuer as if these were simply rituals, without much relevance to the governance of Nuer society. Little effort has been made to go beyond this superficial understanding to discover how regulative ideas about the marriage union marshal activities that help Nuer families solve many of the problems they face in developing peaceful and productive relationships among themselves. The superficiality of the research may reflect a reality for highly individualistic societies, where building alliances that extend beyond the immediate family unit is not a concern.

The purpose of this chapter is to explain how the Nuer build a system of rule and rule-ordered relationships through the medium of marriage and kinship, and to show how these relationships are maintained and perpetuated from one generation to another. In considering the marriage union as part of the constitutional order of the Nuer, we will first describe the formation of a lawful marriage. To do so, we will go back to the common understanding of how the Nuer perceive the basis of marriage in their realm of ideas. This basis is important, because the Nuer marry by the family, and the kin of the groom will transfer many cattle to the kin of the bride. Second, we will describe the kinship system that links the Nuer together in an orderly arrangement of interactions by which particular customs are seen as functioning parts of the social machinery. We will try to explain how the networks of ties of kinship are organized and how they work. Finally, we will explain how the Nuer social order is transmitted over time, from one generation to another.

The Formation of Marriage

In order to understand the regulative ideas of the Nuer concerning marriage and the methods used to marshal actions consonant with those ideas, it is important to conceptualize marriage as a rearrangement of social structure. Social structure is any arrangement of persons in institutionalized relationships (Radcliffe-Brown 1951). As a result of a marriage, certain existing relationships are changed. New social relations are created between the husband and the wife, between the wife and the husband's relatives, and also between the relatives of the husband and those of the wife, all of whom have an interest in the marriage and in the children that are expected to result from it. Marriages, like births, deaths, or initiations at puberty, are structural arrangements that are constantly recurring in human societies. They are moments of the continuing social process regulated by rules and customs.

A marriage union is not based on romantic love between two individuals, although physical beauty as well as character and health are desirable in a mate. The affection that exists after some years of marriage is the product of the marriage itself conceived as a process, resulting from living together and cooperating in many activities, especially in the raising of children.[43]

The primary regulative ideas concern lawfulness and alliance. A marriage is lawful in a modern state system only if it is registered and licensed by the state authority. The Nuer also distinguish between a lawful marriage and an irregular union. In Nuer society, the children born to parents joined in lawful marriage are given "legitimate" status in the society. The lawfulness of a marriage union requires a series of transactions and formalities in which the sets of kin, those of the husband and those of the wife, are involved. The making of a bridewealth payment to the bride's family is an essential part of the establishment of the lawfulness of a marriage. A lawful marriage, therefore, is established by an agreement between two sets of persons, the kin of the groom and the kin of the bride. It is an alliance between the two sets of kin based on their mutual interests in the union itself and its continuance, and in the children born of the union who will be members of both kin groups. An understanding of the nature of alliance is essential to understanding the Nuer kinship system.

The Foundation of the Marriage Union

The Nuer believe the institution of marriage is ordained by God. Man and woman are joined together to establish *cieng* (a human family) for the main purpose of *dieth* (reproduction of human kind) to glorify the Creator. "Sexual activities are from their earliest manifestations given the approval of cultural values. They are from the beginning associated with marriage. It is the chief ambition of a youth to marry and have a home (*gol*) of his or her own. When a Nuer speaks of marriage, he means a home. Having a home symbolizes success and responsibility" (Evans-Pritchard 1951). Sexual activities are associated with the fulfillment of divine will. Even in childhood, it is clear that marriage and the birth of children are the ultimate purpose of the sexual functions.

Children start playing at marriage from the time they begin to walk. They make cattle byres (*lueek muoni*) and huts of sand, and fashion oxen, bulls, and cows of mud. With these toys, they conduct bridewealth negotiations, perform marriage ceremonies, and play at domestic and conjugal life. In its earliest expression, sex is associated with marriage, and the first sexual play occurs in imitation of domestic routines of married life. Sexual play occurs more in response to a cultural urge, rather than to an instinctive one.

The Perpetuation of the Family—Cuong Thok Duel

The Nuer tradition that expects individuals to produce children to perpetuate their lineage should be viewed as evidence of their strong feelings about marriage. As is the case in many other societies, marriage is conceived of as a means by which human beings reproduce their kind as ordained by their Creator. Nuer custom holds that a union that has not been blessed with a child cannot be maintained. Not until a child has been born is the husband accepted by his wife's people as one of them. He is then the father of their daughter's child. Through the child, he acquires kinship with them. Until this happens, the husband continues to live with his own parents.

The extended family suffers anxiety about the birth of the first child. The husband and wife are anxious to produce a son who will become a link in the lineage, or a daughter who will bring cattle to the family when she is married. The parents of the wife and their kin are anxious because they cannot, without risking complications, dispose of the cattle of the marriage until the birth of a child cements the union. Bridewealth cattle cannot be invested in other capital because, if something goes amiss, they might have to be returned to the husband's family.[44]

Individual Autonomy and Parental Control

Among the Nuer, the individual assists in maintaining the acephalous order by being an independent and active participant in the governance of his own affairs. The perception of individual autonomy is grounded in the presumption of equality of individuals in the society. The teaching of the young encourages independent action. As boys reach the age of seven, they are attached to the *luak* (byre) where major family decisions are made.[45]

Initiation to manhood is a major step towards individual autonomy and responsibility. The initiate is given a gun or a spear symbolizing that he is now a warrior. He is required to observe the etiquette that is associated with manhood. For example, he must not milk cows. These steps are necessary but not sufficient to establish his manhood in Nuer society. The young males are made to understand that a Nuer is considered a "man" when he has married and has assumed the responsibilities of running a home and taking independent decisions. Thus, independence and individual responsibility are inculcated in the young at an early age.

Marriage among the Nuer is considered as a means of establishing individual autonomy from the control of parents and other senior kinsmen. A married man ceases to be dependent and becomes his own master. When a man marries, he establishes a home of his own of which he is head. He will have his wife, byre, herd, garden, and children. He makes decisions within his home and takes responsibility for those decisions. At the same time, an individual man's home as a decision unit in the society exists in close cooperation with other units.

The generation of male heirs is important because daughters are not heirs to their parent's wealth. Daughters inherit from their husbands.

The Processes of Lawful Marriage

Matrimony among the Nuer is brought about by payment of bridewealth and observation of customary procedures. In a society where the individuality of the persons seeking attachment is strong, the marriage procedure begins when the young man and girl concerned give their consent to the marriage. Grounding a marriage in the consent of both parties is considered a requirement for its success. The second step is the process of negotiation and payment of bridewealth cattle by the groom's family to bride's kin. Once the cattle negotiations are concluded, and the prescribed ceremonies have been performed, the marriage process is considered complete. The process of distributing the bridewealth cattle among the bride's kin is mainly the responsibility of the father of the girl, who apportions the cattle according to predefined rules.

Courtship and Choice

The young are free to choose their own spouses so long as they avoid certain categories of kin. These categories of kin establish the rules of incest. Girls are arbiters of behavior, and the severest sanction of a breach of good form is their disapproval. Evans-Pritchard (1951) says that the threat of female disapproval is a powerful incentive for making a young man be generous, respectful to his elders, dutiful to his parents and kinsmen, hospitable to guests, industrious, and brave. The girls, on their side, are also eager to earn the good opinion of young men by correct behavior in the home and in society. It is entirely up to the girl to accept or reject a man's proposal of marriage. Sometimes a girl herself makes the marriage proposal:

> The girl can do this by going with some companions of her own set to the *kraal* of her lover and driving away several head of cattle to her father's home. Her father and brother understand what she wants when they see her bringing the cows. If her kin disapprove of the young man they will send the cattle back. If the kin like the young man and his family, nothing will be done to return the cows. After several days have passed and the cattle have not been returned, the young man and his family will know that the girl's family are willing to discuss the matter (Evans-Pritchard 1951).

A father would not risk refusing his daughter's wish when she is in love with a man, even if he is not rich, because she can run away from home or hang herself.

The practice of *Kap dep* is another way in which a girl can make a public proposal of marriage. During the dry season, young men in each cattle camp parade their favorite oxen around neighboring camps. The younger brothers or sisters lead the ox, while its owner follows behind chanting poems (*rauke ka duarke*) and making graceful leaps to attract attention. A girl who loves a young man may on that occasion seize his ox and remove its lead. She keeps the cord and attaches a metal ring to it. Its owner later sends a younger brother to fetch it. This is tantamount to a proposal and acceptance of marriage. If the young man's family has enough cattle to make up the bridewealth, then the betrothal ceremony takes place soon afterwards.

Negotiation and Bridewealth Payment

The initiation of a marriage entails a number of different transactions in which cattle, sheep, goats, and other items are transferred from the groom's to the bride's family (Evans-Pritchard 1940; Kelly 1985). Additional livestock are required to provide ceremonial feasts at various points in the proceedings. However, a major component of the transaction is the bridewealth cattle, a negotiated quantity of animals that are given to the bride's kin by the groom's before she takes up residence with the groom in his community (Kelly 1985; Evans-Pritchard 1951).

The bridewealth payment is apportioned among the bride's family and certain designated close kin in accordance with the preexisting rules of division. These designated kin are *ji cungni*, the "people of rights," who have definitive claims that are recognized in law and custom and voiced at the time the bridewealth payment is negotiated.[46] These kin-based allotments are also inherited and consequently are undiminished by deaths among the members of the bride's kindred. The customary size of bridewealth payments is thus largely determined by the number of recognized claimants and the number allotted to each (Kok, interview, 1989, Kelly 1985). These considerations define the general framework of the transaction.

There is, however, as Raymond Kelly (1985) points out, scope for considerable variation within this framework. First, the specification of claimants and quantities due each one is not uniform throughout Nuerland but varies from region to region. Second, each Nuer region is independent in delineating both "ideal" and "acceptable" rates, effectively defining a range of appropriate payments rather than a single, set value. Third, actual payments vary within this range in accordance with the availability of cattle to the groom's family and kin. Bridewealth negotiations are thus concerned with determining the precise number and kind of cattle to be transferred, taking into account, on one hand, the customary claims and expectations of the bride's kin and, on the other, the economic circumstances of the groom's family (Kok, interview, 1989, Kelly 1985; Evans-Pritchard 1951).

The Process of Distributing Bridewealth Cattle

Cattle are the most valuable assets that Nuer own. The distribution of bridewealth cattle is an important means of maintaining ties of kinship.[47] Distribution is organized according to two principles: (1) equality in the distribution of bridewealth cattle, and (2) fixed apportionment to appropriate persons of right.

There is equal division of the bridewealth payment between the bride's paternal kinsmen (including her father) and her maternal kinsmen (including her mother). The total bridewealth payment is usually forty head.[48] Of the twenty animals that go to the father's kin, ten remain with the father (or his sons) and ten are divided among his family (his parents, brothers, and sisters). Of the twenty head of cattle that go to the mother's kin, ten remain with the mother (or her sons) and ten are divided among her family (her parents, brothers, and sisters). The equality principle in distribution reflects the concept of equality of relationships between the patrilineal and the matrilineal kin of the groom and the bride.[49] Equally important, the principle of equal distribution of bridewealth cattle implies a jointness of endeavor in the business of marital alliances. The two kin groups are both equally responsible for the success of a marriage and the raising of the children produced by the union.[50]

The second principle is that the cattle are distributed in fixed proportions between three groups. These groups are the bride's immediate family, her father's family, and her mother's family. The bride's father and mother each receive ten head of cattle, which are known as the *ghok dieth* (the cattle of parenthood). The families of the bride's father and of her mother each receive ten head of cattle, known collectively as the *ghok cungni rar* (the cattle of the outside claimants), that is, those who are outside the bride's nuclear family.

The bridewealth payment and its distribution to many people are of great importance to the health of the Nuer constitutional order. Peace and order between different lineages are more easily upheld if the marriage union is successful. (Some of this significance will be considered in the section on cross-cutting alliances.) One function of the marriage payment is, therefore, as a form of marriage insurance. The bride's kin have a direct interest in preventing the breakdown of the marriage, since Nuer rules require that a woman's relatives refund her bridewealth cattle in the event of a divorce. Refunding cattle already invested in a variety of productive activities is often difficult and thoroughly disruptive. Another incentive toward lasting marriage is the possibility of losing the right to one's children unless a fee is paid in cattle. The children born of the union after the breakdown of the marriage belong to their maternal uncle, and not to their natural father, until six head of cattle per child is paid as *ruok* (a fee).

Another function is the lawful transfer of the intangible asset of childbearing capacity. Through the payment of bridewealth and the performance of certain ceremonies, the lawful transfer of *dap ciek* (i.e., the "value" of a woman's childbearing capacity) from a woman's father to a husband is effected. A marriage gains recognition only when power over a daughter is surrendered by her father and acquired by her husband through the payment of bridewealth cattle. Among the Nuer, an unmarried woman is in a position of dependence. She lives with her parents, who protect her. If she is killed or injured, her parents or kin can claim damages. After marriage, responsibility for her protection passes to her husband and his kin. The ritual known as *luony dep* (loosing the rope) symbolizes the bride's release from her father's homestead to the groom and his kin. If she is killed or injured by a third party, the husband and his kin claim an indemnity. The woman's kin, however, retain the right to protect her against ill treatment by her husband or his kin.[51]

The transfer of *dap ciek* (the value of childbearing capacity) is the central feature of the Nuer marriage transaction. A lawful marriage gives the husband and his family certain rights in relation to his wife and the children she bears. The husband acquires the right to expect the performance of certain duties by the wife at the same time he accepts his duties towards her. The husband's duties are to cohabit with his wife regularly and to contribute to the economy of the family in those tasks that require not only strength, but also absence from home. The wife, on her part, is tied to the daily chores of the home: preparation of food, cleaning the home, and caring for children. The husband also acquires rights over the person of his wife. As indicated earlier, if anyone kills or injures her, or commits adultery with her, he may claim to be compensated for the violation of his rights. The most important right the husband acquires, however, is control of the children that the wife bears. A Nuer marries because he wants children. A woman's ability to bear children, therefore, is critical to the establishment of the marriage. If a wife proves barren, her kin return the cattle to the husband, and the marriage ends.

The above discussion shows that the distribution of bridewealth cattle is an important means of maintaining ties of kinship. A marriage union is conceived of by the Nuer as an alliance between two kin groups. The Nuer understand marriage as a stable, ongoing system of order that must be transformed from a contractual arrangement into kinship relationships through the birth of children. It is through the children that the husband and wife are united, and the two families are united by having descendants in common. The instrumental function of marriage exchange was, and is still, the creation of a harmonious, enduring social order via a network of alliances among the different Nuer lineages and non-Nuer peoples.

Cross-cutting Alliances and Constitution of Order

In an acephalous society, a marriage exchange is to be understood mainly as creating and sustaining a stable, ongoing system of order. During the exchange process, a series of actors has to be satisfied that each party to the marital relationship will keep the agreement and meet its obligations. The obligation to provide many marriage cattle and distribute them to various individuals is intimately tied into the process of building diverse, long-term relationships. These diverse relationships enable disparate persons to act jointly with one another to accomplish tasks that could not be accomplished as well by individuals or by extended families acting alone.

Marriage Exchange and Network of Alliances

The rule governing the bridewealth transaction is that for cattle transferred, a woman capable of childbearing is received. The transaction can be regarded as an exchange, and as such establishes an alliance between two lineages. It differs, however, from an impersonal purchase and sale, which once completed leaves behind no obligations on the part of either the buyer or the seller (except the claims based on a warranty). The idea of covenant is presumed to be the backdrop of the conceptual context of this exchange.

Bridewealth cattle may be returned or repaid with their increase in certain circumstances, such as barrenness on the part of either the woman or the man, or divorce. The Nuer individual offering cattle in the transaction will, therefore, maintain a close watch on his cattle and follow the increase of his herds until the wife's second or third child is born. By that time, the marriage is thought to be secured. The bridewealth cattle are usually allocated among a variety of capital investments by those who have received them. In many cases, they are used to obtain a wife for a male relative. These transfers are how marriage sets up a network of relationships between sets of kin. These relationships are shown graphically in the Figure 4.1.

FIGURE 4.1   FORMATION OF NETWORK OF FRIENDLY ALLIANCES

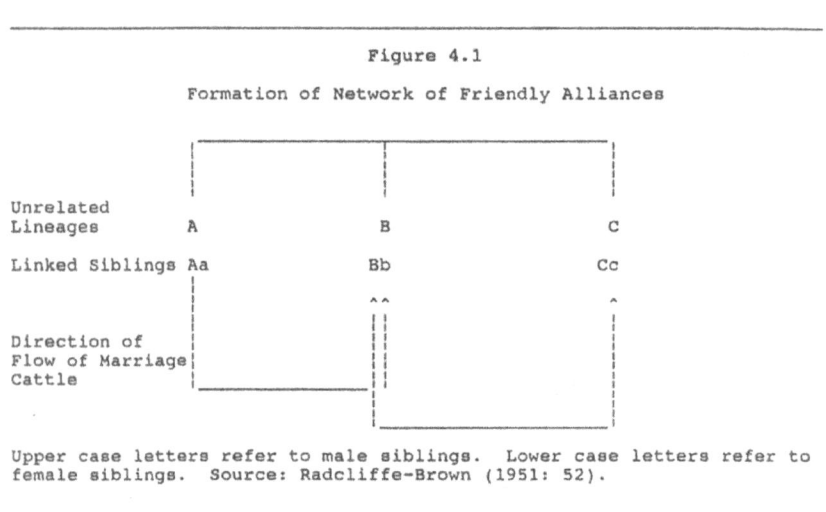

In Figure 4.1, *A*, *B*, and *C* stand for three different lines (lineages) that are not related in any way to each other so that the rule of exogamy does not forbid marriage between them. For each of these three hypothetical lineages, we will trace the marriage transactions of brothers and sisters of the same mother. These individuals are male A and his sister female a; male B and his sister female b; and male C and his sister female c.

The bridewealth payments establish a series of special personal relationships:

- between male B and his sister b
- between male B and his brother-in-law A
- between female b and her sister-in-law c
- between male A and his wife's sister-in-law c.

These relationships are defined in slightly different ways in different parts of Nuerland. We will briefly consider two of them to show how these constructions are multiplied and used.

Between male B and his sister b: When male A marries female b, he makes a bridewealth payment to the *B* lineage. The *B* lineage then uses A's cattle to obtain a wife (female c) for male B. The fact that cattle brought into the *B* lineage by the marriage of female b provides cattle for a wife of her brother male B "links" these two siblings (B and b) for the rest of their lives. Further links are established between male B and his sister b when their respective marriages produce children. For example, when male A and his wife (female b) have children, then because male B is the children's mother's brother, the children of A and b are also "linked" to whatever lineages include their Uncle B. Likewise, when male B and his wife (female c) have children, then because female b is the children's father's sister, the children of B and c are also "linked" to whatever lineages include their Aunt b.

Between male A and his wife's sister-in-law c: In this network of relationships, the transfer of cattle establishes the special relationship between male A and female c, who is the wife male B married with cattle provided by A. When the daughter of female c is married, male A can claim a heifer from female c with which to secure a wife either for himself or his son.

The particular linkages just described between lineages and families are to be continued in succeeding generations. A family's obligations are inherited. There are also sets of rules that regulate the continuity of alliances. One set of rules prevents disruption of the existing relationships. A son of male A cannot marry a daughter of male B, or of any woman related to female c. A son of male B cannot marry a daughter of male C. This prohibition is because these "linked" people are considered related. For example, when the daughter of male B is married, his sister female b will receive a cow because she is a paternal aunt. Any marriage between the linked lines would be considered incestuous because of this transfer of cattle. Because a son of male B will by right receive cattle when the daughter of (his mother's brother) male C is married, children of those lines are prohibited from marrying.

There are, then, established chains of connected families (bound together by "links"). The trust and affection generated by family ties make it easier for the families involved to resolve conflict peacefully and to transact business with one another. A more detailed discussion of the continuity of family relationships is provided in the section on transgenerational continuities.

The Quest for the Alliances

We have shown in this chapter that marriage alliances among families are sought by the Nuer for many different reasons. Alliances reduce the incidence of feuding between clans and lineages in Nuer society. They generate trust and confidence between disparate people so that they can carry out mutually beneficial relationships between themselves. Alliances also place limits on the capacity of each member to decide independently, in order that key tasks aimed at mutual interests may be coordinated within the alliances.

In this discussion of the marriage exchange and the quest for alliances, it is important to keep in mind the larger social context: the "invisible" institutions that order the acephalous way of life. "An institution," writes John R. Commons (1950), "is collective action in control, liberation, and expansion of individual action." The marriage exchange as a governing institution is well understood among the Nuer. Harmonious relationships between members of various Nuer regional groups are facilitated by the creation of alliances via marriage exchange. The relationships among networks of people bound by patterns of reciprocity inherent in the exchange constrain and guide the choices that individuals make.

Prior to the creation of alliances via marriage exchange between any two lineages or regions in the Nuer society, incidents of interlineage or interregional warfare, raids, and theft of cattle were common.[52] Nyuong Nuer, for example, were notorious raiders. The Eastern Jikany and the Lou Nuer fought constantly over the use of Nyading and the *tuoch* (grazing land) along the Sobat River and its tributaries.

The institution of marital alliances formed with outsiders, that is, members belonging to different lineages or regions, is a way of turning otherwise hostile persons into allies. The marriage exchange provides every involved person with friends and allies. For example, the use of spears in fighting (i.e., deadly force) is allowed between unrelated persons, but not between kin. It is a sin to kill kin. Disputes among kin are resolved primarily through negotiation and compromise rather than by violence. Among allies, conflict is settled by reparations for damage. Thus, alliances integrate wider communities of mutual interest and greatly reduce interregional as well as interlineage warfare and raiding. Alliances facilitate the resolution of problems by persuasion and negotiation between members of different lineages.

Building alliances via marriage exchange is also a means of facilitating collective decision making about common problems confronting the individuals entering into these alliances. Individuals can achieve economic well-being only if certain prerequisites are fulfilled in the way institutions order relationships among diverse groups. Nuer families are dependent upon the cooperation of adjacent groups for the success of their productive activities. Resources for cattle are scarce and widely scattered. Neighboring groups have to share these resources and, as a consequence, share common problems. Nuer pastoralists must move about to take advantage of the sparse seasonal rainfall, and, in these migrations, they necessarily pass through each other's grazing areas. Threats of non-cooperation or hostility can result in a breakdown of the migratory patterns upon which all depend. To ensure the maintenance of orderly relationships and collective decision making about common problems, institutional arrangements must be fashioned so that members find themselves under obligations to discharge certain duties that promote the welfare of others.

The establishment of a network of mutual, long-term expectations directly implies a quality of jointness about certain endeavors. It logically follows that the individuals must be able to sustain ordered relationships if they are to benefit from alliances. Each individual must take into account the strategy of others when assessing personal choices. Failure to take the choices and actions of others into consideration can result in error, conflict, and failure. Those who are to cooperate successfully also must trust others to cooperate and act predictably in ways that will give assurance that their investment in joint enterprises will be beneficial. A high level of self-governing capabilities to manage difficulties and tensions embedded in marriage exchange relationships is required of the Nuer, given the benefits to be gained and the difficulties that are involved.

Among the Nuer, marriage exchange creates self-executing arrangements. This means that the marriage union itself contains measures (i.e., systems of governance) that are capable of guaranteeing enforcement without the intervention of external authorities. In the event of conflicts, the appropriate age-set leaders and elders oversee the resolution process. In matters that require religious cleansing, such as disputes over adultery and incest, there is a set of priests who can be called in to mediate between members in alliance. Thus, there is little need of additional executive and legislative action to create and enforce legal obligations under the marriage exchange.

Organization of Kin and Their Obligations

Human beings are the components of a social structure, and a social structure is an arrangement of persons in institutionally defined and regulated relationships. The social function of any feature of a pattern of relationships is its relation to the structure and its continuance and stability (Radcliffe-Brown 1951). In order to continue to exist, kinship must "work" with some measure of effectiveness. Kinship relationships must provide means by which persons can interact and cooperate without too many serious and destructive conflicts.

Tensions and potential conflict exists in all human social arrangements. For a kinship system to work well in an acephalous order, it must provide methods for limiting, controlling, or resolving such conflicts or tensions and for meeting the economic and security requirements of the individuals involved.

To understand the Nuer kinship system and how it works, it is important to understand the Nuer conception of themselves and the way it is expressed in social structures. The kin relationships of the Nuer are defined in terms of rights and duties. Two persons who stand in a particular kinship relationship with each other have specific duties toward each other. A duty may be positive, allowing certain actions, or negative, forbidding certain conduct. Kinship obligations, thus, have the status of customary rights and duties. A system of kinship can therefore be viewed as an institutional arrangement that enables persons to live together and cooperate with one another in an orderly way.

The way the Nuer kinship system works reflects the cosmological conceptions used in the design of institutional arrangements in society. In their past, the Nuer people had to create and act on the organizing principles that were to be used to fashion the constitution of a social order. It is on the selection, method of use, and combination of these principles that the character of the structure of an acephalous ordering depends. Analysis of the Nuer kinship system must, therefore, be in terms of the organizing concepts and their application. These organizing ideas have been elaborated on in chapter three of this study.

In trying to understand the Nuer kinship system, we will first examine the polygynous household, which is the fundamental unit among the Nuer. The household is the primary arena for the expression of age and sex roles, kinship, socialization, security, and economic cooperation. The household is where the very stuff of culture is mediated and transformed into action. Second, we will consider the obligations of kin.

Household and the Span of Significant Kinship

If there is general agreement about the importance of kinship ties, some uncertainty exists among observers about the span at which they remain significant. Evans-Pritchard (1951) claims that ties are respected beyond the tenth generation, by which he probably means beyond the range of fourth order of relationships. For Douglas (1980, 87), the family in the Nuer sense extends to the third and fourth generation, while Rundial (1989) and Bum (1989) say that by the exchange of cattle, the Nuer family extends to the fourth generation.[53] These differing opinions reflect variations among Nuer groups.

Some families maintain shorter or longer periods of effective kinship ties as measured in terms of the negative prohibition of marriage and exchange of bridewealth. It is difficult to say exactly where this span of significant kinship is for all Nuer sections. Hutchinson (1988) says that the Eastern Jikany's prohibition against marriage extended only to the third generation.[54]

A polygynous household is formed when a man marries two or more wives who bear his children.[55] Polygynous marriages imply that fewer males and more females are available for marriage. Polygynous marriages are also the means for maintaining a pattern of population in a feuding society.

The Nuer are a feuding society. In a feuding society, an individual must fight to enforce or to preserve his rights. There are many causes that would provoke the Nuer people who live close to each other to fight. They may fight over a cow, about animal trespass incidents, or because one man struck another's little boy. They may fight over adultery, abduction of girls, theft of cattle, and so on. When a Nuer is wronged, he does not complain to obtain redress from the traditional authorities, but instead he challenges the person who had wronged him to a duel. The challenge has to be accepted. A Nuer hesitates to utter a challenge only when kinship or age-set status inhibits an appeal to arms. Men are frequently killed as a result of fighting.

While there are many children born to a Nuer household, it is the males that are killed off through fighting. Individual killings may lead to feuding between communities and between regions. The desire for large families is partly in regard to feuding. This desire is recognition that institutional patterns work out not only in building social networks, but they also affect aggregate population patterns. Family and kin relationships (that support the polygynous household) have their counterparts in feuding and warfare that maintain population patterns. Therefore, feuding and warfare are integral parts of Nuer society, which emphasizes polygynous marriages and child bearing.

In a polygynous household, there is a socially important difference between the full children of the same father and mother and those children of one father by different mothers. We have already touched on this with reference to the place of complementarity in segmented structures of authority relationship.

As the household continues to grow through the birth of children, it also undergoes partial dissolution as the children marry and leave the household. The household itself does not disappear when the father dies. After the death of the father, the eldest son becomes the "father" of the household, primarily to see that the unity of the family is maintained and that all of his unmarried brothers are assisted in marrying as they would have been were the father still alive. The Nuer patrilineal extended family is formed by sons remaining in their father's lineage, bringing their wives to live with them, so that their children also belong to their father's clan.

The Nuer male at an adult age belongs to two families: to one as son and brother, and to the other as husband and father. It is this connection that gives rise to a network of relationships linking any single person with many others.[56] However, kin relationships are not of the same order as immediate family relationships among the Nuer. An individual Nuer does not think of his father, mother, brothers, and sisters as *ji mara de* (kin). They are members of *ji gole* (family), the intimate circle which he sees as something quite distinct from kin. Kin is anyone to whom an individual can trace a relationship of any kind. If an individual knows that he stands in a certain category of relationship with another person, even without knowing its degree of nearness or distance to establish the exact point of relationship, then that person is regarded in the wider sense of the Nuer concept of *mar* (kin) (Evans-Pritchard 1951). This means in fact, as will become clearer later, that everybody in his village, all with whom he has dealings in the cattle camps, and even those outside these institutions are either true kin or are in one way or another treated as if they are.

Nevertheless, the categories of individuals one can have as kin are limited in number, and they have a definite pattern of arrangement to any person. The Nuer perceive that there is a pattern of kinship relationships that can be described as an abstract system without reference to any particular person (Evans-Pritchard 1951). Where there is no one to fill one of the recognized kinship positions, it is recognized that the actual configuration of kin does not correspond to the ideal configuration. The Nuer attempt to make the actual configuration conform to the ideal by substitution.[57]

Each Nuer polygynous household maintains a large number of relationships that are viewed by members of the family as important to their well being and security. The importance of having a large number of kinsmen is reflected in the following Nuer proverbs, "I want to have kin, even in the devil's house," and "Kinsmen are teeth." The proverb, "Kin are a defense," represents a sentiment echoed by observers.[58] A man, therefore, is esteemed and his alliance courted in proportion as his family is numerous. Numbers of prospective affines (i.e., relatives by marriage) is often a factor in marriage strategy. Because a large circle of kin is the primary form of wealth, when the marriage of a girl is being mooted, inquiries are made first about the number and quality of her relatives. Discussion of the bridewealth only comes afterwards.[59] As will be made clearer later, such considerations are of great importance in conflict between families, since large families enjoy supremacy in their district, especially in conflict situations.

Household Organization and Formation of Lineages

In order to reckon the kin of a person, that person's descent is traced back to his or her four grandparents and eight great-grandparents. All descendants of these ancestors, through both females and males, are his or her *ji mara de* (cognates), because they are of the same origin. For each generation that an individual counts backwards, the number of ancestors is double that of the preceding generation, so that in the eighth generation, a person will have 84 ancestors (Radcliffe-Brown 1951). In practicality, there must be a limit to counting ancestors. The Nuer count back only to 11 generations for important social purposes (Douglas 1980).

Besides cognation, the other way of ordering kindred among the Nuer is by agnation (tracing kinship exclusively through the male lines). Cognates also are agnates, provided they are descended through the male line from the same male ancestor. The Nuer emphasize agnatic kinship, that is, unilineal descent through males. The consciousness of being members of a social group with a common male ancestor, of having shared symbols, and of holding corporate rights in territory and within the limited range of nuclear kin, has a common interest in cattle exchange.

For sons, this consciousness, as well as factors such as spear-names (which are shouted out at ceremonies), honorific titles by which people are sometimes addressed, and reciprocal ceremonial relations, pull the children of their wives to the father's side of the family (Evans-Pritchard 1951). Males descended from a common male ancestor are known broadly as *gaat guanlen* (sons of paternal uncles). Thus, the system of surnames descends in the male line.

Gaat nyiet (children of daughters) is another broad division of kin. These are the persons related to a man through his female relatives who are married and living outside the household organization. *Gaat nyiet* are the individuals who provide the social cement for cross-cutting alliances. It is on these bodies of kin that the security of persons and of property in Nuerland rests.

The significance of unilineal principle lies in its function in defining lineages. Nuer lineages are thought of as deriving from a polygynous house-hold. Unilineal principle identifies persons with common ancestry. They can be differentiated by reference to the founders themselves or to their mothers. The typical lineage structure is conceived of as being present in the structure of the polygynous family and in the distribution of houses in the homestead it occupies. This is why a lineage is generally known as "*thok duel* (the door) of the house of [male ancestor's name is usually given], the founder." The formation of lineages is sketched in Figure 4.2.

In Figure 4.2, clan A is segmented into maximal lineages (*thok dueli*) B and C, and these are divided into major lineages D, E, F, and G. Minor lineages H, I, J, and K are segments of major lineages D and G. Lineages L, M, N, and O are minimal lineages that are segments of H and K.

The smallest genealogical unit that Nuer consider a lineage (*thok du-el*) consists of the descendants of ancestors from three to five generations removed from the eldest living descendant (Douglas 1980). An entire clan organization can be viewed as a genealogical structure, and the letters in the diagram may represent persons from whom the lineage and its segments trace their descent, and from whom they often derive their names.

FIGURE 4.2   THE FORMATION OF LINEAGES

The Formation of Lineages

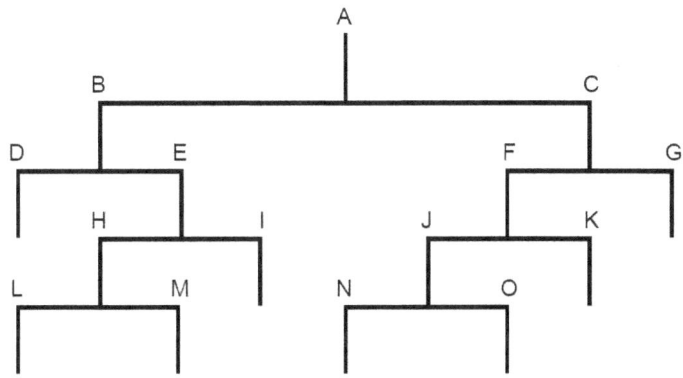

Source: Evans-Pritchard 1940, 193.

A *kar* (branch) of a lineage is itself a lineage. A lineage of ten generations may include two or more branches of nine generations. One of these branches may also contain two or more branches of eight generations, and so on (Radcliffe-Brown 1951; Evans-Pritchard 1951). A lineage of several generations logically includes the dead as well as the living. A lineage group (of living persons) that is socially significant may itself consist of smaller groups, and it may itself be part of a more extended group of related lineages. These lineage structures are made up of brothers and the children of their sisters. These groups have an internal organization determined by sex and order of birth. A group's members, however, are of one flesh and blood, and the Nuer make use of this solidarity between brothers and sisters. Brothers ought to exhibit affection and ought to cooperate and interact without destructive conflict. This unity of brothers is used to build wider structures through marriages.

Clan and Wider Community of Interests

A Nuer clan is a group of individuals who trace their descent from a common ancestor. The Nuer observe a rule of exogamy that forbids marriage between two members of the same clan. Where a clan is divided into line-ages, it is only to the smaller group that the rule of exogamy applies. An in-dividual normally gains membership in a clan by birth. The Nuer tradition of adoption is another way of gaining membership in the larger group through the adopter's family. Where a man is adopted into a patrilineage, thereby abandoning his membership of the clan into which he was born, his children belong to the clan of his adoption, not of his birth.

The clan and lineage are groupings of an individual's relations. In the Nuer kinship system, the members of an individual male's own clan are his own agnatic kin. The kin nearest to him are members of his own lineage. The members of his mother's clan or lineage are also his kin, through his mother. The appropriate classificatory terms for these kin are *nar* (maternal uncle), *malen* (maternal aunt), *gatnar* (son of paternal uncle), and *gat malen* (son of maternal aunt). He is forbidden to marry any woman of his mother's patrilineal lineage. The members of his father's mother's clan and his moth-er's mother's clan or lineage are also recognized as relatives. Members of his wife's clan or lineage are all treated as relatives by marriage. The Nuer con-cept of clan as a system of lineages provides a pattern of organization that divides the Nuer into regions.[18] The clan, therefore, is a more clearly defined territorial unit than lineage.[19]

Among the Nuer, the network of kin and the protection that it pro-vides are extended by means of age-set organization. Links are created be-tween persons of the same age. The rule against marrying the daughter of an age-mate reflects the closeness of the relationship.

Obligation, Rights, and Duties

For ties of kinship to continue in existence, they must enable indi-viduals and families to achieve certain goals. The unilineal lineage groups of the Nuer perform important corporate functions in organizing marriage, ex-changing cattle in marriages, aiding each other in the payment of bloodwealth, settling disputes, and handling external conflicts by negotiation or armed combat.[20]

Among the Nuer, the genealogical relationships are defined in terms of rights and duties. In a society where customary rights and duties are the same for all members, a balanced exchange of goods and services between the kin on the father's side and the kin on the mother's side is maintained in certain important activities, including marriage.

The problems of homicide and vengeance are commonplace among the Nuer. Paternal and maternal kin are from different lineages and therefore have different networks of relationships within which to address the problems of homicide and vengeance. Their common interest is the children born of the union in which they have common descent. Although feuding affects paternal as well as maternal kin, the paternal kin take the most active part. Paternal and maternal kin are not normally party to decision-making processes in each other's territory, but they help each other when it is necessary. Later, we will further discuss relationships in the system of polygynous marriages to feuding obligations.

Individual and Kindred Obligation

The close kin of an individual among the Nuer are the paternal uncles, maternal uncles, and their sons. A paternal uncle's obligation to assist his nephew to marry is an important feature of the Nuer kinship system. As noted above, the payment of bridewealth to kin is an obligation involving the very heart of kinship. It may in no way be avoided.[21]

The entitlement to bridewealth cattle on a niece's marriage also implies a moral obligation for a paternal uncle to contribute cattle, although fewer than those received, to help a nephew to marry. This obligation depends for its strength on personal relation and availability of cattle to pay. The paternal uncle without cattle to contribute may not discharge his obligation, nor does he thereby forfeit his bridewealth rights on the marriages of his brother's other daughters. Nevertheless, shared communities of understanding would censure a paternal uncle or his son, were either to refuse to assist with bridewealth. The obligation on uncles is considered weightiest when they are from the same mother with the father, and when they live with or near the father and are on friendly relations with him. A half-brother of the father, especially if he lives in a different village or district, may feel that he has done all that should be required of him if he gives a cow or a heifer on the marriage of one of his half-brother's sons.

It is understandable that individuals who live together have opportunities for quarreling, and that their common interests, especially in regard to the cattle in which they all have rights, provide many occasions for it. A Nuer is bound to his paternal kin from whom he derives aid, security, and status. In return for these benefits, he has many obligations and commitments. Their often indefinite character offers evidence of and reasons for their force, while at the same time providing ample scope for disagreement.[22]

Duties and rights may easily conflict. Moreover, the privileges of agnatic kinship cannot be divorced from authority, discipline, and a strong sense of moral obligation, all of which are irksome to the Nuer. They do not deny duties and obligations, but they do kick against them whenever their personal interests run counter to these claims (Howell 1954; Evans-Pritchard 1951).

In addition to the assistance he receives from his paternal uncles, a man looks for assistance from his mother's brothers when he wants to marry. If his mother's full brother gives him two or three cows to help him get a wife, then that uncle is regarded as a good relation and may make further contributions on the marriage of the younger sons. As in the case of a paternal half-uncle, a maternal half-uncle considers that he can only contribute one animal for the marriage of the first born son. He regards the marriage of younger sons as the responsibility of his own younger brothers.[23] A maternal uncle is not obliged to contribute to his sister's son's bridewealth. He may be asked to contribute, but if he refuses to aid, he cannot be deprived of cattle on the marriages of the young man's sisters. Any assistance he may give is regarded as an act of friendship and not a return for the cattle he receives. The only cattle the mother's people are obliged to pay to her sons are a male and a female calf, which in Eastern Nuerland are known as the *ghok jookni* (the cattle of the ghosts) (Evans-Pritchard 1951). This claim becomes due when the mother has reached the menopause.

Balanced Exchange Relationships

A deliberate balance between patrilineal and matrilineal is maintained by the Nuer in many different types of transactions. The equality of rights and duties toward each other are emphasized on certain formal occasions, especially when a marriage is being discussed. As noted earlier in this chapter, when a girl is married, the bridewealth is distributed among the following categories of kin in addition to the parents themselves: *guanlen* (father's brother); *wac* (father's sister); *nar* (mother's brother); *manlen* (mother's sister); *guandong* (father's father and mother's father); and *mandong* (father's mother and mother's mother).[24]

When a man is killed and cattle are paid in compensation, the cattle are divided among the kin according to the same principle used when dividing bridewealth cattle. When an elephant is killed, its tusks, or the cattle obtained for them by exchange, are divided among persons standing in the same set of relationships to its slayers.[25]

Cattle are distributed according to the *cung* (entitlements or rights) of each class of the kin listed above. For outsiders who are not familiar with the order of division of meat by age, it is difficult to tell at any particular moment to which person a share will be given. There are two major reasons for the difficulty. First, more than one person stands in a certain category of relationship to a bride, a slain man, or a slayer of an elephant. Second, if the person to whom the share was supposed to go had he been alive is dead, then his right has been inherited by his sons.

The right of entitlement or relationship is an important right. Rules awarding bridewealth rights are the most rigidly formulated rules governing kinship relationships among the Nuer, and are adhered to tenaciously. A head of a household may fail to fulfill the more fluid customary duties to kin without endangering the bonds of kinship. However, refusal to give a man the bridewealth cattle to which he is entitled is viewed by the Nuer as a decisive violation of kinship obligations. The consequence of this act cuts a man off from his kin altogether. The breakdown and consequences of *mar* (kinship relationships) will be further explored in the section on notions of right and right-doing.

The classes of kin entitled to receive marriage cattle, in addition to those discussed above, are clearly defined by their representation in the distribution of sacrificial meat at marriage ceremonies and other important feasts among family and kin. There are variations in the allocations in different parts of Nuerland, but the same classes of kin are everywhere represented in distributions.

The ideal distribution of sacrificial meat is usually described by citing the portions of the animal that are to be given to each particular category of kin. Symmetry is maintained in the distribution. Half goes to patrilineal and half to matrilineal kin. For example, the right hind leg is the right of the father's brother and the left hind leg is the right of the mother's brother; the right foreleg is the right of the father's sister and the left foreleg is the right of the mother's sister; and so forth.[26] The allocation to uncles is further differentiated by defining whether the recipients are full brothers or half-brothers of the father and/or mother. Individuals entitled to meat may be dead or absent, but that right passes to the son or brother of the deceased. On these occasions, age-sets and representatives of collateral lineages, or *ji buthni*, also have rights in sacrificial meat.

The importance of this balance of the patrilineal and matrilineal kin in various activities in the constitution of social order among the Nuer is that a man always has a choice of several homes. If he does not care to reside with his paternal kin, he can attach himself to the home of other male or female kin. It is generally towards his mother's brother's people that he turns when he is not happy with his paternal relatives. Individuals are conscious of this option, or this pull away from the paternal kin, which is personified in a maternal uncle. It signifies not only a balance between paternal and maternal kin within the kinship system, but also a balance between the lineage and the society that contains it—between the lineage system and the total social structure.[27]

Feuding Obligation and Rules

Ter (feuding) arises when a person has been killed but no compensation has been paid by the killer and his or her kin. If compensation in cattle (bloodwealth) is not made, then the kinsmen of the victim avenge themselves by killing a member of the killer's family or lineage. Feuding is subject to law (Evans-Pritchard 1940; Middleton and Tait 1970). Rules stipulate circumstances in which vengeance might properly be taken. These include: (1) when a close relative has been killed, (2) when a woman has been dishonored, and (3) when there has been a transverse killing. A transverse killing is a killing that occurs in the context of inter-clan conflict, where the enforcement of compensation is impossible. For example, in the past, enforcement of compensation for a slain person between the Gaawar and Lou Nuer clans had been problematic. These clans practiced transverse killing until the prophetic period of the 1870s, when the principle of compensation became enforceable.

To function an institution, feuding has to be accepted in principle by a community, at least in the initial stages. If members of a community do not sanction a blood vengeance, then it is virtually impossible to carry out the disputing processes, because the persons involved will be denied support and protection. When the members of a community sanction a blood vengeance, once a person has been killed, both the family of the victim and the family of the killer understand that they are in a state of war. Both parties to the dispute understand who is involved and who is not involved in the dispute. Hostile intentions are nearly always made very clear, because a vengeance killing without sufficient warning is regarded as reprehensible.

Persons engaged in a feud are expected to take prescribed actions that not only publicize their state of enmity, but also demonstrate their recognition that the current situation is sinful and dangerous. These actions include holding religious purification rites, the slayers allowing their beards to grow, and the killer deserting his homestead and placing himself under the protection of *kuar muon* (an earth custodian) until the compensation is paid and the funeral ceremony of the victim is performed. For people living in close proximity and eager to live in peace with one another, a prompt settlement of a feud is the best way to prevent the escalation of conflict. Any delay in resolving the conflict increases the chance of an escalation of the dispute.

The feuding obligation is related to the kinship structures. How binding this obligation is on kin depends on the genealogical distance between the parties concerned. In Nuer society, a clearly demarcated group exists that is based on patrilineal descent. There is a close parallel between the kin participating in the giving or receiving of bridewealth, and those who are involved in the giving and the receiving of bloodwealth.

Many scholars refer to tightly organized vengeance groups, but they differ as regards the boundaries of these groups. This variation is consistent with the differing definitions of the span of significant kinship that has already been discussed. The obligation to pursue vengeance, according to Wicjal Bum (1989), extends to relatives to the fourth generation. Nyang Rundial (1989) refers to the involvement of kin to the fourth, and even the fifth generation.[28]

Feuding obligation continues for generations in the sense that the two parties cannot marry between themselves and cannot share common grazing and water resources if there has been no acceptable settlement. Here, the boundary is the third generation, and more distant relatives and clients are usually regarded as immune. The rule in this area is hazy. Confusion on this point may have been accentuated in the course of the nineteenth and early twentieth centuries as the nature of feuding itself changed. However, obligations and boundaries do exist, reflecting genuine ambiguities as well as providing scope for duplicity and special pleading (Jal, interview, 1989; Wilson, 1988).

The span of significant kinship within which vengeance must be exacted is "regulated by deeply rooted custom," but the application of such rules to particular cases varies according to the local context (Howell 1954).[29] The difficulty of knowing who is a legitimate target in a *ter* (feud) is overcome by the requirement that the man who has killed another may not eat or drink until his blood has been let by a *kuar muon*.[30] This blood-letting requirement is based upon the belief that a slain man's blood will avenge (*cien*). This threat is accompanied by the danger of *nueer* (pollution). A proverb tells us: "*Nueer* keeps people vomiting out the truth; you can't hide the fact that you have killed a man." Thus, the serious consequences of not fulfilling the requirement reduce the likelihood of covering up the deed. By his own actions, the killer is easily identified.[31]

The duty of avenging a murder or other injury falls on the nearest able-bodied male relatives of the victim. Stephen Wilson (1988) observes that this obligation is strongest on the part of those who are the closest relatives of the victim. Sons avenge the killing of their father. Brothers are expected to avenge slain brothers.

Beyond the first degree of kinship, the pursuit of vengeance most frequently involves cousins acting alone or in concert with other closer kinsmen. Thus, vengeance may be transverse. Cousins of the slayer are frequently selected as targets by those pursuing vengeance. A less common, but still significant, category is that of sister's sons avenging mother's brothers. Sister's sons are also potential victims of transverse vengeance. Likewise, mother's brothers are involved in avenging sister's sons, presumably where they are of the right age. In-laws are included within the circle of close relatives upon whom the duty of vengeance primarily falls.[32]

The vengeance obligation, therefore, follows the concentric circles of kinship, being strongest at the center and weakest at the periphery, as one might expect. People feel most obliged to avenge those on whom they depend most. These persons are not necessarily kin, and there is some evidence that residential proximity itself is of some significance in determining the weight of obligation (Howell, 1954; Wilson, 1988).

Transgenerational Continuities and Social Order

As indicated in chapter one, the continuity of a constitutional order depends upon the ability of a community of people to transmit traditions, knowledge and skills, manners and morals, religion and cosmologies, from one generation to another. The Nuer believe that in order for people who live in close proximity to transact activities in common, a set of regulations and rituals must exist for the continuity of social order. In order to explain how the Nuer have maintained their way of life from one generation to another, we will first describe the generational divisions. Then we will describe how regulative ideas which marshal activities are enforced with regard to rights and duties among the kin.

Generational Divisions and the Continuity of an Acephalous Order

Some measure of respect between persons of two or more proximate generations is required for social order. This is the purpose underlying the organization of Nuer society into age-sets. Age-set is based on an initiation process which takes place every ten years, ordering the social and political stratification of individuals into successive groups, each with a given name. The age-set system is regulated by a hereditary cattle custodian (*wud ghok*) who controls the opening and closing of initiation.[33]

From the point of view of an individual man, all other men in his society are formally classed as seniors, equals, or juniors (Evans-Pritchard 1951). The division corresponds roughly to three generations: the older, his own, and the younger. To seniors he must show deference, among his equals he is on free and easy terms, and from his juniors he expects deference. Women are incorporated into this system as daughters, sisters, or wives of members of a particular set. Age-sets occur such that one generation is equal to multiple age-sets. Sexual intercourse with the wife of a man belonging to one's father's age-set is regarded as an offense amounting to something resembling incest. Marriage to a daughter of a member of one's own age-set is also prohibited by rules.

Every person in Nuerland can be addressed as father, mother, brother, sister, son, or daughter by reference to their position in the age-set system. This "kinship" transcends lineage and clan boundaries. Everybody in Nuer society is, in one way or another, kin to everybody else, and the word *mar* (kinship) can be used in this connection: *mar rica* (age-set kin) (Howell 1954; Evans-Pritchard 1951). The use of relationship terminology for a person within the age-set system has important implications for the constitution of social order in Nuerland. The age-set system, like Nuer language and religion, takes all Nuer people as a unit. The kinship system, however, tends to fragment them. Age-set solidarity may account for the informal use of kinship terms among the Nuer, since the terminology of address of the age-set cuts across that of kinship. For example, one man may be the genealogical paternal uncle or grandfather of another, but, if he is of the same generation, he is his age-set brother and they would address each other as brothers.

Contradiction between the two systems (age-set and kinship) is avoided by the assimilation of the values of both into those of the family by the use of the family relationship terms. Although one may not know if a man is addressed as "father" by virtue of his place in the age-set system or the kinship system, it could never happen that a term appropriate in the one would be inappropriate in the other (Evans-Pritchard 1951). The Nuer address all very old persons as grandfather and grandmother; persons of one's parents' generation as father and mother; and persons of one's own generation as brothers and sisters. Others are viewed as sons and daughters. This usage is quite independent of either age-set or kinship. It is merely a courtesy extension of the familial terms to all persons in a way that enhances communication, sympathy, and understanding.

Enforcement of Rights and Duties

In the course of daily living, kin may make mistakes or deny another's rights. There must therefore be ways of enforcing the rights and duties if the kinship system is to continue in existence. Wrongdoing in kin relations is considered deviation, and may be remedied with limited recourse to outside help.[34] Major ways of enforcing rights and duties include the notion of rightness of an act, nullification of marriage, and premarital procedures that require fulfillment of certain conditions before marriage can take place. There are circumstances in life that depend upon ritual as a way of formalizing and emphasizing relationships, thus emphasizing the binding quality that supports potential enforcement. These apply to birth, naming, and death rituals. These are ways of acknowledging important events and occasions in a life cycle. The point is that formalizing patterns and rituals are important in ordering relationships in the lives of people. Formality bestows rights and duties. It also bestows a corresponding obligation to enforcement. Enforcement involves rule ordering and governance structures that are built into the lives of people.

The Notion of Right and Rightdoing

Elders within a kin group resolve disputes between group members and persons from other groups. An essential criterion for arriving at normative judgment among the Nuer is a recognition of the right and wrong of particular sides in a dispute. Most disputes arise because of offenses against individuals and failure to fulfill kin obligations. Some scholars emphasize the extent to which self-interest moves a man to fulfill his obligations. While self-interest is a powerful motivation, it does not deny a Nuer the joy of doing what he and his fellows feel to be right.

It is accepted that a man ought to obtain redress for certain wrongs. Obtaining redress is a process. A case is debated before the elders, who listen to all sides and all witnesses. If the elders find that someone has been denied his right (i.e., someone has failed to perform his kinship duties), then the wrongdoer is asked to pay the cattle due to the appropriate relative. If the wrongdoer refuses to abide by the decision of the elders at the village level, the one seeking redress can go to the council of elders at the district level. If the council at this level confirms the village decision, and the wrongdoer continues to refuse payment of cattle due to his kinsman, then by his refusal he is cut off from his kin group. Relatives will support the man who is right.

To break with his kin means that a wrongdoer can no longer claim rights in bridewealth, bloodwealth, or sacrificial animals. If he is attacked, his kinsmen will not support him. If he is killed, his relatives will not avenge him. He becomes an outlaw—outside the protection of law. To be cut off in this manner from any close kin, either maternal or paternal, invites momentous misfortune. The man or a woman who wrongs a kinsman by denying his right is thereby shamed. He or she also may incur a curse and ghostly vengeance. The fears of these consequences tend to oblige the Nuer to fulfill their kinship obligations and duties.

Nullity and Premarital Procedures

With regard to marriage, the Nuer are not content with the promulgation of rules which prescribe desirable behavior but which have no real sanctions. One of the sanctions available for marriage is nullity. It is a necessary sanction, since it is always possible that persons who conduct marriages may be mistaken in their judgments about kinship relationships. A case of mistaken judgment could foreclose a marriage arrangement, and invalid marriages could be conducted. There are safeguards, and even punishments, in the event that it is necessary to void the marriage. Nullity is, however, a sanction that political or religious authorities desire to prevent. The procedures of conducting a marriage are made public to back up whatever marriage policies are sought to be implemented.[35]

The premarital procedures requiring public ceremony are preceded by publicity and eventually payment of bridewealth cattle. These procedures should be considered as a method of formalizing and enforcing individual rights embedded in the way of marriage in the society. This method of enforcing marriage policies and kinship relationships has been effective in the past. The many requirements that need to be met by the parties to the marriage before a marriage can take place indicate the extent to which the Nuer regulate marriage formation. These requirements include negotiation over the payment of the bridewealth cattle, compulsory ceremonies at different stages of the process, payment of bridewealth cattle, and the distribution of cattle.

In this acephalous society, these requirements are contrived to identify problem cases, to prevent marriages that are in violation of the rules concerning who may marry whom, and to reduce the need to resort to the use of coercive force to enforce violations of marriage restrictions. In the final analysis, the celebration of marriage depends upon compliance with whatever conditions the bride's kin deem important.

Ritualizing the Legitimacy of Birth

In Nuerland, an important event in the life of the kin groups involved in a marriage is the birth of a child. The ritual related to birth is a way of emphasizing the binding quality of the relationships. Birth is publicly acknowledged. Cognates bring goats, sheep, and calf-oxen for *kier* (expiatory offerings), especially at the birth of twins.[36]

After the birth of the first child, the bride's family pays two cows to the groom's family. One cow is paid by the bride's father's side and the other paid by her mother's side. These payments are known as the "cows of the spirit" (*ghok joghni*). They are confirmation of the marriage as symbolized by the birth of the child. The payment is accompanied by a ritual that symbolizes the removal of the prohibition of the two families eating and drinking together and the necessity of wearing *tuac* (cat-skin) in the presence of relatives-in-law (Howell 1954).

Giving Name and Its Importance

Names given to a child are full of symbolism. Names concern not only the child, but also his or her father and his kin and his or her mother and her kin.

> Names, whereby men acquire an idea of a thing which one would imagine ought not to perish, are extremely proper to inspire every family with a desire of extending its duration. There are people among whom names distinguish families; there are others where they only distinguish persons; the latter have not the same advantage as the former (Montesquieu [1748] 1949, bk. 23, chap. 4).

Names among the Nuer are bound up with an individual's identity and with the continuity across generations. After childbirth, a child is named by its father. This is a critical assertion of fatherhood. The father's name is taken as the surname. This custom has a lot to do with the potential enforcement of rules regarding rights and duties within the extended family system. If an unmarried girl's child and its biological parents suffer disgrace it is because the child was not named by its father.

Among the Nuer, a name is to emphasize the separateness and individuality of a person. The presumption of equality does not permit the change of a woman's name to that of her husband, as in Western cultures. In the marital relationship, the equality of husband and wife is preserved in the law of names. Dead persons are remembered in their names. This is an important aspect for understanding naming sentiments. An individual wants his name never to be forgotten as long as his lineage endures. In that sense, he is always be a part of the lineage. To ensure the survival of the dead in their names, the Nuer practice the custom of levirate and vicarious marriage.

A widow neither remarries nor inherits, but continues till death to be married to her dead husband, in whose name she may continue to bear children begotten by her dead husband's brother. The custom of vicarious marriage also ensures that every man will have a son who will be called after him. If a man dies before he has married or before his wife produced a male child, one of his brothers or other close kinsmen must marry a wife for him.

In theory, therefore, every man has at least one son, and through this son his name is forever a link in a line of descent.

The Nuer are interested in the survival of the self in the name as a link in a line of descent —not just survival in the children. This explains why the Nuer do not care to call a son by the same name as his father, and even show aversion at the suggestion that one might do so. If the father and son were to bear the same name, there would arise, in the course of time, some confusion in the recitation of a genealogy.

Death and Mortuary Rites

During the death ritual, or mortuary ceremony for removing the *jiak* (debt) which Nuer feel is due on account of the death, a large groups of cognates and their families are expected to attend, along with the sons-in-law, sisters' husbands, and fathers-in-law of the deceased, if he were a mature man. The Nuer feel that there is a misfortune hanging over them, and the death that occurred was only a part of it. It is therefore necessary to clear the whole debt before any further evil comes to them (Kerjok, interview, 1988; Evans-Pritchard 1940). In addition, the Nuer feel that if the dead were not appeased by mortuary ceremony, he might return in anger to fetch the living, especially his wives, children, and cattle (Evans-Pritchard 1940, 56).

In the Nuer society, to kill a cow is the greatest sacrifice one can make. When an old man who has held an important position in the community dies, the Nuer will consider sacrificing a cow that is still giving milk to his spirit in order to make him feel content. When a man dies, an animal from each wife of the dead must be killed by one of her sons or by some kinsman on behalf of her house. After the cattle are killed, the meat is divided among the kin. It is prohibited for the age-mates of the dead man to partake of the meat of the animal sacrificed at the mortuary ceremony. It is considered dangerous even for them to smell the cooking meat.

People gather and sit to listen to speeches given on the occasion. We have reproduced a speech of a *guan buthni* as recorded by Evans-Pritchard (1949):

> God, now you have given us badness, or is it simply
> the lot of creation? (Is the death you have sent us a special
> evil designed for us or has the dead man merely suffered
> what sooner or later comes to all created things?) Now you
> have taken so and so (he names the dead man), now he has

become one of your people, turn about and take him right away. We who are left in the world, give us rest. Let his children who remain in the world be at peace. He is not finished, his children will carry on his name. In the future they will bear his name Let no further evil befall us.

The *guan buthni* now turns to talk to the dead man: So and so, my brother (or my father if he was a much older man), now you are one of God's people. Do not forget us, let it be your habit to speak (on our behalf) to your Father (God). When we go into the bush let us tread on (*poona*) wild rice (the softest of grasses, hence: let us avoid all dangers of the bush). Let us bear children. May all evil be taken away from us now and may we remain in peace. The *guan buthni* addresses God: God, and you ghosts. You, God, made man and you made death. (You have said) you, man, I made you only that you might perish. God, it is your world. You have shown us death this year. Now we here, we go about with this debt, there has been no laughing with happiness for us this year, you have given us mourning. God, turn about and take away the man you have taken. Breathe on us with favourable breath (*ku ko ngok ni yie mi goa*). You took this man, take also this ox of his together with him. He addresses the ghost once more: and you, so and so, are you now in the great cattle camp (of the dead?) Where are you, our father? Where are all the people of our home? Eh! It is the camp to which we all go at last....You who have gone before do not close your eyes to us. You are a man of God. May there be nothing further bad for us to see.

In the speech above, *guan buthni* reflects deeply upon human life and destiny and the transience of all living things. Mortuary ceremony among the Nuer provides a forum for the related kin to state any grievances they had in their hearts towards one another. If grievances are not aired at this time, then they will not be considered in the future. This is the occasion for amicable settlement of family and kinship quarrels.

The death rituals include a ritual performed by *guan buthni* symbolizing the assumption of new life. Symbolically, the old fire in the dead man's homestead will be put out and the old clay firestones collected and thrown into the bush. *Guan buthni* makes three new clay firestones and places on them a new cooking pot in order to cook porridge. A new fire is started (Evans-Pritchard 1940). When the porridge is cooked, the *guan buthni* ladles it out with a new gourd ladle into a new gourd dish (Evans-Pritchard 1940). All utensils are new and a pot of beer is provided for libation. As each elder rises to speak, he dips a gourd ladle into the pot of beer and pours a libation to the ground.

Evans-Pritchard reports that when the last speech finished, everyone in the ceremony stands and *guan buthni* dips *dhur* (wild rice) into a gourd full of milk and sprinkles the people with the mixture. This is repeated many times until everyone is spattered. Butter is smeared on the backs and chests of those present and on the dead man's spears. Persons who wear mourning cords are called to come forward, and the *guan buthni* cuts the mourning cords and carries them into the bush and throws them away. Afterwards the porridge is distributed and eaten. The *guan buthni* makes a symbolic division of the dead man's possessions, which are divided in the presence of *guan buthni* immediately following the ceremony.

The mortuary ceremonies are concluded by all the people shaving their heads. On this account the ceremony is often known as the *muot* (the cutting). The cutting of the hair of the kin symbolizes the cutting off of the dead from the living. In the marriage ceremonies, there is a similar rite, known by the same word *muot*, in which the bride's hair is shaved off. This is to symbolize the cutting of the ties between the bride and her family and kin. The intention of mortuary ceremony is to cut the dead from the living. The dead man has to be given the full status of ghost and persuaded to accept it so that he will remain as a ghost and not try to return to the living (Evans-Pritchard 1940; Gatluak 1989).

Conclusion

The marriage union is to be understood as a means of establishing an ongoing system of order in an acephalous society. Family institutions are an important part of the way the Nuer govern their relationships with one another. It is through marriage that wide-ranging cross-cutting alliances are created. Individuals, who have no central mechanisms for conflict resolution, have developed their own ways of: (1) resolving conflicts among individuals, (2) punishing those who do not behave according to the rules generally agreed to in society, and (3) insuring the commitments made to the long-term arrangements necessary for productive undertakings. Family institutions are one of the major institutional arrangements used by the Nuer to achieve these objectives.

Marriage involves the transfer of cattle as bridewealth from the groom's family to the bride's kin. A number of reasons have been offered, but the most important is that it distinguishes a lawful marriage from an irregular union. In a society where there is a central administration, a marriage is lawful if it is registered by a person licensed by the central authority. Only children born of such a union are considered legitimate. In an acephalous society, a marriage by which the children who are born gain "legitimate" status in the society requires a series of transactions and formalities in which two kin groups, those of the husband and those of the wife, are involved. The transfer of bridewealth cattle is an important prerequisite for the establishment a lawful marriage. The lengthy process of negotiating the terms of the marriage exchange serves to help each party develop a better understanding of the other.

Marriage is considered by the Nuer to be an alliance between two disparate bodies of persons based on their mutual interest in the marriage itself and the children expected of the union, who will be the kin of both parties. Over time, Nuer marriage rules create multiple memberships and solidarities across communities. Overlapping memberships minimize the cost of conflict and reduce the opportunities for a majority to dominate a minority. They enhance exchange relationships by turning potentially hostile non-kin into friendly allies who can benefit from interdependence. Thus, cross-cutting relationships promote peaceful coexistence in a culture in which local resource scarcities are common. For example, the cattle population regularly exceeds the carrying capacity of Nuer pastureland in dry years. The shortage of pasture can lead to violations of grazing rights that can engender armed conflict, both among the Nuer and neighboring groups. People who depend upon access to each other's resources must have some means of working out cooperative agreements if the full potential of the endowments within each group's jurisdiction is to be enjoyed. If such agreements do not exist, then groups will be in constant conflict about access to resources. Without police and other regulatory mechanisms, people can find themselves constantly at war.

The Nuer kinship system provides an important means of regulating the relationships among individuals. Relationships between patrilineal and matrilineal kin are balanced in formal activities. The household is an important part of the system. The household is the key arena for the expression of age and sex roles. It is the basic kinship unit in which children are socialized, security is ensured, and economic cooperation occurs. Here, the very stuff of culture is mediated and transformed into action. Decisions emerge from the household as the result of processes of negotiation, compromise, conflict, and conflict resolution. Decisions to marry, to move to the cattle camps, to build a byre, or to migrate are made in the context of a family, because such decisions affect the lives of all family members. A polygynous household is stratified and segmented. The man is the household head. He is in charge of the management of cattle and other resources. However, his household is associated with other families within a unilineal lineage. Among the pastoral Nuer, lineages perform important corporate tasks such as sharing resources, arranging marriages, and paying bloodwealth. Elders and age-set leaders within the genealogical group mediate and resolve conflicts. Where it is not possible to resolve a conflict within the group, the problem will be referred to more senior kin. Some cases, such as homicide, adultery, and incest, are handled by an earth custodian, who has special powers to ban and to curse. In these cases, the decision of the earth custodian is considered impartial and final.

The intergenerational transmission of knowledge, skills, manners, morals, religion, and tastes is the means by which the continuity of acephalous ordering among the Nuer is assured. The means of passing on knowledge and values is the family and conformity to established usages. This conformity is maintained by enforceable rules. Among the Nuer the largest share in the control and education of the young falls to the parents and other relatives of the parents' generation. Enforcement of the rules is assisted by the conception of right and right-doing, premarital procedures, and rituals that serve to enforce conformity. Sanctions for nonconformity are imposed by elders at all levels of segmentation. The deprivations imposed on rule breakers include social reprobation, the loss of the approval and the respect of kin and neighbors, and the loss of the privileges that the individual possesses as a member of a community and that the community possesses as part of a given Nuer clan.

Chapter 5 - The Organization of Militia

Introduction

It is a simple matter to understand how defense is organized in a polity governed as a state. A state uses hierarchy as the basic principle for organizing its defense, and attempts to monopolize the use of force. Because in an acephalous society force is not monopolized by anyone, it is more difficult to understand how its defense is organized. It is the task of this chapter to explain how defense as a means of procuring security is organized in Nuer society. We begin by describing how Nuer achieve military capabilities. Second, we examine how the militia works to provide security and defense.

Achieving Military Capabilities

In order to understand how Nuer defend themselves, it is necessary to understand the structure of the Nuer segmentary militia. The conceptions Nuer hold about their relationships with one another affects the way the militia are organized. Individuals are presumed to be equal. This concept of equality is compatible with the development of active individual participation in the defense of a segment of Nuer society.

In describing how military capabilities are achieved in Nuer society, we will first describe relevant early childhood experiences. Second, we will consider the ritual of *gar* (cutting) and its importance. Third, we will examine how military capabilities are mobilized.

Some Experiences of Childhood

The preparation of a child for future responsibilities begins at an early age. When a child is able to play and run in an independent fashion, the lobes of his or her ears are pierced (*mut*).[60] Piercing may take place anytime from the age of four or five onwards. The operation is carried out by the child's mother or elder sister. There is no ceremony for this. When the child reaches the adolescence, he or she wears on festive occasions an earring made from the tail hair of a giraffe.

When the child is eight to ten years old, an operation for the removal of his or her lower front four teeth takes place. This tradition is thought to have originated as a means of feeding persons afflicted with lockjaw. The operation is performed on both boys and girls. It is done by a man who is skilled in removing children's teeth. The specialist pushes a nail-like knife down underneath the tooth and then forcibly pushes it out. Because this causes severe pain, adults have to hold a child down while the operation proceeds. There is no stigma if the child cries. Crying here is not associated with cowardice, and will not be deemed to affect the character of the adult individual.

After his lower teeth have been removed, a boy assumes responsibility for herding calves. This is considered important experience, because much of his life is to be spent in herding animals.

Nuer boys begin learning how to use weapons from the time they begin to walk. Every Nuer boy must learn what is required to defend his person, as well as his own and his family's wealth and good name. Boys play at fighting and engage with sticks and clubs in actual battles that take place between groups in a village or a camp. In such fights, the idea is to learn how to position your stick, held in the left hand, in order to protect your head and chest from your opponent's club. The club is held in the right hand, and the blows are mainly aimed at the head or the chest of the opponent. Sticks and clubs are the weapons are used in fights with closely related persons where the use of spears and guns are not allowed.

Training in the use of the spear involves learning how to spear something near or far away and to *riec* (dodge an oncoming spear). Boys use *dura* stalks to practice spearing and dodging. Young boys first see spear throwing and dodging (*riec*) performed by older brothers who practice this with their peers in the village or camps. The younger boys then try it themselves when they are older. Groups of boys using spear shafts (*tong*, plural; *tang*, singular) sometimes fight other groups from different lineages or adjacent villages or camps. Occasionally, serious injuries are sustained. Boys also learn *riec* in dances where adult males demonstrate this warlike skill. This type of preparation is necessary to the survival of the boys once they reach adolescence. Once a boy has been initiated, he becomes a warrior and must fend for himself against experienced persons in battle.

This kind of early training has made members of Nuer militia renowned for their ability to use the spear. Nuer conquests were carried out with bone and wooden spears. Iron spearheads were scarce among the Nuer during the eighteenth and nineteenth centuries. The Dinka, who suffered the most from the Nuer's eastward expansion and conquests, are reported to have possessed more iron spearheads than the Nuer (Johnson 1980).

Transition from Childhood to Adulthood

There are some Nuer rituals, such as initiation, which have not been identified by past studies as being part of the training of a warrior. However, these can, in fact, be seen to contribute to the acquisition of particular skills and personal attributes necessary to a successful warrior. In the following sections, we will briefly describe the ritual of *gar*, a pivotal event in the life of a Nuer male. We will explain the importance that the tolerance to pain, as demonstrated in the concept of *gar*, plays in preparing a male child to assume adult responsibilities.

The Meaning of the Ritual of Gar

The *gar* is significant both in a general political and religious sense but it also marks changing social status from adolescence to manhood. *Gar* symbolizes inclusion in the covenantal community established through *gar* (initiation) arrangements by adult male members of Nuer society. *Gar* is a sign of the covenant. As such, it brings members of different lineages into a special relationship with one another and binds them into fellowship with people of the covenant. Physical descent alone is not sufficient to become a Nuer. A male must be (*gar*) marked in order to participate in the group of those who have covenanted.[61]

The purpose of the rite of *gar*, in Nuer understanding, is both the propagation and the protection of Nuer society. A number of factors relate the rite of initiation to the question of propagation and protection. It is a general rule that all Nuer males of reasonable age (16-18 in the past) must be marked before they can marry. Neither women nor boys can bear spears. This means that women and boys do not go to war, and also that they cannot perform sacrifice to God.[62] For these reasons, *gar* has significance with regard to the propagation and security of Nuer society.

In Nuer thought, *gar* is intended to have a religious as well as a political dimension. This suggests that *gar* should not be considered purely as a national badge, representing only a physical relationship in the age-set system among the Nuer. While *gar* does serve as a national badge, it also indicates the status of a man in relation to (*kuoth*) God, as well as that man's status in relation to other persons in Nuer society. It is only the initiates that may make sacrificial (*lam*) invocation. The initiates (as compared to boys) are expected to follow a certain code of right conduct grounded in a mature understanding of God's laws in order to serve God and to strengthen Nuer society. The outward sign symbolizes the inner refinement of a life based on reason (*wud*) and love of God (*kuoth*).

The Operation and Objectives of Gar

The actual operation of *gar* (cuts) consists of cutting six marks across the forehead. The operation is performed by a man known as *gaar* (marker) who is skilled at the task. There is no special class of such men, but one who is noted for particular ability may be referred to as *gaar*, a skilled person in the marking of boys. *Gaar* uses a small sharp knife for the cicatrization, or marking with the intent to form a scar.

Initiation begins when the boy's head is shaved clean. All ornaments are removed. Each boy digs a hole from four to six inches in diameter and about six or eight inches deep (Jackson 1923). The earth that is dug out of the hole is pulverized and spread around the hole so that it will absorb the blood. When he is called, each boy lies down with the back of his head in the hole. The *gaar* kneels beside the boy and begins to cut. He starts at the center of the forehead and extends the cut to the ear. The *woc dhol* (first cut to remove boyhood) is made just above the eyes, then the remaining cuts are made parallel to it until they are six in number. Then the man moves over to the left side and, kneeling there, repeats the same process. He then returns to the right side and makes sure that all the cuts are deep and continuous at the center of the forehead.

A boy is told to lie absolutely still, for a show of fear on his part is ridiculed by girls, women, and other members of his age group. If he moves while the *gaar* is operating, it will mean that the *gar* (the cut) will not be straight. For the rest of his life, the crooked scar will be a constant reminder that he flinched while the cuts were being made. The blood from the incisions passes along the cuts and drops into the hole. The wounds are washed by means of a feather of any kind of bird dipped in cold water. If the knife cuts too deeply and arterial bleeding sets in, the fur of a wild cat's skin is applied to the wound in order to stop the effusion of blood. The *gaar* (the marker) does not leave the boy until he is certain that the bleeding has completely stopped.

Initiation has several objectives. The first is to make initiates unafraid of the spear or blood and to accustom them to bearing pain. The second objective is to create age-sets and to train young men in the rules of conduct governing the relationships between initiates and non-initiates on the one hand, and between the members of different age-sets on the other. This implies the grading of age-sets, which is discussed in a later section of this chapter.

Aggregation of Age-Sets

Nuer boys initiated in a number of successive years are aggregated to form a single age-set (*ric*). There is a four-year interval between the end of the series of annual initiations that create one age-set and the commencement of the series of initiations that will create the next set. The interval is known as the time when (*ca ngom kaap*) the knife is hung up. At the end of that interval it is said that the (*ngom ca noong rar*) knife is brought out and boys can be marked again. The cattle custodian of each region controls the creation of age-sets by opening and closing initiation. When he is about to cut the age-sets, the cattle custodian circulates information through couriers to all the elders of a region.[63] The number of years an age-set runs before it is cut is variable. However, evidence shows that ten years between the commencement of one age-set and the commencement of the other may be regarded as the average period (Jal, G. 1987; Evans-Pritchard 1940).[64]

Age-sets are organized independently in each region. If a new age-set is started in one region, the other adjacent regions will follow the lead (Evans-Pritchard 1940). In this fashion, the names and periods of age-sets in neighboring regions are the same. Even though in different parts of Nuerland the names and periods of initiation are not the same, a person moving from one region to another can easily figure out what age-set is comparable to his own.

Segmentation of Age-Sets

Each age-set is internally segmented into two or three divisions. The group of men inducted in each two-year initiation period is given a distinctive name. Although an age-set is composed of divisions that are given different names, all members of the age-sets are known by the first word in the name of the first division. Names of other divisions are not used. Figure 7.1 shows the internal divisions of age-sets in Lou and Western Jikany regions.

Members of each division see themselves as exclusive units in relation to the others. The divisions assist in the mobilization of resources, especially in wartime, but also to solve more mundane problems. The names of subdivisions are, however, rarely heard today. In a case of Luac *indit*, or Luac Karam, one hears Luac, the name of the age-set to which both divisions belongs. The name of the senior division of an age-set is distinguished from the name of the entire age-set by the word *indit* (the greater). Thus, Thut *indit*, refers to the elder division of Thut age-set.

Mobilizing Military Capabilities

Decision making authority is distributed in Nuer militia in accordance with many of the regulatory ideas discussed earlier. Nuer institutions that distribute power widely rather than concentrating it in the hands of a few foster collective identity and openness in the development of defensive capabilities. The creation of complementary opposition and alliances prevents smaller segment from being disadvantaged.

Defensive and offensive forces can be organized at the level of the household, the village, the cattle camp, the district, the regional section, and with other peoples beyond regional boundaries. In accordance with Nuer tradition, elders or household heads, age-sets leaders, custodians, and prophets are expected to serve as trustees for their communities. These institutions are important for the operation of the segmentary militia. The following sections elucidate the role they play.

FIGURE 5.1   SUBDIVISIONS OF THE AGE-SETS IN LOU AND WESTERN JIKANY

	Lou Region		**Jikany Western Region**
Tut	Thut *indit* Muothjang Lilcoa	Lilnyang	Lilnyang Lilcoa Lilcuath
Boiloc	Boiloc *indit* Golyangkakeat Laibuau	Ruob	Ruob Nomalith
Maker	Maker *indit* Nguak	Wangdel	Wangdel Wathcar
Guong	Guong *indit* Carbuoi Nyamnyam	Tangkwer	Tangkuer Karam
Luac	Luac *indit* Karam Camthoari	Rol	Rol Pilual
Lith Gac	Lith *indit* (in bor) Lith *intot* (in car) Cayat (Pilual)	Juong	Juong Majaani
Rial mac	Rial mac *indit* Kuek koryoam	Bildeang	Bildeang

Source: Evans-Pritchard (1940: 252-253).

Household Heads

The head of a household is the leader of the smallest fighting team. The household team is composed of the household head and his sons. Sometimes the sons of the head's married sisters may also live in the household. The team leader organizes the training of the boys within a family, makes cooperative arrangements with other related teams, and resolves conflicts that can weaken the solidarity of the members of a family. Harmony in a team is required for defending their members' lives and property from hostile groups.

Each male in a household is structurally defined in relation to every other male; his status is determined by his birth order. Birth order is also important in determining succession to the leadership of a family team. When the head dies or can no longer effectively lead the fighting team, his eldest son or oldest brother assumes the leadership. If the birth order yields a poor fighter, he will be replace by another more capable brother.

The team is unified by a common interest in defending their lives and their wealth. It is also held together by a common agreement on the rules specifying how decision-making authority over security and defense is to be shared and how compensation for persons killed in the course of hostilities will be paid. Because courage is considered the highest virtue, a man's courage earns him a leadership position of some kind in his community (in the sense that he is respected). Should a man be killed in war, his kin will demand compensation or avenge him. They will also ensure that his name is perpetuated by securing a wife in his name who will produce children named after him.

The implementation of these kinship obligations have important political implications among the Nuer. Individual Nuer have to be ready to defend their rights with force. They risk maiming or death when they start a fight. The confidence that kinsmen will not let your name be forgotten reduces the social consequences of death. Fear of what will happen to his family and his own good name will not stop a man from laying his life on the line. He knows his family will be cared for, and his name will be compensated for, or avenged, and perpetuated (Douglas 1986).

Coordinating Teams of Teams

Leaders of teams are elders of extended families, age-set leaders and custodians in one village or district. When leaders of teams have decided on war, information about the pending hostilities is circulated by means of couriers to neighboring elders, age-set leaders, custodians and prophets (if a prophet resides in the area). Information concerning a war that is contemplated is only circulated among older men and other key personalities in different communities who take decisions on this matter, and who are regarded as less likely to allow the enemy to learn of the plan.

The custodians of defense (*ngul*) who control tactical organizations consisting of age-sets and who decide on war strategy declare at which time the hostilities will start. Then all the men in each village, cattle camp, or in tertiary sections are summoned to a meeting where all are informed of the decision, and war plans are made. The war drums are beaten, and the young men gather with spears and shields at mobilization points within 24 hours. The purpose of the drumming is to speed up mobilization of the militia. Using couriers to inform everyone would take too long.

There two primary reasons for drumming. One is to announce war and the other to announce weddings and ordinary dances. If a wedding is to take place, the people of a village, a cattle camp, or a district know about it before the drumming begins, because the marriage-settlement is openly and freely discussed by all local inhabitants. Therefore, in the absence of any information about a marriage, the villagers or residents of a cattle camp who hear drumming know that the young men are to assemble for a more serious purpose (Jackson 1923). The men notice at once the meaning of this style of drumming and prepare for war by bringing their shields, which they do not carry at festive gatherings such as a dance or wedding.

Mobilization of a Nuer militia is influenced by two major factors. First, the size of the mobilization area is necessarily limited by the distance individuals can travel to participate in a deliberative assembly will make binding decisions for the military unit. Thus, the men will not remove themselves very far from their homes and can mobilize rapidly. Second, the covenantal commitment to defend one's village, cattle camp, or district helps achieve rapid mobilization. Members are armed and ready to move to mobilization points for further instructions from the leaders. At the mobilization point, field tactics and war formation are discussed.

Rapid mobilization tactics are well-suited to Nuerland, which is flat. What ridges exist are low, providing few defensible barriers; they cannot be considered commanding strategic positions. The pattern of warfare in the region consists of a rapid attack and a rapid retreat (Johnson 1980; Bum, interview, 1989). The Nuer adopt a flexible battle formation. They usually advance in three parallel columns, with the center column trying to engage the enemy. The outer columns attempt to encircle the enemy. It is a formation which maximizes their ability to make quick attack and to cover their own retreat (Johnson 1980; Evans-Pritchard 1940).

Prophets

Several prominent prophets from different regions have held leadership positions as warriors and have succeeded in coordinating activities with one another to check foreign aggression (Johnson 1980; Sanderson and Sanderson 1981; Holt 1958). These included Ngungdeang Bong (1850s) and his son, Guek Ngungdeang (1890-1920s), of the Lou Nuer. Deng Laaka, a contemporary of Ngungdeang, was a military leader among the Gaawar Nuer as well as a prophet and earth custodian. All prominent prophets among the Western Nuer, including Kulang Ket, among the Jagei Nuer, Buom Diu, among the Dok Nuer, and Gatluak Nyak of the Nyuong Nuer, were renowned as warriors (Johnson 1980). Both Buom and Gatluak had gained their military reputations before becoming prophets.

These leaders are known among the Nuer as *buuth rem* (leaders of their regions).[65] *Buth rem* is a fighter engaging in violence himself rather than a manager directing the employment of violence by others. A Nuer "officer" both directs the fighting and participates in the fighting. The essential quality of the warrior is courage and bravery. Associated with this is a close bond that exists between the *buth rem* and other team members. This closeness is mainly due to the fact that each and every fighter recognizes the ability of the *buth rem* and participates in selecting him as their leader.

Another factor contributing to the emergence of prophets as military leaders and coordinators of large-scale war against foreigners is the Nuer belief that the *kuoth nhial* (air spirits) are associated with war. The Nuer believe the air spirits, which are another way of thinking about God (*kuoth*), accompany warriors into battle.[66] The prophets are chiefly regarded as the media through which God directs the battle. Before Nuer set off for war, their prophets make a sacrifice and sing hymns to the spirits of the air, while the warriors, kneeling on one knee and with the points of their spears resting on the ground, sing the responses (Evans-Pritchard 1956). The same posture is adopted by the warriors at all ceremonial occasions. People, often led by the prophets, sing hymns of praise and supplication to the air spirits on the occasion of sickness or other troubles.

The Problems of Organizing for Security and Defense

There are problems of security at many different organizational levels in Nuer society. Households in villages or in separate clusters of windscreens in cattle camps share land and water resources. If households come into conflict with each other, the members of each family must be prepared to defend themselves. Members of households, villages, or cattle camps may, upon occasion, need the assistance of others in protecting their lives and property. Kin groups, or political units like villages, however, vary in size. The small size of a political unit increases its vulnerability to aggression by more powerful opponents.

Segmentary complementarity is one way Nuer resolve this size dilemma. When giving support is necessary, related teams or segments can aggregate sufficient forces to defend themselves against an overpowering segment. Each of these segments is composed of lower-level genealogically related individuals that can combine forces to defend their joint interests. Nuer can thus enjoy the advantages of both the large regional organization and the small independent segment. If insurrection occurs in one of the segments, other segments can be mobilized independently to stop the disturbances. If corruption arises in some part of Nuerland, remedies are usually sought through alternative segments of the society. The grounding of segmentary complementarity in genealogical structures and the freedom of action of individuals provide the Nuer with the ability to combine in large numbers against external forces and to cope with internal conflict.

Although segments at different levels of organization can combine to thwart aggression, segments also fight among themselves. A few basic rules govern behavior within a region and also across regional boundaries. First, individuals have a right to demand compensation for injury. Second, aggressors are obliged to pay compensation in cattle. Because of the high value placed on vengeance as a principle among the Nuer, multiple agents with limited jurisdiction are authorized to resolve conflict and take leadership in mediating peace in the community.

All Nuer recognize the right to vengeance where compensation is not paid. The vengeance group is composed of the militia of the segment to which the injured party belongs. The size of the militia depends upon the relative positions of the aggressor and the victim within the existing lineage structure and the number of allies and friends each side can muster. Because of the great distances involved, the membership of the militia is rarely drawn from above the level of the region.

Household Security

In Nuer tradition, homesteads are open, not garrisoned as are homesteads in the Northern Sudan. In a Nuer household, the household *luak* (byre) and the *kraal* are located in front of the houses where each wife and her children sleep. Each house has an open space containing a *buor* (cooking screen) in front of which cooking, the pounding of grain, and churning take place. Each household has a garden behind the buildings and open grazing land located in front of the byre. This property, including open spaces, are resources that must be defended.

Cattle are the chief source of strife among households. *Bok ghok* (cattle theft) is common along the boundaries between the Lou and the Gaawar, and along the borders between the Mor of the Lou Nuer and the Gaajok of the Eastern Jikany Nuer. Evans-Pritchard (1940) reports that the Leek raid the Western Jikany, the Rengyan, and other Western Nuer peoples. *Bok ghok* is also common along borders of other regions.

Bok ghok implies "civil war" among regions. The war of Lueny Yak (*kor lueny yak*) between Gun and Mor primary sections of the Lou Nuer was caused by this practice. Within a region fighting also frequently results from disputes about cattle between individual households in the same village. On the issue of cattle, close kinsmen can fight, and homes can be broken up.

Cultivation land, grazing land, and water sources are resources a household also must defend because they are vital to the survival of a Nuer family. More importantly, the prestige and honor of the family must be protected by responding with appropriate force against attack. Crimes against persons such as rape, abduction, and pregnancy not followed by marriage can also cause fights between households. Members of a household must be able to protect all their resources from raiders. The absence of a credible use of force against raiders can invite further raids and trespasses on household property.

A Nuer family is, however, always attached to *ji mara de*, a kin group. From this association, individuals secure mutual assistance, security and defense, and other means of existence. *Gol*, as noted in earlier chapters, refers to the cattle-dung fire kept burning day and night in the center of the byre. It also refers to the smallest local community that is larger than a single polygynous family. A *gol* consists of at least two or three byres, and the huts of two or three polygynous families. Each of these extended families constitutes the smallest fighting team larger than the family. The heads of the families that compose a *gol* are commonly brothers or a man and his married sons.

Each household unit also has its allies and related individuals outside their *cieng* (village) who can provide support if the household or *gol* are attacked by an overpowering group. An attack on one *gol* will produce some significant reactions in other parts of the village, in other villages, and in the districts inhabited by persons related to the victims. For example, if *A* attacks *B gol* and inflicts heavy damage on life and property, *B* will activate its alliances and will retaliate with equal or greater force. *A* then will activate its alliances in response. Because of the heavy interdependence among individuals, the security network of a Nuer household is complex.

Nuer are considered by many scholars who have studied them to be prone to fight at the slightest provocation. Nuer do not, however, live in continuous turmoil. Because Nuer are contentious people does not also mean that they lack a social order. In fact, the results of contestation and argumentation are such that order and predictable relationships emerge, rather than the expected chaos. Dueling and disputing practices induce prudence in the relations between persons who regard themselves as members of the same group. Persons claim rights because there are rules protecting those rights. The costs of conflict also need to be seen in relation to investment in mediating efforts to reduce or confine overt conflict. Rules are the most important instruments used by individuals to define and protect individual rights. Establishing order by reference to rules generates predictability in relationships. In disputing, Nuer recognize rules as a means of ordering relationships among persons of equal standing.

Defense of the Nuer Village

Hostilities can result when a village's control of its common property resources is challenged. Common property resources are crucial for the survival of a pastoral community in Southern Sudan. Nuer pastoralism cannot be sustained without the resources of the *tuoch* land that supplies water, grass, and species of edible fish. Residents of a Nuer village cultivate common land, use common village water supplies, supplement their diet by fishing in common fish reserves, graze their cattle on common pastures, and herd their cattle in a common cattle camp during the dry season.

Although grazing areas are claimed and operated by different lineages, right claimants of each grazing area invest few resources in herding. In fact, no problems arise if cattle cross grazing grounds to obtain the best grass and water provided they stay within the lineage grazing land or in an area where the prior consent of right claimants has been obtained.

The violation of grazing rules, which most often occurs when grass or water are in short supply, can, however, lead to destructive conflict. The right claimants must exclude others from area by force if necessary. The harder others try to secure benefits from a property over which they hold no rights, the more effort is required by those who hold rights to the resource to maintain exclusive access to the benefits. If the return from the resource is worth the cost of the necessary effort, defensive people will fight to maintain it. If the return on the property right is not worth the effort, the Nuer will not act so as to risk any loss of life.

Residents of Nuer villages are part of larger bodies of people. If a group or a village cannot defend itself, neighbors in adjacent villages come to their aid to maintain the integrity of the village under attack. Individual villages are linked to a multitude of people in other villages by ties of differing strength. The readiness to accept strangers in villages or cattle camps underlies the clustering of persons around the dominant lineage. Individuals who agree to live in a village or a cattle camp consider each other as kin even though no genealogical or marriage relationships exist. The covenantal arrangements are treated as law and enforceable. Relationships become the bonds that regulate their conduct. Shared age-sets membership is an important cross-cutting link among persons. Other ties, even though they are primarily relationships between individuals, have a political significance for large-scale group relations. Marriages between lineages have implications beyond the families immediately concerned. Broadening the ranks of supporting allies is one of important reasons for the existence in Nuerland of marriage agreements between families.

Because it is by nature unexpected, defensive fighting is usually rapidly organized by local communities. Collateral segments within a region can support or reinforce each other if necessary after news of the attack has reached them. Offensive wars in which one Nuer village attacks another, for purposes of conquest, has no place in the Nuer scheme of things. Such conquests are not allowed by the mediation and compensatory schema. If offensive action were to occur it would meet resistance. If such aggression comes to dominate, Nuer culture would be destroyed.

Cattle Camps and the Scarcity of Natural Resources

Shortage of grazing land is a major problem for Nuer pastoralists. Some groups, such as the Lou Nuer, are forced to move into Eastern Jikany territory for grazing and water during the dry season. The rights to grazing lands and water pools in the area are claimed by different households or lineages. The Burjuok cattle camp is, for instance, located in an area claimed by the Wang secondary section of the Gaajok region of the Eastern Jikany Nuer (see Figure 7.2.).

FIGURE 5.2   GAAJOK REGION OF EASTERN JIKANY NUER

....

Laang Primary Section. Thior secondary section
. Duong secondary section
. Kueth secondary section

....

Wangkac Primary Sect.. Mitnyaal secondary section
. Wang secondary section
. Nyathoal secondary section

....

Yol Primary Section . Puot secondary section
. Kual secondary section
. Yic secondary section

. Cam secondary section
. Kuol secondary section
....
Source: Jal (1987); Evans-Pritchard (1940).

Grazing areas and the water sources associated with them are common goods belonging to a community by its capacity to exclude others. These resources can be conceptualized as goods that are "packaged" within appropriate community or lineage boundaries so that others outside the boundaries are excluded from their use (Ostrom, V. 1988). In this way, Lou Nuer communities that live nearby the communities of the Gaajok and/or the Gaawar Nuer may be denied use of grazing land and water claimed by the Gaajok or the Gaawar Nuer. To avoid costs, some lineages are forced to give access to grazing land and water to those who need it.

In addition, cattle populations owned by Nuer communities regularly exceed the grazing resources controlled by these communities in dry years. In each dry season the resulting shortages of pasture characteristically lead to violations of grazing rights that engender armed conflict both among Nuer groups and between the Nuer and the bordering Dinka. Each cattle camp must use force to protect its claims to the resources required by its inhabitants. Failure to do so will result in the suffering of both human beings and their cattle.

District and Regional Divisions

A district is a cluster of villages bound together by common interests and geography. Relationships are characterized by competition, fighting, and conflict resolution. Competition over scarce resources such as land and water source sometimes lead to destructive conflict. Crimes against persons, which include adultery, incest, and homicide also generate violence.

There are, however, social bonds among district residents and members of primary sections of a region that restrain violence. These include the principle of exogamy, the willingness to accept strangers into a district or a village, the clustering around (*dil*) dominant lineage, the ready acceptance of the priestly sanctions of a common mediator, shared age-set membership among villagers, and attendance at feasts and ceremonies. These social bonds link members of one village with members of other villages within a district. Many of these ties extend beyond the tertiary levels.

If a fight occurs between villages within a district or in adjacent districts, any of these links can be activated in order to allow discussion of the problem with a view to resolving the conflict. The segmentary militia are also restrained from carrying on a fight or a feud by the segmentary complementarity of force, by the fact that the Nuer are exogamous, and by the covenantal arrangements that uphold the ideals of mediation. Because Nuer society is exogamous, both disputing parties have kin, allies, in addition to age-set members living among the opposition. These people are expected to press for a peaceful settlement of the feud and prompt payment of compensation cattle. A mutual fear of ritual sanctions, such as the pollution of the earth or the fear of committing a fault against God and fellow men leads the principal adversaries to seek to negotiate a settlement of their differences to prevent breakdown of peaceful relationships. Given the Nuer understanding of God, ritual sanctions are feared. The practical reality that neighboring peoples draw water from the same pool and graze animals in the same pastures is also a restraint against violence. Normal village life and the interaction among villages essential for the welfare of the residents cannot go on while militias of adjacent segments are in a state of feud.

Regionalism and Collective Security

Each Nuer region has a territory that contains natural resources that are used according to specified rules. The segments that constitute a lineage or clan combine in the face of an outside attack. However, a Nuer clan or a region is part of larger Nuerland. The way Nuer think about themselves as a unique community, their relationships with one another and their relationships with other people has a great impact on how they perceive their defense and security arrangements. Their sense of uniqueness as a people is based on some basic bonds in their way of life.

Without a common understanding and the consciousness of participating in cooperative enterprises, the closeness of individuals in the Nuer society would not be possible. A community of individuals dissolves into a disorganized aggregate with no cohesion. Shared understanding among the Nuer grows from a history of common experience, enhanced by a common language resulting in common expectations (Kiser and Ostrom, E.

1982). Nuer cannot constitute a society without coming to an understanding of who they are and how they can maintain their way of life.

The Nuer believe that they are (*gaat kuoth*) children of a common Creator. The unity of the Nuer is analogous to the unity of the (*luak kuoth*) church of God. It is a union (*duol naath*) of the faithful in the workings of (*cak ghoa*) the Creator of the universe. Segmentary complementarity is possible only on the basis of an inner unity in love (*nhok*) to serve God. Thus, religiousness, the common lifestyle, and the fate of the Nuer always exist together. Every connection or link such as blood or marriage relationships and good neighborliness has a religious foundation, leads to collective interest, and is defended by able-bodied males.

The other important idea related to regionalism and collective security, among the Nuer, is the principle of service to God. The Nuer strive to do the right thing in order to realize God's will. The (*lat cungni*) is the most general expression of the ontological essence of the Nuer (Evans-Pritchard 1956; Frank 1987). They consider it as the highest normative principle of social life. *Cung* (rights) are grounded in the right of individuals to fulfill obligation to serve God. Persons of disparate segments unite against non-Nuer aggressors to maintain the peace of God. Equality of persons among the Nuer is seen as the demand for equality of service. As the earlier chapters indicate, the Nuer concepts of *lat cungni* (doing the right) make up the social order. This follows the Nuer conception of freedom of action of individuals.

The task of defense is the highest goal to which the behavior of the Nuer is directed, and a goal for which their lives are often given. The peace of households, villages, cattle camps, districts, and the Nuer people is perceived as the peace of God. Disturbance of that peace is disturbing *kuoth* (God) and must be resisted. The commitment to the service of *kuoth* is expressed in many ways in Nuer society.

There are other affinities that make common military action possible against non-Nuer. Nuer have a homogeneous culture, a common language, and all live in a continuous stretch of land running from west to east across the Nile. There are no isolated sections. Their common language and values permit ready inter-communications between regions. Their feelings of superiority, the contempt they show to all their neighbors, and their readiness to fight them are also a common bond.

Commonalties of the Nuer are symbolized in a common fashion. The spear is a symbol of a commitment to the defense of the peace of God.[67] Nuer clans can suppress internal differences in order to unite in the face of external aggression. Actively feuding sections of the Lou Nuer stopped hostilities to join in a counter-attack against the Anyuak, when the latter penetrated deep into Mor territory in 1911 (Kelly 1985). Shared membership in age-sets is a bond among adult males. *Gar* initiation is thus a national badge that symbolizes membership in a covenantal community. Age-set arrangements facilitate the movement of persons across regions. If a man migrates from his region, he can at once fit himself into the age-set system of the region of adoption. Age mates must support each other in time of trouble. Nuer warriors believe they will be cursed if an age mate dies because he has been abandoned in the face of danger. The obligation to assist an age mate is consistent with the Nuer concept of service to *kuoth* and to one's fellow man.

Successful use of force by a non-Nuer group against any one Nuer region is perceived to undermine the peace of God among the Nuer. The belief in a common Nuer destiny imposes, then, a normative requirement: loyalty to the Nuer commonwealth. The operation of the Nuer commonwealth requires cooperation. It is this cooperation what makes it possible to describe the operation of the Nuer militia as a system of teams of teams.

Nuer clans (and groups within a clan) or lineage combine forces in defensive warfare. Inter-regional cooperation is used to address an existing or potential conflict with one or more other regions or outside aggressors. Nuer conflicts with bordering Dinka are mostly carried out by members of a border group of a single region. Kelly (1985) reports that the Lak, Thiang, and Gaawar jointly participated in some of these attacks, and the Lou and Gaawar in others. Evans-Pritchard (1940) also observes that the Leek, Jagei, and Western Jikany combined in raids on the Western Dinka and the Lou and Eastern Jikany in raids on the Anyuak. These instances are consistent with central features of Nuer segmented structure of authority relationships and point to the importance of segmentary militia organizational characteristics in accounting for the Nuer capacity to mobilize forces in larger numbers.

The combinations of teams are based on shared interests to procure security for the segments involved and for Nuerland as a whole. By combining their military forces, they are able to create a larger force to defeat invaders than one group would be able to create alone. The combined military forces of segments within a clan are coordinated by Nuer prophets, with assistance and cooperation from household heads or elders, age-set leaders, and custodians. *Dayiomni* (minor prophets or priests), elders, age-set leaders, or custodians lead the component segments. (See Figure 7.3).

Limiting Shirking

Individuals working together as a team can accomplish tasks that cannot be accomplished by individuals acting alone. Good teamwork, among the Nuer, yields stability and security for Nuer families. Preventing shirking is necessary, however, for the continued success of teamwork. If there is no accepted means of preventing shirking, individuals will do what they want, disregarding common security and defense requirements. The quality of teamwork will eventually decline, and, in turn, the welfare of the members will suffered.

Among the Nuer, the active participation of each member is an important source of success. It is necessary for members to monitor each other's performance to prevent shirking in order to maintain a high level of participation in teamwork. Responsibility for monitoring performance is assigned to members of a household, household heads, age-set leaders, and *buuth rem* (leaders of the fighting teams). Mutual monitoring and enforcement is possible because people fight in units composed of members of villages or cattle camps. The village and the cattle camp contain the same peoples at different times of the year, which are relied upon for large-scale conflict. These village or camp groups are small enough so that individuals know each other and can monitor each other's behavior. There are costs for individuals who attempt to shirk.

Cooperation is usually preferred to shirking on the basis of self-interest and the interest of one's family. If one villager does not fight, others may decide not to fight. If villagers do not defend their interests, all will lose. It is in the best interest of all able bodied adult males in a village to cooperate to ward off external aggression. Most members of a community want their village to continue to be viable and their way of life to be maintained against disturbances. A variety of factors do affect individual calculations, however. In a small group one individual makes a greater difference than he does in a large group. Joint sacrificing and shared age-set membership also reinforce the commitment of members to a group.

Coordinating the activities of segmentary militia requires trust and experience. Elders, age-set leaders, and prophets are perceived to have the necessary experience to prepare them for the serious business of war. The basic skills learned from earlier childhood are made perfect by practice in fighting through the years. These persons are also believed to be able to guard against momentary passions and irrationalities that might place a community in unwarranted danger.

In the following sections, we will describe the different ways the Nuer organize the monitoring function to prevent shirking. First, we will explain the significance for Nuer defense the common sacrifice and the shared spear name. Second, we will consider how social proximity and belief in a transcendental order help in monitoring. Third, we will examine how shared membership in age-sets prevents shirking.

The Joint Attendance of Sacrifice and Spear Symbolism

Among the Nuer, the unit of moral control is the group that sacrifices together. Joint attendance at feasts and ceremonies means shared experience and accountability. Sacrificing cattle is one of the ways that the Nuer put pressure on each other and recognize claims. Persons who have covenanted for joint sacrifices travel long distances to attend funeral, purification, or peacemaking ceremonies. Claims are reinforced when persons make the effort to travel across country to attend and honor sacrificial rites. Religion as mentioned in earlier chapters, is one of the media in which people communicate with one another and require that deeds support sentiments. Ones presence at sacrifices signals a community of interest and is part of what legitimizes claims to cattle or wives or both. Nuer religion, as Mary Douglas (1980) observes, is a double set of accounts: it enables people to hold each other accountable to a common commitment in rituals that testify to their right-mindedness; it also provides a balance sheet on which their relation to God can be assessed.

A large number of associated persons within a clan or region are brought together by attendance at feasts and ceremonies. These activities are of general importance to the Nuer whether they are in a village or cattle camp in the same district or in another region. The joint effort of creating a Nuer society provides the incentive to resolve problems that undermine its peace and stability. Sacrifice is all about what it means to be a Nuer and to defend a way of life. There is a sense of moral obligation towards one's fellow man, an obligation that decreases as structural distance increases. But there is always a consciousness of obligation towards the members of a clan as well as those within a district who share a common spear name. Members of these institutions are committed to covenantal arrangements to serve God's will. This *nguot* commitment is best express in disputes between groups. In warfare, a man is obliged to aid any man with whom he shares a common (*mut*) spear name. Not to do so is viewed as a failure to discharge an obligation.

Unity in sacrificing is grounded in prior agreement on what the spear symbolizes. The word *mut* means a "fighting spear." *Mut* can also refer to the battle group. The spear is a symbol of strength (*buom*) in collective effort. This becomes clearer when we consider the origins of the spear name. The Creator of all clan spears is thought to be *wiu*, which is another Nuer name for *kuoth*, or God, (i.e., there is only one God). In this broad and symbolic sense, the word *mut*, defined as the battle host, identifies the clan with God conceptualized as the Lord of Hosts (Evans-Pritchard 1956). The association of the spirit *wiu* is essential in the constitution of clans. Thus, there is a community of understanding grounded upon the transcendental order of God. Conduct of persons is ordered by shared commitment to regulative ideas (e.g., *wiu*) marshaling activities when they are acted upon for collective defense.

God is invoked by the clan through the spear of the ancestor held in the hand of one of his descendants offering an animal in sacrifice to God. Thus, the spear symbolizes the submission of kin and clans to God's peace. There is a sense of common bond in the spirit of the spear as the symbol of God that makes men willing participants in the militia as a means of realizing whatever peace can be realized consistent with a right ordering of life.

Social Proximity and Transcendental Order

Living close to one another reveals shared values of individuals. Factors influencing choice of residence include security, the availability of food for the family, and grazing and water sources for the animals. A village or a cattle camp is considered as common enterprise for the common good of the persons involved. This shared interest must be defended by cooperative efforts. Shirking undermines teamwork and must be limited by mutual monitoring. To make interdependence possible, it is necessary that persons have shared interest of some sort. The categories of relationships, however, give the Nuer only a base upon which to build relationship but within a conceptualization of some transcendental order.

Behind every relationship between an individual and an association of persons lies the force of spiritual bonding and an inner unity that acts through this relation among the Nuer. The militia will not fight in coordination with one another or with other segments if the men fighting are not welded together by a feeling of solidarity, if they are not intuitively conscious of themselves as members of one village, one district, one clan, or one Nuer people. This unity of collective spiritual being is the foundation on which the militia is based in Nuer society. This transcendental bonding enables a person to systematize his or her social contacts and so to have the security of living in an ordered world.

The constitution of each segment consists of a network of interpersonal kinship ties that connect all its members to one another and directly to a transcendental order. Living together within the bonds of this transcendental order provides rules for enhancing harmony and security among people. Proximity forces persons to develop common rules to promote their mutual interests and also to protect those interests from aggression. In order to live together, people have to follow rules. One of the rules is to defend a common way of life. Shirking upsets the relationship of trust among people, and the damage must be repaired by social sanctions. For example, running away from a war is considered a breach of covenantal undertakings among people to defend the peace of God. An individual who flees may be banned from the territory.

The Stigma of Cowardice

In Nuer society, courage and bravery are assigned a high value; a coward is despised. A man who does not endure the (*gar*) initiation rite must prove his worth in a fight otherwise the stigma of cowardice remains for the rest of his life. It is difficult for such a man to find a woman to marry. Cowardice is considered incompatible with the Nuer conception of individual worth. A man who cannot defend himself, his family or help his in-laws in a fight is seen as irresponsible. The Nuer also believe that a man who cannot fight with men (*wutni*) prefers fighting with women (*kor*). The reputation of wife-beater is most shameful, and no father can knowingly allow his daughter to marry such a man. It is difficult for such a man, if not impossible, to rise to any social position of prominence in Nuer society. Due to the stigma of incompetence and cowardice he cannot build friendly relationships of any kind. He is seen by his paternal kin as someone who is unreliable in times of a fight with members of an opposing group.

The stigma of cowardice also affects relationships with other families in a village or cattle camp. A man's failure to contribute to the defense of a village, cattle camp, district, clan, or the Nuer people means that the respect and prestige of his family will suffer. A father is blamed for the failures of his son, unless the father's competence and skills in war are known to be good. If the father is not to blame, the traits will likely be ascribed to the family of the mother of that particular son. Indeed, a son might migrate, if he is not banned, to his mother's brother's lineage because in his mother's brother's lineage he can shirk.

Conflicts in a mother's brother's village are viewed as belonging to a different lineage in which one is not directly involved. In this context, a Nuer can escape immediate accountability for not participating in the defense of that community. This is, however, always a temporary solution because, eventually, he will be asked to participate in the defense of his mother's brother's lineage. Within a village or within a patrilineage, it is better to comply with the requirement to fight to the end rather than to face the loss of respect and be treated as a coward.

Age-Set Configuration and Shared Membership

The shared age-set membership promotes mutual understanding, joint association, trust, and sympathy. The key processes in the Nuer age-set seeks the creation, identification, and implementation of shared values. A Nuer age-set is an embodiment and instrument of governance. There is a comradeship between age-mates that springs from recognition of the common experience of having shed their blood together during *gar* (cicatrization). *Gar* creates a bond of brotherhood. It also symbolizes a covenant between adult males of different ages. Members of a junior age-set are expected to show respect to members of senior sets. Their deference to which can be seen more clearly in war situations.

Whenever there is a fight, a column of warriors is a combination of different age-grades, especially the junior elders and the youngest age group. They fight side by side in village or camp units. Arrangements are affected by the exigencies of fighting situations. Junior elders are expected to give "command" or, rather, give guidance. Their directives are followed because of their age and experience within the Nuer age-set structure. For a breach of approved patterns of behavior, including shirking, the sanctions include disapproval, denial of respect, and withdrawal of assistance.

The age-set institution affects the ways in which individuals and groups become activated within and across segments. As time passes, each age-set group changes its position in relation to the whole system, passing through points of relative juniority, seniority, and levels of skill and courage (Jackson 1923; Jal, G. 1987; Evans-Pritchard 1940). This mobility of successive age-sets groups is peculiar to the system and is a necessary characteristic for it is an institution based on the succession of generations. The mobility of groups through the age-set structure and their changing position in it should not be allowed to obscure the constancy of its structural form and its effectiveness in ordering life's activities within a segment.

Conclusion

The organization of segmentary militia reflects the way Nuer conceive of their relationships with one another. Force is not monopolized by any single person. Defense is organized in teams of teams. Polygynous households form themselves into teams of militia for their own defense. The collective choice processes in which power is diffused and widely share rather than concentrated in the hands of a few, involve institutions that foster collective identity, openness, and contestation with respect to security. Nuer defensive capabilities depend on broader processes of competition and coalition formation, within the bonds of a transcendental order that prevents any segment from being permanently disadvantaged.

A household is an institution for training young boys for future responsibility in a segmentary militia. A knowledgeable citizen is one who is familiar with the rules of appropriate behavior in conflict situations. The family is responsible for teaching children the meaning of the rituals of *gar* as well as their responsibilities to kin and age-set members. Because there is no central power to supply equipment to recruits into the militia, each household provides its members with fighting equipment such as sticks, bones, spears, guns, and ammunition. The decentralized supply of weapons and food is an important means of preserving individual freedom of action and family control over its members.

The structure of Nuer authority relationship reflects the segmentation of Nuer regions. Nuer regions are built from smaller segments constituting military units. This is necessary due to the wide dispersal of the Nuer, but it also serves to maintain the rule of active personal participation in the teamwork of fighting. Warriors from different households constitute a team that can act alone or in concert with other teams. When a group is attacked by an overpowering segment, the related segments combine forces to ward off the aggression.

Security and defense among Nuer households, villages, cattle camps, districts, clans, or the Nuerland as a whole is maintained by a team of warriors composed of one or more teams. The complementarity of the segmentary militia based on a common understanding is a key to the security and stability of the Nuer. A pattern of defense organization that would be appropriate for a household team is not fully appropriate for the village, cattle camp, clan, or any portion of Nuerland that involves larger scale warfare. Larger teams are coordinated by the *buuth rem* who have distinguished themselves in warfare.

Chapter 6 - Conflict and Conflict Resolution Among the Nuer

Introduction

Conflict occurs in all human societies. What differs is how people deal with conflict. It is the task of this chapter to explain how the Nuer understand and manage processes of disputing. Conflict occurs in Nuer society on all levels: the Nuer household, the village, the cattle camp, and the larger groups beyond the district levels. Disputes on any level may or may not escalate into destructive violence. An understanding of how the Nuer resolve their disputes will provide an insight into how individuals in an acephalous political system govern themselves.

In this chapter, we will first describe the Nuer conception of conflict. Second, we will consider the major types of conflict and the arrangements for their resolution. Third, we will examine how conflicts are mediated.

Conflict as Contestation and Argumentation

People who are engaged in a dense network of relationships have ample opportunity to violate the rights of others intentionally as well as unintentionally. Their passions make them prone to commit wrongs even though they know what is right. A Nuer thinks in terms of right (*cuong*) and wrong (*duer*). *Cuong* is defined as the right way of conduct of members in a community. Departure from the right requires that somebody takes action to right the breach (*duer*). *Duer* has two meanings: first, it is a wrong when a person actively violates the right of another. Second, it is a wrong when a kin refuses to honor his or her obligations. By his membership in a kin group, a Nuer acquires both rights and obligations.

When a Nuer feels he is wronged, he points to a breach of right or an insult. Where the claim is denied by the person accused (who may make his own counter claim on his own behalf) the dispute takes the form of an argument in which each party supports its case by appeal to rules. A Nuer who feels he is in the right does not seek advice or arbitration. He challenges the man who wronged him to a duel. A person is unlikely to be caught unaware as to whether or not to accept the challenge. It is difficult to refuse a challenge without serious loss of face among the Nuer. The challenge and response to it can be considered as a reformulation of a dispute into a public discourse. This means a stage of a social relationship in which conflict between two parties (individuals or groups) is asserted before members of a community or a third party (Gulliver 1963). The assertion may take the form of club fighting (*duai*), chest pounding (*pat loc*), side slapping (*pat rang ran*), or each man singing a poem of his ox (*tuar*). These disputatious or contentious acts afford the disputants, as well as the people in a community, opportunities to inquire into the conflict with a view to processing and resolving the conflict. This concept of a challenge is mistaken by Evans-Pritchard (1940) for retribution.

Contestation and argumentation help people to learn from one another what somebody else has to say about the problem they are facing. Open deliberation is appreciated by Nuer because it permits them to come to terms with conflict and conflict resolution. This is how they learn how to live together. The disputants tell their side of the story to the other members of a community. Resolution of a conflict comes about as the consequence of learning from what another person has to say about a conflict. Disputation and contestation are accepted as part of the "nature" of things in Nuerland. The posture of independent, aggressive self-reliance is encouraged from childhood. Disputes often end in violent confrontation unless dispute processing is rapidly put in place in accordance with the notion of who is in the right.

Mediating conflict requires an understanding of the nature of the conflict. Nuer distinguish disputes between those problems that turn on rights in material things, such as cows, land, and water, from those that involve rights in persons, such as adultery, abduction, rape, and homicide. The latter are more difficult problems to settle and require more enduring means of conflict resolution. The Nuer system of classifying offending behavior emphasizes the social context in which it occurs. That is, how an act is interpreted, or what reaction follows it, depends on the relationship and interests of the persons involved in a conflict. The closer the relationship between the contestants, the fewer people will be involved, the less severe the retaliatory action taken, and hence the easier the settlement (Epstein 1974). Conversely, the greater the structural distance of a conflict (i.e., the more distant the relationship between the contestants), the greater the number of people involved (i.e., persons taking sides in the disputes), the more severe the retaliatory action taken, and the more difficult the settlement.

A quarrel in Nuerland is of direct concern to the groups to which the disputants belong. Nuer segments are autonomous from one another, and their relationships are characterized by competition, conflict, and fighting. Vengeance is an appropriate mode of redress for any injury sustained at the hands of somebody from a distant clan. This is because the force of law is not the same for all Nuer, but rather, it weakens with the structural distance between parties to a dispute. At the outer edges, with the people not committed to the group, the will to deal justly with all Nuer is checked by natural obstacles, physical distance, and the need to travel. However, everywhere in Nuerland, a complex system of cross-cutting links and exchange relationships hold physical violence in check. Hostility among Nuer is tempered also by the spiritual bonding of the transcendental order to God. This is reflected in many ways as earlier chapters indicate. Elders, age set leaders, custodians, and priests recognize that the interests of their communities are not achieved through fighting and are able to call for amicable resolution of disputes by payment of cattle in compensation. Fighting, however, is a still a viable means of achieving redress.

Types of Conflicts among the Nuer

Different types of conflict occur at different levels of social organization in Nuer society. This poses a critical problem in a society without a central mechanism for conflict resolution. Each decision unit mediates conflict within its jurisdiction. This suggests that conflicts are resolved in different ways in different contexts. In order to explain the different types of conflict and how each is resolved, we will describe disputes arising from:
- matters of honor
- relationships within a family
- conflict in a village
- the cattle camp and water use, and
- clan divisions and the wider society.

Matters of Honor

The notions of honor and shame generate serious disputes but also assist in conflict resolution in Nuerland. The Nuer conception of God is reflected in the idea of honor and dishonor. God is the Creator of man and has given man the capacity to think in order to do the right to glorify His Name. A Nuer sees himself as the guarantor of morality, rectifier of disturbed balances, and the power that reinforces the right in order to protect the sacred person of man in the image of God. Honor depends upon his will, his worth as a person. The role of man as guarantor of morality does not ignore the *muc kuoth* (divine grace). Man defends the fulfillment of the will of God.

The perception of the ultimate source of the sacred within each individual brings honor into the sphere of Nuer religion. It is in this sense that a person's honor is viewed by the Nuer to be sacred, something more precious to an individual than even his own life, of which it is considered the epitome. "Rather death than dishonor!" is the ideal expression of this sentiment, whether on the battle field or in the boudoir (Peristiany and Pitt-Rivers 1992). Nuer perceive that honor is owed to God. Honor must be protected by force if necessary and by the acceptance of danger and hardship among equals. Nuer see that individual and family honor must be preserved even if all else is lost including life.

The opposite of the concept of honor is the idea of dishonor or shame (*poc*). The counterpart of shame is the Nuer idea of *cany*. *Cany* means to despise. Any conspicuous breach of morality or decorum is shameful in Nuerland, as when a man steals or is rude to his father or mother. *Poc* also describes a derogatory situation that can be corrected only by performing an act of honor to cancel out the offense that caused it. In an extreme situation, dishonor can only be washed away by blood (i.e., that is by killing). Dishonor or shame in this sense is differentiated from misfortune.[68] Misfortune occurs in the act of fulfilling the requirement of honor and implies no moral or social disapprobation (Howell 1954).

Nuer Notion of Honor and Possession of Arms

The significance of honor and shame, among the Nuer, is made clearer when different types of conflict are more closely examined. First, male honor demands that men be armed at all times. For a long time the spear has been for a Nuer man an object of necessity. Today it is common to see a Nuer in rags carrying an expensive rifle and a spear. He does not want to part with the spear even though a gun can do more harm than the spear in warfare. This is because the significance of the spear is moral, not merely utilitarian. It is not the spear itself nor its possession that is stressed, but the activities associated with it: war, dancing, and herding. The uses of the spear itself and the evaluations of those uses as an index of social personality are blended, so that the spear is not just a weapon but also something that stands for a very complex set of social relations.[69] It is, therefore, the Nuer belief that the right to carry spears (or arms) is one of the prerogatives of members of a free society where everyone is accountable for his or her own action.

The tradition of arming men is strengthened by the instability that the Nuer experience in their land. Governments seek to license or to ban the carrying of arms, but the ban is rarely complete and not effective. The possession of firearms, spears, and sticks means that quarrels can quickly lead to serious violence and killing. But this does not often happen among the Nuer. Arms are used as deterrence, and the rules do not permit their use without an acceptable reason.

The notions of honor are attached to the possession of spears. Boys are given their first spears as a sign of coming into manhood and of the handing over by one generation to another. It is not just a spear but a new status that he is being given. The boy becomes a man, a warrior, and soon becomes a husband and a father. He can now participate in feuds and wars; he also can engage in dances (*rau*) and displays with oxen, both of which among the Nuer are martial exercise as well as play intimately associated with courtship.[70] Male prowess in the use of weapons is demonstrated in hunting as well as in direct conflict with other men.

Second, challenge and insult, as the chapter on the organization of militia indicates, play an important part in disputes. Because they are always armed, men are at all times ready to enforce rules when they are violated. Nuer society expects men to do so, and failure to enforce rules is considered a dishonorable failure to discharge an important duty. It is punished by withdrawal of confidence. For example, Thiwat Kuany and Ruot Yuol fought in 1978 because Ruot Yuol called Thiwat Kuany *gat jiok* (a bastard). Ruot Yol was seriously wounded in the fight. Kuany and Yuol and other young men had been playing a card game known as *weat*, and Yuol lost. Yuol accused his opponents of cheating. Kuany responded that that was not the case, and Yuol countered with the abusive words.

Ignoring an insult could be interpreted as a sign of cowardice on the part of Kuany, although the insult also could be taken as a joke. But Kuany and Yuol were not in a joking (*leng*) relationship.[71] The village Gok, where the conflict occurred, is composed of two small but opposing segments of Lungngor lineage. These groups are competitors in almost everything. Anything such as an abusive name could be construed as an insult to the honor and prestige of the other group and must be countered with an honorable act to repair the damage.

Female Honor and Dispute Resolution

The honor of men is intimately associated with that of the women related to them by blood or marriage. Therefore, a man is obliged to see that the honor of his wife, sister, daughter, and his close female relatives is respected. It is also the case that, if their honor is compromised, sisters and daughters cannot be married to reliable families. Female honor is articulated in a variety of ways: general comportment, adequate fulfillment of female roles, and sociability; and it can be attacked or questioned by gossip, by physical violence, or in other ways. Its essential expression is, however, sexual. Disputes arising from an attack on female honor may be grouped into the following three categories: first, those involving unmarried woman, where a dispute may be provoked by seduction and particularly by pregnancy that is not followed by marriage; second, by disagreements in bridewealth cattle, and third, by abduction and rape.[72]

Girls in the Nuerland are taught in their early years that sex should occur only within the context of marriage, bearing children, and establishing a home.[73] Once a girl has been compromised, particularly if she is pregnant, pressure is brought on the man concerned and his family to marry her. Violence can ensue if marriage is not agreed upon by the parties involved.

There are circumstances where seduction is, however, not followed by marriage or violence. In cases where a close relationship between seducer and seduced precludes marriage, recourse to blood vengeance is also inappropriate. For example, Luk Kueth was reported to have had illicit sexual relations with Mary Bigoa, a daughter of his relative in the small village of Wec Wukau in 1978-9.[74] The resolution of the problem was to regard it as a religious wrong, a sin, automatically calling for special retribution attended by an extraordinary purifying ritual. A form of violence was, however, also involved in settling this case. Sacrificing the "best" animal of the seducer was a violent expression of disapproval by the community of this behavior between close relatives.

Conflict involving married women is less prevalent than that involving unmarried women.[75] Married women, like girls, are free in their contacts with men. They are not confined to their houses as are the women of the Islamic communities in Northern Sudan. They move about among men and speak freely with men. Affronts to wives generally are answered with violence. Proven or presumed adultery by a wife is usually settled by divorce, provided that the woman involved has no children.[76] Rape is another act that dishonors a woman. The Nuer react violently to rape or abduction, therefore, such activities are rare in Nuerland.

Relationships within a Family

Conflict is present at varying levels of intensity in Nuer families. There is both love and hate among the closest persons within the household, and this is increased by the fact that family ties carry political, economic, and social relationships. Emphasis upon the unity of members of a household in defense against aggression obscures conflict within a family. Killing within a family is anomalous. It cannot be avenged. Rather it is considered a religious wrong requiring a purifying ritual.

To elucidate the issues underlie the recurrent problems existing in Nuer household arrangements, we will examine intrafamilial conflict and its context more closely by considering specific relationships: those between parents and their children, brothers of different mothers, relationships among affines, and so on. Some of these relationships are more fraught with potential for contention than others.

Parents and Children

Although adult sons establish their own homes when they marry, parental influence on them is still considerable, especially when they live nearby their parents. Fathers and sons work together in major family projects and defend their common interests. Sons are strongly obliged to avenge their fathers. Conflict between fathers and sons is rare because it is highly unacceptable behavior. Sons are taught to honor their parents and persons of their parents' age group. The father's position among the Nuer is lawfully predominant. It is through their father that children trace their decent and sons inherit wealth.

Conflict does, however, occasionally occur between fathers and sons. Where a conflict occurs, it is usually related to matters of material things or how resources are used. When the father is perceived to be threatening the family's interest in the allocation of wealth, sons will intervene to prevent mismanagement of the family resources. A father's decision to marry more wives using the accumulated cattle, when his sons are of the age to marry, can cause dissatisfaction in the household. He could be told in a meeting with his sons that the cattle should instead be given to the older son for his marriage. If the father does not listen to his sons, the dispute over the allocation of cattle is reported to the father's brothers who are asked to intervene in order to resolve the problem. Once the fathers' brothers are involved, the problem is mediated and usually resolved through discussions in favor of the sons.

Ties between mothers and sons are close and mainly affectionate. Cases reoccur in Nuerland where a son may defend his mother from his father, who is a wife-beater. Cases of conflict are also common where a son assumes or attempts to wrest control of the family economy from his widowed mother or where a senior son neglects his responsibility to support his mother and her younger children. For example, Pal Mut, age 19, was the eldest of three children in the care of a widowed mother, Nyabiel Reth.[77] Instead of helping his family, he dissipated its resources by taking provisions from the house and even by selling livestock. His mother reprimanded him when she caught him taking milk from a *diar lel* (milk container), a fight developed between them, and he injured his mother. The fight was reported to Pal Mut's paternal uncle who rebuked the young man told him to assist his mother in supporting the younger children.

Brothers of Different Mothers

Solidarity among brothers is valued in Nuerland and contributes to their success in defending their common interests. Armed conflict between sets of brothers is common among the Nuer. In 1977, Bol Ruac abducted Nyak Garejani Dar with the assistance of his brothers, Kek Ruac and Kac Ruac. Tap Lia Kon, their cousin, also helped them. Tap reported that their intention was to force the family to allow the girl to marry Bol Ruac.[78] The two families eventually agreed to establish a union. Cooperation between brothers does not, however, preclude the fact that rivalry and conflicts exist. Quarrels among brothers often occur in the context of the use of family property. Brothers live together before they are married and own cattle in common. This living together provides an added reason for conflict, especially when they are of different mothers.

Although brothers are taught that brothers are one because they belong to one father and one lineage, there is an element of envy, jealousy, and hatred between the sons of different mothers who share a common father. Competition between wives for use of most of the scarce resources of the household leads to this latent bitterness among brothers. Each woman wants to have more cattle use with her children; she wants more milk to make cheese than other women. She wants more attention from the household head. The division of cattle in the household usually reflects the number of children for which each wife has to care. Because all wives do not have an equal number of children, the one that has more children is allocated more cattle for milk and this can engender envy and jealousy among other wives who charge their husband with favoritism. The jealousy (*tiel*) of the mothers is transmitted to their sons and is reflected in the sons' behavior towards their brothers from other women. The problems of *tiel* (jealousy) and competition over household resources are not satisfactorily resolved in Nuerland. As long as polygyny (which remains the ideal form of family) exists, then quarrels among brothers of different mothers will persist in Nuer households.

Relationship among Affines

In Nuerland, in-laws are regarded as members of the family. They cooperate with each other in the exigencies of life. A bride who has many kin is often preferred to one who has more cattle because, through the institution of alliance, kin of the groom can gain access to more labor and protection. As indicated in earlier chapters, affines help each other in a variety of ways. Brothers-in-law easily get involved in each other's conflicts by giving support in difficult times.

Despite high levels of cooperation among affines, conflict does occur. From among the many potential types of disputes among affines, I have chosen the major disputes relevant to the constitutional order of the Nuer to describe here. Conflict is especially common between affines who live close to each other. Because marriage negotiations often include hard bargaining and involve an exchange of honor as well as bridewealth, the affinal relationship is charged with tensions and potential discord (Gatluak, interview, 1989; Wilson, 1988). The direct form of affinal dispute is between husbands and wives. A woman may return to her parent's home claiming persistent ill-treatment from her husband. The problem is usually discussed by the two families involved, that of the groom and that of the bride, to find a solution. If the family of the bride supports her decision to leave her husband, then she may do so. The bride's father then returns the bridewealth to the husband's family.

If a wife leaves her husband after the birth of their first child, his kin may decide to claim the return of all the bridewealth except for six head of cattle. These six are retained by the maternal uncle of the child in order that the father retains his rights in the child. These six animals include the two of "the hairs and the skirts" (cattle for the services the women had given while with her husband). The other kinsmen of the wife must give up their portions of the bridewealth. By this procedure the wife is divorced and can remarry. A wife may also be sent back to her parents' home for a variety of other reasons including difficult personality traits, such as extreme inquisitiveness, nagging, and grumbling. In 1978, Kulia Riak married Nyakuoth Dup, but after a few months the woman was sent back to her parents by her husband where she gave birth to a daughter. In discussions concerning how much bridewealth should be returned, the central problem was the uncertainty as to the paternity of the child, which according to Kulia was prenuptially conceived.

In Nuer society, bridewealth gives rise to all kinds of dispute among affines. The number of bridewealth cattle is arrived at by negotiation between groom and kin and kin of the bride. The agreed upon cattle are usually paid in installments. This method of payment provides plenty of opportunity for disagreement even after the bargain is struck. Some persons on the side of the groom may not readily pay their contributions on schedule. They do not refuse to pay but plead a lack of cattle even if there are animals available that can meet the obligation. The eldest member of the family of the groom mediates conflicts such as this. If cattle are available, the man refusing can usually be persuaded to pay his contribution for the marriage of his kin. Refusal to pay strains the relationship with the groom and undermines kin solidarity.

Affinal relationships are also adversely affected if the man or woman cannot bear children. In such a situation the kin, especially the bride's, will agree to a divorce and let their daughter marry somewhere else. If, however the husband is an old man and the marriage was arranged because the man has lots of cattle or in order to create a political alliance, the girl may be compelled to stay with her husband. But in most cases of male impotence, the man will allow his wife to take a lover and bear him children who are lawfully his children according to the Nuer custom governing family relationships.

A sexual element can also be a factor in conflict among affines, because the affinal relationships place men and women who are not married in a situation of close proximity. Persons are tempted to carry out illicit sexual intercourse with unmarried women, which is considered wrong. The parents want their daughters properly married because the purpose of sexual congress, among the Nuer, is the creation of children. The parents' attitude is a reflection of their desire to see daughters lawfully married so that they may acquire cattle for their sons' marriages. Parents do not tolerate any attention from an outsider that is likely to compromise a daughter's chances of making a suitable match with a man who has cattle.

If illicit sexual intercourse is actually realized, the brothers of the girl will fight the man who committed the wrong, unless he agrees to marry her. If the seducer has no cattle, or if he is not even the man in line to marry in his family, this type of conflict confuses the relationships within the man's family. Such a problem can cause the split of a village or cattle camp. One of the families directly involved may leave the village or camp in order to avoid fighting that could involve many people and families. But moving away is not a resolution and, in fact, complicates the process of mediating conflict and resolution in the future. The members of the man's family usually agree that their son marries the girl to prevent the disruption of relationships.

Conflict between Cousins, Uncles, and Nephews

Gaatguanlen (cousins) are expected to support each other. Cooperation among cousins is expressed in many ways. They fight together, avenge each other, and aid each other in the payment of compensation in case of homicide or injury. Among the Nuer, cousins are supposed to live in one village and move to the same cattle camp in the dry season.

Cousins render to each other services such as loaning equipment, helping in repairing buildings, herding animals, and defending against distant foes. These cooperative activities can bring about disputes. Maluel Kueth borrowed an axe from his cousin Puot Bungjak to cut building poles (*koi*) in a nearby forest. Maluel Kueth later refused to return the axe on the pretext that his cousin owed something to pay for the damage done by Puot Bungjak's cattle. When Puot Bungjak went to the byre of Maluel Kueth to get his animals, a fight occurred in which Puot was injured. Puot Bungjak raised the issue of his axe to the elders.

When the village elders looked into the case, they found that Puot Bungjak was negligent in taking care of his cattle, sheep, and goats and that his animals had destroyed not only Maluel Kueth's crops but also those of other villagers. The decision to resolve the dispute, however, was to appeal to the kinship sentiment and to emphasize the need for harmony. In the end, Maluel Kueth returned the axe to Puot Bungjak, and Maluel Kueth refused any payment for the damage to the crops.

Uncles and nephews quarrel more frequently than cousins. Nephews have many contacts with paternal uncles. Quarrels between uncles and nephews are related in many cases to cattle. Uncles are one category of persons who are obliged by tradition to contribute toward the bridewealth for the marriage of their nephews. When their nephews' sisters (i.e., the nieces) are married, uncles receive a share of the bridewealth. It follows that the uncles who have received a share of the bridewealth of a niece are obliged to pay some cattle towards the marriage of a nephew. In many cases uncles meet the bridewealth obligations, especially when uncle and the father of the nephew concerned are born of the same mother.

Sometimes an uncle refuses. In 1967, Tut Mut Wunbil was to marry Nyadel Ding. When Tut Mut asked his uncle Rundial Wunbiel for his contribution to the bridewealth, he refused saying that he did not have cattle. When this case was reviewed by close relatives, the elders of the family supported Tut Mut Wunbiel and asked Rundial Wunbiel to pay his part. Refusal to comply with the decision of the elders means breaking the kinship relationship (*mar*). This can be costly because everyone else will support the party who is in the right in the case.

Conflict in a Village

In many Nuer villages, conflict is regulated by conditions of land scarcity and continuous production. Where there is no shortage of either land or trees and there have been no vested agricultural interests in any parcel of land for an indefinite period, the principles of land tenure are not clearly defined. The rules that do exist simply refer to the right of an individual to live and earn a living in a village rather than to rights in specific resources. This means that, while each village has a defined territory, it is the active cultivation of land that confers rights of use on the cultivator. A garden that is left fallow for longer than two to five years is regarded as abandoned and may be re-occupied by anyone from the adjacent village. The community attempts to protect the rights of cultivators from damage to their crops by stray animals. Herders who use water from pools or wells without prior permission from right claimants are guilty of trespass.

Trespass and Stray Animals

The destruction of crops by stray animals is a problem of long standing. Resolution of the problem is complicated by the tradition of common rights in grazing land. Pasturing takes place on land subject to common grazing rights, and villagers attempt either to restrict the access of non-lineage members or find ways of accommodating strangers. As noted in earlier chapters, the violation of grazing rights, especially in the dry season, usually results in conflict. Fellow village residents are guilty of trespass as often as are outsiders.[79] Damage of crops occurs most often during the rainy months because the animals are, in most cases, left to fend for themselves without any supervision. Unattended animals inevitably cause trouble from time to time.

The damage of crops by stray animals is not the only problems faced by persons living close to one another. Disputes over water in naturally occurring pools arise, especially in years when the pools dry out early in the year. These disputes may lead to violence. Allowing animals to drink from the water pools of a neighbor is considered a violation of the property rights of the neighbor. Shallow wells are also dug and are the property of the individual who digs them. Mud troughs are built around wells for watering animals, and these can be destroyed by goats, sheep, and cattle. When water is in the trough, stray animals can also drink from it and deprive the well's owner of the water.

The Nuer use the open range rule, which means that the animal owner is suppose to look after his animals and, should they stray onto somebody else's property and destroy crops or drink water, the owner is guilty of negligence. Although fencing is not a lawful requirement, some persons fence their gardens and water troughs to protect from damage by stray animals. They use thornwood for fencing. Disputes that arise are resolved through discussion and payment of compensation for damages. Animal trespass is a common problem to all families, and most people simply accept some damage in order to promote good neighborliness.

Boundaries of Contiguous Gardens

Conflicting claims to rights in land is one of the most common causes of disputes. Disputes over cultivable land and grazing lands are affected by the extremely complex system of property rights. Most land belongs to families and village communities, and not to individuals. Right claimants frequently hold use rights only in land, and they share these rights with others. Use rights in land are mainly transmitted through marriage and inheritance, but they can also be leased. Developed land can also be sold in order to compensate the developer for his labor. In the nineteenth century, the likelihood of conflict over land was increased by two general trends: first, the rise in population, which intensified competition for already scarce resources (Jal, G. 1987; Johnson 1980), and second, the gradual strengthening of individualistic and absolute notions of property as against the complex traditional conception of use rights. This second trend implies the weakening of traditional governance structures.

Most land disputes arise over the location of the boundaries of plots of cultivation land. This is particularly true east of the Nile where the population is larger in relation to the land (Jal, G. 1987). People may verbally agree where the boundaries lie at the time of allocation, but later try to push their claims beyond the agreed upon line. This sort of behavior is a constant source of disputes. Problems are mediated by village elders and age-set leaders. Respected persons in the village who were present when the boundaries were established are called upon to assist in the resolution of these disputes.

Envy and the Evil Eye

Chapter three in this study indicates that the Nuer believe God takes only what is his. He is compassionate, however, and spares a man if he sees that he is poor (*can*) and miserable. All Nuer want to have more cattle and other property. Nuer, however, think it is not safe to be proud of one's good fortune. Pride in having a large number of children or cattle may cause God to take them away. It follows that the Nuer are very uneasy when their good fortune is even so much as mentioned by others. Praising a person's moral qualities of courage, bravery, and generosity is considered proper, but it is more than rude to comment on another person's physical well-being, the size of his family, the number and quality of his cattle, or other possessions because evil consequences could follow. It is what the Nuer call *yol jor*. *Yol jor* is an intent to destroy another person's wealth and property. A Nuer does not praise a cow, especially to talk about its exceptional milk yield, for fear it may cease to give milk. Nuer also believe it is dangerous to tell a young initiate that the *gar* on his forehead are healing well, because such a remark may result in a unhealed spot festering anew.

The idea of *yol jor* overlaps with that of the (*peth*) evil eye. The Nuer consider the evil eye as an act of covetousness and envy (Evans-Pritchard 1956). Covetousness and envy are generated by the act of perception. There is no objective criteria for what it is that generates them in a society of equals. Schoeck (1969) observes that anyone who has a propensity for envy, who is driven by that emotion, will always manage to find enviable qualities or possessions in others to arouse his envy. The envious one dislikes others because of their personal or material assets, and is, as a rule, more intent on the destruction of the assets than on their acquisition. Among the Nuer, a person believed to cause harm and even death to those who come across his or her path, sometimes without any motive at all other than the inherent evil in his or her personality, is thought to have the evil eye (*peth*). Nuer believe that people in that state of mind do not possess the ability to control their own malice. According to the Nuer, *peth* is a diseased state of mind that has no remedy.

If anyone becomes ill shortly after the visit of a person possessing the evil eye—most of whom are well known characters—it is assumed that he has been bewitched. The illness is usually supposed to have been caused by the secret insertion into his body of the bone of some animal, fish, or foreign substance (Kek, interview, 1989; Jackson 1923). A custodian of *juath* (health) can be called in to remove such a foreign substance. According to one informant, there is no scar when the bone enters the body and no marks when it is extracted from the body of the patient.[80] The object that has been removed from the body of the patient is shown to the people who are present to see and to touch it. Persons with the evil eye are often killed with at least the tacit consent of the whole community to which they belonged (Howell 1954). Some informants report that, if compensation is demanded for such a killing, only six head of cattle need be paid to the kinsmen. Others say that no compensation is ever paid for *peth*.[81]

Cattle Camp and Water Use

When the Nuer leave their villages in the dry season, they regroup in large cattle camps located near reliable water sources. In the dry season, a higher level of solidarity, both spatial and moral, exists than does during the rainy season. People in cattle camps live very close to one another in dry season huts and *gauni*; cattle that in the villages are kept in separate *kraals* are tethered in the same *kraal* or in adjacent *kraals*. In the rainy season when the water and pasture are abundant, families herd their own cattle, but in the dry season cattle camps, the cattle of all camp residents are watered and pastured together and the different families take turns to provide herdsmen.

Despite the solidarity of people in the cattle camps, conflicts are easy to begin because people who live very close to one another are competing over limited resources. These conflicts sometimes lead to destructive violence. Fishing and joint herding most frequently provide the context in which disputes arise.

Fishing, at any threshold of supply of fish, may impair the value of the water supply to each individual herd owner. In most Nuer areas, natural pools are used as sources of drinking water for both human beings and animals. Water for human use is stored *waat* (hafirs). Hafirs are built with or without devices to prevent pollution, leakage, and evaporation. They can supply water for a few weeks or even for the whole of the dry season depending upon the rainfall in that particular year.

Fishing in a pool or lake makes the water dirty and undrinkable because of the presence of rotten fish and other debris. Therefore, fishing reduces or drives out other patterns of water use. People and their cattle will suffer, and there will be a deterioration of the quality of life among the population dependent on a particular water source.

Although there are shared interests in the common good of the residents and cattle in the camps, some individuals fish in the pools even though fishing is not allowed. Fish tend to congregate where fishing is not allowed, creating temptations for those who like to fish. This causes conflict between residents of the camps and threatens to undermine the covenantal relationship among the residents. If fishing continues, some camp residents will stop it by force. Because of the danger of breaking down relationships within cattle camps, institutional arrangements are available to repair the damage. The elders who own the cattle, age-set leaders, custodians, and priests mediate these kinds of violations.

Pools also contain plant materials that is used for food, especially in lean times. Because Nuer do not use water vegetable materials extensively, little is known about them. Wild fruits, seeds, and roots comprise a very small portion of the Nuer diet and are not fully utilized in normal times. The seeds and roots of water lilies (*Nymphaea lotus*) are found in pools and lagoons in the early dry season. In times of hunger when some of these plant materials are fully utilized, they become an important source of food and are guarded by the claimants. Ignoring these claims results in disputes that are settled through discussion.

Clan Divisions and Wider Society

Because of the need for a seasonal migration to a limited number of perennial water sources, members of Nuer villages, which are the chief interacting groups in Nuer society, have to cross to neighboring portions of land to share cattle camps, water, and fishing pools. This is why clan divisions (as well as members of different lineages, especially those living in frontier communities) that do not usually share resources during the rainy season may come into conflict during seasonal times of scarcity of water and succulent grazing in Nuerland.

Although the environmental restraints upon Nuer society demand that there should be peace and cooperation between clans and within lineages, and that seasonal migrations should be carried out with the prior agreement of the right claimants, conflicts arise over the use of grazing lands and water sources. Some of the disputes arising from proximity and use of scarce resources in common may lead to destructive violence. However, there are social restraints on the use of violence. These include the marriage role exogamy, the ready acceptance of strangers into a cattle camp, clustering around a dominant lineage, the acceptance of the ritual sanctions of a common mediator, shared age-set membership, and joint attendance at feasts and ceremonies. All these factors link the members of one village, cattle camp, district, and clan or regional section with members of others. But it is in the neighboring villages that they function most effectively and are most necessary. Beyond the district level, although the principles remain, the application of these principles becomes weaker and less effective.

The Slave Trade

For generations, the Gaawar Nuer and their Dinka neighbors on the Arab frontier have suffered more from raids from the Arab merchant camps on the Bahr el Zeraf than have other neighbors of the Nuer such as the Lou, the Thiang, and the Lak. These merchants also exploited internal feuds among different lineages among the Nuer. The intervention of the slave traders in the area led to some sort of centralized leadership among the Nuer, as individuals gathered around the strongest leader for protection. This also led to the breakdown of traditional means of conflict resolution.

The case of Nuar Mer in the late 1800s is an interesting example. Nuar Mer was originally a Thoi Dinka who came as a young boy to Gaawar Nuerland during a time of famine in his homeland.[82] He was adopted by Mer Teng, the earth custodian and priest from the Kerpel division of the Gaawar Nuer clan. Kerpel is a dominant lineage in the area and provided leadership among Gaawar people at the time. After the death of Buogh Kerpel, the Bar section of the Gaawar Nuer split off from the Radh section, who were the immediate descendants of Kerpel (Johnson 1980).

Mer Teng made an alliance with slave traders on the Bahr el Zeraf in about 1865 (Coriat 1993, see chapter notes).[83] When Mer Teng died, he left his adopted son Nuar Mer as the earth custodian as a means to overcome the rivalry between his biological sons. Nuar Mer was reluctant to accept the position because of hostility to his Dinka origins, even though he was supported by the majority of the Kerpel lineage. As an earth custodian the community expected him to stand in a neutral position to the rest of the society. The opposition based on his Dinka background was alien to the Nuer tradition. Because of his adoption into the Kerpel lineage, all rights and privileges that accrued to natural members of the lineage applied to him as well. The opposition led to violence, or threats of violence, after the death of Mer Teng (Diu 1976, see chapter notes).[84]

Threats to his position forced Nuar Mer to seek a closer alliance with the slave traders who were currently based in Gaawar land. He became the most trusted ally of the slave traders. His followers consisted of fugitive communities from the Luc, the Ngok, the Twic, the Nyarweang, and the Dour Dinka who left their country because of famine.

Nuar Mer raided for both cattle and people. He exchanged the people for tobacco, sugar, and other goods. He carried offensive war against the Lake, the Thiang, the Lou Nuer as well as some Gaawar, the Nyarweng, the

Twic, and other Dinka (Johnson 1980). He terrorized people into submission. Children of individuals who disputed with Nuar Mer were captured, or the parents themselves were sold as slaves.[85] Johnson (1980) observes that Nuar Mer also got support from the traders to herd captives of the Nyadikuony section into an enclosure where they were burned to death in revenge for the murder of another man they had killed. The incident is recorded by early administrators, either as the work of a slave trader known as Ali Wad Rahma, or as instigated by Mer Teng (Tangye 1910; Johnson 1980).

Although Nuar Mer was originally a Dinka, he gained the right and ability to function as a custodian through inheritance from his adoptive father. His selection was based on the assumption that he might maintain the neutrality of the office better than the biological sons of his father. However, by allying with slave traders and raiding the Nuer, Nuar Mer violated the neutrality of the office and committed an affront to God. Because he was increasingly more despotic and relied on the Arab merchants for maintaining him in power, discussion to resolve his differences with his people was not possible. Opposition to him was, therefore, to deny his right to political or spiritual authority. Eventually he was killed in a violent civil war led by his chief rival, Deng Lakka, who had the broad support of many Gaawar, Lak, Thiang, and Lou Nuer (Jal 1989; Johnson 1980).

Mediating Conflict among the Nuer

In Nuer society, where persons consider themselves as equal to one another before *kuoth*, mediation is an acceptable mechanism for conflict resolution and the maintenance of lawful relationships. When a person feels wronged or insulted, he challenges the man who has wronged him to a duel. The challenge takes the form of club fighting (*duai*), chest pounding (*pat loc*), and side slapping (*pat rang ran*). These activities are a conscious effort to block any deviation from acceptable behavior and to avoid the breakdown of a relationship. The disputation is based on the Nuer concepts of (*cuong*) right and (*duer*) wrong. Nuer religious conceptions discussed in chapter three contribute to the way in which Nuer think about themselves, their relationship to their universe, and how they relate to one another. These presuppositions shape the common understanding that gains expression in the conception of right.

Conflict over right claims can easily escalate into destructive violence and breach the peace of a community. Disputation and contestation is also a means of illuminating the underlying problems between the parties involved. Given the inevitability of conflict, the institutions developed by the Nuer to resolve a variety of conflicts at different levels of organization are important for an understanding of the working of an acephalous system of order. Processes of mediating conflict among the Nuer reflect the means of supporting and enforcing rule. There are different mechanisms for resolving conflict and formalizing conflict settlement among Nuer households, villages, cattle camps, districts, regional divisions, and in the wider society. The effectiveness of these mechanisms depends on the level of conflict and the extent to which mutually agreeable solutions exist.

In considering the mediation of conflict in Nuer society, we will first describe the processes of mediation that the Nuer use in recurrent problems at different organizational levels. Second, we will consider how Nuer formalize or confirm covenantal relationships in negotiated conflict settlement.

The Processes of Mediation

When a man is injured by another, he prepares to fight. This breaches the peace within a community. The open contestation and disputation brings in persons who seek ways to resolve the conflict. An earth custodian is one of the key persons in a community for the mediation of conflict. He is a neutral mediator with some additional sanctions to curse or ban the individuals obstructing his efforts to settle disputes. In addition to the threat to curse or ban, the earth custodian's power of persuasion and knowledge of traditional law are important in the disputing process. The process begins by making sure the relevant elders of both parties are present. Then the principal parties in the case are called in for a hearing of the case. The hearing usually takes place in the byre of (*kuar muon*) an earth custodian.

The disputants usually describe the circumstances in which an incident occurs. The victim gives his account of the incident and then the offender attempts to justify his action. The elders, and anyone else who is present at the proceedings and wishes to express an opinion on a question, can be recognized by the earth custodian to speak. After the council of elders has listened to all the relevant presentations, the earth custodian and elders withdraw to discuss the matter among themselves and to agree upon the decision. After reentry to the byre, the mediator and the elders acquaint the disputants of their decision. The parties to the conflict accept the decision of the earth custodian and the elders because they believe the verdict is right. Although the sacredness of the *kuar muon* and the influence of the elders carry weight, the verdict is accepted because there is a common understanding among members of the community grounded upon their covenantal tradition. If there are any doubts about the facts of the case, certain oaths, which will be described in the following sections, may be employed, such as swearing statements on the earth custodian's leopard skin.

In order to elucidate the process of mediating conflict, we will first describe the impact of the supporters of the disputants on the process of mediation. Second, we will consider how conflicts are mediated within a Nuer household and extended family, village, cattle camp, tertiary level or district, regional divisions or primary sections, and in the wider society of the Nuer.

The Impact of Supporters and the Audience on Mediation

Supporters and members of the audience have a great impact on mediation of the conflict in Nuer society. Their influence varies according the degree of knowledge, experience, age, social standing, and the number of supporters attending the proceedings.[86] Conflicts between individuals have public consequences among the Nuer. The support each party to a conflict can muster depends upon the relationship between the parties to the conflict and the broader society. In Nuer society, where the forum for mediating conflict is open to any individual or group, the outcome of the case may reflect the influence of the people present.

The influence of the supporters or a particular audience poses a potential threat to the fairness of the outcome of the case. To resolve this problem, a mediator mobilizes his own kin group to support him in persuading the kin group of the victim to accept (*cut ran*) compensation and also to balance the influence of the disputants' supporters. The impact of the presence of the kin of a mediator, as well as those of the disputants, in the disputing process makes it easier to resolve the conflict more objectively. Their presence encourages the supporters and mediators to examine more thoroughly the available evidence so that the decision about who is right or wrong is fair. The role of supporters and the audience can be demonstrated by the following case:

> In 1967, Riek Thijoak and Dep Rundial of Diror village fought over the issue of crop damage by Riek Thijoak's cattle. Dep Rundial was seriously wounded. Close kin of Rundial wanted to avenge him in an open fight with the kin of Riek Thijoak.

Many persons on both sides understood that if the fight started many people could lose their lives and consequently the village was likely to break up. There were other problems between the groups. Pal Thijoak, the brother of Riek Thijoak, was involved in an inter-village fight in which some persons had sustained injuries. Considerable bitterness existed as a result of this incident. Thijoak's kin chose to appeal to kinship sentiment and to emphasize the need for harmony in the village. They decided to accept compensation in cattle for the injury and the damages sustained from stray animals rather than begin a fight that could leave many people dead.

No mediator or explicit third party was involved in this conflict, but the supporters of both men played an implicit third-party role in urging the disputants to compromise. Supporters, in emphasizing common interests, encouraged the disputants to define their dispute in terms acceptable to both. The rephrasing suggested by the supporters also helped the disputants to see the conflict in a more friendly way to include the many cross-cutting relations between them in the village. That is, the broader interests of the supporters and members of the audience to which both men are closely linked altered the way in which the dispute was interpreted by placing it in the context of family conflict.

Household and Extended Family

In a family composed of a man and his wives and children, the man who is the head of the household resolves conflict within his family and requires no outside mediation. If disputants are his wives, the man listens to his wives, each arguing her case before their husband. After listening, he decides about who is wrong and corrects the wrong that has been done. Problems among children are resolved by parents and their older siblings. If a man kills his wife, he pays an ox or steer to the family of the woman for the purification rites, but there is no compensation because the man cannot pay cattle to himself. If she is slain by a third party, her husband is compensated.

The Nuer believe that homicide and incest within a local community are wrong. But a man may be led into breaking the homicide rule by following another rule of approved behavior. Because Nuer teach the young to defend their rights by force, any man can unintentionally kill a cousin in a club fight. The rules prohibiting sexual relationships may not be clear to individuals because the genealogical reckoning in some directions is complicated'.[87] A man may easily be unsure whether or not a particular woman stands to him in a prohibited relationship. The uncertainty of the relationship is compounded by the fact that all the members of a particular Nuer family do not live together in one village. So there can often be more than one view of an action due to a disagreement about what is relevant to moral judgment.

The way these problems are resolved reflects the need to maintain harmony within the extended family. In the case of the fratricide above, there is no outside mediation, no vengeance for the slain, and only a few cattle are paid by the father of the slayer to the paternal uncle as a contribution to the cattle needed in order to secure a wife for the deceased. In this situation, the act is viewed as a sin and the ritual of spiritual cleansing is performed by an earth custodian. Features of the ritual sacrifices are considered in a later section on formalizing covenantal relationships. A man who commits incest with a kinswoman, not knowing her to be a kinswoman, suffers no serious consequences. The act is not considered incest because those involved were unaware of the relationship between them. In all cases, a family head mediates conflicts between his own household with other households.

The responsibilities of mediating conflicts within an extended family or lineage were reduced by the imposition of the British governing authority and appointment of government chiefs. Conflicts that were earlier considered by the Nuer to be strictly private became public problems to be settled in the government chiefs' court. When there was a conflict between Nuer custom (i.e., rule) and the law of the imperial authority, the chiefs usually supported the law of the colonial government. The following case elucidates the nature of the change in rules.

In the early 1950s a widow of middle age was cohabiting with her heir, the brother of her late husband (Hutchison 1988). She committed adultery, and the dispute was whether she should be divorced on charges by her late husband's brother. She had born her husband four children—two of whom were living at the time of the conflict. Of the four children she bore, the first two were fathered by her late husband, the third, by her heir and the fourth (which had died during the delivery), by a lover. The case was reported to the Leek Nuer chiefs' court for a decision on the issue.

During the hearing there were lengthy debates about two compet-ing rules: the widow's late husband's brother has the right to demand di-vorce on the grounds of adultery which violated this right in his wife. The other is that the widow had fulfilled her procreative obligation to the fami-ly of her husband and the children needed to be raised to adulthood within that lineage. These entitled her to permanent membership in her late hus-band's family and lineage.

The judges discussed these issues at length, trying to convince the late husband's brother of his responsibilities to his brother's wife and chil-dren, and the need to make peace with his late brother's affines when a quarrel has separated them. Attempting to reconcile this view with a con-sideration of the brother of late husband rights was difficult. The trial took a number days and achieving a proper balance between the rights of two competing publics became increasingly complex.

The widow defended her decision to take a lover on the grounds that her husband's brother was unable to fulfill his obligations to her and her children because he traveled frequently to Khartoum and often re-mained there for years before returning to see to their condition. All she desired from the court was permission to remain together with her two daughters in her late husband's home and to bear additional children in his name by her lover. Her late husband's brother, however, was adamant about divorce. He did not want the woman in his home. The court ulti-mately dissolved the marriage union.

This decision was unprecedented. During the early 1940s the council of elders of the family of heir and the family of the widow would have certainly resolved this conflict in favor of the widow. Because she had two surviving children at the time of the case, Nuer rules of conduct favor that the children are to be raised to maturity by the father and mother together. The court's decision reflected the colonial influence on the Nuer chiefs, especially when a British official was the legal advisor to the chiefs' court (Howell 1954, 235). The court's decision had a great impact in articulating a new constitutional standard for Nuer society and encour-aging government chiefs and the British courts in Nuerland to challenge the traditional marriage law based on the new rule of constitutional re-quirements (Hutchinson 1988). The general recognition that divorce was possible at all, particularly after the conclusion of a marriage union and after children have been born of the union, had the effect of encouraging divorce.[88]

Village and Conflict Resolution

The rules governing levels of relationships are different from one type of relationship to another. A village is composed of different social groups, and residents hold membership in multiple groups. These overlapping ties are taken into account in conflict situations and in mediating disputes. The smaller the group is, the stronger the sentiment of solidarity among members. For this reason, relationships in the village are stronger than the feelings of unity among members of a regional segment.

A village is a segmentary unit of governance to facilitate active individual participation in the affairs of the village. Each Nuer village is divided into hamlets. Each hamlet provides its own mediative services for it residents. Hamlets are residential units built not on kinship ties alone, but also they are built within a conceptualization of transcendental order to God. This common understanding affects the way conflicts are handled among residents in the village. Disputes between members of two hamlets are mediated by elders and age-set leaders of the two hamlets. In cases of general interest to all members of a village, representatives of the hamlets, who are chosen on the basis of age and competence, constitute the council of elders to work out resolutions to problems affecting all villagers. Decisions are made by a majority of the council members often after long discussion. Where there are doubts about the truthfulness of the statements, persons are made to take an oath before an earth custodian and elders. The following case elucidates how Nuer mediators resolve the problem of obtaining "truthful" evidence in troublesome cases.

There was a dispute between Ruot Nguany and Yiei Garekui in January 1964 in Ler, which is west of the Nile among the Dok Aak.[89] Nguany gave his garden to Garekui for use for grain production in the coming rainy season. Garekui cleared the plot and planted when the rains came in May. In early July, Nguany contacted Garekui that he wanted his garden back. Garekui refused and argued that they had an agreement that he should use the garden for the 1964 rainy season. Nguany denied he leased his land to Garekui. Garekui insisted that he was using the land with his (Nguany's) permission for one season. There was only one witness, Kedoa Tap Kong, the wife of Nguany. Nguany reported the problem to his father's brother

Manguet Per. He said that his garden was being taken by force by Yiei Garekui, who had planted the garden with grain and vegetables without obtaining prior permission. Ruot Nguany and Manguet Per decided to cut down the flowering grain.

At night the two men went to the garden and cut all the flowering grain and vegetables. Garekui visited the garden the following morning and found the crops destroyed. He immediately concluded that the disaster was committed by Nguany and his Uncle Manguet Per. Garekui decided to fight it out with Nguany, but on the way to Nguany's home he changed his mind. He went instead to report the case to the *kuar muon* (who was also the head chief of the local government) of Ler area and took with him samples of the crops which were cut down. The samples of crops were shown to the chief, and Garekui related the story.

Deng Luth, the *kuar muon*, summoned Ruot Nguany and Manguet Per for questioning. When the two men were asked whether or not they destroyed the crops of Garekui, they denied that they did. The two men related that the garden belonged to Nguany and that Garekui took and planted the garden without the prior consent of the owner. They again denied having any knowledge of who destroyed the crops. The chief then called Kedoa Tap Kong, thinking that she would tell the truth. When she was asked, Kedoa Tap Kong confirmed that there was no prior agreement between her husband and Garekui about the garden. Garekui reiterated his claim to the *kuar muon* that there was an agreement to use the garden and that there was no force used to get the garden. He said that the statements made by Nguany, Per, and Kong were false. The chief told the parties to the conflict that the case was a serious one and he was going to perform *kueng* (oath) unless somebody told the truth.

Kueng is a hole, dug under the instruction of an earth custodian. The hole represents a tomb. A bed-like arrangement is made for the dead body to rest upon, and then the hole is covered with mud. The accused usually supplies the sacrificial animal, but sometimes the accuser provides the animal. Accused, accuser, and their witnesses are told that, if they are innocent, they should step over the grave as they make their declarations of innocence. If they are lying, they should not cross the grave. The custodian then utters an invocation over a tethered victim (a sheep) that whoever crosses the grave falsely declaring their innocence will die. Mary Smith (Evans-Pritchard 1956) recorded the curse of the custodian on a similar occasion:[90]

'. . . now, sheep, thy blood is shed to death on account of the man who is at fault.' He then calls on God: God of heaven, God of our fathers God who created all things, God of the universe, God of the flesh (*ring*), I call on thee to look upon these persons, that the man who is at fault may die. Now, I know that thou, O God, listenest to my speech (*rietda*).

Nguany, Per, Kong, and Garekui all stepped over the *kueng*, that is, they declared that they were telling the truth. *Kuar muon* gave them three to six months to live. He told Kedoa Tap Kong, the wife of Nguany, that if she is lying she will be first to die followed by Per, then her husband, and then other members of their extended families. The same was applicable to Garekui. According to Wicjal Bum (1989), Kedoa Tap Kong died from birth complications after some months, and the other, Manguet Per, died afterwards.[91] Ruot Nguany became sick and confessed to *kuar muon* that he had lied. He asked if *kuar muon* could retract his curse, but *kuar muon* responded that it was too late to do anything because some persons had already died. Nuer believe that if *kuar muon* retracts the curse for any reason, he or his children will die because that is seen as a corruption of the power of *kuoth*. Ruot Nguany could not be saved but died in fulfillment of the curse.

Cattle Camp and Mediating Conflict

A cattle camp is divided into clusters of windscreens used by groups of household who jointly herd their animals. Conflict mediation is carried out within these smaller units by heads of households, age-set leaders, and other influential community leaders. Dividing a camp into smaller groups reduces the size of conflict that each body of persons must deal with. Everyone is known by everyone else so that mutual monitoring of behavior is nearly without cost. The enforcement of decisions is also easier.[92]

However, conflicts of general interest also arise in a cattle camp. Such disputes are mediated by an assembly composed of the representatives of all the clusters of windscreens. Loss of cattle to predatory animals is often attributed to negligence on the part of the person who was responsible for herding on a particular day. The herdsman is considered liable for any loss of cattle. If the loss of a cow can be traced to negligence on the part of a herdsman, the person who has lost a cow raises a case against the herdsman before the council of elders. The decision is usually unanimous that the family of herdsman is required to compensate the loss.

Mediating District and Clan Disputes

Conflicts within a district are usually between villages that share a cattle camp, attend common feasts and ceremonies, share age-set membership, and share a common belief in the transcendental order of God, etc. The significance of this is that most of the villages are linked, and all accept the ritual of a common mediator and the mediation of disputes carried on by elders, age-set leaders, and custodians of the villages involved.

If, however, conflict cannot be resolved by the members of the leadership of the villages, then neutral persons from another village or villages are called in to mediate. Their decisions on the issues are binding on all the disputants. Disputants accept the decisions of mediators from outside their villages or districts because they are considered impartial and also because the parties to a dispute are willing to resolve the conflict. The elders, age-sets leaders, and custodians enforce the decision after the two groups have performed the necessary rituals that formalize the settlement of the conflict.

Primary sections of a clan are not in frequent contact, because they live in geographically separate regions. When conflict between sections or regional divisions of a clan occurs, it is expressed in terms of the lineage of the dominant clan associated with the division or section. In this event, someone outside the dominant lineage who has extra power to sanction is needed to mediate. This is one of the special conflict situations in which the *kuar muon* (earth custodian) functions as a mechanism for mediating.

If a man refuses to accept the decision of *kuar muon* as arbiter, after everyone else, including his elders, has accepted the decision, then the *kuar muon* may pass his official badge, the leopard skin, to the man refusing to accept the decision. An action of this kind is tantamount to a curse. The man must give an ox or a cow to the earth custodian in order to convince him to take the leopard skin back.

Conflict Resolution among Clans

Conflicts between clans usually are seasonal because of the need to share cattle camps, water, and fishing pools in the frontier districts during the dry season. It is usually encroachments on grazing lands and water sources by other people that brings about disputes. Theft of cattle, sheep, and goats is also a source of conflict between regions.

Relationships across clans restrain the use violence and work to promote peaceful resolution of conflict through negotiation. The Nuer recognize kinship alliances between persons of different clans, the Nuer readily accept strangers from other areas as members of their cattle camps, and Nuer of all regions share memberships in an age-set system. All Nuer accept the priestly sanctions of a mediator. Mediating conflicts between regions is carried out by age-set leaders and prophets. The most senior age-set members have authority across clans in Nuerland because of their age. Because younger men respect them, older persons can mediate conflicts using *ric* (age-set relationship) as the source of their authority. Negotiated settlements are enforceable because they can "command" the junior men and also because of the willingness of the parties to resolve the dispute.

The prophets are able to resolve of conflicts among peoples who share a common border such as the Lou and the Gaawar Nuer. From the 1850s to the late 1920s, prophets represented different clans and their peoples, but their influence extended over clan boundaries. Because of this influence, Guek Ngundeang of the Lou Nuer as able to negotiate between the Lou and the Eastern Jikany Nuer (in particular with the Gaajok and Gaaguang, the Gaajak primary sections) payment of compensation for homicide. Deng Laaka of the Gaawar clan had similar influence among the Thiang Nuer.[93] Bum Dieu of Dok Nuer, Gatluak Nyak of Nyuong Nuer, and other Western Nuer prophets were able to unite neighboring regions for raids against non-Nuer. The prophets are not a mechanism of lineage or a local community structure like earth custodians or cattle custodians. They are pivots of federation between adjacent clans representing the idea of states and personified the cohesion of the Nuer. This position enables the prophets to mediate conflicts between regions.

Formalization of Covenantal Relationships

Restoration of covenantal relationships between individuals takes more than an agreement over the terms and conditions of reconciliation. Sacrificing cattle to God is the most popular way of formalizing covenantal relationships. It is important, however, to realize that Nuer sacrifice animals on many occasions: when a person is sick, when sin has been committed, when a wife is barren, sometimes on the birth of a first child, at the initiation of sons, at marriages, at funerals and mortuary ceremonies, after homicide and at settlement of feuds, before war, when persons or property are struck by lightning, and sometimes before large-scale fishing enterprises.

Nuer perform two broad types of sacrifices: personal and collective. These terms refer to the distinction between sacrifices offered for persons who may be sick and those offered on behalf of social groups. There also are two types of intentions of the persons in offering these sacrifices. The first type has primarily a piacular *(kok,* i.e., expiatory or atoning) intention and the second a confirmatory one. Hubert and Maus ([1899] 1968) observe that the first are sacrifices of "desacralization" (they make the sacred profane, that is, they remove a Spirit from man) and the second are sacrifices of "sacralization" (they make the profane sacred, that is, they bring Spirit into man). We will limit our discussion here to the role confirmatory sacrifices play in the formalization of covenantal relationships, but reference to personal sacrifices will be made when it is necessary.

The main function of collective sacrifices is to confirm, legitimize, reestablish, or add strength to something. A collective sacrifice may change in social status (war to peace, hostilities to harmony, separation to bonding) or re-new relationship between social groups, such as the ending of a blood feud by making God and the ancestors, witnesses of it (Dung, interview, 1989; Gatluak, interview 1989; Evans-Pritchard 1956: 199). Many ceremonies are incomplete and ineffective without sacrifice, but sacrifice may be only one aspect in a complex of ceremonies, dances, and rites of various kinds, that have no religious significance in themselves. The importance of sacrifice lies in the fact that it sacralizes the social event and the new relationships brought about by it. It solemnizes (consecrates) the change of status or relationship, giving it religious validation. On such occasions sacrifice has generally a conspicuously festal and Eucharistic character (Evans-Pritchard 1956, 199).

Confirmatory sacrifices give religious validation to conflict resolution achieved among individuals in households, villages, cattle camps, districts, regions, and in the wider Nuer society. This explains why such rituals are performed by specially appointed representatives of the groups concerned or by public functionaries. In Nuer society, confirmatory rituals are performed as part of the reestablishment of social relationships that have been breached.[94]

Ritual Sacrifice among Kindred

When homicide or incest occurs among close kin it is usually considered to be a religious sin. The remedy for sin is sacrifice, which a cleansing of blood performed by a priest. Looking closely into the cleansing of blood, however, we see that it is combined with peacemaking and a affirmation of kinship solidarity. An ox is sacrificed for a cleansing of blood. The cleansing of blood, like all other Nuer ritual sacrifices, both personal and collective, consists of four basic features that require brief consideration.

The first act of the process of sacrifice is the *puot yang* (the presentation and tethering of the sacrificial animal). When an animal is identified for sacrifice, it is brought to the place where it is to be killed. The *puot yang* (the tetherer) drives into the ground, with *puot ghok* (a wooden club for the purpose), the *loc* (tethering peg) of the animal. After an ox is staked, the *puot yang* (the tetherer) pours a libation of water, milk, or beer under the tethering peg that completes the presentation of the animal for sacrifice. The second act of sacrifice is the *buk yang*, during which ashes of cow dung are placed on the back of the sacrificial animal and then lightly rubbed with the right hand of the participant. This is the act of consecrating the animal to God. The *buk* (rubbing) is finished before a person speaks the *lam* (invocation). Every speaker repeats these actions in turn. Some persons place ashes on the back of the animal without speaking. The act of placing and rubbing in ashes consecrates an animal for sacrifice symbolizes the substitution of the life of a beast for the life of a man and hence also the identification of man with beast (Evans-Pritchard 1956).

The third stage of the process is the *lam yang* (invocation), which requires the officiant to speak to God over the sacrificial animal. The *lam yang* defines the intention of the sacrifice and includes other matters that are relevant in the case. Speakers address the audience as well as God. They state the purpose of the sacrifice as well as all sorts of affirmations, exhortations, reflections about life, anecdotes, and opinions. The invocation is given by the priest or earth custodian because of a fear of slipping away from known efficacious procedures. During *lam yang* (invocation) grievances are made public, not with the intention of inflaming passions, but because it is the rule of such assemblies that everything a man has against others must be related in order to be discussed and resolved. As a result of such open discussions, it is less likely that parties will harbor unresolved bitterness.

In his invocation, the earth custodian calls upon *kuoth cakda* (God of our creation) and relates the history of whatever has happened. Nuer say a man must make invocation in truth (*thuok*). Every statement made in the presence of God must be true, even the minute details of the history of the events that led to the situation that occasion sacrifice. Evans-Pritchard (1956) observes that the victim (ox) offered to God has placed on its back by the earth custodian and other speakers what is said in the *lam* (invocation), and if the sacrifice is to be efficacious, then what is said must be true.

Fourth stage of the ritual is *nak yang* (killing of sacrificial animal). After the end of his address, the *kuar muon* spears the ox. An ox is speared on the right side; sheep and goats have their throats cut. People rush to cut up (*kuak*) the carcass. It is a custom in such rituals of cleansing that meat is not subject to orderly division. You take what you can get out of the carcass. When *kuak* (rush to cut meat) is over and people resettle, the priest cuts off some of the hair of the head of the man who has slain another. This symbolizes that he is free from contamination.

To formalize the reestablishment of relationships between close kin who commit incest and to prevent fatal disease, a custodian is called in to perform the ritual known as the ritual of separation of incestuous parties (*bak ruali*). At the end of this type of sacrifice, the ox is held to the ground while the priest inserts the point of his spear in its throat and cuts towards the breast. He severs the ox in two, dividing the head into two pieces with an axe. As the priest or his representative makes the final cuts, and then the parties to the offense tug at the carcass on either side and pull it apart. This is the process of *bak ruali*. The separation of the carcass symbolizes that the parties to the incest are not supposed to have sexual intercourse because they are kin and must keep apart to maintain kinship ties.

Village and Cattle Camp

The ending of hostilities in a village requires some sort of a ritual to formalize the renewal of relationships. Insults and club fights among members of a village or a cattle camp that strain relationships are brought to an end through the resumption of sharing food, beer, milk, and common activities. Mutual friends, age-sets leaders, elders of the parties in dispute, or allies call the persons who are separated by quarrels together for some beer, food, or a work party that affirms the fact that the past conflict has ended. Among the Nuer, eating together or drinking milk or beer together symbolizes good relationships. A Nuer will not normally share food with another if he is in a serious conflict with that person.

Some events involving members of a village or cattle camp require more elaborate confirmatory activities. These events include settling the act of homicide, adultery, or incest. Ritual performance is always necessary in formalizing the end of a blood feud, the consequence of adultery (*kor*), and incestuous relationships. Need for harmony in a village or a cattle camp makes speedy confirmatory sacrifices absolutely necessary. Persons living close to one another and relying upon each other for important tasks cannot survive a lengthy feud. A feud is incompatible with the normal life of a village or a cattle camp. Confirmatory sacrifices related to conflicts requiring the cleansing process are carried out by religious functionaries. The process of reestablishing relationships is described earlier in this section.

In order to renew intimate relationships between groups and families, another ceremony, known as *maath* (bringing parties to friendship again), is held. It takes place some time after the compensation cattle have been paid if the geographical distance between the groups concerned is not too great and if both parties are willing. This ritual to reestablish covenantal relationships includes drinking water, milk, or beer from a common bowl to express the reinstatement of relationships between the groups. An ox (*thak*), called *yang tol coka* (the cow of the breaking of the bone), is supplied by the slayer and sacrificed. After the sacrifice, which seals the covenant with blood, one of the ox's bones is held at either end by representatives of the two parties while the earth custodian severs it in two. The left half of the bone is thrown away. The two parties then consume the flesh of the ox together (Bum, interview, 1989; Howell 1954, 46; Evans-Pritchard 1956, 256).

District and Clan Division

Members of an extended family do not live in one village or in one district but are usually found in several different villages and districts. There are social links between persons in such settlements that include common belief in a transcendental order of God, marital alliances, and age-set membership. Family members also share cattle camps, grazing, and water and all accept the ritual sanctions of common mediator. These links facilitate communication among persons in villages.

Shared feasts and ceremonies occur between primary groups of a region when some of their members share a cattle camp in the dry season. The Lou Nuer share cattle camps with the Gaajok of the Eastern Jikany Nuer during the dry season along the Sobat River. A similar mix takes place between Gaawar and Thiang Nuer of the Zeraf communities.

When individuals in different villages in a district want to seal an agreement with blood to end hostilities, the identity of the officiant in the sacrifice depends upon the nature of the conflict. The officiant is usually the *diel* (oldest member of the dominant lineage) in the district. Where there is religious sin involved in the conflict, a priest is often asked to perform the sacrifice. Hostilities are finally put to rest by calling upon God and common ancestors to witness the change of relationships through confirmatory sacrifice. Once a covenant is made and sealed with blood a violation of the established covenant is viewed as affront to divine will.

Ritualization of Covenantal Relationships among Groups

People who do not have constant contact have little to quarrel about because they do not share scarce resources. During the dry season, however, some groups come to share grazing and water sources in frontier communities. As mentioned in earlier chapters, sharing grazing grounds and water can result in abuses such as fishing in protected water. This leads to conflict.

The mutual need to share limited resources, however, provides incentives to seek the binding resolution of conflict. Reestablishment of covenantal relationships grounded upon common religious presuppositions across regions is necessary for Nuer survival. This is possible because of a common language that makes communication between regions relatively easy. Shared age-set system also assists in ending conflict.

Senior age-sets of each region are entrusted with facilitating the implementation of agreed upon settlements for conflicts that have arisen between groups. In a majority of cases, custodians perform the sacrifices that confirm settlements between groups from different regions. Nuer believe a prophet can sanctify a covenantal relationship between persons of different clans. They also believe in the power of the ritual sanctions of a prophet.

Sanctification is believed to be important because it transforms a relationship between persons from different regions from hostility to harmony and changes the attitudes of parties to the conflict so that they can adopt the terms and conditions of the settlement. The act of consecration of life does not by itself make permanent peace among persons. It succeeds only because the community of understanding among individuals involved recognizes its importance and value. Universal credence, which exists before the rituals are performed, is the condition of ritual efficacy.

Conclusion

Conflict that sometimes escalates into destructive violence exists in Nuer society at various levels of segmentary organization. Considering how conflict is resolved provides one means of elucidating features underlying the organization of the Nuer household, the village, the cattle camp, and larger groups beyond the district levels.

Nuer conceive of conflict as contestation and argumentation. Making claims and counter claims is grounded upon the Nuer concepts of *cuong* (right) and *duer* (wrong). Claiming a right may in some sense be divisive, although it need not be disruptive. In many cases disputes over claim of right in some way sets one person or part of a segment against another person or part of the segment. A dispute can lead to fighting that undermines the covenantal relationships among persons in the community. Contestation and argumentation can be mediated by a variety of persons who wish to find an equitable solution to a conflict.

There are many types of conflicts at various levels of organization in Nuerland. They occur in the contexts of households, villages, cattle camps, and beyond tertiary sections or districts. Each type of conflict is resolved within its context through discussion and whatever arrangements are agreed upon as appropriate to its resolution.

Mediation is necessary only when the principal adversaries are unable to discuss a problem without the assistance of a neutral person. In Nuer society, the mediator's task is to listen to a presentation of the facts of a case by the litigants and other persons in order to find out who is in the right or is more right.

Disputes within a Nuer household (or within households that are closely related to one another) require no outside mediation. An extended family is capable of governing itself.

A variety of different ties link the members of cattle camp and one village with members of others. These relationships extend across boundaries, although they are more effective in cattle camps and neighboring villages. Beyond the sectional, district, or clan level, even though the same social principles operate, practice may be moderated by expediency.

Formalizing of the reestablishment of covenantal relationships depends upon a sincere expression of remorse by the individuals or groups for the act that requires confirmatory sacrifice. In the ritual process of sacrifice, a number of steps are taken to ensure that the members of the two communities understand and are committed to peace in addition to the expression of remorse. Individuals walk long distances to be present for the ritual. It is during the sacrifice that problems between individuals and between groups can be thoroughly discussed and resolved. This is done in the presence of God and the ancestors, who are concerned about the reestablishment of peace.

Chapter 7 - Continuity of Historical Patterns of Change

Introduction

The withdrawal of the British from the Sudan in the early 1950s led to the creation of an independent nation-state in the Sudan. It was accompanied by the emergence of modern societies fashioned by a new Sudanese elite drawing from the British intellectual traditions in science and technology. The key problem of this chapter is to explain the continuity of historical patterns of change in the Nuer society. First, I will describe the problems Nuer encountered during British rule. Second, I will consider the organization and constitution making of Sudan as an independent nation-state. Both periods of history posed numerous threats to the Nuer as well as a range of potential opportunities.

Problems Encountered During British Rule.

The establishment of British rule in Nuerland, effectively 1927-1956, gave rise to institutions alien to the Nuer. These foreign institutions were mainly concerned with the maintenance of lawful relationships among members of Nuer society. The task was to establish links between the rules governing the Nuer people in a shared community of relationships, as well as to maintain the public order and civil administration. Claiming the right to govern embodies the claim to authority in law and the prerogative of administering the autonomous system of order.

The problem of controlling the Nuer led the British imperial government to create courts and to appoint chiefs [95] to administer the colonial system of law and order. The British solution to the problem thus relied upon what they thought to be "indirect rule." These imposed institutions radically undermined the Nuer way of life.

The Courts and the Emergence of Autocracy

The colonial government was interested in building a system of indirect rule in Nuerland that was grounded substantially in British conceptions of government. The Native Court Ordinance of 1931 was an explicit effort to administer justice through local courts. The British administrator did not initially know anything about the Nuer traditional system of justice. Ironically, resorting to the traditional system of justice was regarded as a violation of the Native Court Ordinance (Howell 1954). The British did not realize how broadly the Ordinance undermined Nuer political and judicial institutions.

The British Government representative in the local administration issued warrants to men they appointed chief. The warrant allowed chiefs to sit in British courts for the purpose of judging cases. The warrant also empowered each of the chiefs to assume executive powers that were territorial in scope. The assumption of exclusive executive and judicial powers ran counter to the acephalous political traditions of the Nuer. There was no tradition that recognized one man or group of men as paramount rulers over other persons or communities. Religious Leaders and community spokespersons commanded some measure of influence, but they never wielded executive power in Nuer society.

Santandrea (1968) describes the Nuer *kuar muon* (earth custodian) as a powerful ruler. It would be a conceptual error, however, to equate the power of *kuar muon* in pre-colonial Nuer society with the power of the warrant chief under the colonial administration. The power of *kuar muon* was limited by the check and balance system in Nuer political organization. The power of the warrant chief, on the other hand, was arbitrary and virtually unlimited; it was naked despotism, unparalleled in Nuer political history. Whereas the people could remove the *kuar muon* from his position as spokesman, it was only the colonial government that could remove the warrant chief. This was because the government, and not the people, had made him a chief. By empowering the warrant chief with both executive and judicial powers, the British government overturned that portion of the indigenous political system of the Nuer that was grounded in a clear tradition of local accountability.

The basic rule changes introduced by the imperial government during the 1930s and 1940s included the following: (1) the elimination of contestation in the process of conflict resolution, especially in the settlement of feuds; (2) the introduction of capital punishment, terms of imprisonment[96], and collective cattle fines as deterrents; (3) the elimination of the right of vengeance of the relatives of the slain; and (4) the redefinition of several forms of homicide that for the Nuer warranted compensation. The colonial administration also did not agree with the Nuer belief that the type of weapon used in a slaying (that is, whether club, fishing spear, fighting spear, or gun) should affect the sentence of the court. This change had the effect of weakening certain parts of the Nuer code of warfare.

The procedure adopted by the imperial government for resolving feuds was described by a British officer who himself served as a district commissioner in Central Nuer District (Howell 1954). The procedure was as follows: first, the swift suppression of hostilities by the warrant chief with the assistance of the police or the army. Second, the seizure of all the cattle of the parties to the conflict pending the arrest, trial, and sentencing of the persons who have killed, wounded, or participated in the hostilities. Third, discovery by the court of the parties at fault and imposition of a collective fine on their kin segments. The last step included the transfer of the cattle for compensation and a sacrifice to formalize the resolution of the conflict by a *kuar muon* (earth custodian).

The courts tried persons for deviating from accepted conduct and imposed fines ranging from a *ruath* (bull-calf) to a pregnant cow or even more. They also had the power to assign the wrongdoer to a term of imprisonment, if the British district officer agreed (Howell 1954). Cases involving premeditated killing were beyond the jurisdiction of the warrant chiefs' court. Persons charged with murder were tried by a magistrate using a British statute known as the Sudan Penal Code. Thus, capital punishment was imposed on Nuer by an alien law. Moreover, when a person was sentence to death by a magistrate's court and executed, there was no payment of compensation by his kin to the kin of the victim.

The colonial prison system was an innovation that undermined and overrode the Nuer forms of punishment for serious deviations. In Nuer society, it was understood that persons found by the council of elders to have committed a fault were obliged to repair the damage by payment of compensation or banishment. Many Nuer, however, drew a false similarity between the district jailhouse and the priest's sacred homestead. They thought slayers were confined to prison not for punishment but rather for protection from the spears of avenging kinsmen. In addition to imposing terms of imprisonment, the British courts also administered corporal punishment, of which public flogging was the most detested. Both men and women were flogged, a practice unheard of before in traditional Nuer society.

The most immediate effect of the establishment of the British court system was its impact on the indigenous institutions for adjudicating disputes. Prior to the colonial period, the assembly of the people (that is, the council of elders, age-set leaders, custodians, prophets, the supporters of the disputants, and the public following the court proceedings) all played important roles in dispute resolution and the administration of justice. The establishment of the British courts drastically curtailed the ability of these participatory groupings to play their indigenous juridical roles. Instead of complaints being sent to elders, age-set leaders, or custodians, they were now sent to the courts or to the British district commissioner. Howell (1954) complains that the Nuer people "have for the past few years been in the habit of bringing the most trifling complaints to the courts." Yet under the traditional Nuer system, trifling complaints would not have stood the chance of so much as being reported to the council of elders or to the age-set leaders. Petty issues were formerly viewed as family problems and better addressed through the family mechanism. The British court system fostered a passion for litigation that invariably proved injurious to the Nuer way of life and undermined the foundations of the Nuer social order. Certainly, the multiplicity of cases at the courts reflected a heightened degree of social and political disintegration. The impact is still being felt among the Nuer today.[97]

Chiefs and Corruption

With the increase in the number of cases, the chiefs could not give sufficient attention to every individual problem. Nor were the chiefs disposed to settle the cases. Most of them were ready to take advantage of opportunities for personal benefit rather than to serve their own people. The result was that many persons who should have been found innocent were convicted. In many cases, the corruption of the chiefs was the direct cause of the miscarriage of justice.[98]

When the British learned that the chiefs could act contrary to tradition and that this would, in turn, undermine the administration, the administration devised a new referral policy (*luoc*). In many cases, according to Wicjal Bum (1989), when it was discovered that a chief for one reason or another did not hear the evidence available in individual cases, such cases were sent back to the chiefs to complete the hearing. The effect of the referral policy was that it reduced the number of persons being sent to prison. The district commissioner was authorized to overturn the decision of the chiefs in any case.

The referral policy of sending some cases back to the chiefs can be viewed to reflect a genuine desire on the part of the British, and also a personal interest on the part of a district commissioner, to render justice.[99] Its shortcoming, as Howell (1954) observed, was that every Nuer who lost a case appealed to a district officer, who could not possibly review all cases.

The burden to the officials of case overload was intensified by the fact that the courts provided revenue for the local administration. Increasing in the number of cases, therefore, was important to the operation of the government in the locality since the revenue produced largely by court fees and fines rose in proportion to the number of cases processed in the court. The need to increase revenue levels also led to the appointment of court clerks to record court proceedings and to keep account of court receipts. The power to appoint the clerks, or the "missionary boys" as they were known locally by the Nuer, enhanced the popularity of the office of the chief. The clerks, who were mainly primary school graduates and whose salaries were relatively low, tended to enrich themselves from the court proceeds and from bribes taken from litigants. Many examples can be given of these clerks pocketing court fees and fines.[100] As cases at Diror, Walgak, Pathai, and Langken Courts reveal, clerks often failed to enter into the cashbooks the correct amount of revenue collected (Bum, interview, 1989; Banak, interview, 1989; Rambang, interview, 1996). In some cases no entries were made at all.

Chieftaincies and Involuntary Servitude

Chiefs were empowered by imperial ordinances to compel men to work on roads, to serve as couriers, and to build government rest houses, court houses, and public facilities without compensation. The Nuer were not accustomed to participating in mass construction projects such as the building roads and public buildings. More importantly, they were not accustomed to being ordered to engage in collective labor. Since anyone who disobeyed the chief in the exercise of his executive duties was liable to be prosecuted in court, work details ordered by the chiefs often resulted in a person being fined or imprisoned or both. When in 1927 Guek Ngundeang, the Lou Nuer Prophet, refused to report for road work on the pretext that the Lou people did not need the roads, he was harassed and eventually killed by the colonial authorities for resisting road work (Johnson 1980).

Having the power to force people to work without compensation offered more opportunities for chiefs to enrich themselves. Chiefs often detained persons pending trial to work on their private farms or diverted laborers from public works projects to farm work. Persons who did not want to work on roads or on the chief's farm circumvented the law by offering the chief a ram, a calf, or a sum of money, hoping thereby to escape a sentence of imprisonment in the court. Chiefs were then bribed by litigants to decide cases in their favor. British officers were aware of these offenses, and chiefs caught taking bribes were dismissed from their jobs.

Although chiefs heard cases throughout the year, the government paid the chiefs a sitting fee only once a year. This was because the British officers visited the courts only in the dry season. There were no all-weather roads in Nuerland. In most locations, court centers were built on higher land far from the rivers.

Taxation also was imposed on the Nuer by the British government. The decision to collect a direct tax, even a small one, was another symbol of external control over the Nuer. The Nuer clearly understood that to pay a tax was to recognize the over-lordship of the person to whom it was paid. In England, as one administrator remarked, "each [tax] payer, even the unwilling and slippery one, regards himself as merely contributing to his country's finance. This is not so in Africa." Roads were built in the Sudan to facilitate the movement and supply of the troops defending the colonial regime. The Nuer felt that the users of the roads should bear the costs of constructing and maintaining them. Similarly, the Nuer did not see any benefit to themselves in contributing toward the other infrastructure the British wanted built. Nuer viewed British taxes as a form of tribute.

Nuerization of the Court as a Method of Adaptation

Administrative insensitivity was reduced as a result of the eventual admission of the inappropriateness for Nuerland of the system of executive chiefs. In March 1927, the Governor of Bahr el Ghazal admitted failure in applying chiefs' courts to the Nuer. The governor acknowledged that he and his colleagues in the province had not realized that:

> Cattle cases are only heard by the cattle chief, land cases by the land chief, and so on.....Unfortunately, when we first started administering this province, this ancient system was not known and it has only recently been realized. In our ignorance we presume that a chief was a dispenser of justice in every case and generally paramount in the tribe. . . . Through lack of knowledge and inexperience we failed to grasp this point, and jumping

over this stage, we appointed chiefs to whom we looked as the responsible head. This being so, it can readily be understood that many cases of failure of a chief to hear cases and of the loser to accept the decision was due to the chief knowing that he could not deal with the case and to the parties to the action not recognizing his authority in the particular class of case. Hence much trouble arose which at times developed into misunderstanding and his people being erroneously regarded as contumacious of government control.[101]

Thus, in Nuerland, many district officers regarded the chiefs' court as fundamentally a European innovation in which some Nuer judicial concepts were applied. Howell (1954) points out that often decisions were made in the mistaken idea that justice had been done, without realizing that Nuer ideas of justice were different than British ideas. In addition, some decisions in the chiefs' court were based directly on the British Penal Code in the Sudan (Howell 1954). The Nuer persistence about the maintenance of segmentation in the court led to important changes in the chieftainship.

The search for a new social order resulted in a return to the indigenous way of life. In the 1940s and 1950s the colonial administration made a sustained effort to understand how the Nuer governed themselves. The primary objective of this effort was to determine how best to adapt British rule to Nuer patterns of governance. Reports by Dr. Edward Evans-Pritchard, the American Presbyterian Church, the Catholic Church missionaries, and colonial administrators provided insight into Nuer institutions and the general pre-colonial history of some segments of regional communities. These reports contain the first recorded versions of the oral traditions regarded as common to most Nuer segments.

These accounts of the oral traditions are not based upon reliable sources, as is made clear by Douglas Johnson's *History and Prophecy Among the Nuer of the Southern Sudan* and Gabriel Giet Jal's *The History of the Jikany Nuer Before 1920*. First, the validity of the evidence is questionable. Most of these investigators were involved with a government that was killing and banishing Nuer leaders, taking cattle, burning villages, and forcing Nuer out of their villages. Because the Nuer did not trust the investigators, information was obtained with difficulty. Different men living in the same village might give vastly different accounts of the history of the same clan. Then, on a subsequent visit to the village, the informants might deny information previously given. In spite of the weaknesses in the early recorded oral traditions, historians and social scientists still find them useful in the study of many aspects of Nuer life.

In the end, Nuer elders, the custodian chiefs, and the administrative officers, using the information collected by various groups in the colonial regime, restructured the courts in order to reflect the Nuer concept of justice. Thus, in place of the small number of territorial courts that had forced unrelated and autonomous segments under one chief, the government created additional courts so that each original group had its own court. This action restored the social order and replaced rule by a few with rule by many chiefs.

The political aspect of the reforms was manifested in response to the demands for representation in the courts by *gaat tutni* (segment headmen) who were leaders of smaller lineage groups. The purpose of giving a segment headman a seat in the chiefs' court was to ensure that each member of a segment who made claims in disputes received backing from his own chief in the court. Increased group representation transformed the British court system into an acephalous system of order, and the composition of the court ensured that contestation was part of the procedure of the Nuer courts. Thus, the principle of contestation was made clear in joint meetings conducted between two secondary segments. The attitude of the chiefs in such a Nuer court was: if you settle these cases, we will settle those.

For example, a man of *cieng Both* secondary segment will be supported by court members who represent *cieng Both* in arguing a case against a man of *cieng Lungor* secondary segment. The decision that is reached in the case will be a resolution achieved among the groups. Because the judgment is reached as a covenant between the groups, the implementing chief will be bound by the spirit of the covenant to implement the judgment. There is also present, to ensure justice is done and that the implementation of the decision is carried out, a neutral body represented by the chiefs of other segments who, with the segments concerned, make up the sum total of the people over whom the court has jurisdiction. These persons will act as arbitrators, while those who represent the segments to which the disputants belong are acting as advocates rather than judges. It was, however, the latter upon whom the responsibility for implementation would fall. This is the way the court works. If there is a joint meeting between Eastern Jikany and Lou clans or regions, all representatives of each side, who might have been at loggerheads with each other over internal affairs will join together in forwarding the interests of their own people.

Their covenantal approach to problem solving has been a blessing to the Nuer in that the spirit of compromise often prevails. In disputes that have adversely affected communication within a region, the chiefs have followed the Nuer tradition of bringing in persons or chiefs from other regions to act as third party intermediaries. It is on the basis of this tradition that appeal courts have been formed, removing a British officer who earlier had acted in this capacity.

The complementarity of segmentary groups thus remains an essential feature of the Nuer court system, and in this sense the courts are a stabilizing factor in the maintenance of group identity. Representation reflects the Nuer concept of equality and freedom of action. Because the members of the court are selected freely by the individuals involved, the individual Nuer is expected to support the efforts of his or her representatives in the court. Family members also can remove their representative in the court if he proves to be oppressive or works contrary to their aspirations (Howell 1954; Bum, interview, 1989; Rambang, interview, 1996).

The Socioeconomic Changes and Urban Growth

Political changes of such degree could not have occurred apart from changes in the economy and in the social structure connected with the economy. Such changes did take place, but it is difficult to determine their relationship to the political changes. In some instances they can be considered to have been the cause, in others the conditions, and in still others the effect.

During the British rule in the Sudan, new technological developments and new methods of cultivation contributed to a rapid increase in agricultural productivity and a consequent expansion of trade surpluses in some areas, especially Gezira, Nzara farming centers, and, later on, Renk.[102] These factors, in turn, facilitated a rapid increase in population. Although reliable figures are scarce, it seems likely that during the conquest of the Sudan by British and Egyptians in the second half of nineteenth century, the population of Sudan as a whole increased more than half and possibly doubled.[103] The expanding population spilled over into many cities and towns that emerged in the Sudan, especially in the Southern Sudan. But since the independence of Sudan in 1956 and during the civil war, the population has declined.[104]

The emergence of cities and towns is perhaps the most striking socioeconomic change of the late nineteenth and twentieth centuries. In the 1800s, almost all settled places in the Nuerland either were villages, fortified havens, or British government outposts without an adjoining market. The "city" was the location of the seats of British administrative centers. Cities in the Northern Sudan include Khartoum, Port Sudan, and Suakin. These are of Arab orientation. Cities in the Southern Sudan include Juba, Malakal, and Wau.

In the twentieth century, trading and manufacturing centers sprang up in the Southern Sudan in places with sufficient population. Such sites include Nzara, Juba, Watoka, Malakal, and Wau. The merchant class, which at the beginning of nineteenth and early twentieth centuries had consisted of a relatively few itinerant peddlers, increased sharply in number and changed drastically in character in the late nineteenth and twentieth centuries. The change was seen first in cities and towns, and then in the villages. Commerce over land and the Nile River and its tributaries quickly became important aspects of Nuer and southern Sudanese economic and social life, as they already were in the Northern Sudan. Markets became important social institutions. Institutions for credit, banking, and insurance sprang up in the major cities and towns for funding trading activities. Concomitant with the growth of commerce was the demand for manufactured handicrafts. This was accompanied by the wide spread of formation of crafts cooperative societies in the Southern Sudan. Often the cooperative societies played a major role in city and town government. Thus the expansion of commerce and the growth of towns and cities went hand-in-hand with the political changes that occurred during the British rule.[105]

The gradual acceptance and incorporation of money (silver coins and paper) by Nuer during the British era in the Sudan accelerated change and commerce. The acceptance and incorporation of money was primarily linked to the British government imposing taxation, developing cattle markets, and wage labor. Wage labor opportunities were universally rejected by the Nuer as equivalent to slavery.[106] The experiences of the Nuer with work parties were associated with specific tasks that could not be achieved by the family workforce alone.

The following example shows how the introduction of "labor tribute" by the British local administration in the mid-1930s slowly started to change the Nuer view about wage labor. Local conditions greatly accelerated the change. The rinderpest epidemics that swept through the Upper Nile between 1931 and 1933 were especially disastrous among the Gaawar and Lou Nuer due to accompanying floods and crop failures (Johnson 1979; Hutchinson 1988). The situation in that region became so critical that the British government was soon forced to suspend tribute collection in cattle and to subsidize the importation of large quantities of grain.

In 1933, the British Commissioner of Eastern Nuer District proposed to initiate a program of "labor tribute" in which the distribution of famine relief would be coordinated with compulsory cutting of wood for government steamers. A "small pecuniary reward" for conscripted Nuer laborers was also advocated on the grounds that it would teach them the value of currency and eventually speed the tribute collection. The potential benefits of the project were heralded by the British Governor of Upper Nile Province.[107]

The creation of governmentally sponsored and supervised cattle auctions in various small court and market centers of Nuerland for the purpose of buying and selling of cattle with money was a point of economic departure for the Nuer. The mutual convertibility of these two media of exchange (cattle and currency) began to be established for most Nuer. At the beginning, these auctions were held mainly for the disposal of cattle collected as court fines by the colonial government. This became a significant economy, since chiefs' courts were established in all parts of Nuerland by the late 1940s. In addition, government revenues generated through court fines had risen by that time to as much as one third of that collected as tribute (UNPMD, September 1946). Cattle fines were imposed as "social deterrents" in most cases of fighting, homicide, theft, slander, and in certain types of "adultery" and "fornication" (Howell 1954).

The cattle the government collected as fines usually included a large number of heifers. In light of the availability of heifers, it became possible for Nuer to use money to purchase young and fertile female cattle to increase their herds.[108] It was this opportunity that first motivated Nuer to enter the cattle market as buyers, and cash paying ones at that. Because these government auctions were run strictly on a cash basis, they had the added effect of stimulating the export market. This happened because most Nuer desiring to acquire the cattle collected as fines were forced to sell an ox in an open market prior to the auction so as to have the required cash available.

The Cultural and Intellectual Changes

In the late nineteenth and the twentieth centuries Nuer not only experienced political and socioeconomic changes but also a cultural and intellectual changes. During this time education was introduced to the Nuer and other Southern Sudanese peoples, the school curriculum was developed, and Christian theology was taught in schools. The period marked the beginning of closer interactions between the Nuer and the Western World. It is also marked a transition in Nuer architecture, from traditional-style structures to those of European-style.

It was during this period of British administration that the responsibility for literacy education and other services were assigned to missionaries by the protectorate government with some government support (Sanderson and Sanderson 1981). The education the missionaries were expected to offer in Southern Sudan was "to fit the ordinary individual to fill a useful part in his environment with happiness to himself . . ." (Lugard 1930). In keeping with the principle of indirect rule, this required a conscious effort to retain "native institutions" while at the same time teaching the African "to adapt himself and his institutions to changing ideas and conditions" (Lugard 1930). From this principle, it logically followed that education should not attract an African away from his social unit. This principle, however, was impossible for missionaries to implement (Sevier 1975). Under this influence, the Nuer vernacular language and literature took on its modern form. This led to a remarkable growth of literacy among the laity and the development of national cultural sentiments in most of countries in modern Africa.

Developing literary education among the African pastoral Nuer in the nineteenth and early twentieth centuries was no small problem for the British administration. British imperial sovereignty meant that the system of indirect rule attempted to deal with and through traditional institutions. But among the Nuer, there was no centralized system of religious order or written literary tradition through which to rule. Indirect rule in the Southern Sudan therefore, meant something quite different than indirect rule in the Northern Sudan. The missionaries and district officers were critical in bringing literacy, Christianity, and technology to the South. The political expediencies of indirect rule thus introduced the English language and the Bible to the Nuer. In fact, everything from writing their own language to more advanced forms of agriculture, industry, science, and medicine were brought to the Nuer by the missionaries and a wide variety of peoples from different parts of Europe and the United States. It is likely that Arabic literary traditions would have been introduced at some point.

It is important to know how indirect rule shaped and sharpened the differences between the Northern and Southern Sudanese. These differences profoundly influence the Nuer people and the way they approach the challenges of a changing world. Evelyn Baring, Lord Cromer (British agent and consul general of Egypt, 1883-1907, and author of the Anglo-Egyptian system of government) was a man experienced with governing in Turkish and Arabic Egypt. Cromer had an orientation to Islam rather than to the Christian churches of England. In Northern Sudan, the British relied upon the Mullahs, dervish orders, and places of prayer to spread their hegemony. The Southern Sudanese were viewed as hopelessly primitive. This bias explains Cromer's rejection of conversion to Islam or Christianity and their educative complement as either possible or desirable for "the pagan" of the Southern Sudan (Sanderson and Sanderson, 1981). However, as a result of political pressure from England, Cromer finally allowed the Christian missionaries to enter Southern Sudan.

Organization of Sudan as a Nation-State and Constitution Making

On January 1, 1956, the Republic of Sudan was established as an independent state within the territorial boundaries that had existed under the Anglo-Egyptian Condominium. From its inception, the independent government had to face many problems, including the problems inherited from the previous regime. Many of these problems have become even more severe over the years and have remained part and parcel of Sudan's precarious existence as an independent and united country. The discussion that follows will focus primarily on those problems that are directly concerned with the organization of the Sudan as a sovereign state. As will be noted, some developments have direct repercussions for this topic. For instance, the Islamic resurgence that started in the 1960s, although a phenomenon of international dimension, had direct implications for the organization and constitution making in the independent Sudan. In addition, the Sudan's ethnic and religious diversities and current conflicts, which spread into the Horn of Africa's subregion, burdened Sudan's relations with most of its neighbors, including Ethiopia, Eritrea, Kenya, Congo, and Uganda.

The discussion here will deal with how the Government of independent Sudan is organized, statehood and problems of constitution making and the viability of Sudan as a multicultural, multilingual and multi-religious State.

Structure of Government of Sudan Immediately After the British

Basic institutions in human societies are organized to create structures of incentives and deterrents that lead people to behave in predictable and thus ordered ways. There is a type of rationality imbedded in the structure of human institutions. The organization of Sudan as an independent state was accompanied by efforts to conceptualize a new political order using the European conception of the nation-state. The European idea of a nation-state refers to a people who share a common language, literature, and cultural tradition. It is the concept of state that has become increasingly important in the organization of Sudanese society. Fundamental to the conception of state is the belief that the peoples of the world are or should be organized as nation-states in global family of nations. This was the pattern followed in non-Western societies following the collapse of the British, Dutch, French, German, Japanese, and Portuguese empires in the period immediately following World War II.

The achievement of independence from the British raised hopes among the Sudanese that at the end of imperial control better conditions of life would come to pass. Every citizen would have the same rights, enjoy the same freedoms, and peace and prosperity would characterize the common good. But disillusionment among the Nuer and other Southern Sudanese followed very quickly. The independent state of Sudan not only condemned the South to poverty, but the prevailing constitutional structures had totalitarian overtones. The rulers of the Arab North imposed on the Sudanese people a repressive, predatory regime. Independence was seen by Southerners, therefore, to serve almost no purpose, and their world was made even worse than it had seemed during the British colonial rule.

The Sudan as sovereign nation-state was organized on highly centralized, restrictive and directive principles. This conception of sovereignty (i.e., of rule by an elite governing authority) was alien to the Nuer and to the majority of peoples in Southern Sudan. They accepted, however, the definition of the independent state as a set of heavy, centralized structures imposed upon the disparate social structures and processes of Sudanese civil society. This definition was commonly held across Africa. Wunsch and Olowu (1990), among others, have acknowledged that the post-colonial structures in most African countries are heavily centralized structures.

In Sudan, this is especially problematic, since theory of the centralized state carries with it a corollary of a single, comprehensive, and uniform code of law (which for Arab Sudan is Islamic law, or Sharia law). A single, uniform, overarching structure of governmental arrangement is presumed to serve the public interest of all citizens. The organization of local government and inter-governmental arrangements is within the domain and scope of the central government authority. However, given the diversity of ecological conditions applicable to various regions in the Sudan and the cultural diversity of its peoples, acceptance of a single, comprehensive, uniform, code of law has been impossible to achieve.

The Sudan concentrates its power in the executive arm of government, the Council of Ministers. The Council of Ministers is the source of a single, uniform set of law and regulations. Such law and regulations are presumed to serve the public interest of all citizens, yet those who exercise this authority not only are the source of law, but also are beyond the reach of legal remedies.

The Sudan is an interventionist state; it restricts the social life of citizens by using variety of means to assure its dominance. It also exercises total control over all economic activities. Materially, the choice of goods and services provided by local and inter-governmental arrangements is within the authority of the central government. Supervision over the provision of public goods and services by public officials is the exclusive jurisdiction of the government (i.e., only other officials do the checking on public officials). Politically, the marketplace of ideas is also under government control. The Sudan government has not been opened to public discussions of public issues. The government in 1985 publicly hanged Mahmud Muhammad Taha as a heretic because he dared to expound opposing views on public issues such as the government's 1983 implementation of Sharia (An-Na'im 1987).

The Sudanese experience as an independent nation-state has been largely that of a colonial creation struggling through protracted adaptations to become an organic part of Sudanese social processes. This experience is analogous to the European experience in which nations as "cultural-speech communities" struggle to obtain independence as nation-states. Thus, the lack of linkages between diverse Sudanese societies and the monolithic post-colonial state in the Sudan is not surprising. Neither is it surprising that many of these discontinuities are manifested through violent conflict.

Statehood and Constitution Making

After the declaration of independence, the Sudan adopted in December 1955 the Self-government Statute of 1953 as the country's first national constitution. British constitution experts had drafted the Statute, which served as the Transitional Constitution. As a transitional document, it was intended only to lead Sudan to independence and enable it to produce a permanent constitution later on. It has remained the most resilient constitution in the continent of Africa (Warburg 2003).[109] It has survived three military coups, appearing in resurrected form with some changes and modifications after each regime has seized power.

The reasons for the failure to attain a permanent constitution are partly due to the irreconcilable conflicts of interests of the socio-religious forces in Northern Sudan. These forces represent two major historic Islamic groups: the Mahdiyya or Ansar (followers of the Mahdi of the 1880s) and the Khatmiyya (who opposed the Mahdist movement of the 1880s). Concurrent with the independence movement of the 1940s, the groups organized into two major sectarian parties: 1.) the Umma Party (UP) backed by the Ansar, and 2.) the National Unionist Party (NUP), which in 1968 became the Democratic Unionist Party (DUP), backed by the Khatmiyya.[110] A third Islamic party, representing a yet smaller base of support, consisted of an educated Islamist elite organized into the small but radical Muslim Brotherhood. After 1985, the Muslim Brotherhood became the National Islamic Front (NIF) and since 1998, the National Congress. The Muslim Brotherhood (and its descendant forms) was intent upon enforcing an Islamic constitution, but was too weak to do so without collaboration from more broadly based, traditional Islamic parties (Warburg 2003; Kok, P. 1996; An-Na'im 1985).

Each of these political groups, and also a large number of the military officer corps, had economic and social interests in common and were always seeking to consolidate their privileged positions. All of the Northern elite groups have a common vision that entails the adoption of Islam as the religion of state, the Sharia as the main source of public laws, and Arabic as the official language. The majority who support an Islamic state and Sharia law prefer to impose their vision democratically through the majority vote. However, as we shall see, coercion has been used more often than democratic means, especially in the Southern Sudan. Although the supporters of this vision never agree on the details, they are united in keeping the hegemony in the hands of the Muslim, Arabic speaking, northern riverain elite, and to exclude the peripheral regions, whether Muslim or Christian, from the center of political and economic power.

Failure to Achieve a Federal Constitution

In the face of an elite-controlled, centralized government, the South and other marginalized regions advocated the redistribution of national wealth in order to create a just and fair society. In addition, the majority of Southern Sudanese rejected the centralization imposed upon them by the Northern Sudanese majority. They demanded a federal secular state in which power was shared and in which other cultures and languages could flourish alongside the Islamic and Arabic.

To the Nuer and most of the Southern Sudanese, who are acephalous peoples with a democratic cultural tradition that supports the idea of democratic self-governance, federation 1s a logical solution to the problems of constitution in an independent Sudan. Federalism is one common strategy of accommodating polyethnicity, diversity and national minorities.. For many Southerners, to accept centralization would undermine their cultural traditions as polycentric or acephalous societies. Moreover, as non-Muslims, they would remain second-rate citizens in their own country.

These two contradictory visions have remained at the center of Sudan's constitutional conflict since 1956. All Northern political parties except the Communist Party have consistently rejected a federal solution. They insist that Sudan's permanent constitution should be Islamic, and that a democratic majority should make that determination. The uniformity of the vision held until 1986, when following a coup d'etat the Democratic Unionist Party broke rank and indicated a willingness to compromise on the issue of Sharia. To make centralization more palatable, the Northern parties promise to preserve the rights of non-Muslim and non-Arab minorities and to allow them to use their own languages and to develop their indigenous cultures. This promise, however, is conditional upon establishing the predominance of the Arabic language in all educational institutions and state offices, and establishing Islam unchallenged as the religion of state.

The Northern parties view federation as a political system of governance in the Sudan as a first step toward political separation from the Islamic and Arab hegemony. Northerners also argue that the Southern Sudanese lack the political and legislative experience to govern themselves. The bias is not entirely undeserved. Douglas Johnson (2003) points out the failure of most of the members of parliament from the South during 1950s to translate the slogan of federalism into a concrete proposal. Sadly, some members of parliament from the Southern Sudan were susceptible to Northern manipulation in order to gain opportunities for distinction, prestige, and personal power. Self-interest distracted them from serious concentration on the constitutional problems at hand.

Ironically, the rejection of a federal constitution by the government and Northern parties brought about unity among the Southern people. A new federal party contested the 1957 elections and won almost all the constituencies in the Southern provinces. These elections brought along new members to parliament such as Fr. Saturnino Lohure, leader of the Federal Bloc. Common political aspirations for democratic autonomy enabled the Southern members to constitute a loose alliance with members of parliament from the Eastern and Western Sudan to jointly fight for federal constitution.

The Beginning of the Search for Acceptable National Constitution

The formation by 1956 of a committee for drafting a permanent constitution was the beginning of the search for a nationally acceptable constitution. The committee argued about the nature of the constitution, and the possibility of an Islamic constitution became real for the first time. By early 1957, the Northern members of the Constitutional Committee had committed themselves to the principle that Islam was to be the official religion of the state and the Sharia one of its main sources of legislation. The two most powerful sectarian leaders supported this commitment: Sayed Abd al-Rahman al-al Mahdi (of the Ansar) and Sayed Ali al-Mirghani (of the Khatmiyya). The two leaders demanded jointly that Sudan be declared an Islamic parliamentary republic with the Sharia as the main source of legislation. By this demand they fell in line with the Muslim Brotherhood, who had advocated the adoption of an Islamic Constitution since 1954. The Muslim Brotherhood wanted to establish an Islamic republic under a Muslim head of state with a parliamentary democracy based on Islamic law. This republic would legislate in accord with the dictates of Islam and would also uproot social evils and corruption as required by Islam.

The Constitutional Committee laid out a transition period of five years, in which the Sudan would become fully Islamized and all laws brought into compliance with Sharia. According to Abdelwahab El-Affendi, under the Islamic constitution there would be no discrimination on the basis of race or religion, and non-Muslim citizens would enjoy all rights granted to citizens under Muslim law (Affendi, 1991).

However, the Southern Sudanese and other non-Muslim and non-Arab minorities did not accept the claim that an Islamic constitution would allow them to practice their own religions freely, or that they would be granted full citizenship and equal rights under Islamic law. The unrest posed a serious threat to the future of a united Sudan. Although the Constitutional Committee agreed upon the draft constitution, it was never ratified. By April 1958, when it was finally presented to the Constituent Assembly, the Assembly was otherwise engaged. They failed to ratify before the military coup of November 1958, led by General Ibrahim Abboud.

The Constitutional Model of Abboud Military Regime

General Abboud's policies codified the issues of the on-going political and military struggle in the Southern Sudan. Abboud and his civilian supporters (the Umma Party) devised policies for maintaining the power of the Revolutionary Government. The process of working out arrangements to make the change of government stick required Abboud and the Umma Party to specify the basic conditions for achieving stability in a government undertaken by military rule. Their policies were of fundamental importance to the new government and are of constitutional significance. Abboud's formulation also served as a model for aspiring military leaders in the Sudan, such as Nimeiri and Beshir, as well as military leaders in other third world countries.[111]

A constitution can be conceived as specifying the terms and conditions of government. In Abboud's case, these terms and conditions provide us with an understanding of the way his systems played out in the Sudan as a nation-state. Abboud's formulation provided two important principles about how to maintain the military in power. First, power is based on either repressive action or constructive action. Second, everything that a government does has an effect on its power base. That power base, in its essential structure, rests upon instruments for repressive action. In consolidating the government, Abboud, and other military dictators who followed him, relied upon repressive power exercised through: 1.) decrees, 2.) police, 3.) an organized intelligence service, 4.) propaganda facilities, and 5.) military force. Abboud's revolutionary government was not subject to any legal constraint in monopolizing all legal political activity. The military junta suspended the constitution, closed the parliament, and banned political parties. All opposition was made illegal. Legislation in the form of presidential decrees became the foundation of state security and formulated the duties and obligations of citizens. Magistrates did what the government wanted.

General Abboud's government favored the Islamic orientation of the Ansar and the Khatmiyya. He decreed that the Arabic language was to be the medium of instruction in the school system in the South in order to achieve unity of religion and national integration. Although the English language was maintained for a time as a medium of instruction, it was to be phased out. Indeed, it was phased out eventually. New Koranic schools and mosques were built in various parts of the Southern region. The government funded the Islamic school programs. Control of the Christian mission schools was transferred to government. Conversion to Islam was encouraged, especially among students. The Koranic school is widely accepted throughout the Islamic world as an appropriate agency for indoctrinating the young with Islamic culture through reading and reciting the Koran.

Christian missionaries were blamed for the Southern resistance to Arab-Islamic ways. Abboud's regime limited the rights of Christian churches to offer medical, relief, and educational activities, and regulated churches through the (foreign) Missionaries Societies Act of May 1962. These and other measures provoked numerous strikes throughout the Southern schools during the early 1960s. Early in 1964, the government transferred many Southern officials and teachers to the North on the pretext of national integration and to learn the Arabic language. In fact, they were transferred because they were thought to be instigating hatred against the Arabs and Islam.

Since police are the bulwark of the national security system, control over police is viewed as key to control of government. This meant for Abboud that police were to be politicized as a partisan, paramilitary arm of the revolutionary government. Abboud's government formed a carefully concealed secret service capable of penetrating and dealing with any suspected anti-revolutionary activity in the Southern Sudan.

The repressive apparatus was given priority in laying the foundations for the constructive measures that were to be initiated on behalf of the revolutionary movement. During this time the army carried out a limited campaign in the South against the remnants of the 1955 mutiny in Torit,[112] many of whom were still hiding in the bush. As unrest spread in the South, the army began to burn villages and to destroy properties, including livestock. Such repressive activities, especially those aimed at educated Southern Sudanese, increased Southern opposition to the government. Opposition was met by further repressive action, including arrest and torture of civilians. The repressive actions of the government forced many people to seek refuge in the neighboring countries.

The Transitional Constitution for the Sudan made by the British survived the military junta of General Ibrahim Abboud, who was ousted by a civilian uprising in October1964. The Transitional Constitution was revived when Sudan started its second democracy in 1965 under the Umma Party leader Sadiq al Mahdi. It is reported that the constitution was slightly amended, but the original text remained unchanged. The demand of the Southern Sudanese parties for the right of self-determination for the Southern Sudan and for a referendum that would enable its inhabitants to decide on its relationship with the Muslim North had, therefore, no chance of being accepted, even by moderate Northern parties.

There was some agreement that the Constituent Assembly to be elected in 1965 would approve a permanent constitution, but this did not happen. After the caretaker government was dismissed, the Umma Party (UP) and National Unionist Party (NUP) returned to power advocating ideas and programs similar to those they had proposed in 1956 through 1958 that supported the establishment of an Islamic parliamentary republic with Sharia as the main source of legislation. Thus, the Round Table Conference in March 1965 on the Southern demand for self-determination failed to reach an agreement (Beshir 1968).

Al Turabi and Islamic Constitution

At this time, the Muslim Brotherhood was under the leadership of Hassan al Turabi (a brother-in-law of Sadiq al Mahdi). The Muslim Brotherhood reconstituted itself with the addition of some minor Muslim groups (or *sufi*, i.e., Islamic "followings" that have characteristics of lineages) into the Islamic Charter Front (ICF). Their aim was to implement an Islamic system of order in the Sudan. The ICF was at that time still small and weak and had to look for an alliance with the Umma Party and the National Unionist Party (NUP). Sadiq al Mahdi of Umma Party provided support to Islamic Charter Front in order to implement an Islamic Constitution.

Turabi and other members of Islamic Charter Front were active participants in a Constitution Committee. The three options discussed were: 1.) an Islamic constitution proposed by the ICF; 2.) a secular constitution proposed by Southern Sudanese and some members of the Northern intelligentsia; and 3.) a "constitution with an Islamic orientation" proposed by the NUP. The NUP option, which was rather similar to the Transitional Constitution, was finally adopted and its draft presented to the Constituent Assembly on January 15, 1968.

Turabi presented to the committee a memorandum showing the advantages of the Islamic constitution. It said:

1. The constitution should represent the will of the people and since the majorities are Muslims their will should prevail.
2. Unlike other religions, Islam is a religion and state and it instructs (the believers) to govern in accordance with Allah's Revelation.
3. The adoption of a non-Islamic political system in the Sudan had not been in response to popular demand, but rather a work of despotic rulers with Western culture and orientation.
4. The ostensibly Islamic states that ruled Muslims were bad models whose knowledge of Islam was very poor.
5. An Islamic constitution would be a rule of sacred law and not a rule of men because in Islam there is no place for theocracy or "clergy".
6. Islam opposes dictatorship.

7. Islam protects private freedom and guarantees freedom of opinion and participation in public affairs.
8. Islam encourages *iftihad,* because the final opinion is the public's and every individual, group of individuals, or political party had the right to advocate their views and to work for the assumption of power through *shura* (consultation).
9. Islam recognized freedom of religion before Europe had ever thought about it and calls for the protection of citizens with other religious beliefs.
10. Islam calls for equality before the law and in public rights.

This memorandum, according to Gabriel Warburg (2003) demonstrated Turabi's political-ideological pragmatism and flexibility, "since it claimed that Islam protected private freedoms and guaranteed freedom of opinion, while at the very same time he [Turabi] was actively propagating the outlawing of Communist ideology and the expulsion of the democratically elected Communist members from Parliament". Turabi's interpretation of *iftihad* (the evolution of jurisprudence through legal reasoning) was opposed by more conservative members of the Islamic Charter Front who were against his unprincipled opportunism.[113]

The three parties were allied in shutting out the Communist Party, which opposed their Islamic agenda in favor of a secular one. However, Turabi's main opponents in the Constitution Committee were Southern Sudanese and the Muslim leaders from Dar Fur, the Nuba Mountains, and the Red Sea Hills. Muslim leaders in these regions regarded an Islamic constitution as a ploy for consolidating the hegemony of northern central Sudan under the umbrella of an Arabic Islamic culture, which would thus consolidate the marginalization of Sudan's southern, western and eastern population (Alier 1990). On May 23, 1969, all the political parties in the Sudan arranged to meet in order to discuss the constitution proposals of the Constitution Committee, but, less than forty-eight hours before that meeting took place, the military seized power under the leadership of Colonel Ja'far Nimeiri.

The Nimeiri Secular Constitution

Nimeiri wanted to establish a socialist state in Sudan, and he had the support of the communist bloc. The new military government was a coalition of Marxist-inspired radicals. The ruling elite immediately suspended the

Constitution, outlawed all political parties, and nationalized important components of the economy. As for Nimeiri, he immediately began to neutralize or eliminate opposition to his rule. This included a military action against certain members of the Ansar Party.

Fighting between North and South had been ongoing for fourteen years. It would continue as long as there was Southern resistance to the creation of a united Islamic Sudan. Nimeiri's commitment was to a united *socialist* Sudan; this explains why he was open to the possibility of Southern regional autonomy. Two Southerners were appointed to Nimeiri's cabinet: Abel Alier, a Dinka lawyer who had been involved in Southern politics on the national level since the independence, and Joseph Garang, a member of the Sudan Communist Party. Garang was appointed to head the new Ministry of Southern Affairs. On June 3, 1971, Nimeiri announced that the "Southern problem" was political and must be resolved politically, rather than militarily.

Yet as Nimeiri tightened his dictatorial grip on Sudan, his coalition of radical socialist and communist officers felt apart. In July 1971, the communists staged a coup to push Nimeiri out of power. The coup failed after three days. After Nimeiri regained control of government, the communists were purged from government and several were executed. Joseph Garang was hanged. Abel Alier replaced him as Minister for Southern Affairs. After the shake-up, Nimeiri took steps to court the Islamic political leadership. As we shall see, the sectarian leaders worked to undercut Nimeiri's design for a united socialist Sudan.

Nimeiri's government promulgated the Sudan's first permanent constitution on May 8, 1973. This came to pass seventeen years after independence. The importance of Nimeiri's Sudan Permanent Constitution was his attempt to resolve the two major problems to constitution making in the Sudan: 1.) the status of the South and 2.) the question of religion and politics. Nimeiri's rule (1969-1985) was the first time Sudan was governed as a secular state *by design* since its inception as an independent country in 1956. Yet Nimeiri's rule was clearly one-party rule. After the 1971 coup, he declared that the Sudan Socialist Union (SSU) was the only legitimate political party in the Sudan.

The Constitution of Sudan proclaimed the Sudan as a "unitary, democratic, socialist and sovereign republic." It said, "Islamic laws and customs shall be the main sources of legislation. Personal matters of non-

Muslims shall be governed by their laws." Article 16 of the Constitution is even particularly important because it attempts to resolve the problem of religion in the state in the following manner:

1. In the Democratic Republic of the Sudan, Islam is the religion and society shall be guided by Islam, being the religion of the majority of its people and the state shall endeavor to express its values.
2. Christianity is the religion in the Democratic Republic of the Sudan, which is professed by a large number of its citizens who are guided by Christianity, and the state shall endeavor to express its values.
3. Heavenly religions and the noble aspects of spiritual beliefs shall not be abused or held in contempt.
4. The State shall treat followers of religions and noble spiritual beliefs without discrimination as to the rights and freedoms guaranteed to them as citizens by this constitution.
5. The abuse of religious and noble beliefs for political exploitation is forbidden. Any act which is intended or is likely to promote hatred, enmity or discord among religious communities shall be contrary to this constitution and punishable by law (Sudan Constitution 1973; Warburg 1985; Sidahmed 1997).[114]

Unfortunately, the attempt to find a political solution to the Southern problem by accommodating all religions on the basis of equality and promoting a culture of secularism failed. The 1973 Constitution remained in force for less than twelve years. By 1975, it had already been amended, drastically curtailing basic human rights in the South.[115]

The Permanent Constitution was followed by the National Reconciliation of 1977. This reconciliation led to admission of the leaders of the banned sectarian political parties [Turabi (NIF), Sadiq al Mahdi (UP), and Mirghani (DUP)] into the Sudan Socialist Union Politburo. By admitting leaders with an unshakable Islamic agenda into the decision-making processes, Nimeiri thereby undermined the secular basis of the 1973 Constitution (and also the Addis Ababa Agreement of 1972, which established regional autonomy in the South). By 1983, Nimeiri had embraced politically the Islamic Way, a decision that was in contradiction to the secular intentions of his own constitution, which, by his presidential decrees, he overruled.

Nimeiri's experience raises the question of whether or not a constitution imposed by a military regime, supported by a centrist Northern minority can survive in the Sudan at all. Peter Nyot Kok defined Nimeiri's government as: "secular, presidential, one-party state, quasi-federal, pseudo-constitutionalist, mixed economy oriented." Since Nimeiri's socialist revolution was based solely on the support of the ruling elite represented in the 1972-73 Peoples' Assembly, it could not, according to Peter Nyot Kok, expect to win a national consensus.[116]

After Nimeiri was removed in 1985, an elected government came to power. It was led by Sadiq al Mahdi. During that third democratic government, in the years 1986-89, a different approach was adopted, which advocated winning a national consensus as a precondition for the formulation of a Permanent Constitution and its subsequent ratification by Parliament. A National Constitutional Conference (NCC) was formed to carry out the task. The proposed conference was never convened during the three years of the tenure of the regime because of NIF opposition. While the NIF had sufficient influence to delay the conference, it was aware of its own weakness should a constitution advocating multicultural rights and the freedom of religions be promulgated. Without yet having gained the support of the Umma and DUP for an Islamic constitution, the NIF needed time in order to consolidate its hold on state power. This situation led to NIF support Omer Hasan al Beshir in a military coup d'etat in June 1989.

Peter Nyot Kok observes that the search for a permanent constitution under liberal democratic regimes in Sudan has been fundamentally flawed by the assumption that a special parliamentary majority could impose such a constitution. Such an assumption is the very antithesis of a constitution by consensus (Kok, P. 1996). Yet why, despite the fact that Muslims were and still are the overwhelming majority in Sudan, has the dream of an Islamic constitution in the Sudan failed to be realized? The reason why Islamic constitution did not materialize until 1998 may to be found from the very nature of Sudanese Islam. "Its origin," writes Abdel Salam Sidahmed, "was in popular Islam in which *Sufism* played an important role." The political power of the Ansar and the Khatmiyya was due more to the hereditary loyalty of their adherents, rather than to their ideological commitment to an Islamic state. The leaders of these sects had impressed their continuous commitment to an Islamic constitution and Islamic state upon the Sudanese people; however, being astute politicians, they moderated their language whenever they were in power. They were careful to safeguard the unity of their base of power: a multi-religious, multi-cultural, and ethnically diverse Sudan (Sidahmed (1997). According to Abdel Salam Sidahmed "the conduct of their politics and government was virtually secular." He maintained that the sectarian leaders are "neither fanatics nor advocators of vigorous Islamization of Sudanese politics" (ibid). The resistance of the Nuer, the South, and non-Arab groups was also a big factor moderating the behavior of sectarian leaders. Also, the popular Islamic belief system as practiced by the Ansar and the Khatmiyya was traditionally more relaxed. It relied more on the goodwill and loyalty of adherents, and less on a rigorous set of orthodox rules, such as are propagated and implemented by the radical Islamists. This is why the Islamic constitution had to wait until 1998, when it was imposed upon citizens by an alliance between President Omer Hasan al Beshir's military regime and the National Islamic Front (Warburg 2003).

Nimeiri Shifts to the Islamic Way in the Sudan

Nimeiri wanted to use religion to suppress opposition in the North, to subjugate the "infidel" in the South, and to keep the Communist at bay. To silence his critics, Nimeiri announced on April 30, 1984, that:

in order to protect the faith [Islam] and the fatherland from schemes of schemers and the mischief Satan, and in order to protect the gains of the believing people and fulfill my national duties and constitutional responsibilities, I have issued Presidential Decree number 258 [1984] announcing the imposition of martial law throughout the country; this, in pursuance of the aims of the revolution.(Khalid 1985).

Nimeiri's published works indicate that his shift from a secularist-leftist position to embracing the Islamic Way had to do with the abortive communist coup of July 1971, which opened his eyes to the truth. Francis Deng portrays the President's "encounter" with God in *Seed of Redemption* (1986). Deng writes that Nimeiri was ordered to reform his ways and return to the path of a true believer; following his encounter the President sent for his local spiritual leader in order to receive guidance. The guide reportedly said, "Mr. President, by revealing Himself, it is clear that God has chosen you to be the leader of this country. You are President, but you are also the Imam of God. He will change you as He desires. I am but a tool of His will. The power to transform you has already descended from God."

As mentioned previously, reconciliation between Nimeiri's Regime and the sectarian and Islamist groups was effected in 1977. Immediately after achieving reconciliation with the opposition, Nimeiri appointed a committee to "return the laws of the land to compatibility with Sharia" (*lajnat muraja't al qawanin li'tatamasha ma'a al shari'a*). Dr. Hasan al Turabi was committee chairman.

The committee was given the task of bringing the Sudan's legislation into full harmony with Sharia law. It drafted seven bills on matters such as the prohibition of alcoholic beverages and the banning of usury (*riba*) and gambling. Other bills drafted were concerned with the implementation of the *hudud* penalties contained in Sharia for murder, theft, adultery, and the like. The most important bill was the one outlining the sources of judicial decisions (*usul al ahkam al qadiyya)*, since it provided for the application of the Sharia in all matters not covered in other legislation. This bill became law of the land, but could not be implemented fully until after the third democratic government led by Sadiq al Mahdi was removed by the Beshir coup.

The Islamist Coup and Islamic Constitution

On June 30, 1989, a military coup headed by Lieutenant General Omer Hassan Beshir took place. This military regime has ruled the Sudan ever since (at least, until this writing of October 2004). Some primary documents at my disposal, as well as some printed secondary materials, assign blame to the NIF, and particularly to Turabi, as being the main instigators of Beshir's Islamist military coup.[117] Many Northern and Southern Sudanese I have spoken with, who were living in Sudan at the time of the coup, believe that the NIF used deception on a systematic basis to confuse public opinion and to cover up the fact that the coup was carried by the military and aided by civilian (i.e., NIF) collaborators.

The immediate justification for the coup, it appears, was that the Islamists led by Turabi (both in the NIF and in the army) realized that a draft peace agreement with the Southern opposition movement (Sudan Peoples' Liberation Movement) would become a reality. The DUP's Muhammad Osman al Mirghani had signed the agreement in November 1988. It later was endorsed by Sadiq al Mahdi's coalition government. The NIF feared that a political solution to the Southern problem would undermine their chances of gaining power and enforcing an Islamist agenda in Sudan. According to Sadiq al Mahdi:

The NIF-led Salvation Regime had, since 1989, left behind a catastrophic legacy with regard to the civil war. It had not only aborted the peace process, which had been almost brought to a successful end, but also injected a religious element in the civil war and increased its bitterness and violence. By declaring *Jihad*, Sudanese society, not only in the South, was polarized to such an extent that the conflict "boiled over regionally to Sudan's neighbors", who exploited religious differences to meet their own political needs.(Sadiq 2000).

Hassan Beshir and his military colleagues simply provided the umbrella for an NIF take-over. The NIF then played the role of ideological mentor to the new regime (i.e., they served as the *ulama*, a group of learned men guiding the people and their rulers in the true content of Islam). The Islamists viewed Islam as the only means to resolve the problems prevailing in the Sudan, including the Southern problem. They not only refused to abolish the Islamic laws (i.e., Nimeiri's 1983 September Laws which implemented Sharia), but also implemented a new Islamic Penal Code in March 1991. The executions, amputations, and other punishments prescribed by the Sharia were restored. Moreover, public order emergency courts, whose judges were military officers, were empowered to arrest or flog illegal vendors, confiscate their goods, and destroy their equipment. Hassan Beshir stated that he and his fellow-officers had recruited cadres from the NIF when they seized power in June 1989 in order to implement their Islamist program (Lesch 1998).

On the international front, the Islamists had a close relationship with Ayatollah Khomeini's Iran, a nation viewed by many as Sudan's regional mentor. The Sudanese Islamists "maintained that Islam, the majority religion, and Arabic, the language of the *Quran*, represented the essential bases of the country's nationalism." Consequently, adherents of traditional African faiths could be compelled to convert, since they were not monotheistic "People of the Book" (i.e., they were not people having in common the principles of the one true religion sent by Allah through his prophets). More explicitly, the Islamist *ulama* issued a *fatwa* (a legal statement) in 1992 ordering soldiers to kill apostates and heathens who opposed *da'wa* (the "invitation" to Islam) and who defied the Islamist regime (Warburg 1971).

Nine years after the Islamists seized power, the Sudan became an Islamic state ruled in accordance with an Islamic Constitution. The Islamic

Constitution was adopted by referendum in June 1998. In Part I, Article I of the constitution, under the heading "Nature of the State", the following formulation about the diversity of religions and cultures is offered: "The state of Sudan is an embracing homeland, wherein races and cultures coalesce and religions conciliate. Islam is the religion of the majority of the population. Christianity and customary creeds have considerable followers." The question of languages is defined in Part I, Article 3: "Arabic is the official language in the Republic of the Sudan; and the state shall allow the development of other local and international languages." Part I, Article 4 concerns supremacy and sovereignty and suggests the following definition regarding religion and state: "Supremacy in the State is to God the Creator of human beings." According to Sadiq al-Mahdi, "this concept is a conduit of theocracy, because it allows humans to speak on behalf of God, and exercise that sovereignty...However Sovereignty is a political concept which should be vested in the people" (Sadiq 2000; An-Na'im 1985).

Part IV of the constitution deals with the Legislative Power. Article 65 defines sources of legislation as follows: "Islamic law and the consensus of the nation, by referendum, constitution and custom shall be the sources of legislation; and no legislation in contravention with these fundamentals shall be made."[118] This "consensus" provision offered the status of *ahl al-dhimmah* (People of the Book) to non-Muslims in the Islamic state as a compromise. The South rejected this compromise. In practice, it meant that the supremacy of Islamic law remained the un-challengeable source of legislation and that the government remained free to adopt strategies to make non-Muslims fit for membership within an Islamic state.

Strategies for Assimilation and Incorporation

In January 1962, the Minister of Education Ziada Osman Arbab asserted in a speech at Juba that national unity implied the universal adoption of Arabic as the national language and Islam as the national religion. In his first address to the constituent Assembly in October 1966, Premier Sadiq al Mahdi said: "the dominant feature of our nation is an Islamic one, and its over-powering expression is Arab, and this nation will not have its identity and its prestige and pride preserved except under an Islamic revival." Dr. Hassan El Turabi, the leader of the National Islamic Front, known now as Popular Congress Party (PCP), expressed himself in a similar vein. He argued that since the people in the Southern Sudan had no culture, this vacuum would necessarily be filled by Arab culture in the course of an Islamic revival. In this spirit, attempts were made by the Sudan Government during the 1960s to create an Islamic national identity. By 1964, all Christian missionaries were expelled from the South. Arabic was introduced as the administrative and educational language; Islamic conversion and Koranic education were encouraged. Education became the means of promoting Islam and the Arabic language.

Language as an Instrument of Assimilation

In the historical experience of the Southern Sudan, as in other African countries bordering Arab and Islamic countries, the principal sources of cultural assimilation and the effacement of African culture are Arabic language and Islam. In both instances the underlying processes have been closely linked to the integration of local economies into wider markets. In the Afro-Arab borderlands the steady erosion of African cultures and languages has been in process for over a millennium. Among the population on the Western *Sahel* (the southern boundary of the Sahara), the Horn of Africa, East Africa, and the West Africa littoral (coast), the African languages have been relatively able to hold their own. Arabic there is used for mainly religious purposes. However, along the neck of the Nile and the central areas of the *Sahel* many African languages have died out.

Today, the Southern Sudan is one of the most violent cultural and territorial interfaces in the Afro-Arab borderlands. The war which started in August 1955 continues with brief pauses to the present. One of the most contentious issues in this conflict is the factor of Arabization which most Southerners in the country reject. Its imposition as a matter of policy by successive governments based in the north of the country since the beginning of the era of independence has, at the cultural level, contributed to the making of the conflict. Ushari Ahmad Mahmud has observed that in the Southern Sudan:

> Arabic spread and vernacular recession are inextricably related. The development of Arabic entails the underdevelopment of the vernacular. The on-going process of language change in the Southern Sudan indicates clearly that Arabic is progressively displacing the vernacular languages in all contexts and functions. This process is presently at an embryonic stage of development. But its direction is obvious; and indications of its ultimate product are visible in the language

practice of Southern families that are already monolingual in Arabic (Mahmud 1983).

This phenomenon is discernible among the young Nuer families as it throughout the whole of the Afro-Arab borderlands.[119] Among the contradictory forces confronting each other in Africa, it is important to mention the concerted southward drive of Arab and Muslim Africa. The movement relies on training Black African Muslims in the Koranic schools of Arab countries (e.g., Saudi Arabia, Kuwait, Egypt, and Libya) and then having them return home to set up Koranic schools where primary education is given wholly in Arabic and centers on the Koran. This missionary process has been ongoing since 1970-71. According Gerard Chaliand (1982), the propagation of the Arabic language "represents a qualitative change from what was the situation in Koranic schools some years ago where the students learned by heart a few ritual phrases."

Transformation of Educational Institutions and Expansion of Islam

The drive to assimilate the Nuer and other Southern Sudanese into the Northern Sudanese cultural system was to be achieved through education, especially through changes in primary teacher training. The government followed the practice used by the British Government in cooperation with Christian missionaries in the Southern Sudan. The missionaries, with the support of the British administration, established and operated the Mundari (Protestant) and Busere (Catholic) primary teacher training centers. These centers supplied the primary school teachers who taught in English, as well as in the indigenous languages such as Nuer, Dinka, and Zande.

The Sudan Government established a new primary teacher training center at Maridi. Students at Mundri and Busere were transferred to Maridi. There the medium of instruction was Arabic and English, with the goal of preparing students to teach exclusively in Arabic. The two missionary primary teacher training centers were turned into middle schools. Teachers who had taught in the two missionary centers were to be retrained in the Arabic language so they could teach in the new primary institute at Maridi. Most of the teachers sent to Arabic training in the North did not return to the institute in Maridi. While some who succeeded in their course of Arabic training were placed in the schools in the Northern or in the Southern Sudan, others were said to have failed the course and lost their jobs or else they were assigned to jobs in government departments. In addition to these problems in the primary schools, a significant number of sub-grade teachers, who had for many years been teaching school children through the medium of Nuer and other languages lost their teaching jobs when Arabic was introduced as the required medium of instruction.

Nuer teachers who were suspected of disagreeing with the Northernization of offices held earlier by the British and foreign Christian missionaries, as well as teachers and workers from other groups who were suspected, were transferred to Northern Sudan. There they found the living conditions to be different and difficult. For example, rent was comparatively high, and the Nuer and other Southern teachers did not have a good command of Arabic language. Because of their deficiency in Arabic language they could not be assigned classes to teach. They therefore did nothing and this led to bitterness.

The passing of the Missionary Act in 1962 restricted the evangelistic activity of the Christian churches, while at the same time the government encouraged Islamic missionaries in the South to promote Islam. The abolition of Sunday as a day of worship for the Christians in the South, and the establishment of Friday as an official weekly holiday, was another overt attempt at assimilation.

Decades of effort to promote assimilation through education and Arabic language have not yielded positive results in Nuerland. Many Nuer have learned the Arabic language. They learn it in schools and in work places because now Arabic is the language of commerce and serves as a common language among several disparate peoples. Knowledge of the language has not, however, transformed the Nuer into Arabs. Islam has not made inroads into Nuer society because its teachings and requirements about the ways of life are inimical to the Nuer way of life.

After independence the Sudan government opened more primary schools, and the enrollment of primary school children increased dramatically. The Northern Sudanese helped to build and to staff middle schools, which would produce both administrative officers and religious scholars. This new school building program included the establishment of Koranic schools. It was funded by USAID. In the South, there were numerous aspirants for high school education. Higher education opportunities would have prepared many students for the university or for higher-level government jobs. However, opportunities were not made available by the government in the South, and Christian groups were not permitted to build and operate higher educational institutions in Nuerland.

The Failure of Sudan as a Nation-State

The failure of the successive systems of government in Sudan (elected or military) to meet the political aspirations of the Sudanese people and to provide for the essential values of security, stability, and productive relationships among its citizens is due to many factors. One of them has been and still is the lack of genuine appraisal of the "fitness" of its institutional arrangement for the ways of life of its disparate language communities. To analyze Sudan's institutions is to understand the complexity of factors that has caused the failure of the Sudan as a nation-state. Political authority structures are most likely to win popular support if they evolve as a part of a common heritage rather than being imposed from outside. No linkage has been established between the political institutions prescribed in the state constitutions and the indigenous institutions of the Nuer and other African peoples in the South. Instead, a centralized hierarchy has been imposed upon the South.

Hierarchy is a legitimate type of institutional arrangement that is well suited to organize some, but not all, activities. The imposition of a centralized system as the most important source of governmental energy and problem-solving capability, however, does not make full use of the governing and problem-solving capabilities of many indigenous institutions. Resistance to centralized governmental control in the form of the current civil war, uprisings and repressions, massacres, language and religious conflicts, and coups and counter-coups is evidence of the poverty of this institutional form. Sudanese have alternative institutional forms to draw upon, which include non-hierarchical conceptions based on self-governance, rather than on dominance.

The Arab in the Northern Sudan believes that he can create Sudan as a nation-state *de novo* without a social or cultural base. On the contrary, it is a fantasy to believe it is possible to create and define the geographic space known now as Sudan without taking into serious account the Nuer and other African's historical experiences, institutions, and preexisting social environments. Scholars recognize that nation-states are founded upon common language, literature, and cultural traditions. The effort to construct a national identity in a territory in which citizens lack any sense of common social characteristics and values has resulted in human tragedy and is perpetuating miseries upon the majority of people in the Sudan.

It is important to understand how the Nuer and other African peoples in the South govern themselves within villages and towns, how individuals acquire and transmit property, how civil disputes are resolved in courts, how offenders are brought to justice, and how citizens make decisions about the conditions of life which are the most important to them. Such analysis will also reveal how persons create linkages with others. It is also important to understand the habits of the mind and the heart of the Nuer people and how they think, feel, and behave in relation to one another. Standards of respect, the conception of what is right (and wrong), and the measures of justice and well-being are based on presuppositions that inform normative inquiry, moral reasoning, and juridical inquiry. In addition, institutions and culture, geophysics, geopolitical, demographic, and historical factors, over which a society may have very little choice, affect the political regime. Thus, institutional arrangements, culture, and environmental conditions are definitely relevant for any serious analysis of the failure of the post-colonial State in the Sudan.

The vision of the *ulama* of the National Islamic Front for transforming the values of diverse communities in order to constitute one nation under one religion (Islam) and one language (Arabic) called for radical policies. The rulers of Sudan have chosen an assimilationist approach that will culminate in full Arabization and Islamization. This is a process of imposing the values of one ethnic group at the expense of many other ethnic groups. They are imposing through the educational system and other cultural vehicles the Arabic language to unify different language groups. They are constructing civic buildings and monuments, composing self-consciously nationalistic music based on the Arabic songs and dances, and creating literary societies and publishing houses as part of the Arabist effort. Some civic rituals have been developed that are grounded in events from the recent Arab history or from the distant past. Those events are reinterpreted in light of contemporary political circumstances. Islamic tenets and practices are transformed to become the conceptual underpinnings for the nation-state. In the context of assimilation, the languages, cultures, histories, and religions of non-Arab and non-Muslim peoples are not relevant factors and do not serve as preconditions for nation building.

The assimilation approach has not succeeded in transforming Sudan into an Islamic utopia. To achieve a radical revolutionary transformation in ways of life from one day to the next is not a possibility in the Southern Sudan or any other human society. The potential for learning is possible and substantial. However, the cycle of the ordinary routines of daily life are deeply embedded in the intergenerational cycles of life that are critical to that which is cumulative for human psychological and cultural development. Conditions conducive to favorable patterns of adaptation will depend on principles of democratic self-governance that allow for diversity and complementarity, rather than on coercive uniformity. This fact of life was recognized to a large extent by the British imperial government in the Sudan.

The participative arrangements left by the British administration in 1956 were, however, seen by the new government of independent Sudan as instruments for permitting national policies to penetrate rural areas to elicit greater support for national government programs. They were never recognized as a means of strengthening the administrative capacity of local governments and private institutions to take over functions usually not performed by central ministries. Within a very few years, local government had become the local "administration" in the whole of Southern Sudan. The substantial devolution of local government was achieved. This was largely done by re-defining the authority of local government. Since that time, attempts at decentralization were swept away by military intervention or political opposition at the top.

The failure to formulate and enforce rules satisfying the different cultural groups, the failure to honor the Southern Sudan's desire to maintain cultural traditions and autonomy, the failure to ensure equal access to national institutions and public resources, and the failure to provide for autonomous government institutions with the power to deal with local issues undermined the central government's credibility among the Southern Sudanese. The result has been constant strife and growing regional inequality that is a menace to the stability of the regime and offers the Nuer and other Southern Sudanese peoples little recourse but revolt and secession to ensure their rights and to maintain their cultural identity.

Conclusion

The traditional way of life of the Nuer people has confronted its most serious challenge during the twentieth century. Resistance to the early intrusion of Islam made the Nuer vulnerable to the slave trade, and that vulnerability reinforced their resistance to Islam. Likewise, the intrusion of the British Empire, through its exercise of hegemony over the Egyptian-Sudanese protectorate, resulted in the imposition of subject status upon the Nuer.

The British imperial commitment to indirect rule, initially presuming to rely upon traditional institutions, ended up having a corrupting effect by institutionalizing the rules governing relationships among the Nuer into a formal code of law. The imposition of Western systems had the effect of separating those rules from the processes associated with conflict resolution. Furthermore, it imposed upon the Nuer a system of chiefs' courts subject to British concepts of penal law associated with terms of imprisonment. In time, however, the commitment of British colonial officials to a better understanding of the Nuer way of life led to anthropological investigations. Edward Evans-Pritchard was commissioned by the Colonial office to conduct the investigations. As a result of his findings, modifications were made in the native courts that allowed for more viable accommodations to the Nuer way of life. The establishment of an internationally recognized sovereign state in 1956, the Republic of Sudan, marked the end of the period of British imperial rule.

Today the constitutional commitment of the Government of Sudan to Islam and its association with a civilization grounded in the primacy of the Arabic language poses a serious challenge to the Nuer people. Submission to the basic constitutional commitments of the government would spell the extinction of the Nuer culture and way of life. The demand for alternatives implies resistance. The Southern Sudanese resistance has taken the form of armed conflict. How patterns of conflict and conflict resolution are to emerge in the course of time that has already extended over decades cannot yet be determined.

Those seeking to resolve problems of governance in the Sudan may draw upon the ideas associated with acephalous systems of order including American polycentricity, the Swiss cantonal system, and others. Those ideas must, however, not be imposed upon people, but rather assimilated into the cultural heritage that different peoples draw upon in fashioning their own institutions.[120] It is in this way that the emerging way of life turns upon the development of a collegiality where people draw upon one another's experience in constituting and reconstituting systems of self-governance that can be adaptive to their local environment.

It is difficult to anticipate the future of the ways of life in the Sudan. Achieving national potential depends upon a culture of inquiry that relies on processes that allow for the emergence of complementary communities of relationships among persons, rather than on violence as a way of resolving conflict. The future of the African, Arab, Christian, and Muslim peoples in the Sudan depends upon civic openness and potentials for restructuring that can be achieved through contestation and argumentation, carried out in a respectful spirit that enables people to elucidate information, clarify alternatives, and facilitate innovation. The Nuer acephalous system of order, American federalism, and Swiss confederation have important implications for achieving such a culture of inquiry. If efforts to achieve order in the Sudan were patterned in this way, a way of life grounded in principles of self-governance, and in which "reflection and choice" might function in the affairs of all Sudanese, could emerge.

The challenge the Nuer face is to mobilize their resources to restructure patterns of association in the context of diverse collectivities and communities of relationships. Whether or not the Nuer can mobilize the analytical capabilities to devise constructive ways to meet the demand of the modern world is problematical. Yet the existence of many segments independent of each other and a web of different associations provide opportunities for innovation and experimentation, as well as for conflict and conflict resolution. Acceptance of the need to reform institutions is an important element of the Nuer system of order that will help them successfully compete in the modern world.

Autocratic systems are at risk in the modern world. The presumption that the state is the mechanism that governs society is now subject to challenge. Indeed, the creation of the centralized, bureaucratic state in Africa has been revealed as a serious failure. Historical patterns of change indicate that the self-governing features of democratic societies are more consistent with African acephalous systems of order. We have much to learn from diverse acephalous societies in working out new systems of order that offer the peoples of the world alternatives to imperial and autocratic systems. It is important to keep in mind that democratic societies are not sustained by the activities of voting, political parties, and parliaments alone. These institutional arrangements will succeed only with the support of a self-governing tradition and many autonomous units organized at all levels of society. Nuer traditions may have an important place in the constitution of viable African systems of government built upon principles of self-government.

FIGURE 7.1 MAP OF NUERLAND WITHIN UPPER NILE PROVINCE (NUER REGIONS)

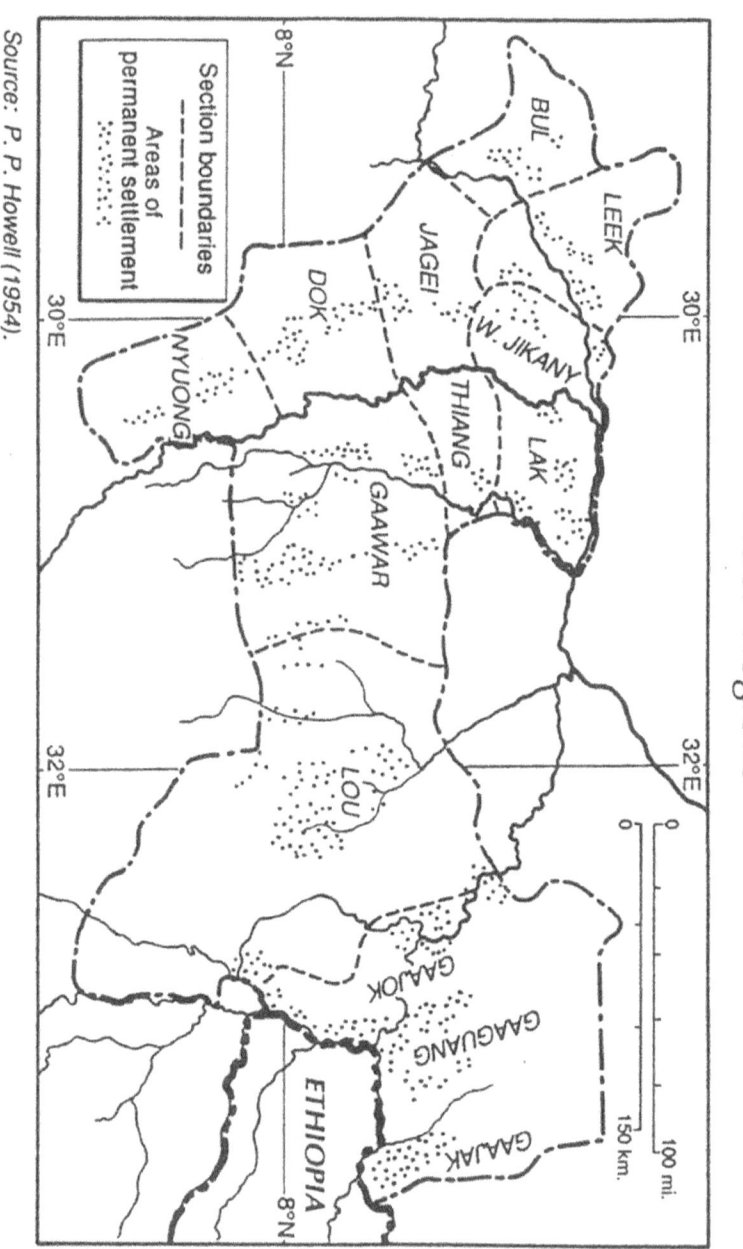

Chapter 8 - The Nuer People and the Sudanese Civil Wars

Introduction

When Sudan became an independent state, there was a clear expectation of democratic self-governance among the African peoples. For the Nuer in particular, it was an expectation rooted in antiquity and demanded by modern times. Thus, the failure of the Sudanese to reach consensus on an acceptable constitution to govern an ethnically, religiously, and culturally diverse society has been a bitter disappointment. Conditions of sustained political and economic marginalization of the South have accentuated the historic North/South cleavages, resulting in a nearly constant state of civil war. Southern disappointments were compounded after 1989 by the National Islamic Front (NIF)/military coalition government's overly-centralized governing structures, use of the military in support of arbitrary and autocratic governance, and implementation of Islam, Sharia laws and Arabic language in the South. These actions are fundamental elements in the institutional failure of the Sudan as a nation-state and of the cause of the civil war that has devastated the South.

Suffering because of civil war is now a common denominator for all Southern peoples. We will at times in this chapter speak of the Southern experience in generalities. However, the differences among the Nilotic, the Bantu, and other people groups are what shape the political landscape on the ground in the South and have a direct bearing on the possibilities for achieving an end to the civil war. In this chapter, we will examine briefly the Nuer experience during the first Sudanese civil war. Second, we will discuss the 1972 Addis Ababa Accord and its subsequent failure. Third, we will show how the second civil war devastated the civilian population in the Nuerland and other Southern Sudanese populations. Fourth, we will consider peacemaking role the Christian church plays in the South. Finally, we will discuss the imposition of Marxist-Leninist practices in the Southern Sudanese liberation movement.

The Beginning of the First Civil War

The Northern Sudanese monopoly of the prerogatives of government was resented and resisted by the Nuer because it relegated them to second-rate citizens. They were not permitted to take an active role in local schools, police, or government. When mission schools were nationalized during 1956-1965, Northern Sudanese were brought in to replace all the mission personnel. Thereafter, headmasters and headmistresses of all Southern schools were from the North.[121] Police officials were brought in from the North and assigned to the small towns. This meant that Southern people were not recruited for the police, public administration, or military colleges. Lack of Southern participation in these forces meant that the way conflict was resolved reflected the Northern perceptions of the police, state officials, and military. Recruiting police from outside the locality made cooperation between the police and the citizens more difficult to achieve. Consequently, the work of police from the North assigned to Nuerland was characterized by a lack of understanding for the way the Nuer are organized. The police were seen as an occupation force and were avoided as much as possible. Thus, the absence of a common understanding and cooperation between the police and local population undermined and reduced the effectiveness of the police services.

This cultural gap is important, since effectiveness of police services is closely related to the concept of "co-production." Scholars investigating the determinants of police services developed the concept of co-production nearly two decades ago (McGinnis 1999). In a regular production process, a commodity is produced or a service is rendered by one actor and consumed by another. Under a process of co-production, both actors must interact to produce the desired result. For example, if police officials and neighborhood residents coordinate their efforts to monitor crime in that neighborhood, then public safety results from a process of co-production. In the Nuer case, if there had been a continuing cooperation between the police and the Nuer, then public safety would have resulted from a process of co-production. In reality, there is no co-production between the imported police and the Nuer.

The Northern Sudanese were alarmed by the continued resistance of the Nuer to Arab culture, which Northerners considered to be the superior (Albino 1970). Northern Sudanese have always under-estimated the intelligence, self-respect, and commitment to their way of life by the Nuer and other Southern Sudanese. The Northern Sudanese blamed the American Presbyterian missionaries working among the Nuer for having manipulated "the simple minded Nuer." It never occurred to most of the Northern Sudanese administrators, merchants, and political leaders that it was their own unwillingness to deal respectfully with the Nuer and to take into account the way they organized themselves that might explain the Nuer acceptance of Christianity over Islam. Governmental officials accused the missionaries of poisoning the minds of the Nuer because exposure to Western education enhanced the ability of the Nuer to resist Northern pressures.

According to the Northern administrators working in Nuerland, the Nuer had been inoculated with the "virus" of an alternative religion and culture at least a generation earlier (Sanderson and Sanderson 1981).[122] By the 1950s and 1960s the "infection" of the missionaries was self-sustaining and self-extending. It had reached a point that Nuer evangelists thought the foreign missionaries were irrelevant and obsolete (Dung, interview, 1989).[123] This meant that Christianity in general, and Presbyterianism in particular, had already taken root in the indigenous Nuer culture and was not dependent upon the foreign missionaries to flourish. The government then limited contact between missionaries and the Nuer by closing missionary hospitals and dispensaries. Closures included medical facilities at Leer, Nasir, and Wanglel. The government claimed that these facilities were being abused as tools for missionary purposes, and that they could not meet government standards (Abdel-Rahim 1968; Sanderson and Sanderson 1981).

A Strategy of Forced Unity

The Islamic leaders' ambition was to consolidate the Sudan into an Islamic nation-state. The central government which they dominated embarked on a program of forcible conversion of non-Muslims to Islam. They used various methods including the politics of discrimination. Thus, the participation of the Southern Sudanese Christians and non-Muslims in the political process is contingent upon their acceptance as assimilated individuals within the context of the Muslim community of believers. The Muslim/Arab did not think of this discrimination as violating the rights of others. The social, religious, and cultural background that shaped Muslim/Arab thinking—and even the Arabic language—made impossible the expression of civil and human rights as the Nuer understood them.

To forcibly consolidate the Sudan into an Islamic nation-state is at the same time to deny the Nuer and the majority of non-Muslim Southern Sudanese people the right to participate in the governance of their own affairs. It imposes upon the Nuer a system of governance that is contradictory to their most basic beliefs. Rather than unity, coercion has created a condition of national insecurity: civil war.

National unity as an end had not been the question in the late 1950s. There were, and still are, two key problems with achieving it. The first problem is the inability of the Government of the Sudan to articulate the kind of system of governance that would nurture the national unity. The second problem is whether or not force may be employed as a proper means of achieving national unity. History has shown that efforts to coerce uniformity of sentiment in support of assimilation into Islam (essential to the Islamist regime) among the Nuer have failed.

When moderate actions, such as assimilation, did not succeed, those bent on the accomplishment of national unity resorted to ever-increasing severity. For example, students who resisted Islam were subject to lashes or other corporeal punishment that was acceptable in the Northern Sudanese *khalwa* (Koranic schools). Western educated Southerners were perceived as subversive elements and persecuted. Over time, physical violence by agents of the central government became more frequent in the villages in the various Southern districts. State violence ultimately drove many of the Nuer and Dinka people to take their children out of school, flee into the bush, or leave the country. The destruction of homes, burning crops, and theft of livestock were key elements in the government's campaign of coercion.

The Sudan African National Union and the Anya-nya Guerrilla Army

The first armed rebellion involved a military unit in Torit District, Equatoria, in 1955. At that time, most of the Southerners in the army were Equatorians (including the Latuka, Bari, Madi, Acholi, Zande, Mandari, and other groups). After the Torit mutiny, scattered guerrilla forces began to form in the South. Sharon Hutchinson (1996) observed that at first there were few Nuer directly involved in confrontations with the newly established Sudanese state. Indeed, it took years for some Nuer communities to become convinced that the government army and the *jellaba* (Northerners) were their principal enemy. Nevertheless, once it became clear that the Sudanese government intended to impose a policy of forced Arabization and Islamization on the South, growing numbers of Nuer joined the incipient secessionist movement.

Campaigns of forced displacement and other abuses compelled Southern Sudanese leaders in exile to form the political organization called Sudan African National Union (SANU) and the *Anya-nya* guerrilla army to defend their people. The choice of the name was influenced by the East African Nationalist parties. The Southern Sudanese, however, were divided in their aims. Some advocated unity with the North; others advocated Southern independence. Either way, however, what the Southern Sudanese were really fighting for was recognition of their basic human rights: They wanted freedom with justice.

The military wing of SANU became known as *Anya-nya*. The name was meant to strike fear into the hearts of the Arabs. It comes from the Madi[124] word "*Inyi-nya*" or "*Inya-nya*" (Fuli, 2002). *Inya-nya* is deadly poison extracted from a rare snake. The non-Madi people in Torit District could not pronounce the word *Inya-nya* and said *Anya-nya* instead.

The SANU's policy strategy was (1.) to wage a strenuous liberation war against Arab Imperialism for complete independence of South Sudan, and (2.) to wage war against illiteracy in South Sudan through education. Regarding the guerrilla forces, SANU leadership felt that the *Anya-nya* had to work together with citizens in full cooperation in order to defeat the Arabs.

SANU's leadership was not able to overcome the divisions and suspicions among the Southern leaders. Initially, Nuer were a majority of the SANU leadership, but the movement broke in two after a conference in Kampala in 1964. After that, it was known as SANU-outside and SANU-inside. SANU-outside was composed of mostly Nuer, Equatorian, and some Dinka leaders in exile who wanted independence for Southern Sudan. SANU-inside was based in Khartoum and led by William Deng, a Dinka. Later, William Deng was murdered and SANU weakened.

Another political group inside Sudan at that time was the Southern Front, led by Abel Alier (Dinka), Paul Logale (Bari), and Peter Gatkuoth Gual (Nuer). The Southern Front took advantage of the opportunities presented to them by the weakness of SANU-inside and the divisions among SANU-outside, and came to be seen as the more effective of the Southern political groups. The Southern Front took the leadership of the Regional Government in the South after the Addis Ababa Agreement.

The *Anya-nya* was never a completely unified military force and it was never completely under the control of SANU. Most of the soldiers recognized that they had taken up arms to liberate and protect the citizens of the

South Sudan. They were not to victimize, torture, rape, or rob them of their property. The *Anya-nya* did not have external military support. At first, they armed themselves with machetes and Molotov cocktails to attack police and military outposts in the South. Guns were obtained this way, and through the occasional ambush of army patrols or the defection of Southern police and military personnel.

The overthrow of President Abboud in 1964 improved the *Anya-nya's* opportunities to acquire military hardware. SANU was able by then to tap external financial resources from friendly countries including Israel.[125] There was at that time a great deal of military equipment flowing from East Europe through the Sudan to Congo, and the *Anya-nya* was able to seize many of these weapons through ambush.[126]

The First Civil War and the Nuer Involvement

The burning of the Christian Literature Center in Khartoum and the expulsion of all foreign missionaries in 1964 was a crucial turning point for the Nuer in their attitude toward the central government, and hence in their willingness to take up arms against it. At that time, there were relatively few Christian converts among Nuer population, outside of a small group of mis-sionary-trained, literate elite. The expulsion of foreign Christians woke up the Nuer to the reality of what was closing in on them.

By the mid-1960s, a pattern of guerrilla warfare emerged: swift at-tack-and-retreat rebel raids on government-held positions during the rainy season, countered by massive Government of Sudan dry season offensives in which the army, bolstered by the Egyptian Air Force, plundered and razed the surrounding countryside. Most of the armed clashes with government forces took place in eastern Equatoria, eastern Upper Nile, and western Bahr el Ghazal Regions. Of the estimated one half to one million Southerners killed during this seventeen-year-long civil war, the vast majority were civil-ians caught in the cross fire between *Anya-nya* and government forces.

Local patterns of inter-community fighting and feuding were exacer-bated and frequently manipulated by both government and *Anya-nya* troops. In an attempt to consolidate local support, light weapons were distributed widely among the Nuer in eastern and central Upper Nile Region by both sides in the conflict. Many Nuer, particularly those in the east, were trained in the laying of traps and the mining of roads (Hutchinson 1996). A number of powerful Nuer prophets emerged among the central and eastern Nuer, some aligning themselves with the *Anya-nya* rebels and others with government arms suppliers.

More than a million Southerners were forced out of their homes and sought refuge in the neighboring countries. Of these, approximately 40,000 were eastern Nuer who sought sanctuary across the Ethiopian frontier. Large sections of the western Nuer were shielded from the worst effects of the first civil war by a decade of extremely high floods[127] (1961-72), as well as by the inscrutable military priorities of the time.

The Addis Ababa Peace Negotiations

Over time, political situations developed both in the North and in the South that pointed to the need for a negotiated settlement of the conflict. In the Northern Sudan, Colonel Nimeiri and other military officers staged a successful coup d'etat in Khartoum on May 25, 1969. The new military government was a coalition of socialist-inspired (rather than Islamist inspired) radicals. Nimeiri announced that the problem of the Southern Sudan was to be resolved through peaceful negotiations. The Nimeiri regime contacted SANU to negotiate with the government for a peaceful resolution of the Southern Sudan problem. SANU accepted the offer to negotiate peace. As already discussed, it was during this period that Nimeiri's coalition of radical officers fell apart and the communists staged a coup to push Nimeiri out of power. The coup failed after three days. In spite of, and sometimes because of, the political uncertainties in the North, the position of the guerrilla movement in Southern Sudan dramatically improved after 1969.

Global political changes also affected SANU's position. After the 1967 Arab-Israel war, the Sudan government adopted a militant espousal of Arab causes. This meant that not only did the Ethiopian government become more sympathetic to the Southern guerrilla (because of the Sudan government's support for Eritrean secession), but also Israel became interested in the Sudan's civil war. With the overthrow of Obote in Uganda in 1970, Idi Amin came to power. Amin was friendly toward the Southern Sudanese cause. He not only came from the border region between the Sudan and Uganda, but he also had absorbed many Southern Sudanese into the Uganda army, and was himself, at that time, a willing client of the Israelis (Johnson 2003). Thus, SANU's guerrilla army secured a regular supply of arms and access to modern military training.

Anya-nya leader Joseph Lagu was Israel's main beneficiary. Lagu, a Madi from Equatoria, engineered the series of coups that divided SANU, leaving the exiled SANU politicians (the mostly Nuer and Dinka SANU-outside) without sources of military supply. Through 1970, Lagu increased his standing with the benefit of military hardware and supplies received from Israel, and persuaded a number of *Anya-nya* commanders of smaller guerrilla forces to join him. In January 1971, Lagu formed the Southern Sudan Liberation Front under the command of his now expanded *Anya-nya* armed forces. The group was later renamed the Southern Sudan Liberation Movement (SSLM). With a unified command and a secure supply of weapons, Lagu began to show greater military strength and activity in engagements outside of Equatoria. As the SSLM became a force to be reckoned with, the government accepted the SSLM's demands to recognize it as an equal negotiating partner, and to meet in neutral Ethiopia. As far as the South was concerned, conditions for a negotiated settlement to the war were far better than they had ever been before.

The peace talks between the Government of Sudan (GoS) and the SSLM began with a united Sudan as the one precondition. Many Southern Sudanese in the Diaspora were unhappy about abandoning the goal of independence, and there was a clear difference of understanding between the government and the SSLM delegations about the meaning of "regional autonomy" as then proposed for negotiation. To the SSLM, autonomy meant federation. The delegation came armed with a proposal for a full federal structure. The negotiation concentrated on the establishment of a regional government, the security needed to provide a basis for ending the fighting, and a plan for absorbing the *Anya-nya* forces into the national army, police, and prison and wildlife enforcement services. There was neither discussion of the economic powers of the new regional government, nor of the national development policy as it applied to the South. In the end, the SSLM delegation accepted an agreement that offered far less regional autonomy than they had hoped to achieve.

Addis Ababa Agreement

In spite of its flaws, the Addis Ababa Agreement of February 27, 1972, as negotiated between the GoS and SSLM, brought fame to the signatories. This peaceful resolution of the Sudan conflict has rightly been regarded as the most important achievement of the Nimeiri's regime. The agreement put an end to seventeen years of internecine strife and courageously granted recognition to the pluralistic nature of Sudanese society, which had hitherto been ignored by all previous Northern leaders. In granting the South some measure of autonomy within the union, the Muslim-dominated regime acknowledged that the realities of culture, race, religion, and economics would dictate a new approach to the internal structure of Sudan and its constitution.

This recognition was, in fact, the basis for a plan to decentralize the Sudan, especially in the field of economic development. Such a plan had been announced by Nimeiri in 1971. The demand for decentralization was brought about by the size of the Sudan, the immense differences between its regions, and the concentration of economic and political power in the hands of a minority Northern elite. The imbalance of economic and social development in the country had raised repeated criticisms. The central Northern Sudan had been granted special treatment at the expense of the so-called marginalized regions. These regions included the South, Darfur, Kordofan (especially the Nuba Mountains Region in southern Kordofan), and the Beja peoples of the Red Sea Hills in the east. Because of this neglect, attempts had been made since independence by the South and these other marginalized regions to gain autonomy.

The Addis Ababa Agreement provided for equality of all citizens regardless of race, color, or religion. As already mentioned in the chapter on continuity of historical patterns of change, the Agreement recognized the Southern cultural identity and granted the South the right to legislate in line with its traditions, modified by adaptation to the changing environment. Free elections to the Southern Regional Assembly were embodied and the assembly was empowered to elect its own president. However, before it ever took effect, the Addis Ababa Agreement was undermined by amendments to Sudan's 1973 secular constitution. Indeed, after seven years, the end of Addis Ababa Agreement was in sight.

The Regional Government in the Southern Sudan

The regional government created by the Addis Ababa Agreement consisted of a Regional Assembly which was empowered to elect and remove the President of the High Executive Council (HEC), subject to confirmation of the President of the Republic (Chapter V, Article 13. 1, Chapter VI, Article 19). The Regional Assembly could also vote to request the President of the Republic to exempt the Southern Region from any national legislation it considered detrimental to Regional interests. The Agreement granted the Southern Regional Assembly power to raise revenues from local taxation, corporate taxation, business profit taxation, and royalties.

The Agreement further promised additional revenues from the central government. The regional government was specifically denied the right to legislate or exercise any power over economic planning (Chapter IV, Article 7, viii). It was able to legislate on matters of mining, but without prejudice to the right of the central government in the event of the discovery of natural gas and minerals (Chapter V, Article 11, x1v).

The implementation of the Addis Ababa Agreement was hampered by not only by Nimeiri's efforts to manipulate Southern polities and control the economy, but also by divisions among Southern politicians. When the war ended the Southern Sudan economy was in shambles. Agriculture needed rehabilitation, destroyed roads and bridges needed to be reconstructed, and houses and offices needed to be rebuilt. Despite the desperate need, the central government starved the South for funds to carry out rehabilitation of the infrastructures and other important services. The South was very much disappointed and the North-South development gap continued to widen. Even though arrangements for control over revenue from resources and development efforts had been spelled out in formal agreements, a tug-of-war ensued. The central government used its power to withhold funds and withdraw rights. The South, as minority in the national legislature, lacked power to retain those rights. Southern autonomy eroded and changes to the Agreement were made by arbitrary assertions of power by the central government.

The Security Arrangements and Reintegration of Ex-Anya-nya

Both the regional government and the central government were empowered to integrate the *Anya-nya* forces into different branches of the regular armed forces. The SSLM wanted the Southern soldiers to remain in the South Sudan in order to protect the Southern civilians from the Northern army. Southern leaders accepted the retention of an equal number of Northern soldiers to allay the fear of the central government that a Southern garrison made entirely of former guerrilla troops was a potential secessionist threat. The interim provisions for security were set out in a separate protocol (Protocols on Interim Arrangements, Chapter II). The Southern Command was composed of equal numbers of Northern and Southern troops.

The implementation of the security arrangements and the absorption of *Anya-nya* into security branches of the government of Sudan were the most difficult parts of the post-Addis Ababa Agreement challenge. The integration of the guerrilla forces was to take five years. There were to be an equal number of *Anya-nya* and government troops (6,000 each) stationed in the Southern Region. Those *Anya-nya* who were either not eligible or did not want to join the army were to be absorbed into the police, prison services, or wildlife enforcement ranks under the regional government.

Of the ones taken into the Sudan army, many were dissatisfied with the low ranks they received. Those who had wanted to join the army but were not deemed eligible were bitter. They thought the selection process was not fair. Many of the older, more experienced fighters had low formal educational qualifications and did not receive the consideration that they thought their service in the bush warranted. Overseeing the absorption of ex-*Anya-nya* into the army was the responsibility of the Joint Military Technical Commission, made up of senior officers of *Anya-nya* and government army officers.

The pace of absorption was controlled by the central government. Problems began to surface because the pace of integration was proceeding too quickly. There was a need to slow the pace in order to allay the suspicion of *Anya-nya*, since many *Anya-nya* were themselves not happy with the idea of integration into the Northern-dominated army. Some ex-*Anya-nya* soldiers refused to accept integration, and of those not absorbed, some returned to exile in Ethiopia. The regional government made its concern about the rapid pace of absorption known to the central government.

The integration of *Anya-nya* into the army was completed in five years, as stipulated in the Addis Ababa Agreement, but still many remained dissatisfied. Problems continued. While the quota of *Anya-nya* in the army was set at slightly over 6,000, the number of government troops in the Southern Sudan was not reduced to 6,000 soldiers. Senior ex-*Anya-nya* officers were retired early from the army. When the government began transferring ex-*Anya-nya* soldiers out of the South for duty, the remaining ex-*Anya-nya* began increasingly to resist.

In May 16, 1983, government soldiers from Juba Garrison under the Command of Major Kasiano attacked Bor Garrison because the Southern troops at Bor were alleged to have refused transfer to the North. The government of Sudan maintained that integration of ex-*Anya-nya* into the

Sudan Armed Forces had been completed; therefore, these forces could be transferred to any location in the Sudan. Thus, when Southern troops refused transfer, it was considered mutiny. The Bor mutiny generated disastrous consequences for the civil population. Law and order quickly broke down and violence broke out. In the Upper Nile Region (Nuerland), the widespread possession of light weapons drastically increased the destructiveness of the violence. Many Southern Sudanese fled to the neighboring countries as refugees, or to towns and cities in the Northern Sudan as internal displaced persons. Immediately following the Bor mutiny, a presidential order abolished the Southern Regional Government.

The Beginning of the Second Civil War

President Nimeiri had already dissolved the Southern Regional Assembly in 1980. This arbitrary, unconstitutional act was justified by increasing tension between the Dinka and the Equatorians. The Equatorians complained that they were being marginalized in the government by the Dinka. They demanded division of the South into three regions (Bahr el Ghazal, Equatoria, and Upper Nile). Nimeiri liked the idea of dividing the South in order to "weaken" it.

President Nimeiri's Republican Order Number 1 of June 5, 1983, divided the South into three regions. This Republican Order directly abrogated the Addis Ababa Agreement. It was seen as a coup against the Southern Sudanese Regional Government. When Nimeiri reached out to the SSLM in 1972, he gave the impression that he realized, more than had his predecessors, the true nature of the Southern problem and the cultural uniqueness of the region. Yet in fact, Nimeiri had never been genuinely committed to the principles of the Addis Ababa Agreement.

For those who worked to achieve the settlement of the first civil war, the Addis Ababa Agreement was the keystone of the preservation of national unity. For Nimeiri, the Agreement had a completely different political significance. Autonomy was a price he was prepared to pay to the Southern Sudanese in return for their support against his enemies in the North. As the Southern Sudanese began to exercise their autonomy, Nimeiri felt that his role in the South was reduced to that of mere participation in ceremonial activities. He found himself passing decrees or appointing and dismissing Ministers on the advice of the Regional President of the High Executive Council. In the cases when Nimeiri was not willing to rubber stamp regional recommendations, the Southerners stood firm against him. He could not tolerate this defiance, because it came from a power center beyond his jurisdiction. Moreover, he feared such behavior might encourage the institutions of the North to follow suit and play their constitutional role (Khalid 1985).

Nimeiri, to overturn Southern autonomy, used the divisions within the ranks of Southern Sudanese leadership to his advantage. The Dinka dominated the regional government, and this was resented by many non-Dinka. Indeed, it was the Equatorians, unhappy about their subordinate share of power, who asked Nimeiri to effect the division of the Southern Region into smaller autonomous regions in order to let them exercise independence. Although the Addis Ababa Agreement provided adequate means for conflict resolution, it nevertheless was not silent on the mechanics of division. Dividing the Southern Region into smaller regions amounted to an amendment of the Agreement. Article 4 of the Addis Ababa Agreement provided that "the provinces of Bahr el Ghazal, Equatoria and Upper Nile as defined in Article 3 (iii) shall constitute an autonomous region within the Democratic Republic of the Sudan and shall be known as the Southern Region." Thus, the Act speaks of one integrated region. Abolishing that region could be construed as a violation of the Agreement unless the decision to do so were taken in the manner prescribed by the law.

In the end, Nimeiri's treatment of Southern leaders, his high-handed actions toward the ex-*Anya-nya* troops (resulting in the Bor mutiny[128]), and his abrogation of the Southern Region ignited the South against him. Many Southerners again saw armed resistance as their only recourse. Two months after the Bor mutiny, as many as 2,500 Southern soldiers had defected to the new guerrilla base in Ethiopia and another 500 remained in the field in Bahr el Ghazal. This was in addition to the mostly Nuer troops already organized and under arms as *Anya-nya II*. Many old *Anya-nya*, who themselves had opposed the integration into the Northern army, rededicated themselves to separation from the North. At this time, there were some 15,000 Northern troops in the South, supported by American-made aircraft.

The Second Civil War and Loss of Human Lives

The Government of Sudan continued to encourage divisions and chaos in the South by supplying arms to groups functioning as proxies. These groups included Southern guerrillas in the south and east, and Arab militias (*murahallin*) in the west. By 1989, the major guerrilla forces, including

Anya-nya II, had joined with Colonel John Garang's Sudan Peoples' Liberation Army (SPLA). The SPLA's objective was to establish a united, Socialist Sudan, but not a separate, independent Southern Sudan. Its primary support came from the Communist Bloc countries and Communist Cuba, channeled through the Marxist regime in Ethiopia.

The loss of human life through gunfighting, hunger, disease, and other related causes in the second civil war is estimated to be over two million persons. According to reports, most of the deaths occurred in Upper Nile Region, which is the Nuerland (Burr 1993). Many who died were civilian: mostly women, children, and the elderly. This figure is as of 1995, and is considered as an estimate, rather than as a reflection of the total losses in the South. Many deaths from inter-communal fighting have not been recorded.

The 1991 split of the SPLA into Nasir (Nuer-dominated) and Torit (Dinka-dominated) factions led to increased destruction, maiming, and massive killings. Factional fighting spilled over into regional and ethnic conflicts, such as the Jikany-Lou Nuer conflict of 1992-1994 and the Dinka-Nuer conflict of 1991-1999, which took lives in large numbers (Duany, W.; Lowrey; and Duany, J., 1997). The pre-war population of Southern Sudan was estimated at some five to six million. In 1993, the population of Southern Sudan was estimated at four and half million. The UN estimated the population declined by 1.9 percent in 1993, and the excess mortality in that year alone was 220,000.

The GoS and the SPLA factions each have employed different methods of violence to subdue the Southern civilian population during the war.[129] The violent acts committed by the government include: killing civilians; pillaging civilian cattle and grain; burning civilian homes; abducting women and children; and giving impunity to profiteers, whether army or civilian. Abuses committed by the Nasir and Torit factions of SPLA include: indiscriminately attacking the civilians living in the opposing faction's territory; pillaging civilian cattle and grain; destroying and burning civilian homes in the opposing faction's territory; taking food from civilians, directly or indirectly, by force, or by fraud; abducting civilians, principally women and children, from the territory of the other faction; and creating tens of thousands of "unaccompanied minors."

The unaccompanied minors were boys who were originally brought or lured to Ethiopian refugee camps by SPLA with promises of educational opportunities. They then were segregated from their families and trained and deployed as soldiers. Some of the boys had not reached fifteen years old (the minimum age under international law). Later, SPLA-Torit was guilty of similar practices with boys inside Sudan. The Torit faction is guilty of denying unaccompanied minors the opportunity to be voluntarily united with their families.[130]

In addition, both the GoS and SPLA were guilty of placing severe restrictions on relief efforts by international and U.N. agencies. They especially cut off efforts to Nuer regions of Upper Nile that did not fall into either the GoS or the SPLA camps.

Refugees and Internally Displaced Persons (IDPs)

The following sections discuss features of the war experience that are common to the Southern Sudanese population in the South. The Nuer and others have suffered the loss of life, they have been driven from their homes, witnessed the breakdown of the traditional family, seen their children suffer adversity and abuse, and have had their food production and assets stripped from them. The civil war effected an exodus of Southern Sudanese refugees to neighboring countries: Ethiopia, Kenya, Uganda, Congo, and Central African Republic. Over one and one-half million Southern Sudanese are refugees in these countries, and many others have taken refuge outside of Africa. When fighting broke out in 1983 and afterward, civilians all over the South were on the move, seeking safety but rarely finding it in Northern cities such as Khartoum or other locations in the South. It has been reported that up to 85 percent of Sudan's Southern population has been displaced (Winter, 1990). Displacement has a negative effect on the food supply. As starvation increased, thousands died.

The displacement of families and prolonged violent conflict in the Southern Sudan has had a dramatic effect on gender relations. The numbers of female-headed households are increasing. Many women have little choice but to assume the many roles traditionally assigned to men. This is a difficult position for many women in war-torn Sudan to find themselves in. A woman's physical and emotional insecurity increases dramatically with the breakdown of the traditional family and community support systems. The roles and responsibilities of women are drastically altered as they become the sole income earners in the household. Both sets of factors will create problems in the post-war reintegration.

A bleaker picture emerges when the duration of displacement is considered. There is a loss of dignity and diminished hope associated with a long separation as a refugee or displaced person. This also could create problems in the future, since self-confidence and optimism are vital human characteristics for self-reliance and self-governance.

Breakdown of Traditional Family

Sudan's civil wars have contributed not only to the large destruction of life and life-sustaining assets (such as cattle), but also to the erosion of indigenous governance systems. When war and violence disrupt indigenous governance, a degenerative cycle is set in place. A weak and ineffective indigenous governance system allows the spread of lawlessness and criminal violence, which in turn result in poverty and insecurity in Southern communities.

Among the Nuer, shared standards of judgment, having to do with the common sense of justice (fairness), underpin the interactions of mutual trust and accountability. The Nuer local community, as shown in preceding chapters, is characterized by cultural homogeneity with patterns of interaction girded by common history, norms, and values. The civil wars have brought about the cracking of the communal framework. Before the war, everywhere in the Nuerland the individual was more or less integrated into a family, a clan, a cohesive rural unit, or a compact religious or political body. From childhood to adulthood, the Nuer individual never felt alone, never felt lost, and never felt himself or herself to be a speck of life floating in eternity of nothingness. The war has weakened (and perhaps destroyed) this corporate pattern of family and communal life; it has undermined the framework of lawful conduct of communal living.

The civil war has led to the dispersal of people in ways that deeply affected the Nuer traditional family. There are family members who have not been able to reunite for the last forty-nine years (i.e., since 1955). A serious erosion of values stems from declining ability or capacity of the family to function as an effective socializing agent, and from the collapse of the school system in the Nuer Region. One of the most pronounced signals of the erosion of values can be seen in the growing preference for the use of force and artifice, rather than the reliance on achievement through merit and mastery. Children now choose as models those who carry weapons, rather than those who excel in education and demonstrate productive skills. A generational shift in authority relations has exacerbated the decline of the family and further eroded community values. This, together with other factors, constitutes a crisis of order among Nuer young people, which now poses a fundamental challenge in the task of reconstituting the social order to ensure lasting peace and good governance in the region.

Crisis of Southern Children

Children have been adversely affected by the armed conflict in the Southern Sudan. They have experienced their homes being raided and demolished; they have been beaten and abused; many have seen family members beaten, raped, or killed. There is extensive trauma associated with massacres, and children often witness these horrors. Countless children have been separated from their families. Many cope with life-threatening danger in their daily lives. They have been denied education; they endure poor quality living conditions. Social and psychological disturbances associated with children's war-related experiences are commonly manifest in behaviors which include: sleep disorders; concentration impairment; nightmares; withdrawal; aggression; fear of unexpected sounds and movements; clinging behavior; depression; inability to form close relationships; stealing and lying; and lack of trust in adults and/or other children (Riak, G. 2002). Without question, Sudan's war has exerted profound, negative effects on all aspects of the lives of children in the South.

The family is an important institution in minimizing the impact that war has on a child. For instance, if the family remains together, the child can tolerate many deprivations. However, once the family is dispersed and disconnected, such as many families are in the Southern Sudan, then the situation is indeed critical for the child (Riak, G. 2002).

Many children are active in the war. This development is a dramatic change in the culture of warfare among the Nuer. The Nuer tradition protects minors. Boys were not allowed to go to war because they had not yet learned the art of warfare, and also because (1.) a boy's family would not be compensated if he were killed and (2.) if a boy killed any person, then that person's family would not receive compensation. During the civil wars, however, boys have been (and still are) easy targets for recruitment after they have lost parents. Boys are also vulnerable after their school life has been disrupted in their areas. This disruption may include the destruction of school buildings and the conscription of school staff into the liberation army. In some cases, boys have been taken directly from their families and communities by SPLA, and made to perform atrocities as part of a deliberate de-socialization process. In other cases, child combatants have been imbued with a code of ethics that sanctions violence in specific circumstances.

Famine, Asset Stripping, and Disruption of Seasonal Patterns of Life

The general chaos of civil war and the deliberate government starvation strategies are largely responsible for devastating famines in the Southern Sudan. Famine can be considered as an outcome of the political process of impoverishment, resulting either from the destruction of productive assets, or from the transfer of productive assets (including cattle) from the politically weak to the strong.

A number of groups were used by the government to destroy and/or seize productive assets; these groups are chiefly responsible for the famines that have taken so many Southern Sudanese lives. Alex de Waal identified three of the groups that have been vehicles for state policies and utilized as proxies by the government to attack the Sudan Peoples' Liberation Army and its supporters. The use of proxies allows the government to inflict damage at a relatively low cost and without having to put too much military recruitment pressure on Northern citizens (de Waal 1993).

The first group de Waal identified as being government proxies were independent militias, such as the government-aligned Nuer *Anya-nya II,* and the Arab militias (*murahallin*).[131] Their responsibility was to attack supporters of SPLA and take their reward in the form of looted cattle. They were also free to harass and loot famine migrants. The *Anya-nya II* had a political agenda of building a separate state independent from the North, and had sharp political differences with their fellow rebels in SPLA. The *murahallin,* on the other hand, never had a political agenda. The second group de Waal identified was the Sudanese army itself. The army isolated certain garrison towns by preventing citizens to flee and denying food entry in order to create artificial scarcities. The third group were the traders who cooperated closely with the Sudanese army. Since military control over the entry of commodities to garrison towns created scarcities, the situation enabled the traders to extract maximum profits.[132]

The government proxies were not alone in inflicting deliberate civilian devastation. The Sudan Peoples' Liberation Army also employed starvation strategies. Three elements in SPLA's military policy were responsible for creating famine conditions: (1.) the siege of government-held towns, which included obstruction of relief; (2.) raiding and the destruction and looting of villages; and (3.) the forced requisitioning of food from the rural people. The SPLA later modified these policies because of pressure from the UN and the United States, but continued to deny relief food and other health services to areas not supporting SPLA, especially the Nuer regions, both east and west of the River Nile.

Widespread raiding, displacement, and asset destruction did not adversely affect all parts of Southern Sudan simultaneously, but instead created at various times and places situations of extreme instability in which ordinary economic activities and survival strategies became impossible (Mayotte 1992). Crop production, for instance, was drastically reduced in most areas of the Southern Sudan because of the fear of anti-personnel mines planted in the household farms and gardens. The scorched-earth tactics used by both the SPLA and the government military jeopardized food supplies. Both sides burned villages, frequently killing many villagers and their cattle.

Thus, the use of food as a weapon of war in the Southern Sudan has taken a great number of lives. In 1988 alone, more than 150,000 Southern Sudanese died from starvation because military leaders on both sides of the conflict refused to allow food to reach civilian populations they thought were loyal to their opponent. The Northern Islamic-based government hoped that depopulating the South would bring ultimate victory.

The leaders on either side cared little for the fate of the ordinary people. As a priority, humanitarian needs ranked far below the concerns of military strategy and international diplomacy. Only a few thousand victims of starvation were members of the military forces; the greatest numbers of dead were among the women, children, and elderly. One hundred eighty thousand of the dead were children. These segments of the population, the least able to defend themselves, suffered as pawns in the war. The magnitude of their fate was similar to that of the Khmer people of Cambodia during the 1970s.

Because the Nuer reside within one of the primary war zones in the Southern Sudan, their cyclical pattern of life has been disrupted. The Nuer move to cattle camps during the dry season and back to their permanent villages at the beginning of rainy season to grow variety of crops. In this war zone, the population has been repeatedly targeted for raiding by the Sudanese army, the Popular Defense Force (the military arm of the National Islamic Front), militia, and opposing liberation movement factions. The cattle camp only invites raids. Such a large aggregation of people and resources is fool-hardy. Cattle-raiding is intended to deny civilian support to the opposing side.

The subsistence village economy also became an important target. Domestic livestock were captured, houses were burned, and water resources such as wells were destroyed. The split of SPLA in 1991 into factions intensified the inter-factional fighting and the asset-stripping nature of such attacks, where food stores and standing crops have been seized or put to the torch, relief inputs have been captured, and cattle camps have invited attack. As specific populations have been denied the opportunity or the means to feed themselves, they have fled to seek refuge elsewhere.

The pattern of the second civil war indicates that resource depletion and economic subjugation are objectives of the war, not just incidental consequences. The government population pacification program among the Nuer is advanced when villages are demolished in and around the Nuer regions, and when the Nuer are forcibly displaced to resettlement areas along Ethiopian borderlands. These populations are deliberately deprived of economic independence when they are stripped of their capital (cattle and other assets).

The SPLA economic war strategy is similar to that of the Government of Sudan. Concentrations of displaced civilians have been used to attract relief resources, partly to help the displaced persons and partly to feed the SPLA. This strategy was enacted among displaced populations in Equatoria Region and in refugee camps in Ethiopia. This strategy was particularly effective for SPLA in Ethiopia, especially before the 1991 split. It has not been as effective among refugee populations in Kenya and in Uganda, where SPLA does not exert political and administrative control.

Thus, Sudan's civil war is being fought as a resource war. Battles between organized, armed groups with the intention of seizing or holding territory are only one aspect of this specialized form of warfare. Civilians have been systematically targeted for asset stripping raids since the outset of the conflict. The intention has been not only to seize whatever resources the civilians possess, but also to deny these resources to the opposing side. Moreover, entire civilian population is regarded as a resource to control.

The net effect of these disrupting activities has been a massive displacement of population. In some cases, families and groups moved far away from their homes to escape the fighting. In their new locations, they may have no seeds, no equipment, or no cattle for establishing new homes. Thus, they will often move from one place to another in search of peace.

Role of the Christian Church in Peacemaking

Before the foreign Christian workers were expelled from South Sudan in 1964, there were close relationships between the various Christian denominations and the civil society organizations in the Southern Sudan. (These types of organizational relationships did not exist in the wider, and predominantly Muslim, Sudanese society.) There was among Southern Sudanese, therefore, an expectation regarding the role of the church as an institution in the midst of war, displacement, and social breakdown.

The role of the Christian church is that of custodian of values for the Southern Sudanese society. As a custodian of values, the Christian church as an institution has reinforced the traditional principles that have fashioned the political and behavioral orientations of disparate peoples, and the terms under which those orientations are justified. Christian teaching thus became a measuring stick by which social action was evaluated. The institutional role of the Christian church is perceived as mutually reinforcing. The institution has been viewed as the source of values, and because of this perception by the society, it also is seen to be the best judge and authoritative interpreter of social values.

The Presbyterian Church (USA) first began establishing its work in the Nuer country of Upper Nile in 1902. Later, other Christian groups, such the Roman Catholic, Episcopal (Anglican), and Seventh Day Adventist churches, began working in the Nuerland. The aim of these groups was to spread the Gospel of Jesus of Nazareth and to promote Western ways of life among the African population. The effort of the American Presbyterian mission among the Nuer was directed mainly towards evangelism. The training of preachers, catechists, and church leaders for work among the indigenous population was the primary interest of the American missionaries. Education through the medium of the English language was considered prerequisite for

Christian conversion, and the American ways of life was perceived to be important in encouraging proselytization. The whole education system in the Nuerland, therefore, was geared toward promoting the mission of winning Christian converts and civilizing the "savages." This explains the Presbyterians' disregard for technical and secondary education.

The Christian doctrine of the fundamental equality of all human beings before a Creator God was consistent with Nuer traditional covenantal theology. There also was a common belief in the equality of women and men, slave and free, poor and rich, and child and adult. Christian beliefs, however, were institutionalized in a way that Nuer beliefs were not. During the 1950s and 1960s, in reaction to forced Islamization, Southerners were more willing to embrace a Christian identity.

In addition, the Christian missionaries taught that the role of the church as an institution was to call attention to injustice and moral faults in the society. The performance of this function only intensified the conflict between the church leadership and the political leaders of the Islamic faith. Thus, in the Southern Sudan, people came to expect that the churches have a role to play in promoting justice, in seeking reconciliation, in offering forgiveness, and in helping both adults and children reaffirm the process of reconstruction.

After the SPLA split in 1991, in response to the out-of-control violence, the people of the diverse Christian congregations emerged as a formidable grassroots peacemaking force in some areas of the South, particularly among the Nuer. They were armed with the commandment, "love thy neighbor." The historic duty of the Christian to serve in the midst of the suffering and to care for those in need led the New Sudan Councils of Churches in 1996 to formulate a call for peace in the declaration: *Here we Stand, United in Action for Peace*. The churches then took this message to the parties engaged in the civil war and to the world at large. Since the churches began to take action, the realities of the war in the Sudan have been widely publicized and discussed in Europe, the United States, and Africa (New Sudan Council of Churches, 2002; Duany, J. 2003).

Marxism-Leninism and Disruption among the Nuer

The most important issue here has to do with the nature of the relationship between the Sudan Peoples' Liberation Movement/Army and the constitution of order among the populations of the Southern Sudan, particularly the Nuer. The way people think of themselves, their relationships with one another, and their organization are the important ingredients in what constitute a civil society. Some Southern Sudanese have turned their backs on their history and have dismissed the ways their civilization is traditionally constituted. The structure of the institutions of the SPLM/A has consciously ignored the traditional ways of life of the Southern Sudanese. The incompatibility of their program has been obvious to the Nuer, who rebelled against the way the SPLM/A treated them. The following sections describe the disruptive institutions of the Marxist-Leninist order in the Southern Sudan and how the SPLM/A struggled to impose by brute force this alien social system on the Southern Sudanese.

Assault on Indigenous Institutions and Values

While not explicitly a communist party, the SPLM/A, under the leadership of Colonel John Garang, aspired to liberate the Sudanese people from the minority clique of "oppressors" who have dominated governance in the Sudan since independence in 1956. From its founding in 1983, the SPLM/A was supported by the Marxist (Soviet Bloc supported) government of Mengistu of Ethiopia in this endeavor.

Establishing a "Socialist System" in all of Sudan was the main goal of the movement. The SPLM/A and its *Manifesto* were associated with efforts to achieve the salvation of all people in the Sudan, to liberate the oppressed, to eradicate their oppressors, and to transform Sudanese society from a bourgeois one (i.e., a society in which the means of production are privately held) into a "new" Socialist Sudan. This vision comes from the gospel of Marx and Engels as articulated in the *Communist Manifesto*. It explicitly repudiates all religion, morality, and eternal truths. It presumes to act "in contradiction to all past historical experience" ([1848] 1967), yet is as "devoted to Salvation as any Abrahamic prophet" (Ostrom, V. 1992).

A Soviet-style institutional design was adopted by SPLM/A and introduced as the ultimate means of solving Sudan's problems. A class struggle was presumed to exist between "oppressors" and the "oppressed." The struggle could end only in a revolutionary reconstitution of the Sudanese society into a "New Sudan" under the leadership of the socialist elite. The term New Sudan has a familiar ring: Chairman Mao's revolutionary creation was called "The New China."

The SPLM/A's *Manifesto* (1983) divided the world into two camps: the "friends" and the "enemies" of the SPLM/A. Similarly, Sudanese Society was divided into a class system as described in the philosophy of scientific socialism. This system classified people as socialists, revolutionary intellectuals, peasants, bourgeois, or petty bourgeois. The existence of these contrived classes was propagated in the refugee camps in Ethiopia and within the units of fighting men in the Southern Sudan. Class warfare was the gospel drilled into the minds of the Southern Sudanese who were sent to Cuba and other socialist countries for training.[133] Individuals were taught that they always had enemies within close proximity.

The young people were primary targets for Marxist indoctrination. Some Marxist ideas are so radical that the young will only accept them when detached from their indigenous culture, or when traditional cultural relationships are weakened. The drive to recruit child soldiers into the SPLM/A ranks can be partly explained on this basis. The acceptance of communist teachings is greater among the young who are either drawn away from or removed from their parents' influence.

Within the ranks of SPLM/A, some intellectuals claimed that they were the socialist elite. The Socialists were to be the beneficiaries, as well as the custodians, of the SPLM/A revolution.[134] These individuals went about identifying people to stamp as bourgeois, so that they then could be isolated and destroyed (Aleu, 1992). The majority of intellectuals, former government ministers, representatives in parliament, college and high school students, and former military and police officers were all branded as reactionaries. They were considered as the "enemies within the movement" (Oduho, 1992, Aleu, 1992). Traditional Nuer elders were labeled bourgeois by the young and the uneducated. Children and other family members began calling their parents and elders "comrades" in defiance of indigenous, respectful ways of referring to such people in society. A wife was taught to address her husband as "comrade." People began to wonder what that situation would lead to. The new vocabulary was perceived by many as a deliberate policy to destroy the way of life of the different communities in the Southern Sudan. The SPLM/A itself became the ruling class in the areas under its control. Autocracy prevailed; the SPLM/A was to serve as the instrument, and Southern Sudanese civil societies to be the object molded.

Understanding the Need for a New Strategy

The SPLM/A has attained possession of adequate means of coercion and has terrorized the Southern population into passive compliance. It has not managed to wipe out traditions or integrate society around any positive political values. The SPLM/A is able to persist only as long as it successfully coerces, disintegrates, and demoralizes its social environment. Because the cooperation of the civil population is needed in order to carry out the liberation struggle, coercion has not been a successful strategy. Corruption, in various doses, might have worked to secure cooperation for some time with some people, but in the end, it demoralizes both the commanders and the people. Reforms that are able to counter the power interests of the commander class are very few. For some, breaking away from the SPLM/A may be the only recourse.

This happened in 1991, when the SPLA split produced the Nasir faction, the Torit faction, and several minor factions. The split occurred along ethnic lines and had the effect of removing the majority of the Nuer in Upper Nile out from under the direct control of John Garang's Dinka-dominated SPLM/A and its agenda for social-transformation. In 1997, the Nasir faction and several others signed a Peace Agreement with the Sudan government. Riek Machar was leader of the Nasir group at that time (it was re-named the South Sudan Independence Movement). The Southern leaders who signed the 1997 Agreement were given government positions in Khartoum. This move had several consequences. Among them, it politically marginalized the Southern faction leadership by removing them from the field. It also opened the field to a tradition-based grassroots peace movement among the Nuer and Dinka peoples.

The Nuer political, religious, and civic groups have not been able to mobilize resources and come together in sufficient strength to compete with the SPLM/A politically on the national and international levels. Nevertheless, the Nuer and other Southerners are beginning the processes of dialogue and are calling on their leaders and scholars to rethink and to map out a new way for the South to mobilize their God-given resources to win the peace. The quest for self-government and regional self-respect will not be fulfilled suddenly on the day a Sudan Peace Agreement is signed. Rather, it requires that Southern Sudanese people achieve a common understanding. Otherwise, to use de Tocqueville's words, they will be "unable to discern the causes of their own wretchedness and [so] fall sacrifice to ills of which they are ignorant" (Tocqueville [1835] 1945, 1:231). If they are to emerge from Marxist-Leninist tyranny and present a united Southern front in the face of Islamist oppression, the Southern Sudanese people and their leaders are challenged to use their resources better, to think more creatively, to plan more wisely, and pray more effectively. As we shall see in the next chapter, those resources include the traditional constitution of order.

Conclusion

The failure of the Sudanese to reach consensus on an acceptable constitution to govern themselves has resulted in two devastating civil wars. Muslim groups who captured the central government authority dominate the whole society. They imposed an Islamic constitution upon Southern Sudanese Christians and non-Muslims. They imposed Islam as the religion of the state, the Sharia as the main source of public law, and Arabic as the official language of the Sudan.

The heavy centralization of governing structures and the use of the military in support of arbitrary and autocratic governance were the fundamental elements in the situation of institutional failure and civil war. When, after Independence, the Northern government sent senior security operatives, teachers, and merchants to the South to fill the positions once held by British and Egyptian personnel, this move was perceived as an act of Northern domination. Southerners feared this would lead to forced assimilation into Islamic culture. Arbitrary arrests, detention of suspected persons, and destruction of properties led to the exodus of political leaders, students, and leaders of civil society organizations. This led to a net loss of experienced and educated citizens who subsequently became refugees in other countries. Many of these leaders and students in exile joined together to form SANU and the *Anya-nya* guerrilla army to pressure for internal re-structure of Sudan. The geographic size of Sudan, the immense differences between its regions, and especially the concentration of economic and political power in the hands of a minority Northern elite brought about the Southern demand for decentralization.

As the *Anya-nya's* war against the Government of Sudan intensified, the Government of Sudan was pressured both internally and externally to find a peaceful resolution of the conflict. The Addis Ababa Agreement was concluded in 1972. It was abrogated in February 1980 by Nimeiri's unconstitutional act of dissolving the Southern Regional Assembly and its government. The abrogation of the Southern Region led to the second civil war.

The second civil war devastated the civilian population in the South by taking a heavy toll of human life and weakening the social structure. Both the Government of Sudan and the SPLA (and its factions) targeted the civilian population, either to prevent production and/or to seize resources. The same SPLA that aspired to liberate the Sudan from domination by people of Arab descent ended up alienating the Southern people and exacerbating ethnic divisions by adopting and imposing an oppressive, Soviet-style institutional system of order. The desire of the Southern Sudanese is for freedom with justice. The Nuer people will adapt to change, but they will not allow others to impose change upon them.

Chapter 9 - Response to Imperial and Autocratic Challenges

Introduction

Geo-political forces—British imperialism, Islamic dominance, Socialist transformation, and civil wars—have bent and shaped the branches of Nuer indigenous culture; however, the root still lives. The Nuer people continue to fall back on the basic patterns of their acephalous social order for strength to face modern challenges.

How does the Nuer indigenous culture demonstrate its viability in the contemporary world? This chapter attempts to answer this question. We will first consider how the Nuer maintain their autonomy. This will entail consideration of how the Nuer organize their relationships with one another to enable their indigenous development to continue as a society, despite alien disruptions. Second, we will describe how the Nuer build their relationships with the other neighboring Nilotic peoples. Third, we will demonstrate how Christians and Muslim Arabs relate to one another in the Sudan. Fourth, we will explore Occidental influences on the African ways of life.

Autonomy and Federation as a Means to Cope with Imperial and Autocratic Challenges

How the Nuer are able to maintain their autonomy and adapt to the changing environment turns upon the value placed on autonomy and freedom of association.[135] The Nuer perceive freedom as a collective property of the community as a whole. In so far as the citizens rule themselves by actively participating in political decision-making, they remain free both internally and externally. This takes into account the internal dynamics of Nuer social processes as well as the value attached to autonomy and federation. Today, autonomy and federation are a means used to cope with the imperial autocratic system of government in the Sudan.

Autonomy connotes the capacity of human beings to reason self-consciously, to be self-reflective, and to be self-determining. It involves the ability to deliberate, judge, choose, and act upon different possible courses of action in private as well as public life. The idea of an autonomous individual could not develop among the Nuer as long as political rights, obligations, and duties were closely tied (as they were in the European medieval worldview) to property rights and religious tradition (Held 1996). Individual autonomy is closely related to democratic consent.

The Nuer habit of consent giving is a continuous activity permitting perpetual evaluation of individual ideals and beliefs. Historically, Nuer belief was measured against individual experience and challenged by the experiences of other people in ways bounded by a framework of processes. These processes included open discussions and common beliefs, customs, and norms. Public deliberations, the rules of assembly, and decision models were geared to maintaining amicable relationships among the persons involved. Decisions that effected basic ways of life, such as marriage or the location of a cattle camp, were negotiated, as were the traditions on which these constitutional decisions were based. Presumption of equality and consent propelled the development of institutions. Nothing less could have allowed the Nuer to cope with the rapid change they faced in the twentieth century. Their belief system offered a firm moral foundation.

The Nuer world is neither static nor ungoverned. The Nuer tradition perceives the purpose of community as concerned with the well-being of individuals and groups involved (Evans-Pritchard 1956). The individual's well-being is associated with his or her participation in an open public realm in which people engage in a variety of instances of collective decisions in a vital self-governing society. Traditionally, the processes of deliberation aim at broad consensus. Maintenance of consensus requires openness to established modes of discourse and decision-making that distinguishes thoughtful decision-making from mere conformity, indifference, or hypocrisy. The Nuer, as an open acephalous society, work to preserve freedom of action rather than to submerge individual thinking to group conformity.

In Nuerland, the institutions of governance are grounded in the self-organizing principles of the peoples at the local level of village, town, clan, district, and county. These indigenous institutions are organized around principles of democratic autonomy, equality, and individual responsibility. Self-governance must be free from pretense and deceit. Thus, self-organizing systems become democratic self-governing systems because those being governed have equal liberty and equal standing in the constitution of an order where rulership prerogatives are subject to effective limits among multiple agents, each exercising a limited public trust.

Autonomy and Federation among the Nuer

The Nuer commonwealth emerged in response to needs among different clans. The boundaries of their existing political associations were not strictly identified as geographically determined political bodies. In Upper Nile Region, as in other parts of the Sudan, the division of the provinces into administrative districts attempted to follow the divisions of the ethnic groups and their sub-groups. This internal consistency was never fully achieved, for the populations of the region were far too mixed to be contained within administrative boundaries. The creation, for example, of two new states out of the greater Upper Nile boundary produced three separate administrations. This division introduced administrative tensions into the area that further aggravated Nuer and Dinka relations with each other and with the government.

The pre-colonial Nuer confederation was composed of small, almost entirely separate nations. The Nuer understood the historical principles of autonomy. Not only did each province (or clan/region) form a nation, but also each village within a district (or a district within province) formed a little nation.[136] Even the *pek dhoar* or *pek cieng* (the hamlets or neighborhoods) were autonomous polities, each with its own particular interests, minimal government, and its representatives in the village councils. In other words, each autonomous unit has its own political life. Accordingly, laws vary among the Nuer according to local circumstance. (Howell 1954). Even the objectives of regulation can change from place to place. In some respects, the way the Nuer understand the law and rights in different regions poses significant variation in meaning assigned to the terms they use as well as creates important differences in the values emphasized by particulars.

Autonomy and federation have been key elements in the constitution of order among the Nuer. Clans, lineages, and sub-lineages, conscious of their separate identities, have desired and maintained self-governing capabilities, yet have at the same time achieved vital objectives by combining their efforts and domains into a confederation of Nuer, both distinct from and interacting as a unit with other cultural groups. The Nuer confederation is made up of eleven federations based on kinship and local affiliations. The confederation occupies a continuous land mass from east to west containing water and land resources. A confederate council of elders is called in to take leadership whenever the need for joint action arises. The habits of self-governance, the spirit of compromise and self-reliance, and the strong moral basis of Nuer religious beliefs are sources of social capital available to each member of the confederation. Each of the eleven federations has known boundaries, its own police and militia, its own system of law and order, and common language.

The common objective that the Nuer achieve through federation, combined with a division of powers, is the defense of their way of life against the influence of external military forces and external social influence. There is an awareness of a prior covenant of people-hood with a single God and a bond and a hope for the preservation of equality, autonomy, and equal justice among persons. Federation protects individual and communal rights in grazing lands, fishing reserves, and water resources. Military and economic concerns, however, have usually not been sufficient in themselves to maintain the Nuer federation. In William H. Riker's words, "some deeper emotion than mere geographic contiguity with cultural diversity" must be present (Riker 1964).

Nuer covenantal arrangements give individuals the opportunity to take advantage of both large regional organizations and small independent autonomous units. Political units such as villages and/or cattle camps vary in size. The practical reality of the ecosystem and the management of the natural resources often limits the size of units to those that can benefit from ecological niches and variability. The small size of a political unit increases its vulnerability to aggression by more powerful opponents. Federation is one way Nuer resolve this size dilemma. It is a means of securing autonomy and self-preservation. Different levels of organization can combine to thwart aggression and internal corruption. Federation is also used as the means of building the Nuer commonwealth and enhancing collective action.

The people involved regulate the use of natural resources shared by two or more federations. The colonial-era Nuer, as self-organizing and self-governing people, had instituted arrangements for a cycle of conferences to deal with constitutional matters. Prior to Sudan's independence, elders and the chiefs across clan lines met every five years at Fan-gak in the Central Nuer Region to see that basic constitutional arrangements kept pace with their changing environment and to address new challenges to the Nuer way of life.[137] After the Sudan became independent, the representatives of the Government of Sudan in Nuerland discouraged such conferences. The central government viewed arrangements of indigenous governance as a usurpation of central governmental functions. The last conference of Nuer elders, chiefs, and officials was in 1963, nearly 40 years ago. The Nuer way of life did not dissolve with the demise of the Fan-gak federal conference. There were and still are multiple agents with limited authority to resolve conflicts arising between the groups using a resource held in common.

Jikany-Lou Nuer Conflict and Akobo Conference.

A 1992-93 outburst of warfare between the Jikany and the Lou Nuer illustrates how the Nuer way of life has become vulnerable to disintegration and destruction. Patterns of behavior manifested in this conflict violated the historical accepted norms among the Nuer. For example, it is not accepted practice for Nuer to raid other Nuer or to kill women, children, and elderly persons. These categories of persons are perceived to be non-combatants. Action such as burning of homes, destroying property, and killing persons who have run to a private home for refuge or sanctuary were prohibited by Nuer customary law. The Jikany and the Lou Nuer war, however, included the raiding of cattle, the loss of sanctuary, the burning of homes, and the killing of women, children, and elderly persons. Because the combatants used modern weapons, it was often impossible to know from whom the fatal bullets came. Personal responsibility therefore was lost, moral precepts collapsed, and lawful order disintegrated into near anarchy.

The conflict started when the SPLA leadership issued a decree annexing all lands south of the Sobat River to the Dinka Administration in Bor. The Ngok Dinka, Lou Nuer, and Jikany Nuer resisted this decree because it divided their people.

The Nuer consider lands, water, and fish reserves as common properties. However, the Nuer themselves are divided into units of governance. Rights to portions of Nuerland are divided among these units. Rights to resources are further divided among lineages. Each lineage has its own cultivation land, pastures, water supplies, and fishing reserves. Members of lineages alone have rights to exploit the resources.

The Jikany and the Lou represent the two largest Nuer groups on the east side of the Nile. The Lou traditionally have occupied the belt between Kongor and Akobo, including the Ayod, Waat, and Yuai areas. The Jikany are located along the Sobat River, including the Ulang, Nasir, Chotbora, Jekou, and Maiwut areas. Jikany communities extend across the Pibor and Akobo Rivers into Ethiopia. The Lou have their rainy season grazing areas and permanent villages in the area where there is no river. During the dry season, from December through May, they customarily move to the Jikany area along the River Sobat to graze and fish. This suggests a joint ownership of resources by the two communities.

The Jikany have challenged these prior arrangements in recent years, and this has led to fighting over the joint use of these common pool resources during the dry season. Attempts to exclude the Lou from the use of the *tuoch* and fishing grounds were costly, but the feasibility of excluding them from these natural resources was directly related to the willingness of Jikany to bear the cost required to accomplish that task. Property rights acquire effective meaning only when the cost of denying access is worth bearing.

Constitution of Akobo Conference

The war between the Jikany and Lou Nuer was resolved in a September 1994 peace and reconciliation conference held at Akobo. Initially, the constitution of the Akobo Reconciliation Conference reflected the principles of federation and autonomy. The organization of the conference included the assembly of the invited delegates, *ad hoc* committees, and the secretariat of the Conference. The Conference itself operated along the lines of the traditional court. It was a conference setting where anyone could ask questions or make statements from the floor. A technical committee analyzed the issues and made recommendations. One purpose of the Conference was to acquire reliable information about the Jikany-Lou Nuer conflict.

The assembly of the invited delegates consisted of 18 delegations of mediators (Duany, W. 1994). Members of the delegations represented the eleven different federations within the Nuer confederation and specialized groups such as the South Sudan Women Association, church groups and religious associations, and the Nuer in Diaspora. There also were mediators from some of the Dinka federations, including people from Ngok, Twic, and Dungjol. Other people from different parts of the South Sudan also came to help in the process of conflict resolution.

Community leaders from the Liech federation functioned as the court that would hear the case and manage the process of reconciliation in the Nuer way of doing things. Malual Wun Kuoth, an elder drawing on his 44 years of experience as a custodian and official of the Government of Sudan, was nominated to preside at the Conference. The organizing committee to the Conference recommended Malual, and the assembly confirmed him as the Chairperson of the Conference. He was assisted by Yot About, head of the Dongjol

Community Council, and by George Along, the head of Latuka Region of Eastern Equatoria.

The choice of the Liech delegation to act as court was based on the Nuer tradition of inviting an impartial third party to help resolve the problems of the parties in conflict. The Jikany and the Lou Nuer considered the elders and custodians of Liech Region as impartial. Thus, the role of the Liech custodians at the Akobo Conference was a transient responsibility.

The delegates to the conference deliberated issues including:

1. Should both sides to the conflict compensate each other for their losses or should the losses be canceled?
2. Was the administration of Cie-Dhuor Bang and Cie-Dongjak to be under Lou or Jikany administration?
3. The rights to grazing land.
4. The rights to fishing areas.

An open process was used to call forth testimony, free expression of grievances, and wide input to finding solutions to the conflict. Public contestation helped the Conference mediators to learn from one another about the problem they were facing. Both Jikany and Lou were encouraged to argue their side of the dispute in the hearing of the other members of the Reconciliation Conference. Open deliberation was appreciated because it permitted the Nuer to come to terms with the conflict and its resolution in a way that was consistent with their tradition. Public discourse is how they learn to live together in a self-governing society.

The resolution of the conflict over the grazing grounds came about as the consequence of learning from the open discussions on the floor of the conference. Open deliberation provided information and clarified issues. Disputation and contestation were accepted as part of the nature of things at the Conference. In the end, the Jikany and Lou Nuer agreed to share the use of the grazing land as a common pool resource. The agreement was in fact a re-affirming of the traditional pattern of use. The two communities have used these *tuoch* lands as common-pool resources for centuries.

The most important indication that both sides to the conflict perceived the agreement as mutually satisfactory was the sealing of the covenant with blood. Nuer will not accept sealing the agreement with blood if they are not sufficiently satisfied with the agreement. This means that when an approach to the reconstruction of relationships is dominated by reconciliation initiatives that are charades and void of genuine expressions of remorse, the agreement that results will not be accepted.

The spirit of reconciliation signified by sealing the covenant with blood is known in Nuer as *nguot* (singular). The word *nguot* means "to cut." It means here "to cut a covenant." People negotiate and compromise to reach an agreement, but the formalizing element of the *nguot* commitment is the essential element in establishing the renewed relationship among the parties. The Jikany and the Lou Nuer first made a *nguot* commitment verbally to declare the nature of the agreement that was in the making. Even when the Peace Agreement was committed to writing, symbolic action was required to accompany the verbal as well as the written agreement. These actions included the offering of sacrifice by killing oxen in order to seal the covenantal commitment with blood and participating in the feast in celebration of reconciliation. The dismembered animal(s) represent the curse that a *nguot* maker calls upon down on himself if he should violate the commitment he has made. This curse also would include the punishment prescribed by the covenant mediator, designated by God or His representative.

To implement Conference resolutions, including the agreement on grazing land, the Jikany-Lou Reconciliation Conference established a special court, a police force, and a military unit to enforce decisions of the conference. Copies of the Peace Agreement and the creation of institutions for implementing and monitoring the conference resolutions were deposited with every federation of the confederation and other peoples who participated in the conference. The police force, the church groups, the women associations, and the ordinary citizens were the monitoring institutions. The court was to resolve disputes or challenges to the accord.

Building the Future of An African Civilization

Prior to the British colonial period, a number of features could be discerned in patterns of interaction among the peoples of the Nilotic region of the South Sudan. These included the dominant influence of the Nuer over other groups in the region as manifested in patterns of alliances, mergers, accommodations, and conflict; the spread of Nuer language in the Nilotic region; and Nuer territorial expansion. These patterns made for an extended moral community that included neighboring peoples. The Shilluk, however, were located too far from the Nuer to fall within the direct orbit of their influence. The Nuer were a feuding society, but stability in the region rested upon patterns of alliances, mergers, and accommodation of conflicting interests. The processes of Nilotic commonwealth during the pre-colonial era were characterized by autonomy and federation—the prevailing pattern of authority relationships in this region (Kelly 1985).

In order to amplify the constitution of order of the Nuer people—as bequeathed by tradition—the Nuer people need to be cognizant of how to find constructive ways to relate to other language and cultural communities in building the future of an African civilization. Long-term accommodations depend on patterns of reciprocity. Christians and Muslim Arabs, Occidentals and Africans will need to learn to live together in order to cope with the modern world. Open discussions and the efforts of reformers such as the Muslim Imam Mahmud Muhammad Taha (who called for a revision of Sharia that is more in line with contemporary human rights norms) need to be appreciated as providing the foundations for reconciliation.

Autonomy and Federation with the Other Nilotic Peoples

The Nilotic peoples have differential resource endowments. These differences are due to variety in altitudes, rainfall patterns, flood conditions, land types, and vegetation. These variations provide reasons for cooperation, population movement, and the alternation of grazing and cultivation patterns.

The social dynamics working within and among the peoples in the region are accordingly concentrated around the need to minimize the risks of living in a harsh environment. Harmonious achievement of common interests in trading, grazing lands, use of water sources, fishing resources, and other productive endeavors requires development of patterns of interdependencies. This has led to the institutionalization of diverse communities of relationships.

In order to mitigate the effects of adversity, the peoples of the region create voluntary arrangements within a number of regional economies and federations that help to link them together. Markets, trading centers in villages and cattle camps, and towns are the most formal nodes in the voluntary network of exchanges that operate within particular societies and bind together peoples from differing regional economies and climatic conditions.

An association of cattle owners initiated the emergence of a Nuer-Dinka federation. No one knows the exact date of the emergence of the Nuer-Dinka federation, but its existence may be traced back as far as the 1830s. Douglas Johnson (1980) suggested that the Nuer prophet Guek Ngundeang established the right of compensation by cattle. This meant if a Nuer or a

Dinka were killed, then the relatives of the deceased would have the right to claim cattle to compensate the kin of the dead. This rule was instituted in the mid-1800s. The Nuer-Dinka cooperative arrangements may have begun earlier, and Guek Ngundeang only formalized them. In 1839, an Egyptian flotilla succeeded in penetrating the vegetation-choked channels of the Upper Nile, gaining access to the Bahr el Jebel, which was explored as far south as Bor and Aliab Dinka territory (Gray 1961). The report of the voyage indicates that by 1839 the Nuer already occupied both banks of the Bahr el Jebel, which were formerly Dinkalands (Johnson1980).

During the emergence of Nuer federations with the Dinka, herders associated themselves together in cattle camps. *Kuaar* (custodians) of adjacent villages associated themselves in an effort to solve common problems between their peoples. One of the problems was cattle raiding in the *tuoch*. The federation was an attempt to normalize relationships and to make individual members accountable for their actions. Federation as a method of problem solving also was applied to the Anyuak and Murle in the region. Such arrangements were not made with the Shulluk, because they did not have as many cattle as other communities bordering the Nuer. Therefore, competition between the Nuer and Shulluk over the use of common-pool resources was not as acute as compared with others.

Among the Nilotic peoples rich networks of voluntary associations within and between communities frequently involve ties of reciprocal obligations and social contracts. The loaning or bonding of livestock, the sharing of labor, and ultimately the arrangement of marriages, forge sets of more profound and lasting links between individuals and within communities. These functional and voluntary associations are complemented by rules that take account of communities of relationships that were, and still are, multinational in character.

Dinka-Nuer Conflict

The Dinka and the Nuer peoples are the largest in population groups in the Southern Sudan. Of all the Nilotics in the Sudan, they are the closest in their ways of life and language. They live in the same provinces or states in the Upper Nile Region and some parts of Bahr el Ghazal. Intermarriage between the two communities is common. Water points, fishing grounds, and grazing areas are shared in Upper Nile and Bahr el Ghazal. In times of flood or any natural disaster, it is common to find one community migrating to the place of another for safety.

Traditional feuds over grazing areas, water points, and fishing grounds are not uncommon today, but, historically, indigenous methods of conflict resolution were well established and respected. However, the introduction of modern assault rifles into inter-community disputes increased the destruction and bitterness between the Dinka and the Nuer.

Wunlit Peace and Reconciliation Conference

The Dinka-Nuer West Bank Peace and Reconciliation Conference held in Wunlit, Bahr el Ghazal, Sudan from February 27 through March 8, 1999, was a major step in a much larger process. This process is designed to bring reconciliation to many groups and peoples of South Sudan who are in conflict with one another. As this process grows and expands it carries the potential to transform the dynamics of the macro-Sudan conflict.

In June 1998, the New Sudan Council of Churches (NSCC) established an organizing team and hired short-term staff to focus exclusively on the Dinka-Nuer peace process. These are the two major groups, if they will cooperate, who can make a difference to the cause of the South Sudanese. During the initial eight months, the team included field mobilizers and organizers, women, civil community leaders, liaisons from the Sudan Peoples' Liberation Movement (SPLM), the United Democratic Salvation Front (UDSF), intellectuals from the Sudanese Diaspora, and peacemaking facilitators.

Working under the direction of a local custodian, nearly three hundred citizens labored for three months to build an entire village for the peace conference. One hundred fifty *tukul* (houses) and a large meeting hall that could accommodate one thousand people were built. Some food was provided locally; additional food was imported. Extensive arrangements for transportation of participants and supplies were planned, requiring relationships to be maintained at all levels of society: from the local custodians on up to the highest levels of the political movements.

Prior to the Conference an exchange of high profile of leaders took place between Dinka and Nuer areas. This was to make sure the security arrangements were in place in the Dinkaland (where the Conference was held) and to make certain that the Nuer were serious about the peace conference. These visits ignited the enthusiasm of local populations, demonstrating to all that the peace was underway, and convincing the key leaders that security would be guaranteed.

Hundreds of delegates chosen by counties and provinces from Dinka and Nuer communities began moving toward the site. The Conference site became a living peace village with hundreds of security personnel, teams of women cooking and serving each of five "villages," and youth working through the night to service the water needs of a total community of approximately 1,500 people. International observers and journalists were free to observe and report on the peace process. The Conference was co-chaired by Wal Duany (the author of this book) and Dr. Peter Nyot Kok. At the end of the Conference, a total of 318 people signed the Covenant.

Wunlit Dinka-Nuer Covenant

The Conference closed with the signing of the Wunlit Dinka-Nuer Covenant and Resolutions.[138] Each person placed his or her thumb print on the final document, and some also chose to sign their names. The Covenant was sealed with Christian worship and the traditional sacrifice of a bull and festivities. The Dinka and Nuer participants declared an end to seven years of intense violent conflict.

The Wunlit Dinka-Nuer Covenant is a step toward developing a culture of peace, but it does not suggest an aspiration for a society free of disagreements and conflicts. Disagreements and conflicts can also be evidence of a systemic search for solutions to problems. The striving for the development of a culture of peace expresses the desire for the creation of human institutions that will prevent, manage, and resolve conflict. The creation of effective human institutions ensures not only that the fabric of the Dinka-Nuer societies are not destroyed by conflict, but also that their creativity is advanced in the process.

The Wunlit Covenant between Dinka and Nuer is a morally informed agreement or pact based upon voluntary consent, established by mutual oaths of reconciliation or promises, and involving or witnessed by some transcendent higher authority (Duany, W., et al., 1999). The covenant was made to provide for a joint obligation to achieve peace under conditions of mutual respect, which protects the individual integrity of the parties. The Wunlit Covenant, like every Nuer covenant, involves consenting, thinking together, agreeing, and promising cooperation for mutual benefit. Such covenants are meant to be perpetual or unlimited.

In modern law, covenant is defined as a promise or agreement under consideration or guarantee between two parties. It is the seal or symbol of guarantee that distinguishes covenant from a modern contract. Theologically and politically, a covenant is a promise that is sanctioned by an oath accompanied by an appeal to the Deity to see or to watch over the behavior of the one who has sworn, and to punish any violation of the covenant by bringing into action the _lam_ (curses) implied in the swearing of the oath.

The theological form of the Wunlit Covenant relating to the oath is shown in ritual or symbolic act such as the slaughter of the White Bull. Thus, two words used as synonyms for *ngut* in the Nuer translation of the Bible are *yai* and *guk*. The first means oath and the second is used as a synonym for covenant but has its origins in the word *lam* for cursed. This reflects the way in which a covenant embodies mutual oath taking. The oath-taking basis of covenanting is evident in the Medieval Latin term for confederacy: *coniuratio*, with *iuratio* the Latin term for oath (Elazar 1996). Later this was translated into the German e*idgenossenschaft* from *eid*, the German word for oath. Both Nuer and Dinka understand the relationship between covenant and mutual oath-taking.

In its political form, the Wunlit Covenant expresses the idea that the Nuer and the Dinka peoples can freely create or recreate communities and polities, peoples and publics, and civil society itself through such morally grounded and sustained compacts, thereby establishing enduring partnerships. In all its facets, the key focus of Wunlit Covenant is on *relationships*. A covenant is the constitutionalization of a relationship of peace between the Dinka and Nuer peoples. As such, it provides the basis for the institutionalization of that relationship, as is shown in the Wunlit Resolutions that provide for the monitoring and maintenance of the peace.

Christians and Muslim Arabs

Religion has been a continuing problem in the Southern Sudan. The war in the Sudan is not simply a matter of religious differences (Christianity and African religions vs. Islam), but it is made more complex because various factors contributing to violence have found expression in religious terms. Issues such as racial discrimination and the disparity in wealth and power between Northern and Southern Sudan have been perceived by many as inseparable from religion. Government policy since the inception of the Sudan as a nation-state has by and large disregarded the Sudan's multi-religious and acephalous character. Thus, violent conflict has remained endemic.

Common Understanding and Standards of Moral Judgment

Common understandings must exist among Christians and Muslim Arabs as a basis for arriving at standards of moral judgment. Common standards are important because they become the basis for the evaluation of individual conduct as well as for the discharge of public prerogatives. While the difference between Christian and Muslim is acute, common understandings do exist.

First, the idea of one God as the source of Creation has important implications for harmonizing relationships among different cultures. Jews, Christians, Muslims, and some traditional African religions share this idea. A common commitment to the laws of the Creator has significance for the constitution of order in any human society.

Gratian, the Italian monk who codified canon law in the twelfth century, identified methods of normative inquiry permitting the development of impartial standards of moral judgment. He relied upon the concept that, "a principal foundation of all law [is] the timeless principle that we should do unto others as we would have them do unto us" (Tierney, 1982). This is one version of the Golden Rule that is at the core of religious teachings in many religious traditions. This rule might be regarded as "[a] general law, which bears the name of justice" (Tocqueville, [1840] 1945, II: 259). Hillel, the great Jewish teacher and contemporary of Jesus of Nazareth, identified the same basic core of religious teaching when he said, "what is unpleasant that do not to thy neighbor; this is the whole law, all else is its exposition." (Ostrom, V.1991). Similarly, Jesus taught, "Thou shalt love thy neighbor as thyself" (Matthew 22: 39 KJV).

The Koran suggests that the variety in humankind is one of the riches in God's world. Thus the principle is clearly established that God is the God of all Creation, and that one is to recognize and embrace all His children (K. 49:13).[139] The Prophet Muhammad teaches through tradition (the Hadith, the second-most authoritative source of the Sharia) that "one won't attain true faith until he loves for his brother what he loves for himself" (Sahih Bukhari, Vol. 1, Book 2, No. 12). The Nuer Prophet Ngundeng Bong taught the Nuer that "all people are children of (*kuoth*) God" (Duany, W. 1992; Evans-Pritchard, 1956). Whereas all people are children of God, to love thy neighbor as thyself implies that neighbors are equally entitled to a fellow-feeling of brotherhood. Thus, the generalizations offered by Gratian, Hillel, Jesus, Muhammad, and Ngundeang Bong stand as the fundamental principle for constituting self-governing communities of relationships in the Sudan or in any human society.

Second, the key idea is that a covenantal relationship exists between God and those who have chosen to govern themselves in accordance with God's law. Judaism, Christianity, and Islam draw upon the teachings embedded in Abraham's tradition, as well as others. The Nuer govern with similar religious principles. This conception of a covenantal society is consistent with Judaic, Christian, and Muslim teachings, as well as other religious teachings.

It is, of course, not enough to highlight the universality of God's embrace of all human beings. A presentation of the facts will not, of a sudden, arrest the suspicion among the Jews in Israel that Arabs are treacherous assassins, waiting for the chance to put a knife into the back of a Jew. It will not undermine the distrust of Christians in Southern Sudan of Muslims and Arabs in Northern Sudan or *vice versa*. The skepticism is that the appeal to Scripture *per se* is no guarantee that peace and harmony will result.

A basic problem with the appeal to Scripture is the presuppositions that various all-too-human interpreters bring to it. The other is that Scripture itself is a collection of many pieces of writing by many authors at different periods of time. The writings are naturally shaped by each author's personal experience with the Divine and the world. Thus, when one reads Scripture, one should remember that the writer of a given passage claims that God said what is recorded. Thus the encounter with God is necessarily indirect. Carl Evans says, "God is reflected in Scripture, yes, but just as importantly God is beyond Scripture as the living, sovereign deity of the universe" (Evans, 2000).

Nevertheless, there are ways that the embracing of the universal values of scriptures can be integrated in ongoing dialogue among adversaries and injected into the more public discourse in conflicted relationships. Beyond efforts at cognitive and moral persuasion, the international community can increase its pressure on regimes and groups that commit human rights violations or threaten to do so. Reinforced by our understanding of the pro-human ethics of the great religions, advocates of the defense of human rights, including the leading democratic governments, can be made militant for good governance and healthy conflict resolution processes.

Christian and Muslim Arabs in the Sudan

The majority of Muslims and Arabs in the Northern Sudan are expansionists. They also believe in the necessary supercession of Islam over Christianity, Judaism, and traditional religions.[140] Thus, they believe that the government and constitutional system must be Islamic. Muslims claim a legitimate right to rule by virtue of their religious choice, their democratic weight, and their claim to natural justice in order to practice the values and rules of their religion to their full extent in personal, familial, social, and political affairs (Affendi 1991). This drive to implement the Islamic Constitution is a serious concern among the Northern Sudanese liberals, as well as among Christians.

Among the concerned Northern Sudanese are those of the Republican Brotherhood. They do not share the argument that Muslims are unitarian or that the Sudan constitution must be a unitary and/or theocratic document. As far as a resolution to the conflict in South Sudan is concerned, the Republican Brotherhood has advocated a federal-socialist-republican-type of rule. As early as 1955 the Republican Brotherhood called for the division of the Sudan into Eastern, Northern, Central, Western, and Southern Regions. The Republican Brotherhood welcomed as a starting point for a peaceful settlement the Addis Ababa Agreement of 1972 that granted South Sudan administrative autonomy. In 1983, the Republican Brotherhood was the only Northern Sudanese party which called for Islamic Sharia Law to be immediately rescinded after its declaration. The party believes that rescinding Sharia Law is essential for building the necessary trust for peace negotiations with the South.

The form of Sharia that the Republican Brotherhood advocates is based upon Mahmoud Mohammed Taha's controversial *Second Message of Islam* which attempts to reformulate Sharia to take into account a modern sense of community practice (An-Na'im 1986). Taha's approach would mean the evolution of a modern form of Sharia that would be more accommodating to Sudan's diverse population and to the legal, political, and economic challenges of the twenty-first century.[141]

The philosophy of the Republican Brotherhood is based on a modern liberal conception of the Islamic system, including a belief in the equality of the sexes.[142] The Islamists in the Sudan government consider these views heretical. In January 1986, the government of Sudan executed the Republican Brotherhood's septuagenarian leader Mahmoud Mohammed Taha on the charge of apostasy. This effectively removed the possibility of the establishment of Islamic tradition based on federalism under the Islamist regime. To federalize the Sudan will require a radical change of political and Islamic attitudes in the Muslim in the North. Sadly, a cadre of elite who presumes that the autocracy of the early Caliphates is the only possible way of life controls the government of Sudan.

Nevertheless, despite the seemingly unassailable political power of contemporary radical Islamists, there is no necessary impasse between the basic teachings of Islam and the basic teachings of Christianity. In twenty-first century Sudan, Islam faces the challenge of applying the teachings of the Prophets to a republican way of life.

African and Occidental

Many different cultural and historical circumstances have helped shape the lives of the Nuer and other Nilotic peoples. The exposure of the Jikany and the Lou Nuer to larger human experiences has forced them to adapt their thinking. Contacts with the larger world evoked a sense of awareness of their existence within the cultural heritage of the body of human civilization. In other words, they began to recognize that what happens in one society affects others.

The meaning of the past experience has an essential relationship to understanding the Jikany-Lou conflict and the emergence of events in the future. Much, of course, will depend on how ideas inform actions, and what can be accomplished in Nuer society. The key to keep in mind is that the relationships among individuals in the Jikany and the Lou communities occurred through patterns of association with one another. Peace processes were worked out through networks of covenantal arrangements that depended more on mutual understanding and reciprocity than on command and control by central authorities.

Secularism and the Nuer Way of Life

In the course of the nineteenth and early twentieth centuries, as has been shown in earlier chapters of this work, the Nuer world increasingly came under the direct or indirect influence of European expansion and colonialism. Along with political and economic domination came the social and cultural impact of post-Enlightenment Europe. Western laws, systems of education and political institutions were introduced in the Nuerland and formed a parallel network that increasingly competed with the traditional, religiously legitimated institutions such as customary law, marriage law, conflict and conflict resolution methods, and systems of governance.

The significant doctrine that accompanied all these new institutions and ideas was called secularism. It advocated human moral autonomy and a retreat of the moral authority of religion—particularly that of religious institutions—from the public into the private sphere. A process of secularization was believed to have been an essential component of the modernization process in Europe, and now it was viewed as a necessary precondition for the modernization of Nuer society. Secularization is also used in a narrower sense to refer to a doctrine that seeks the separation of religious authority from political power, particularly the state. It may be more accurate to call this doctrine *laicism*, which is a political system characterized by the exclusion of ecclesiastical control and influence (Waterhouse 1943). The idea of secularism was a novelty only in insofar as it propagated a complete break with religion as a source of legitimacy in worldly affairs.

Nilotic peoples implicitly opposed the process of secularization and the idea of secularism from the very start. Thinkers and religious leaders such as Ngundeng Bong of Lou Nuer, Aianhdit of the Abiem Dinka of Northern Bahr el Ghazal, and many Muslim leaders argued against it. What exactly were the objections of the Nilotic leaders to secularization and secularism? To understand these leaders' argument, it is important to realize that it is built on what would be called in Western social science an "idealist" perspective. A basic premise of the Nilotes is that the source of strength of a society is primarily located, not in its economic or military power, but in its culture and in the consciousness of its members. The idea here is that it is of vital importance for any society to remain (with modification and adaptation) loyal to its tradition and cultural self. If it does not, then it will lose the self-confidence which is the source of its self-reliance and power, and it is bound to fall prey to disintegration and decay.

The society, in the view of the Nilotic traditional leaders, is held together not by material wealth but moral solidarity and by loyalty to a generally agreed body of values and norms. The institutions of society—the law, the system of education, and so on—are viewed as organically related to these cultural values. Efforts to replace indigenous institutions by others based on alien, non-indigenous values would inevitably result in a separation between the outward institutional structure of society and the internal structure of the consciousness of its members. This would create a mental cleavage that would lead to alienation and eventually to the disintegration of society.

The British government, in trying to subject the Nilotes and other Sudanese societies, weakened indigenous cultural foundations. The British intent, however, was not to transform Nilotic society, as the Muslim and the Socialist wanted to do, but rather, to govern it. The British government sent Evans-Pritchard and other anthropologists in to learn about the constitution of order among acephalous societies. The lessons learned contributed to better governance of the Nuer in particular. Nevertheless, the lack of correspondence between the structure of indigenous institutions and the formal structure of state is a root cause of the failure of the state (and its attendant conflict) in the Sudan, in Africa, and elsewhere.

The African traditional religious values affirm the "equality of men before God" with their gesture toward the possibility of a community in which no one has superior moral or political rights. The religious affirmation was the only basis upon which values of political equality could be preserved for society as a whole, but this was not always applied without prejudice. On the one hand, the religious vision of equality was, at least, a way of maintaining the vision of a better life. On the other hand, religion was used to justify in human institutions a diverse array of inequalities, including slavery and serfdom.

The British government, during their colonial involvement in the Sudan, did not demonstrate in practice the value of tolerance of different religious groups. Nilotic prophets Ngundeng and Arianhdit became victims of secularization when their peacemaking efforts attracted the adverse attention of the British administration, which saw the prophets as competitors to their own authority. The removal or neutralization of prophets was actively pursued as an administrative policy throughout most of the 1920s, and was effectively completed by the 1930s (Johnson 1994; Majok 1984; Beshir 1968). The suppression of the Dinka and Nuer prophets by the Anglo-Egyptian

Condominium government was followed by the constructions of hierarchies of chiefs and chief's courts within the British system of Native Administration. Because of the information learned by Evans-Pritchard, religious figures were not removed completely from the daily life of the Nuer, but some form of separation between religious and secular authorities was imposed. Regulated and supervised law replaced spiritual inspiration in the settling of dispute. A similar process was experienced among other peoples throughout Southern Sudan. The religious confrontation with the colonial government was more pronounced for some Southern peoples and less for others.

Influence of Judaism in Africa

In ancient times, the peoples of the Upper Nile Basin had contact with those who practiced the Jewish faith. Centuries later, shared ideas relating to principles of organization and relationship are clearly discerned among their descendant peoples (Weiner, et al., 2000; McFall, 1970; Evans-Pritchard, 1956; Steinberg, 1947). For example, an indigenous people of Hamitic origin known as the Agaw live in Ethiopia. Most of the Agaw-speaking peoples are Christian, but the Falasha practice an archaic form of the Jewish faith. The central feature of Falasha religion, common to Jews everywhere, is a belief "in the one and only God, the God of Israel, who has chosen His people and who will send the Messiah to redeem them and return to the Holy land" (Kessler 1985). The Falasha practice male circumcision on the morning of the eighth day after birth, are rigorous in their observance of the Sabbath, and pay meticulous attention to the laws of cleanliness and purity.

The most distinctive characteristic of the Falasha is that they adhere strictly to the teachings of Torah (in particular, the Pentateuch: the five books of Moses). Because of their historical and geographic isolation from the larger Jewish community, they are not familiar with the Oral Law, the Halachah (also known as the Talmud). It is equally a consequence of this isolation that the Torah used by the Falasha is not written in Hebrew, but rather in Ge'ez (an archaic Semitic dialect; also the liturgical language of the Ethiopian Orthodox Church). Falasha synagogues are called *masgid* (a word that means "Mosques" among Islamic people). Whether the Falasha are true Jews, or whether they are "Hebrao-Pagans," has been the subject of considerable controversy since at least the middle of the nineteenth century. Indeed it was not until 1973 that the Sephardi, the Chief Rabbi in Jerusalem, ruled categorically in favor of the Falasha. Two years later the Ashkenazi Chief Rabbi followed suit, opening the way for the Israeli Ministry of Interior to declare that the Falasha were indeed Jews, and thus entitled to automatic citizenship of Israel under the terms of the law of return (Beckwith 1990). Some of the Falasha migrated to Israel in the late 1980s following the declaration of their automatic Israeli citizenship.

Over the centuries, the Ethiopian Jews have had direct or indirect contact with the Jikany Nuer and Lou Nuer in the area. Today, the Black Jews still are neighbors to the Jikany and the Lou Nuer that live to the east of the Nile. Indeed, J.E. Merdinger (1997) observed that for a long time, North African Christianity retained a decidedly Jewish cast. This is another indication that Judaism has had an important influence in traditional Nuer society in shaping the way they think about their relationships with God.

Influence of Christianity in Africa

Saint John Mark the evangelist is reported to have brought Christianity to Africa through Egypt during the first century A.D. The religion spread to Ethiopia, Nubia, and other parts of North Africa. We know that there existed a constant flow of trade between the Christian kingdom of Axum (Abyssinia/Ethiopia) and the African interior (Tafla 1967).

Early Christian contact with the Meroitic Empire to the south of Egypt is mentioned in the New Testament. Acts 8:26-40 records the story of a Meroitic court official. This man, a eunuch with authority over the queen's treasury, visited Jerusalem with a strong desire to workshop the One True God. He purchased a scroll of the Book of Isaiah and read it. According to Biblical scholars, the scroll was the Septuagint translation of the Old Testament into Greek. This language was taught and maybe even spoken at the Meroitic Court (Werner, et al., 1988). There also was Meroitic contact with a Jewish colony on Elephantine Island opposite to modern Aswan. These Jews may have provided the knowledge of the One and Only God (in contrast to the many gods of ancient Egypt and Meroe), which had reached all the way to the Meroitic capital. This would be the most natural explanation for the court official's interest in traveling to Jerusalem and worshipping the God of Abraham, Isaac, and Jacob.[143]

Thus it seems clear that it was a Meroitic court official who heard the Gospel of Jesus from the deacon Philip and brought back this new found faith to the Meroitic capital of Napata. This Sudanese man was therefore the first recorded non-Jewish believer in Jesus of Nazareth, before the Roman centurion came to faith as reported in Acts 10, and long before the Gospel reached Europe. Therefore, the message of Jesus was sown in Sudanese soil only a few years after the crucifixion and resurrection of Jesus of Nazareth, certainly before the year A.D. 40. However, there is no evidence that any Christian community sprang up in Meroe at this time (ibid).

The Meroitic Empire collapsed and was succeeded by a Nubian Kingdom. Nubia is the name given to the stretch of land along the Nile River starting from Aswan all the way down to the confluence of the Blue and White Niles near modern Khartoum. Nubia is the land in the Nile valley between the first and the sixth cataracts. In the period between the fifth and the fourteenth century, it was the homeland of the Nubian people, who organized themselves first into three and then into two kingdoms. Some Biblical scholars say that the influence of the Nubian Christian kingdoms was not confined to the Nile valley, but extended even further South, and well into Western and Eastern Sudan. It encompassed at certain times, part of the Nuba Mountain and Darfur regions, and bordered on the Christian kingdom of Axum in the southeast (Werner, et al., 2000).

Modern Christianity came in contact with the Nuer people during the nineteenth century. The Nuer found Christianity, as delivered by the Presbyterian denomination, to be a "democratic and republican religion," which they deemed comparable to their own conception of religion. The practice of Presbyterian Christianity is similar to the Nuer indigenous religion in that both emphasize that divine covenants bind people together (Robertson 1980). Through the covenant, persons are committed to one another. *Nhok* (divine love), ritual efficacy, and sin are all common elements in the Nuer covenantal theology. These values and rules are rooted in the belief that the *cak* (creation) is an expression of God's loving kindness.

The Nuer covenantal theology has a profound influence over the way the Nuer constitute their relationships with one another. Equality pervades all their institutional arrangements. Among the Nuer, the indigenous idea of man created in the image of God provides a basis for affirming the dignity of individuals, human rights, and democratic procedures. It suggests that human beings have a God-given dignity and worth that unite humanity in a universal covenant of rights and responsibilities within the family of God. The perspective of the covenantal approach is used in organizing their life as a cause-and-effect factor, and in generating a configuration of indigenous institutions that has assisted in adaptation to the changing environment of the modern world. All persons are entitled to the essential conditions for expressing their human dignity and for participation in defining and shaping the common good. The Nuer render to other people their due because of their loving respect for their God-given dignity and value of humanity.

Conclusion

The Nuer people have endured the encroachments of nineteenth and twentieth century conquerors: European/Christian, Arab/Islamic, and Marxist/Leninist. These have taken a toll, but also they have delivered benefits. These encroachments are human events, and apart from how we may judge them, they are part of the universe of cultural evolution. At least now, the Nuer have gained first-hand experience with the devastating consequences of colonial subjugation, *jihad*, and social experimentation based on the theories of Western intellectuals. As a result, they are gaining a new appreciation for the time-tested values of their ancestors. In this chapter we have demonstrated that the Nuer acephalous order with modification has so far preserved and expanded substantive freedom for the Nuer people. The covenantal way of organizing life is a causally effective factor in generating a configuration of indigenous institutions that has assisted the Nuer in adaptation to imperial and autocratic challenges.

Autonomy and federation have been key elements in the constitution of order among the Nuer. Clans, major lineages, and minimal lineages, each conscious of their separate identities, have desired and maintained self-governing capabilities. Yet, they have achieved vital objectives by combining their efforts and domains into a confederation, both distinct from and interacting as a unit with other cultural groups.

The Nuer as a people accept the principle of resolving conflicts through mediation. The Jikany–Lou Nuer conflict is a case to illustrate the method of traditional conflict resolution. However, in building the future of an African civilization, the Nuer need to be cognizant of how to find constructive ways to relate to other language and cultural communities. Long-term accommodations depend on patterns of reciprocity. Christians and Muslim Arabs, Occidentals and Africans will need to learn to live together and lay a foundation for reconciliation.

Contact with the Islamic and the Occidental worlds has opened the door for the emergence of new customs, mores, and beliefs that have become part of the process of adaptation and transformation of Nuer traditional society, along with the development of commerce in exchange relationships, education, church, and other institutions. The viability of the Nuer way of life—how the Nuer society has transformed in the past, how it is connected today, and how it will adapt to change in the future—depends upon the integrity of its organizing principles.

For now, the Nuer must work together to overcome the setbacks caused by decades of civil war, poverty, disease, illiteracy, and dependence upon international relief. The external political environment complicates these internal struggles. If the Nuer are able to free themselves from those who would today subject them to mass enslavement in uniformitarian dictatorships, then perhaps they can build upon their self-governing capabilities to realize undreamed of social, economic, technologic, and political possibilities. Whether or not these possibilities include the architecture of palaces or prisons is for the Nuer to decide.

About the Author

Wal Duany was born in Akobo, Upper Nile, Sudan. He received his M.A. degree in International Politics with a concentration in the Middle East from Syracuse University, and his Ph.D. from a joint Ph.D. program of the Department of Political Science and School of Public and Environmental Affairs, Indiana University.

He has held a number of positions in the Government of Sudan: Regional Minister for Cabinet Affairs in the High Executive Council, Regional Director of Regional Minister of Finance and Development, Controller of Regional Peoples Assembly, Chairman and Managing Director of Southern Sudan Regional Development Corporation, and a member of the National and Regional Assemblies.

Wal Duany is a mediator and a consultant on negotiations and conflict resolution, and helps to resolve disputes and assist negotiators to be more effective.

He is a former Research Associate in the Workshop in Political Theory and Policy Analysis at Indiana University, where he worked on Comparative Customary Law and Development.

Photo: Wal Duany, taken in Akobo, Southern Sudan, during the 1960s

Notes Regarding Nuer Oral Traditional Texts

The Nuer Oral Traditional Texts are a collection of interviews, songs, and stories that I recorded from the Nuer peoples, both in Africa and in the United States. Interviews cited in the text of this work are indicated as follows:

A

Interview with Manaseh Abraham on September 15, 1989, in Khartoum.

B

Interviews with Thigin Banak during August and September 1989.
Interview with Wicjal Bum in Khartoum during September 1989. Wicjal was an old administrator in the Sudan for a very long time.

C

Interviews with Kor Can on August 26, 1989.
Interview with David Chang on September 23, 1988 in Atlanta, Georgia.
Interview with Michael Cot on October 13, 1989 in Khartoum.

D

Interviews with Yoal Dok during September 1989, in Khartoum. Yoal Dok is former governor of Upper Nile Region and a citizen of Gun primary section of Lou Nuer.
Personal communication received in 1983 from Thabac Duany of Juba, Sudan.
Interview with Rev. Kang Dung on September 12, 1989, in Kosti, Sudan.

G

Interview with Magany Gai in October 1988 in Atlanta, Georgia and October 1989 in Khartoum.
Interviews with Gatluak Gatloa during September 1989 in Khartoum.
Interview with Mabor Gatluak during October 1989 in Khartoum.
Interview with Riel Gatluak on September 13, 1989, in Kosti, Sudan.

J

Interviews with Koryom Jal of Lak Nuer during August and September 1989 in Khartoum.

K

Interview with Nyagony Kek on September 25, 1989, in Khartoum.

Interviews with Riek Kerjok during September 1989 in Khartoum.

Interview with Chief Luak Kok during late 1989 in Khartoum.

Interviews with Lutlut Kok during August and September 1989 in Khartoum.

Interviews with Tap Lia Kon during September 1989 in Khartoum.

Interview with Ezekiel A. Kutjiok on September 15, 1989 in Khartoum.

M

Interview with Gai Majoak on September 2, 1989.

Interviews with Rev. Thomas Maluit during October 1988, in Atlanta, Georgia, and September 1989, in Khartoum.

R

Interview with Cuol Rambang on July 15, 1996, in Nairobi, Kenya.

Interview with Koang Reth during October 1989 in Khartoum.

Interview with Andrew Wieu Riak during January 2004, in Syracuse, New York.

Interview with Pal Riek on August 25, 1989 in Khartoum.

Interviews with Nyang Rundial during August and September 1989 in Khartoum.

T

Interview with Thoan Teny on September 17, 1989, in Khartoum.

Bibliography

Abdel-Rahim, M. (1968) *The Development of British Policy in the Southern Sudan, 1899-1947*. Khartoum: University of Khartoum Press.

Affendi, Abdelwahab El. (1991) *Turabi's Revolution: Islam and Power in Sudan.* London: Grey Seal.

Albino, Oliver. (1970) *The Sudan: A Southern View*. London, England: Oxford University Press.

Aleu, Dhol Acuil. (1992) "Leadership and Political Crisis in SPLM/SPLA: A Contribution Towards Solution." Rome, Italy: Sudan Peoples Liberation Movement/Sudan Peoples Liberation Army.

Alier, Abel. (1990) *Southern Sudan: Too Many Agreements Dishonoured.* London: Ithaca.

Allen, Barbara. (2005) *Tocqueville, covenant, and the democratic revolution: harmonizing earth with heaven.* Lanham, MD: Lexington Books.

An-Na'im, Abdullahi Ahmed. (1985) "The Elusive Islamic Constitution: The Sudanese Experience." Orient 26/3 (September): 329-39.

———. (1986) "The Islamic Law of Apostasy and Its Applicability: a Case From the Sudan." Religion, 16: 197-224.

———. (1987) "National Unity and the Diversity of Identities." The Search for Peace and Unity in the Sudan (pp. 71-77). Francis Deng and Prossor Gifford (eds.). Washington DC: Woodrow Wilson Center Press.

Barbour, K.N. (1961) *The Republic of the Sudan.* London: University of London Press Ltd.

Barkun, Michael. (1968) *Law Without Sanctions: Order in Primitive Societies and the World Community*. Yale University Press.

Beckwith, Carol. (1990) *African Ark: People and Ancient Cultures of Ethiopia and the Horn of Africa*. New York: H. N. Abrams.

Beshir, M. O. [Mohamed Omer]. (1968) The Southern Sudan; background to conflict. New York, F. A. Praeger.

Berman, Harold J. (1983) *Law and Revolution : The Formation of Western Legal Tradition*. Cambridge, Massachusetts and London, England: Harvard University Press.

Burr, J. Millar. (1993) "Quantifying Genocide in the Southern Sudan, 1983-1993." Washington, D.C: U.S. Committee for Refugees.

Cabral, Amilcar. (1970) "National Liberation and Culture." Speech delivered on February 20, 1970 at Syracuse University, Syracuse, New York, under the auspices of The Program of Eastern African Studies. It was translated from the French by Maureen Webster. See http://www.cwo.com/~lucumi/cabral.html (accessed 26 January 2005).

Chaliand, Gérard. (1982) *The Struggle for Africa: Conflict of the Great Powers*. New York : St. Martin's Press.

Coleman, James S. (1988) "Constitutions and the Construction of Corporate Actors." Paper presented at the Colloquium at the Workshop in Political Theory and Policy Analysis. Bloomington, Indiana: Indiana University.

Colson, Elizabeth. (1974) *Tradition and Contract: the Problem of Order*. Chicago: Aldine.

Collins, Robert O. (1968) "Autocracy and Democracy in the Southern Sudan: The Rise and Fall of the Chiefs' Courts." In Arnold Rivkin (ed.), *Nations by Design* (pp. 154-178). New York: Doubleday and Company.

Commons, John Rogers. (1950) *The Economics of Collective Action*. New York: Macmillan.

———. ([1924] 1959) *Legal Foundations of Capitalism*. Madison: University of Wisconsin Press.

Coriat, Percy. (1993) "Governing the Nuer: documents by Percy Coriat on Nuer history and ethnography, 1922-1931." Edited and introduced by Douglas Johnson. *Journal of Anthropological Society of Oxford*: Occasional Papers 9. Oxford: JASO.

Crazzolara, J. P. (1933) "Outlines of a Nuer Grammar." *Modling*. Instituti Anthropos.

———. (1953) *Zur Gesellschaft und Religion der Nueer.* Wien-Mödling: Missionsdruckerei St. Gabriel.

David, N. (1982) "Prehistory and Historical Linguistics in Central Africa: Points of Contacts." In *The Archaeological and Linguistic Reconstruction of African History*. Edited by C. Ehret and M. Posnansky. Los Angeles: CA.

Davidson, Basil. (1992) *The Black Man's Burden: Africa and the Curse of the Nation-State.* New York: Times House, a Division of Random House, Inc.

Demsetz, Harold. (1967) "Toward a Theory of Property Rights." *American Economic Review*, Vol. 57 (May): 347-459.

Deng, Francis Mading (1986) *Seed of Redemption: A Political Novel*. New York: Lilian Barber Press.

de Waal, Alex. (1993) "Some Comments on Militias in Contemporary Sudan." In M.W. Daly and Ahmad Alawad Sikainga (eds.) *Civil War in the Sudan*, London: British Academic Press: 145-146.

Douglas, Mary. (1980) *Edward Evans-Pritchard*. New York: Viking Press.

———. (1986) *How Institutions Think*. Syracuse, New York. Syracuse University Press.

Duany, Julia. (1996) "Sudanese Women and Education: A Struggle for Equal Access and Participation." Ph.D. Dissertation. Bloomington, Indiana: School of Education, Indiana University.

———. (1997) "Making Peace: A Report on Grassroots Peace Efforts by Women in South Sudan." *African Journal of Institutions and Development (AJID)*. Ile-Ife, Nigeria: Obafemi Owolowo University, Vol. 3, Nos. 1 & 2, pp. 19-34.

———. (2003) "South Sudan: People-to-People Peacemaking: A Local Solution to Local Problems." In Mary Ann Cejka and Thomas Bamat (eds.), *Artisans of Peace: Grassroots Peacemaking among Christian Communities*. Maryknoll, New York: Orbis Books.

Duany, Wal. (1992) "Neither Palaces Nor Prisons: The Constitution of Order Among the Nuer." Ph. D. Dissertation. Indiana University, Bloomington, Indiana: Department of Political Science and School of Public and Environmental Affairs.

———. (1994) "Jikany and Lou Nuer Reconciliation Conference." A Report for Briefing the African Bureaus of the Department of State, National Security Council, Congressional Committee on Africa, and the Non-Governmental Organization Community. November 15-18 (Washington, DC). Indiana University, Bloomington, Indiana: Workshop in Political Theory and Policy Analysis.

———. (1999) "Customary Law and Ways of Life in Transition Among the Nuer." In Maryam Niamir-Fuller (ed.), *Managing Mobility in African Rangelands: The Legitimization of Transhumance*. London: Intermediate Technology Publications.

Duany, Wal, et al. (1999) Wunlit Dinka/Nuer Peace Documents. Nairobi, Kenya: New Sudan Council of Churches. Also see http://www.southsudanfriends.org/wunlit/index.html (accessed 26 January 2005).

Duany, Wal and Peter Nyot Kok. (1999) "The Diaspora Briefings: A Report on the Wunlit Dinka-Nuer Peace and Reconciliation Conference." Nairobi, Kenya: New Sudan Council of Churches.

Duany, Wal, William O. Lowrey, and Julia A. Duany. (1997) "The Indigenous Peace Process: A Case Study of the Jikany/Lou Nuer Conflict and its Resolution." Indiana University, Bloomington, Indiana: Workshop in Political Theory and Policy Analysis.

Ehret, C. (1974) *Ethiopians and East Africans*. Nairobi. Kenya

———. (1982) "Population Movement and culture contact in the Southern Sudan, c.300 BC to 1,000 AD: A Preliminary Linguistic Overview." In *Culture History in Southern Sudan*. Edited by J. Mack and P. Robertshaw. Nairobi, Kenya

Elazar, Daniel J. (1996) *The Covenant Tradition in Politics: and Commonwealth*. New Brunswick: Transaction Publishers.

Equatorial Nile Project. (1954) *The Equatorial Nile Project*. 4 bd. n.p. Khartoum. n.d. Maps and Diagrams, map E 12 (1954).

Evans, Carl. (2000) "The Scriptural Basis for Peace among Islam, Judaism, and Christianity." In Raymond G. Helmick, S. J. and Rodney L. Petersen (eds.), *Forgiveness and Reconciliation: Religion, Public Policy and Conflict Transformation* (chapter 5: p.108). Foreword by Desmond M. Tutu.. Philadelphia and London: Templeton Foundation Press.

Ekechi, F.K. (1989) *Tradition and Transformation in Eastern Nigeria*. Kent, Ohio: Kent State University Press.

Ellickson, Robert C. (1986) "Of Coase and Cattle: Dispute Resolution Among Neighbors in Shasta Country." *Stanford Law Review*, Vol. 38 (February): 623-687.

Epstein, A. L. [Arnold Leonard]. (1974) *Contention and dispute: aspects of law and social control in Melanesia*. Canberra: Australian National University Press; Portland, Oregon: International Scholarly Book Services.

Evans-Pritchard, Edward, E. (1940) *The Nuer: A Description of Modes of Livelihood and Political Institutions of a Nilotic People*. Oxford: Clarendon Press.

———. (1951) *Kinship and Marriage Among the Nuer*. Oxford: Clarendon Press.

———. (1956) *Nuer Religion*. Oxford: Clarendon Press.

Frank, S. L. (1987) *The Spiritual Foundations of Society: An Introduction to Social Philosophy*. Translated from Russian by Boris Jakin. Athens, Ohio: Ohio State University Press.

Fuli, Severino. (2002) *Shaping A Free Southern Sudan: Memoirs of Our Struggle 1934-1985*. Limuru, Kenya: Kolbe Press.

Gasser, Adolph. (1939) *Geschichte der Volksfreihit und der Demokratie* [*History of Freedom and Democracy*]. Aarau, Switzerland: Verlag H.R. Sauerlaender.

Glickman, Maurice. (1972) "The Nuer and the Dinka: A Further Note." *Man* (New Series), Vol. 7, No. 4 (December): 587-594.

Gluckman, Max. (1955) *The Judicial Process among the Barotse of Northern Rhodesia*. Manchester: The Manchester University Press.

Goody, Jack and S. J. Tambiah. (1973) *Bridewealth and dowry*. Cambridge Papers in Social Anthropology, No. 7. Cambridge: Cambridge University Press.

Gowlett, J.A.J (1988) "Human Adaptation and Long-Term Climatic Change in Northeast Africa: An Archaeological Perspective." In *Ecology of Survival*. Edited by Douglas Johnson and David Anderson. London: Lester Crook Academic Publishing.

Gray, Richard. (1961) *A History of the Southern Sudan, 1839-1889*. London: Oxford University Press.

Gulliver, P. H. (1963) *Social Control in an African Society*. Boston: Boston University Press.

Held, David. (1996) *Models of Democracy. Second Edition*. Cambridge: Polity Press in association with Blackwell Publishers Ltd, Oxford UK.

Hoebink, Michael. (1998) "Thinking About Renewal in Islam: Towards A History of Islamic Ideas on Modernization and Secularization." Utrecht University.

Holt, P. M. [Peter Malcolm]. (1958) *The Mahdist state in the Sudan, 1881-1898: a study of its origins, development and overthrow*. Oxford, Clarendon Press.

Howell, P. P. (1954) *A Manual of Nuer Law: Being a Account of Customary Law, Its Evolution and Development in the Courts Established by the Sudan Government*. London: Oxford University Press.

Hubert, Henri and Marcel Maus. ([1899]1968) "Essai Sur la nature et les fonctions du Sacrifice." In *Oeuvres I*, Paris (First published in L'Annee Sociologique, 2 1899). English ed., *Sacrifice: Its Nature and Function*, London, 1964, 9-94.

Human Rights Watch/Africa. (1994) *Civilian Devastation: Abuses by all Parties in the War in Southern Sudan*. New York: Human Rights Watch/Africa.

———. (1995) *Children of Sudan: Slaves, Street Children, and Child Soldiers*. New York: Human Rights Watch/Africa.

Hurst, H. E. and P. Phillips. (1957) *The Nile Basin*. London: Constable.

Hutchinson, Sharon. (1988) "The Nuer in Crisis: Coping with Money, War and the State." Ph. D. Thesis. University of Chicago, Chicago, Illinois: The Division the social sciences, Department of Anthropology.

———. (1996) *Nuer Dilemmas: Coping with Money, War, and the State*. Berkeley: University of California Press.

Jal, Gabriel Giet. (1987) "The History of the Jikany Nuer before 1920." Ph.D. Dissertation. University of London, London, England: School of Oriental and African Studies.

Jackson, H. C. (1923) "The Nuer of the Upper Nile Province." *Sudan Notes and Records*, Vol. 6, No. 1 and Vol. 6, No. 2 (Part C).

Johnson, Douglas H. (1979) "Colonial Policy and Prophets: The Nuer Settlement 1929-1930." *Journal of the Anthropological Society of Oxford*. Vol. 10:1-20.

———. (1980) "History and Prophecy Among the Nuer of the Southern Sudan" (Parts 1 and 2). Ph.D. Thesis. Los Angeles: Graduate School, Department of History, University of California. Ann Arbor, Michigan and London: University Microfilms International.

———. (1994.) *Nuer Prophets: A History of Prophecy From the Upper Nile in the Nineteenth and Twentieth Centuries*. Oxford: Clarendon Press.

———. (2003) *The Root Causes of Sudan's Civil Wars.* Oxford: James Currey, Bloomington and Indianapolis. Indiana University Press and Fountain Publishers, Kampala.

Johnson, Douglas H. and David M. Anderson, eds. (1988) *The Ecology of survival: case studies from northeast African history.* London, England: L. Crook Academic Pub.; Boulder, Colorado: Westview Press.

Kaminski, Antoni Z. (1992) *An Institutional Theory of Communist Regimes: Design, Function, and Breakdown.* San Francisco, California: ICS Press.

Kelly, Raymond C. (1985) *The Nuer Conquest: The Structure and Development of an Expansionist System.* Ann Arbor: The University of Michigan Press.

Kerreri, S. G. S. (1931) (Office of the Western Nuer District Administration) "Western Nuer District Notes." *Upper Nile Province Handbook*, chapter 3. Durham: University of Durham, School of Oriental Studies, Sudan Archives, 212/14/9.

Kessler, David. (1985) *The Falashas: The Forgotten Jews of Ethiopia.* New York: Shocken Books.

Khalid, Mansour. (1985) *Nimeiri and the Revolution of Dis-May.* London, Boston, Melbourne and Henley: KPI Limited.

Khogali, Mustafa M. (1978) "Nomads and their Sedentarization in the Sudan." Khartoum: Department of Geography, University of Khartoum. (Unpublished manuscript).

Kidder, Robert L. (1983) *Connecting law and society : an introduction to research and theory.* Englewood Cliffs, N.J.: Prentice-Hall.

Kiser, Larry; Ostrom, Elinor (1982). "The Three Worlds of Action, A Metatheoretical Synthesis of Institutional Approaches." In Ostrom,

Elinor, ed. (1982), *Strategies of Political Inquiry*. Beverly Hills: Sage.

Kok, Peter Nyot. (1996) *Governance and Conflict in the Sudan, 1985-1995, Analysis, Evalution and Documentation.* Hamburg: Deutsches Orient-Institut, Mitteilungen 53.

Llewellyn, Karl N. and E. Adamson Hoebel. (1941) *The Cheyenne Way: conflict and case law in primitive jurisprudence*. Norman: University of Oklahoma Press.

Lesch, Ann Mosely. (1998) *The Sudan : Contested National Identities*. Bloomington and Indianapolis: Indiana University Press and James Currey, Oxford, England.

Lienhardt, R. Godfrey. (1975) "Getting Back Your Own: themes in Nilotic myth" In J.H.M. Beattie and R. Godfrey, *Studies in Social Anthropology: Essays in Memory of Evans-Pritchard by Former Oxford Colleagues.* Oxford: Oxford University Press.

Lugard, F. D. (1930) *The Dual Mandate in British Tropical Africa, 1858-1945*. Edinburgh and London, W. Blackwood and Sons.

Mahmud, Ushari Ahmad. (1983) *Arabic in the Southern Sudan: History and Spread of a Pidgin-Creole.* Khartoum, Sudan: FAL Advertising and Print. Co.

Majok, Damazo Dutt. (1984) "Resistance and Cooperation in Bahr el Ghazal 1920-1922", In M. O. Beshir (ed.), *Southern Sudan: Regionalism and Religion.* Selected Essays, Khartoum: University of Khartoum, Graduate College.

Makec, John Wuol. (1988) *The Customary of the Dinka People of Sudan*. London: Afroworld Publishing Company.

Marx, Karl [and] Friedrich Engels. ([1848] 1967) *The Communist Manifesto.* Penguin.

Mather, Lynn and Barbara Yngveson. (1980-81) "Language, Audience, and the Transformation of Disputes." *Law and Society Review*, Vol. 15, No. 3-4: 775-825.

Mayotte, Judy. (1992) *Disposable People: The Plight of Refugees*. Maryknoll, New York: Orbis Books.

McFall, Ernest A. (1970) *Approaching the Nuer of Africa Through the Old Testament*. South Pasadena, California: William Carey Library.

McGinnis, Michael D. (1999) _Polycentric Governance and Development*. Ann Arbor: The University of Michigan Press.

Merdinger, J.E. (1997) *Rome and the African Church in the Time of Augustine*. New Haven and London: Yale University Press.

Middleton, John and David Tait, eds. (1970) *Tribes Without Rulers: Studies in African Segmentary Systems*. London : Routledge & Paul.

Montesquieu, Charles de Secondat. ([1748] 1949) *The Spirit of the Laws*. New York: Hafner Pub. Co.

Neryl, Lewis. (1995) "Women and Children the Recovery Process" In Geoff Harris (ed.), *Recovery from Armed Conflict in Developing Countries: and Economic and Political Analysis*. London and New York: Routledge.

Newcomer, Peter J. (1972) "The Nuer are Dinka: an Essay on Origins and Environmental Determinism." *Man* (New Series). Vol. 7, No. 1 (March): 5-11.

New Sudan Council of Churches. (2002) *Let Justice Prevail: Position Papers of the Sudanese Churches on Peace and Self-determination*. Khartoum and Nairobi: A Co-Publication of the Sudan Council of Churches and the New Sudan Council of Churches.

Niamir-Fuller, Maryam (ed.), (1999) *Managing Mobility in African Rangelands: The Legitimization of Transhumance*. London: Intermediate Technology Publications.

North, Douglass C. (1990) *Institutions, Institutional Change, and Economic Performance*. New York: Cambridge University Press.

Oduho, Joseph. (1992) "Crisis in the SPLM/SPLA." Kampala, Uganda: The Vision Newspaper.

Ostrom, Elinor. (1989) "Microconstitutional Change in a Multiconstitutional Political System." *Nationality and Society* 1, No. 1 (July): 309-317.

———. (1990) *The Governing the Commons: The Evolution of Institutions for Collective Action*. New York: Cambridge University Press.

———. (1992) *Crafting Institutions for Self-Governing Irrigation Systems*. San Francisco: Institute for Contemporary Studies Press.

Ostrom, Elinor, and T. K. Ahn, eds. (2003) *Foundations of Social Capital*. Northampton, Massachusetts: Edward Elgar Publishing Ltd.

Ostrom, Vincent. (1987) *The Political Theory of a Compound Republic: Designing the American Experiment*. 2d rev. ed. San Francisco: Institute for Contemporary Studies Press.

———. (1988) "Crytoimperialism, Predatory States, and Self-Governance." In Vincent Ostrom, David Feeny, and Harmut Picht (eds.), *Rethinking Institutional Analysis and Development: Issues, Alternative and Choices*. San Francisco: Institute for Contemporary Studies Press.

———. (1991) *The Meaning of American Federalism: Constituting a Self-Governing Society*. San Francisco: Institute for Contemporary Studies Press.

———. (1992) *Constituting order: The Uses of Language, knowledge, and Artisanship to Inform Choice*. Bloomington, Indiana: Indiana University: Workshop in Political Theory and Policy Analysis.

———. (1997) *The Meaning of Democracy and the Vulnerability of Democracies: A Response to Tocqueville's Challenge*. Ann Arbor: The University of Michigan Press.

Ostrom, Vincent and McGinnis, Michael D. (1998) "Democratic Transformation : From the Struggle for Democracy to Self-Governance." Working Paper W98-7. Indiana University, Bloomington, Indiana: Workshop in Political Theory and Policy Analysis.

Packard, Randall M. (1981) *Chiefship and Cosmology: An Historical Study of Political Competition*. Bloomington, Indiana: Indiana University Press.

Peristiany, J.G. & Julian Pitt-Rivers, eds. (1992) *Honor and Grace in Anthropology*. Cambridge: Cambridge University Press.

Radcliffe-Brown, A. R. (1951) *African Systems of Kinship and Marriage*. London: Oxford University Press.

Robertson, Palmer O. (1980) *The Christ of the Covenants*. Phillipsburg, New Jersey: Presbyterian and Reformed Publishing Co.

Riak, G. Galou. (2002) "My Observation of the State of Children in Bieh State." A paper given by Dr. G. Galou Riak during an interview.

Riker, William H. (1964) *Federalism: Origin, Operation and Significance*. Boston: Little, Brown.

Rondnelli, Dennis A. (1981) "Administrative Decentralization and Economic Development: the Sudan Experiment with Devolution." *Journal of Modern African Studies*. 19/4: 595-624

Sadiq, Al-Mahdi. (2000) *Second Birth in Sudan: in the Cradle of Sustainable Human Rights.* Khartoum: Umma Party, n.p.

Sahlins, Marshall D. (1961) "The Segmentary Lineage: an Organization of Predatory Expansion." *American Anthropologist*, Vol. 80 (March): 53-70.

Sanderson, G.N. and L.M. Sanderson. (1981) *Education, Religion, and Politics in Southern Sudan 1899-1964.* London and Khartoum: Ithaca Press.

Santandrea, Stefano. (1968) *The Luo of the Bahr el Ghazal*: Bologna: Editrice Nigrizia.

Sawyer, Amos. (1992) *The Emergence of Autonocracy in Liberia:Tragedy and Challenge.* San Francisco,: Institute for Contemporary Studies Press.

Schilde, W. (1947) *Die Niloten und ihre Nachbarn.* Africa Handbuch Angewandten Volkerkunde. Herausg. H. A. Barnatzil. Bd 1-2 Innsbruck.

Schoeck, Helmut. (1969) *Envy: a theory of social behaviour*. London, Secker & Warburg.

Sen, Amartya. (1999) *Development as Freedom*. New York: Anchor Books.

Sevier, Candida E. (1975) "The Anglo-Egyptian Condominium in the Southern Sudan, 1918-1939." Ph.D. Thesis. Princeton: Near Eastern Studies, Princeton University.

Sidahmed, Abdel Salam. (1997) *Politics and Islam in Contemporary Sudan.* Richmond: Curzon Press.

Simmel, George. (1978) *Conflict and the Web of Group Affiliations.* Glencoe, Illinois: The Free Press.

Southall, Aidan. (1976) "Nuer and Dinka are People: Ecology, Ethnicity and Logical Possibility." *Man* (New Series), Vol. 11, No. 4 (December): 463-491.

Steinberg, Milton. (1947) *Basic Judaism.* New York and London: Harcourt Jovanovich (a Harvest/HBJ Book).

Tafla, Bairu. (1967) "The Establishment of the Ethiopian Church" in Tarikh, Vol. 2., No. 1. Nigeria: Historical Society of Nigeria.

Taha, Mahmoud Mohamed. (1987) *The Second Message of Islam.* English translation and introduction by Abdullahi Ahmed An-Na'im. Syracuse, New York: Syracuse University Press.

Tangye, H. Lincoln. (1910) *In the Torrid Sudan*. Boston: R. G. Badger.

Tierny, Brian. (1982) *Religion, Law and the Growth of the Constitutional Thought 1150-1650.* Cambridge: Cambridge University Press.

Tocqueville, Alexis de. ([1835, 1840] 1945) *Democracy in America.* In 2 vols., Phillips Bradley, ed. New York: Vintage Books.

———. ([1856] 1955) *The Old Régime and the French Revolution* (Stuart Gilbert, Trans.). New York: Doubleday.

Tothill, John D., ed. (1948) *Agriculture in the Sudan: Being a Handbook of Agriculture as Practised in the Anglo-Egyptian Sudan.* London: Oxford University Press.

UNPMD. (1940, 1946) *Upper Nile Province Monthly Diary* (UNPMD). University of Khartoum Library, Khartoum, Sudan.

Wai, Dunstan M. (1978) *The African-Arab Conflict in the Sudan.* New York: Africana Publishing Company.

Wantok, Amon Mon, et al. (1992) "For a Strong SPLA: What is To Be Done?" Nairobi, Kenya: by a Group of Former SPLA Political Detainees.

Warburg, Gabriel R. (1971) "Ulama, Popular Islam and Religious Policy in the Northern Sudan, 1899-1916", *Asian and African Studies*, Vol. 7: 89-119; also in Hebrew in G. Baer (ed.), *Ulama and Religious Problems in the Islamic World.* Jerusalem: Magness Press.

———. (1985) "Islam and State in Numayri's Sudan" In J.D.Y. Peel and C.C. Stewart (eds.), *Popular Islam South of the Sahara.* Manchester: University Press.

———. (2003) *Islam, Sectarianism and Politics in Sudan Since the Mahdiyya.* Madison, Wisconsin: The University of Wisconsin Press.

Waterhouse, E. S. (1943) "Seculaism." In J. Hastings (ed.), *Encylopedia of Religion and Ethics.* Vol. XI. Edinburgh and New York, 1934: 347-348.

Werner, Roland, William Anderson, and Andrew Wheeler. (2000) *Day of Devastation, Day of Contentment: The History of the Sudanese Church across 2000 Years.* Nairobi, Kenya: Paulines Publications Africa.

Wildavsky, Aaron. (1987) "Choosing Preferences by Constructing Institutions: a Cultural Theory of Preference Formation." *American Political Science Review*, Vol. 81, No. 1 (March): 3-21.

Wilson, Stephen. (1988) *Feuding, Conflict, and Banditry in Nineteenth-century Corsica.* New York: Cambridge University Press.

Winder, J. (1942) "Note on the Evolution of Policy in Regards to Chiefs, Sub-chiefs, and Headman," Nasir: Eastern Nuer District, File 1.

Winter, Roger P. (1990) "War and Famine in Sudan." Testimony before a Hearing of the U.S. House of Representatives Committee on Foreign

Affairs. U.S Committee for Refugees, Washington, DC: American for Nationalities Service (May 25).

Wunsch, James S. and Deli Olowu. (1990) *The Failure of the Centralized State: Institutions and Self-Governance in Africa.* First edition. Boulder, CO: Westview Press

Notes

Chapter 1

[1] Acephalous societies were seen as having no history of their own and as responding only to external problems. Such societies were considered primitive, backward, and needing to progress to statehood. Until recently, many scholars did not see an acephalous arrangement as another system of order. What people want or what a people think they want—that is, their desires, preferences, values, and ideals—were not subject to sensitive inquiry. Preferences in regard to political objects, however, are not external to a way of life. They constitute the quintessence of political life. They are the constitution and reconstitution of the way that people live their lives together (see Douglas, 1980; V. Ostrom, 1991; Wildavsky, 1987, 3-21).

[2] The word "chief" is used in this study as (and should be understood as) an agent of British colonial government and successive governments of the Sudan. Custodian(s) on the other hand, refer to traditional governance agents who are (or can be) called on by the Nuer to assume leadership when the need arises. Custodians are sometimes referred to as *kuar* such as *kuar muon*, *kuar ghok*, or *kuar tuac*.

[3] The British courts in Nuerland were established as a vehicle to carry out multiple functions for the British colonial government. Courts were the basis of the system of judicial and executive control in the Nuerland. The British colonial government relied upon the chiefs' court for the dispensing of justice among the Nuer. The chiefs' court was also an agent for the establishment of law and order, for carrying out all administrative and executive work, and for promotion of trade, education, agriculture, etc., in Nuerland (Howell, 1954, 2, 36-37, 66; Johnson, 1980).

[4] H. H. MacMichael (1929) quoted in Abdel Ghaffar M. Ahmad's "Some Remarks from the Third World on Anthropology and Colonialism: The Sudan." In Talal Asad (ed.) *Anthropology and Colonial Encounter*, London, 1973, 267.

[5] In his *Leviathan* ([1651] 1960, 56), Thomas Hobbes defines the power of a man in a society or in a commonwealth of persons as his present means to obtain some apparent future good. Man is perceived as restless in his search for power. This is the foundation of Hobbes's postulate about human behavior. Anxieties to gain power on the part of humans, who are continually striving to use the present means to obtain some future apparent good, implies, according to Vincent Ostrom (1992, 41), that human reflections and communication organized with reference to speech will yield knowledge. The capacity to understand one's experience, to articulate this understanding in communication with other human beings, and to act on the basis of that understanding produces not only knowledge, but also introduces the dimension of culture. According to V. Ostrom (1992, 39), Hobbes's definition is characteristic of all forms of artisanship and, coincidentally, to all forms of action (the use of present means to obtain some future apparent good). This principle applies as much to the mediations of *kuar muon* (the Nuer Custodians) as it does to practices of other Nuer key religious and political functionaries.

[6] I obtained this information in an interview with Rev. Kang Dung on September 12, 1989, in Kosti, Sudan (see Jackson, 1923, vol. 1, no. 1, p. 72; Diu Garadin, 1975; Johnson, 1980, 90). On the principle of segmentation, "in Evans-Pritchard's analysis, the entire (or rather, the entire male) social structure presents itself as a consistently executive tree diagram (dendrogram), whose humblest, smallest twigs are formed by the individual members, united at the nodes into groups of brothers, the latter in their turn united at higher-order nodes into groups of cousins, groups of cousins in their turn into even larger groups, into still larger groups, into yet larger groups... until finally, at least in theory, the dendrogram encompasses the entire society. The branches of the dendrogram make both for integration...and for opposition at the same time: for the nodes at the same level, although united in their turn by a higher-order node at the next level, are still in opposition vis-à-vis one another, and in fact this also applies to all groups and individuals tied to each other by the node immediately above them. For this type of structure anthropology has coined the term of 'segmentary system'." See Wim Van Binsbergen (1999) "Reconciliation: a major African technology of shared and recognised humanity (*ubuntu*)" http://www.shikanda.net/general/gen3/invoeg_15_mei_99/reconcil.htm (accessed 26 January 2005).

[7] A mediator draws on his special mediative skills and knowledge of traditional law. This gives him some power of expertise not enjoyed by all Nuer. The power to curse those who obstruct the processes of mediation is an added source of inequality in power reserved for the Custodians.

[8] Range of kinship is the structural distance between two persons within a kinship system. (For further reading on this subject, see Evans-Pritchard, 1940 and Radcliffe-Brown, 1951, 6-8.) Since the concept of range of kinship is so important for this study, a detailed description will be presented in chapter four.

[9] Herders covenant as to how to govern the common-pool resources before they place animals in the grazing fields. Elinor Ostrom (1990) observes that the temptation for rule breaking is always present, but persons who have agreed to use resources in common monitor each other to enforce their rules. This is possible in the close proximity of the cattle camp, because individuals repeatedly communicate and interact with one another in a physical setting. Camp members develop levels of trust on the basis of respect for the covenant. That level of trust influences the effects their actions will have on one another, on the sharing of the common pool resource, and the way they will organize themselves to gain benefits and avoid harm. In line with Elinor Ostrom's findings (1990, 183-84), when Nuer come seasonally to a cattle camp, the covenant becomes the binding rule governing their relationships.

Chapter 2

[10] Betthwell A. Ogot maintained that migrations of Nilotic (Luo) people to Kenya, Uganda, and the Lakes Region took place during the sixteenth century. They migrated from their cradle homeland into the Southern Sudan. This is suggesting to me that the occupation of Upper Nile Region had been earlier than 1500. The Luo are not to be confused with the Lou Nuer.

[11] Geographically, the Nilotic peoples are widely distributed, stretching, with gaps, from about Latitude 12 degrees North, to Latitude 4 degrees South. The Shilluk of the White Nile are the northernmost group. In the South are the Luo in Tanzania. See Betthwell A. Ogot 1967. Of course there are other Nilotic peoples further South than the Luo, such as the Zulu people.

[12] See Gowlett 1988; Ehret 1974; David 1982; and Johnson 1986.

[13] The terms "highland" and "intermediate land" are defined in greater detail in Wal Duany 1992.

[14] Chuol Cot Pear, who served as a Government of Sudan (GoS) official during the late colonial period and also during the independent Sudan taught some of us this song at American Missionary School at Wanglel. I am not sure whether he composed the song himself or if somebody else did. The song tells the world of the ecology of Southern Sudan, especially of the Nuerland. It praises God Almighty for the coming of the Christian Missionaries to the South, and perhaps recognizes the positive role played by the colonial government in stopping the Arab harassment and the Arab enslavement in some parts of South Sudan.

[15] This theory is elaborated by Evans-Pritchard 1940 in many of his writings on segmentary societies, especially the Nuer; also see Mary Douglas 1985: pp. 64-65.

[16] Some Bible translations, such as most of the English language Bibles and translations into some African languages, adopted the term "Ethiopia", where the original Hebrew has Kush. This word choice is unfortunate, because it creates the false impression that the country referred to is the one we now call Ethiopia. Modern Ethiopia traditionally was known as Abyssinia (in Arabic, *Al-Habash*). For further information about this confusion, see Roland Werner, William Anderson and Andrew Wheeler, chapter 1, p.23.

[17] The art of constructing pyramids is also found among the Nuer. See Douglas Johnson 1994:196.

[18] The Arabs who married into the Nubian royal family took advantage of the custom of the Nubians. To win the favor of the Arab intruders, the Nubian king offered his daughters in marriage to Arabs. The result was that the kingdom broke up, passed by inheritance to certain sons of the Arabs on their mother's account, according to the customs of the Nubians. Nubian custom establishes the succession of the sister or sister's son. In this way the Nubian kingdom broke down and the Arab took possession of it. The Arab considered the Nubian to be an "infidel."

[19] The source for writing this section is Wal Duany, "Customary Law and Ways of Life Among the Nuer of Southern Sudan" in Maryam Niamir-Fuller, ed., *Managing Mobility in African Rangelands*.

[20] In chapter seven of this book, I discuss autonomy and federation with other Nilotic peoples, and indicate in more detail how Nuer resolve their problems by using indigenous approaches.

[21] Such an analysis is briefly given in the section in this chapter on "Patterns of Village Life."

[22] For a modern example of how mediation in conflict resolution has been applied over the years between Dinka and Nuer, read "Wunlit Documents", New Sudan Council of Churches, Nairobi, Kenya. Wunlit Documents also may be found online. See: http://www.southsudanfriends.org/wunlit/index.html (accessed 26 January 2005).

Chapter 3

[23] A cosmological view refers to basic presumptions about a universal order.

[24] Most of the other Nilotic peoples have organized themselves quite differently than the Nuer. The Sudanese Nilotic peoples include: Anyuak, Bari, Dinka, Mandari, and Shilluk (see Raymond Kelly 1985, 157B225; Evans-Pritchard 1940, 111; Marshall D. Sahlins 1961, 322B24; Peter J. Newcomer 1972, 5B11; Maurice Glickman 1972, 585B87; Aidan Southall 1976, 463B91; Lienhardt 1958, 110B31; Douglas Johnson 1980, 53B120; Gabriel Giet Jal 1987, 13).

[25] Nuer do not believe that God causes anyone's death, but rather that He can be angry and allow angry spirits to cause harm. Father Crazzolara (1953) reported that the Nuer told him that if God kills a man or destroys property by lightning, He has only taken what was His, what was His right to take.

[26] The source of this information is an interview with Rev. Kang Dung on September 12, 1989, in Kosti, Sudan (see also Mary Douglas 1980, 107; Evans-Pritchard 1956, 18B20).

[27] Information obtained in an interview with Riel Gatluak on September 13, 1989, in Kosti, Sudan; and Riek Kerjok on September 27, 1989, in Khartoum (see Evans-Pritchard 1951, 49B65).

[28] There are a variety of family associations among the Nuer. Vicarious and leviratic families are the most important family groupings besides simple, lawful (nuclear) and compound families. A vicarious family is made up of a wife married to a man who died without a male heir and a husband closely related to the dead person and their children. A leviratic family is made up of a woman and her children and a brother of a dead man inheriting the wife of his brother to continue to bear children in his name. Leviratic marriage also prevents the breakdown of relationships between the two covenanting families. For more information on the variety of family associations, see Evans-Pritchard 1951, 49B65.

[29] The concept of *nguot*—a cutting process—relating to the establishment of covenantal commitment manifests itself throughout the ancient languages of the Middle East, North Africa, and most of Africa south of the Sahara. See Dennis J. McCarthy 1963, 53; Erich Isaac 1961, 447, "Circumcision as a Covenant Rite," suggests that the calling of heaven and earth as witnesses to the covenant in Deuteronomy 4:26 relates to the "cutting" of a covenant by means of allusion to the Babylonian creation myth, which involved the cleaving of a primeval being to form heaven and earth. The concept of covenant is used in two senses here. The first is covenanting between God and man. This covenant is characterized by fundamental inequality between God and man. God promises to give man protection from evil, and man to obey God. This is the theological meaning of covenant. See Exodus 2:24; 3:16, 17; 6:4B, 8; Psalm 105:8B, 12; Palmer O. Robertson 1980. The second use of the concept of covenant, as cutting an agreement between man and man, is perceived among the Nuer as marked by equal standing of these parties to the covenant. The terms and conditions of the covenant have to be understood clearly by the parties, and they are enforceable in human terms.

[30] *Yang ruali* is the cow sacrificed for purification of closely related persons who committed an incestuous act. The cow is usually cut in half, one part for each of the parties involved, and symbolizing shedding of blood if one should repeat the prohibited act.

[31] For a full presentation of evidence, see Dennis J. McCarthy 1963, 52; Evans-Pritchard 1956, 107B200; Genesis 15:18.

---

[32] Sharon Hutchinson has ably described the relationship between life and blood as the Nuer see it, and the political implications of that connection. See Hutchinson 1988, 184B93.

[33] Information was obtained in an interview with Rev. Kang Dung on September 12, 1989, in Kosti, Sudan (see Douglas Johnson 1980, 127B40).

[34] An interesting comparison is found with the Levites of the tribes of Israel. God appoints them as priests and judges of these tribes (Numbers 1:47B-54). They are not counted in the census of Numbers which is used for the tribal political divisions. God gives them no territory, but scatters them throughout all the tribes. While receiving no territory, they are allotted cities (Numbers 35:2B-8). Especially fascinating is Numbers 35:6, "The cities which you give to the Levites shall be the six cities of refuge where you shall permit the manslayer to flee."

[35] Among the Western Nuer, only a few lineages provided the various peoples with *kuar muon* (earth priests or earth custodians) and *wud ghok* (men of cattle or cattle custodians). The Gatleak originated from the Leek Nuer, and the Jimem originated from the Bul Nuer, who were the most likely sources of both (Douglas Johnson 1980, 100; Rev. Kang Dung 1989; Evans-Pritchard 1956, 292; Crazzolara 1953, 11B-12). Gatleak priests are now found among the Jikany and Lou Nuer. Jimem are also found among Lou.

[36] A captured foreign boy of non-Nuer descent, if adopted by his captors, counts as a son, and he cannot marry into his adoptive lineage. The reason has to do with the exchange of the bridewealth cattle. When the captured boy marries, his captors (adoptive family) will contribute cattle to the marriage payments for his wife. This contribution gives them a claim to some of the cattle that will come in when his (future) daughter eventually marries. It is impossible, therefore, for a family to arrange a marriage in which they are both contributing *and* claiming cattle. For a son to marry a girl at whose marriage his family is entitled to claim cattle—it would be an incestuous union. The rule by which they forgo sex gives related persons a claim to the bridewealth cattle due to kinfolk. This also applies when a girl is adopted. Her adoptive kin perform a religious rite and say, "she will become our daughter and will receive her bridewealth cattle." The cattle of her bridewealth give her kinship status, and with it the right to receive the cows due to the paternal aunt on the marriage of

her captor's sons. Marriage is forbidden between her descendants and the descendants of her captor's sons, by virtue of her bridewealth, for several generations.

[37] Gea and Ghaak are the principal ancestors of the Nuer. Most of the Nuer clans claim to be descended from these two ancestors. Not all Nuer clans can claim direct descent from Gea or Ghaak. Some stories of origin, while associated with Gea and Ghaak, clearly show an origin from outside the ancestral Nuer (Johnson 1980, 88). This is the case with the Jimem (a priestly lineage), the Jikul, the Jidiet, the Kakar, and the Gaawar of Gaawar clans. In each story, the ancestor is invited into a Nuer settlement and is incorporated through some ritual into the existing kin structure. See Douglas Johnson 1980, 88B89; Mary Douglas 1980, 80B81; Evans-Pritchard 1940, 1951; Magany Gai 1988; Thomas Maluit 1988.

[38] The Nuer contribute a negative example to the theory of the state. See Max Rheinstein 1967; T.M.S. Evens 1978, 100B16; Elman Service 1975; Aiden Southall 1976; Henri J.M. Classen and Peter Skalnik, eds. 1975; Rev. Kang Dung 1989.

[39] According to the Nuer, the original priests were Gea, Ghaak, and Kir who have been reported as the ancestors of all Nuer, except the incorporated Nuer. See Douglas Johnson 1980, 53B120; Gabriel Giet Jal 1987, 13; Riel Gatluak 1989; H.C. Jackson 1923, 69B74, "Legendary History," Khartoum: Central Record Office (CRO), Dakhlia (DAK) 112/15/99; Evans-Pritchard 1933, 125B26; Evans-Pritchard 1954, 139.

[40] The cosmological conception of "subduing" the earth to the glory of their Creator can be said to have led the Nuer to massive assimilation of their neighbors who do not acknowledge the same worldview. Raids and land appropriation can be considered to result from this conception.

[41] Vincent Ostrom's (1991, 199B244) treatment of cooperation, competition, conflict, and conflict resolution in his *The Meaning of American Federalism* clarifies ways of achieving coordination in a covenantal society.

Chapter 4

[42] Titles of functionaries are different for different regions, but mean the same thing. For example, *kuar muon* is known in some areas as *kuar tuac*, the leopard skin chief. *Wud ghok* (and not *wut ghok*) is called *kuar ghok. Guan thoi* is also called *kuar yier*,

kuar bieth or *kuar tuoi*. Jackson 1923, vol. 1, no. 1, p. 89 mentions that among some Nuer segments, the office of *kuar muon* and *kuar tuac* are different. One therefore must be careful in describing an office or position by using the title alone. There is confusion in titles. The function is one "office" described by different names in different sections of Nuer society.

[43] Nuer believe love is built by learning how to sit down and discuss problems and to accommodate individual differences. For further discussion of this aspect (Frank 1987; Radcliffe-Brown 1951; Evans-Pritchard 1951).

[44] The underlying purpose for this rule is discussed in the section devoted to giving name and its importance. For further discussion of this rule is found in Radcliffe-Brown 1951 and Evans-Pritchard 1951.

[45] In some parts of Nuerland a boy is attached to *luak* at the age of 6 or 7. This depends upon the availability of older boys in the household who could teach him about what boys are supposed to do.

[46] Many persons on the groom's side and kin on the bride's side attend the bridewealth negotiations. The following positions within each family are represented:
- Groom and Bride's Kin
- *Guan buthni* (master of ceremony)
- Father
- Brother by the same mother
- Brother by a different mother
- Father's elder brother by the same mother
- Father's brother by a different mother
- Father's younger brother by the same mother
- Father's sister
- Mother
- Mother's elder brother by the same mother
- Mother's brother by a different mother
- Mother's younger brother by the same mother
- Mother's sister
- Father's best friend
- Witnesses from both sides

(see Evans-Pritchard 1951, 76; Howell 1954, 92; Raymond Kelly 1985, 119; Gatluak, interview, 1989; Kok, interview, 1989).

[47] For the maintenance of kin relationships these cattle exchanges are made by the Nuer as long-term rights. They do not end by the death of the parents, but are inherited by their sons (see Kok, interview, 1989; Gatluak, interview, 1989; Howell 1954, 92; Evans-Pritchard 1951, 76; Kelly 1985).

[48] The distribution of bridewealth cattle may not be identical in all sections of all Nuer regions. There might be shifts here and there of an ox or calf or heifer, but the balance and proportions would be the same as recorded here (see also Lutlut Kok 1989; Raymond Kelly 1985; Evans-Pritchard 1951, 75-76).

[49] I obtained this information from an interview with Lutlut Kok on August 13, 1989; Riel Gatluak 1989 (See Evans-Pritchard 1951, 75-76).

[50] It is the children that create the kinship bond between two groups and that generate the ties of affection. The failure of a marriage will hurt them equally. Cattle will be returned to the husband by the bride's kin. The groom and kin who might have contributed cattle to the marriage may not get back all their cattle. Some cows would have died of natural causes and others may be hidden. The consequence is that the man may not be able to remarry for a long time. The divorced man's subsequent marriage will be regarded as second rate. If the divorced woman marries, the number of bridewealth cattle for that marriage will be reduced to half of the bridewealth cattle that otherwise would have been paid if she were still a girl.

[51] Ill treatment of a woman by her husband is considered as a legitimate reason for dissolving marital relationship among the Nuer. It is, however, difficult to prove that a woman has been ill-treated by not providing her food, clothing, or sexual services. Physical beating is often justified and can be argued as to who is in the right.

[52] I obtained this information from Wicjal Bum in September 1989 in Khartoum.

[53] The variations in the span of significant kinship has a lot to do with each lineage and internal management of relationships. As previous chapter indicates, *guan buthni* has the function of performing certain rituals that would permit intermarriage or cohabitation between individuals who were otherwise considered improper spouses. Reasons given that permit marriage usually have to do with the descent of one of the parties. For example, one of the parties may be of Dinka or Anyuak ancestry and that

can be overlooked for the purposes of marriage. The major source of this information is interviews with Nyang Rundial 1989 and Wicjal Bum 1989.

[54] The shrinking of the span of significant kinship in Eastern Jikany might be ascribed to the widespread influence of Christianity.

[55] Barren men marry, but his wife or wives bear children with one of his brothers or an outsider, and the children are considered to be his children. A barren woman remains with her parents and makes her house close to her parents. She cannot be married because she would not bear children to any man.

[56] Relationships of the first order are those of parents and child, husband and wife, brothers and sisters, and between older and younger children (Radcliffe-Brown 1951; Evans-Pritchard 1951). Relationships of the second order are those traced through one connecting person, such as those with father's father, mother's brother, stepmother (father's wife), sister's husband, brother's son, wife's father, etc. Those of the third order have two connecting links, such as mother's brother's son (*gat naru*), father's sister's husband (*cio wacdu*), and so on. It is possible to go to fourth, fifth, or nth order. In each order the number of relationships is greater than that in the preceding order. The strength of the relationship is indicated by the number of cattle given as bridewealth payments and the gifts that are given when needs arise. The network of relationships includes both *mar* (cognatic) relationships and relationships resulting from marriage (i.e., a person's own marriage and the marriages of his relatives). An important characteristic of a kinship system is the range over which these relationships are effectively recognized for social purposes of all kinds, including wealth distribution, group control of a common property, related segments combining forces against external aggression, bloodwealth payment, etc. The differences between wide-range and narrow-range arrangements are important for understanding different kinship systems (Radcliffe-Brown 1951). The Shilluk system of the present day, for example, is a narrow-range system. Although among the Shilluk a wider range of relationship, to second, third, or more distant cousins, is recognized, there is no obligation to distribute cattle or goats to these kin at the time of a marriage. The Nuer, by contrast, have a wide-ranging system. An individual may have several hundred recognized relatives by kinship and by marriage that he must treat as relatives.

[57] A process of openly adjusting genealogies so that history accords with the current distribution of authority has been described in J. A. Barnes 1967; L. Bohannon 1952:

Africa XXII, no. 4; I. G. Cunnison 1959; R. F. Murphy 1967: 167-70; Edward Evans-Pritchard 1951.

[58] I obtained this information from an interview with Lutlut Kok and Wicjal Bum on September 18 and 20, 1989, in Khartoum. Persons who have recorded similar information include Evans-Pritchard, 1951; Howell, 1954; Stephen Wilson, 1988, Douglas Johnson, 1988; Mary Douglas, 1980.

[59] I obtained this information from an interview with Lutlut Kok and Wicjal Bum on September 18, 20, 1989. This requirement of a large family is common among other Nilotic peoples (also confirmed in interviews with Ezekiel Kutjiok, 1989; and Magany Gai, 1988) and Mediterranean societies (see Stephen Wilson, 1988).

[88] A Nuer clan is here understood to mean a region of the Nuer people who live within a common territory such as Lou, Gaawar, Eastern Jikany or Jagei Nuer. A clan is segmented into lineages. Lineages are further segmented again and again until the smallest local community or village (see Evans-Pritchard 1940, 1951; Radcliffe-Brown, 1951).

[99] A lineage is not a residential unit. It is wealth distributing arrangement (see Mary Douglas, 1980; Evans-Pritchard, 1940, 1951).

[00] People who live in one village treat each other as kin although they may not be of common ancestry. A Nuer will treat as kin anybody who has some dealings with him.

[11] Those of us raised in Nuer society have learned from a young age that the paternal uncle is expected to contribute cattle in the marriage of his brother's sons. This custom was confirmed in an interview with Riel Gatluak in Kosti, Sudan and Lutlut Kok 1989 in Khartoum 1989 (see Evans-Pritchard 1951, 158).

[22] When a man dies, he leaves his brother to care for his sons and to see that they marry to maintain his lineage. This means the paternal uncle assumes the father role and the boys are expected to submit to him.

[33] There is an arrangement that the maternal uncles contribute toward the marriage of their sisters' sons according to the birth order of sons and that of the uncles. Elder maternal uncle (full or half maternal uncles) contribute cattle to the marriage of the

first born son of his sister. This is followed in the subsequent marriages. This rule may not be applicable in all cases, but deviation is usually resented (see Riel Gatluak September 13, 1989; Lutlut Kok 1989; Evans-Pritchard 1951; P. P. Howell 1951).

[44] This balancing of relationships is grounded upon the Nuer presumption of equality of relationships between parties to a marriage or family producing children. Paternal and maternal uncles are equally responsible in the success of their kin (see Evans-Pritchard 1951; Howell 1954).

[55] Elephant meat is not subject to the rules of division that apply to the distribution of meat of the sacrificial cow. In the case of elephant, individuals get what they can (see Howell 1945; Evans-Pritchard 1951).

[66] Among the Nuer, one of the key responsibilities of a young man is to learn the rights that guide the distribution of meat. Thus a boy raised in Nuer society to manhood is expected to know the way meat is distributed to kin and non-kin (see Evans-Pritchard 1951; Wicjal Bum September 1989; Riel Gatluak September 13, 1989; Lutlut Kok 1989).

[77] The covenantal tradition underlies the balancing of relationships between paternal and maternal kin. It is grounded upon Nuer religious conception that gives a person an equal standing with one another. The relationship between the lineage system, segmentary complementarity, and the total social structure is further elucidated in the discussion in Chapter Seven on "Problems of Security and Defense."

[88] I obtained this information from an interview with Wicjal Bum and Nyang Rundial on September 1989 in Khartoum.

[99] I obtained the information from interviews with Riel Gatluak on September 13, 1989 in Kosti, Sudan; Pal Riek on August 25, 1989 in Khartoum; Manaseh Abraham on September 15, 1989 in Khartoum.

[00] A person who has killed someone may not eat or drink until *ca bier* or his blood has been let out by earth custodian in a ceremony. The ritual is known as *bir*. A sharp knife or a fish-spear is taken and the arm of the killer scratched therewith until blood flows (Wicjal Bum 1989; Gatluak, interview, 1989; Howell 1954). The Nuer believe that the performance of this ceremony should neutralize the potential spiritual con-

tamination in the blood of the slayer when the blood of the slayer and that of the dead meet in the earth (Hutchinson 1988, 211-36).

[11] I obtained this information from interviews with Kor Can on August 26, 1989; Yoal Dok on September 26, 1989; Gai Majoak on September 2, 1989 (see Hutchinson 1988).

[22] The information was obtained from interviews with Thigin Banak on August 25, 1989; Wicjal Bum on September 2, 1989; Pal Riek on August 25, 1989 in Khartoum.

[33] Between the opening and closing of initiation, boys are initiated at the age of 16. A ceremony called *gar* is held every year by families with boys who were initiated in that year. Evans-Pritchard 1940; P.P. Howell 1948; Douglas Johnson 1980; Gabriel Giet Jal 1987: 383-385.

[44] Homicide, adultery, and incest which require intervention from an earth custodian will be discussed in more detail in chapter six of this study.

[55] I obtained this information from an interview with Thigin Banak on August 25, 1989; Thoan Teny on September 17, 1989 in Khartoum (see Mary Glendon 1989, 55-66).

[66] After birth of twins, kinsmen do not visit a home of another kinsman who has begotten twins without bringing something to sacrifice. Expiation (*kier*) is to remove the "impurities" that may bring death (*nueer*) to the twins.

Chapter 5

[60] *Mut* can also mean "spear."

[61] Nuer women play a crucial role in warfare. They help in carrying spare spears, food, the wounded, and water for the fighting men. Women also sacrifice animals to God, but a woman may not slaughter the sacrificial animal. This is understandable when we think of the spear as representing strength and masculinity. The one who slaughters the sacrificial animal among the Nuer does not reduce the importance of the offering. A woman also gives sacrificial invocation with her mouth and sometimes with the spear if she chooses to do so. The iron head of the spear is a

modern invention. Sacrificial invocation was done in the past with a spear made out of wood and bone, and which did not require a lot of strength to carry.

[62] I obtained this information from an interview with Wicjal Bum on September 13, 1989; Riel Gatluak on September 27, 1989 in Kosti, Sudan (see Evans-Pritchard 1956).

[63] The elders and other citizens maintain the calendar for closing and opening periods of initiation. It is not only the cattle custodians who keep the dates.

[64] The names of the age-sets are not included because they are irrelevant to understanding the Nuer age-set system. For lists of names of age-set see Evans-Pritchard (1940: 251); Gabriel Giet Jal (1987: 383). The order of age-set is ill-remembered. Informants do not remember the order in the same way. It is, however, important to note that the names of the age-sets are not the same in all Nuer regions. Adjacent regions, however, tend to have the same names.

[65] *Buth rem* is not necessarily a prophet or a priest. A person who has distinguished himself as a skilled warrior and has the ability to bind people can become a *buth rem*.

[66] *Kuoth* (God of heaven) and *Kuoth nhial* (air spirits) are both names for God. The spirits of the air are not thought of by the Nuer as independent gods, but rather as hypostases of the modes and attributes of a single God (Evans-Pritchard 1956: 49).

[67] Most Nuer lineages do not possess an actual spear, only spear-names. Two Nuer clans, however, have been identified in published work as possessing actual spears. The Gaatgankir who trace their origins to the Anyuak (Gabriel Giet Jal 1987) and also to the Dinka (Evans-Pritchard 1956: 241) possess a *mut wiu* to which a mysterious origin and power are attributed. The Gaatgankir believe that the spear was held by Kir, the ancestor of the clan, when he was cut out of the gourd in which he was found (see Douglas Johnson 1980; Gabriel Giet Jal 1987; Evans-Pritchard 1940). The spear is also associated with the air spirit *wiu*, who is regarded as being in some sense immanent in it. The Thiang Nuer are also said to have an actual *mut*, called the *mut baar Thiag*.

Chapter 6

[68] For further reading see Wilson, 1988; Peristiany and Pitt-Rivers, 1992: 1-7.

[69] Information is obtained from an interview with Rev. Maluit October 12, 1989 in Khartoum; also see Evans-Pritchard, 1956: 239.

[70] Uninitiated males dance in ordinary festivals, but they are excluded from dancing (*rau*) and displays with an ox.

[71] *Leng* are jokes made by cousins or closely related persons. *Leng* are sometimes abusive (see Evans-Pritchard 1951). The joking relationship in its reciprocal form can be regarded as a kind of friendliness expressed by a show of hostility. The mutual abusive behavior is hostility in other connections, but the joking relatives are required not to take offense but to respond in the same way (see Radcliffe-Brown, 1951, 57).

[72] Recorded from interview with Riel Gatluak on September 26, 1989 in Kosti, Sudan and from Thigin Banak on September 29, 1989 in Khartoum.

[73] This point has already been discussed in some detail in the section on courtship in chapter four of this study.

[74] Thabac Duany furnished this information in a personal communication in March 1983 in Juba, Sudan.

[75] Recorded from an interview with Riek Kerjok on October 12, 1989 in Khartoum.

[76] Divorcing a woman with two or more children was extremely difficult, if not impossible, in the 1930s among the Nuer. It was thought that the woman had met her procreative obligations and should not be divorced (Evans-Pritchard 1951, 91-92; Howell 1954, 145, 149; Hutchinson 1988, 301-02; Gatluak, interview, 1989; Kek, interview, 1989).

[77] This information is obtained from an Interview with Yoal Dok, former Governor of Upper Nile Region, September 15, 1989 in Khartoum.

[78] This information was obtained from an interview with Tap Lia Kon, on September 17, 1989 in Khartoum.

[79] Information obtained from Magany Gai, on October 21, 1988 in Atlanta, Georgia.

[80] Information obtained from Nyagony Kek on September 25, 1989 in Khartoum.

[81] Howell (1954, 218) observes that such compensation is never paid. Riel Gatluak maintained in an interview on September 26, 1989 in Kosti, Sudan that there is no strong retaliation from kin of *peth*.

[82] Malual Mayom 1975 (originally cited by Douglas Johnson 1980, 600). He maintains that Nuar Mer was a Thoi Dinka, which confirms Struve's (1908, 8) observation.

[83] Coriat claims that the contacts occurred during the life time of Teng Kerpel. This is not important because others such as Mer Teng might have been involved as an intermediary in the establishment of friendly relationships. The merchant camp was established in around 1865 (see Johnson 1980, 601, endnote 81).

[84] This was first cited by Johnson 1980, 210.

[85] Originally cited by Johnson 1980, 210.

[86] See Mather and Yngveson (1981, 780).

[87] This information was obtained from an interview with Wicjal Bum, September 1989, in Khartoum.

[88] The consequence of permitting this divorce was the rapid rise in the frequency of divorce (Hutchinson 1988, 349).

[89] I obtained this information in an interview with Wicjal Bum, September 17, 1989, in Khartoum.

[90] Originally cited by Evans-Pritchard (1956).

[91] Information from an interview with Wicjal Bum, in September 1989 in Khartoum.

[92] The average human population of a Nuer cattle camp varies from one camp to another. It is affected by the amount of available grazing land, the type of water

sources available, the availability of fish, and how far it is from the permanent villages. The range is from 300-10,000 persons.

[93] Recorded from an interview with Wicjal Bum in September 17, 1989, in Khartoum. Similar information is found in Evans-Pritchard (1940, 189).

[94] Nuer perform no regular and obligatory rite to bring rain, to ensure the fertility of the soil, to mark the onset or the end of the cultivation season, or to ensure the success of hunting or fishing. If in certain circumstances a ritual is performed, such as before large-scale fishing effort, it is rarely regarded as necessary or important. A lack of interest in crop production and hunting may explain the absence of obligatory rituals. Nuer take the physical conditions of their land as given. They believe they can do very little to affect change in the nature of endowment. They must fit their organizations and activities to the situation as it is (see Barbour 1961; Evans-Pritchard 1956, 200; Tothill 1948).

Chapter 7

[95] The British Colonial Authority viewed the office of "chief" as having traditional basis in the indigenous society. Within the limited period of their rule during the twentieth century, the British decided there was a certain justification for believing in the ritual basis of the chief. Yet even within this context there was a wide gap between the British ideas and expectations about the nature of chieftaincy and the Nuer political perspectives. The British saw the chief as the local administrator who would assist them in implementing social, economic, and political policies. The chief would oversee the collection of taxes, assist in the procurement of agricultural produce, and help in the recruitment of labor. All these functions were largely alien to the Nuer conception of a leader's role. Among the Nuer, a "chief" was first and foremost a ritual figure and had no executive powers. Thus, in place of the term "chief", I use the term "ritual chief" or" custodian". The failure of the British to perceive the ritual character of the Nuer chieftaincy may have been based upon the prior assumptions about the political nature of traditional African leadership.

[96] The response to the introduction of terms of prison is similar in a number of acephalous societies in sub-Saharan Africa. F.K. Ekechi (1989) observed that prison was the most hated colonial innovation in Iboland (Nigeria). See also John Wuol Makec (1988) for further reaction to confinement to county jailhouse in Dinkaland.

[97] In his *Dispute and Conflict Resolution in Plymouth Colony, Massachusetts 1725-1825,* W. Nelson observes that Plymouth's most litigious individuals during the 1725-1774 period tended to be people who were poorly socialized. Robert C. Ellickson (1986: 623-687) has also noted that socially marginal people were disproportionately represented in civil and criminal litigation. In Sudan, in the days of the operation of the British court system, resort to litigation was usually viewed as an irreparable breach of a relationship. Litigation tended to be relied upon by persons who were not closely related by blood or marriage.

[98] The problem of corruption of the chiefs, according to Wicjal Bum (1989), was a widespread phenomenon in the world of the Nilotic people. It was widespread among the Dinka and the Mandari as well. It was also a problem in Nigeria among the Ibo, according to Ekechi (1989).

[99] If the chiefs had been able to render balanced judgments, then the need for appeal would have been reduced. Taking into account the fact that the appeals were numerous, it is reasonable to infer that the purpose of insisting that the chiefs render more acceptable judgments was to lighten the load on the appeal officers.

[100] I obtained this information from an interview with Wicjal Bum (September 27, 1989), and Thigin Banak in Khartoum (September 29, 1989). For further reading, see F. K. Ekechi (1989); J. Makec (1988).

[101] Correspondence from the Governor of Bahr el Ghazal Province to the Civil Secretary, March 21, 1927, Civ. Sec. 1/10/34 (see also Robert Collins 1968: 168).

[102] See K.N Barbour (1961): Nzara Textile Scheme at Yambio. See also Douglas Johnson (1994), p.28: The Renk grain growing scheme of Upper Nile was developed by northern merchants, although the Closed District Ordinance of the 1920s was introduced to facilitate the final abolition of the internal slave trade and to halt the spread of Islam into non-Islamic districts. The ordinance did not apply to Renk District in Upper Nile, which was further north. This exception was to protect the interest of northern merchants.

[103] During the first thirty years of the condominium period, various merchants benefited from the increased prospects for trade throughout the country. Religious leaders and tribal notables in the northern Sudan benefited from an administrative system which allowed them to accumulate rights to labor and land, and which, by the

granting of government contracts, gave them a stake in the new political economy of the country. The Mahdi's posthumous son, Sayed Abd al Rahman al Mahdi, for instance, gained considerable wealth through government contracts for wood, fuel, and meat; he became staunch supporter of Britain as a result. The same pattern did not happen in the South where commerce continued to be in the hands of Greek, Syrians, Armenian, and northern merchants (See Douglas Johnson, 2003, p. 17).

[104] The civil war since 1955 has not enabled the Southern Sudan to develop humanitarian services such as medical services (e.g., hospitals have been destroyed, famine and disease have taken toll on the population, and child mortality rates are extremely high). War casualties have taken nearly two million lives. War-related consequences have been the main cause of the population decline of the country as a whole.

[105] Personal interviews including Wicjal Bum (1989) in Khartoum. Wicjal, now an old man, was an administrator in the Sudan for a very long time. I also interviewed Chief Luak Kok in the same year.

[106] The main sources for writing this section are Sharon Hutchison's Nuer Dilemmas, Coping with Money, War, and the State University of California Press and Douglas Johnson's Nuer Prophets. Oxford 1994.

[107] See Sharon Hutchinson (1988: 65-72). Also, letter from Pawson, Governor of the Upper Nile, to Civil Secretary October 27, 1933 (Civ. Sec. 30/2/3, p. 5). This experiment was originally proposed by Sherratt, Assistant District Commissioner of the Zeraf Nuer (see J. Winder, "Note on the Evolution of Policy in Regard to Chiefs, Sub-chiefs and Headmen," 1942; Nasir, Eastern Nuer District Files, File 1.).

[108] The ratio of female to male cattle collected by the government in cases of homicide was about seven to three (Appendix, UNPMD, November 1940).

[109] I was able to write this section on Constitution Making with the great help of the materials and sources made available from Gabriel Warburg: *Islam, Sectarianism and Politics in the Sudan since the Mahdiyya,* 2003.

[110] The formation of the parties was charged with religious and nationalist polarization. The name of the Umma or Ansar Party is "electric" in the Islamic context. *Umma* is an Arabic word denoting a concept of Muslim unity (as in people who are part of a divine plan), and *Ansar* denoting followers of the Mahdi's

Messianic vision of an Islamic state. The Mahdiyya, who in the 1880s drove Egypt out of Sudan, favored a Sudan independent of Egyptian and British ties. The National Unionist Party (now the Democratic Unionist Party) is more broadly based than Ansar, but, because it is more characterized by factions than is Ansar, it is less effective politically. The Khatmiyya have a long history of friendship with Egypt. For summaries of Sudanese political parties, see http://countrystudies.us/sudan/.

[111] This section benefited from Vincent Ostrom's *Cyptoimperialism, Predatory State, and Self-governance* (p. 166-178) and *Polycentric Governance and Development*, edited by Michael D. McGinnis.

[112] In August 1955, a battalion of Southern soldiers mutinied in Torit (Equatoria Province), thereby igniting the first civil war. The Torit Mutiny occurred five months before independence was attained on January 1, 1956. For more details on the Torit Mutiny, see Severino Fuli's *Shaping a Free Southern Sudan.* (Kolbe Press, Lumuru, Kenya, 2002: pp. 187-195) and also Douglas Johnson (pp. 21, 28, 108-9).

[113] See *Al Sahafa*, November 1, 1983.

[114] The author was a member of the National Assembly at the time, and participated in the debate of the 1973 constitution.

[115] For more detail on the amendments to the 1973 Permanent Constitution, see Mansour Khalid (1985).

[116] Peter Nyot Kok is quoted from Gabriel Warburg, *Islam, Sectarianism and Politics in Sudan since Mahdiyya* (2002: 150).

[117] Accusations were also leveled against other politicians for corrupting the army. For example, in *Thawat al-Inqath al-watani* (pp. 31-4), it was stated that Sadiq al Mahdi's son graduated from the Jordanian military college by "special arrangement."

[118] The main sources for writing this section is from Na'Im, *Islamic Constitution*, 2002; Gabriel Warburg, *Islam, Sectarianism and Politics in the Sudan since the Mahdiyya*, 2003; Kok, Peter Nyot, *Governance and Conflict in the Sudan*; Affendi, *Turabi's Revolution*.

[119] Gerald Chaliand. *The Struggle for Africa*. London. 1982. pp. 54-55. The author goes on to say that; "In the Ivory Coast for example, whereas the number of Francophone students was 700,000 in 1976-77, the number of students in Koranic

schools, where teaching is in Arabic, was nearly 100,000" (ibid.). In my own experience in the Southern Sudan during the early 1980s, various agencies based in Saudi Arabia and the Arab Gulf paid Southern Sudanese parents to send their children to Arabic language schools.

[120] Vincent Ostrom (1987: 25) observes that Federalism can be conceptualized as "constitutional choice reiterated." This is similar to acephalous conditions of governance among the Nuer. Such conditions are constituted and reconstituted according to choices of individuals involved and modifications dictated by the environmental changes.

Chapter 8

[121] The Northernization of teaching positions held by British women in the South was delayed due to the shortage of women teaching staff in the North and the restrictions of Islam on women to move freely.

[122] This attitude is a confirmation of Dr. Turabi's and Sadiq Al Mahdi's position that there is a cultural vacuum among the Black Africans that needs to be filled by Islam. They blame the acceptance of Christianity and rejection of Islam by the Nuer on foreign missionaries. They do not recognize that the tutelage of Islam is incompatible with the traditional Nuer way of life (see Sanderson and Sanderson 1981).

[123] I obtained this information in an interview with Rev. Kang Dung on September 12, 1989, in Kosti, Sudan.

[124] The Madi are a people and language group of Southern Sudan, Equatoria Province, Madi Subdistrict, Opari District, West Nile District. *Alternate names:* MA'ADI, MA'DITI, MA'DI. *Dialects:* PANDIKERI, LOKAI, 'BURULO. *Classification:* Nilo-Saharan, Central Sudanic, East, Moru-Madi, Southern. See: http://www.ethnologue.com/show_country.asp?name=Sudan (accessed 26 January 2005).

[125] See Severino Fuli (2002) and also Douglas Johnson (2003) for further reading.

[126] The author was the Secretary of Finance of SANU at the time, and has first-hand information.

[127] "Since 1961, inflow to the Sudd has increased substantially, presumably due to increased rainfall in the headwaters around Lake Victoria. The inflow was 26,831 billion m³/year of water prior to 1960, but from 1960-1980, it averaged 50,324 billion m³/year (Hughes and Hughes 1992). The wetland area consequently increased dramatically until 1980, but the trends in recent years are not known." See: Hughes, R. H. and J.S. Hughes. (1992). A directory of African wetlands. IUCN, Gland, Switzerland and Cambridge, UK. See http://www.worldwildlife.org/wildworld/

profiles/terrestrial/at/at0905_full.html (accessed 18 February, 2005).

[128] As dissatisfaction increased among ex-*Anya-nya* troops, mutinies at this time were not uncommon. Ex-*Anya-nya* were finding a haven in Ethiopia and organizing into *Anya-nya II*. The mutiny at Bor in May 1983 is key because it led to the founding of the Sudan Peoples' Liberation Army (SPLA) by Colonel John Garang, Maj. Kerubino Kwanyin Bol, Lt. Colonel Samuel Gai (Nath) Tut, and others. For a summary of these events, see the section "Resumption of Civil War" on the Human Rights Watch website http://www.hrw.org/reports/2003/sudan1103/10.htm (accessed 26 January 2005).

[129] See *Civilian Devastation: Abuses By All Parties in the War in Southern Sudan,* (Human Rights Watch/Africa 1994).

[130] See *Children of Sudan: Slaves, Street Children, and Child Soldiers* (Human Rights Watch/Africa 1995) and *Civilian Devastation: Abuses By All Parties in the War in Southern Sudan* (Human Rights Watch/Africa 1994).

[131] Baggara Arab militias called *murahallin* were formed by the Baggara federation or by cattle-keeping nomads in northern Sudan near the border of Bahr el Ghazal, Southern Region.

[132] Movement inside the South was difficult, and the civilian population in garrison towns such as Torit, Kapoeta, and Juba were virtual hostages. GoS imposed restrictions on movement within the country, and on travel outside the Sudan. It was government policy and practice to prevent civilians from fleeing to other African countries. The Government of Sudan feared that the potential for a large refugee population in neighboring countries would provide a reservoir for recruitment of armed insurgents. This was how *Anya-nya* began. Also, the GoS wanted to conceal from the world what it called then and today "an internal matter."

[133] The rule of terror in the Southern liberation movement has been partly documented and partly learned from insights gained in one-on-one interviews. The resources to confirm these statements include (but are not limited to) the works of Dhol Aleu, Oduho, Wantok, and other former political detainees; Amnesty International report July, 1993; and reports by the U.S. Committee on Refugees. I interviewed, on numerous occasions, leaders and officials of each of the liberation movement factions.

[134] The model of infallible, absolute control by an enlightened elite in pursuit of utopia on earth is ironically similar to that employed by the *ulama* of the National Islamic Front described in chapter seven.

Chapter 9

[135] This section benefited from the chapter, "Customary Law and Ways of Life in Transition among the Nuer", in Maryam Niamir-Fuller's (editor), *Managing Mobility in African Rangelands: The Legitimization of Transhumance.*

[136] I share the observation of Elizabeth Colson (1974), who views clanship not as an entity in itself, but as a principle of organization which is utilized in different fashions according the nature of the other institutions existing within the social field. Among the Nuer, then, a clan is a policy decision. Under some circumstances clans become corporate groups making alliances with one another. Under other circumstances, they are categories used as recruiting devices. A clan can be perceived as a state or a province within Nuer federal arrangements.

[137] Fan-gak, traditionally known as Pan-gak (a contested area) suggesting that this area was originally inhabited by Dinka and occupied later by the present occupants. During the colonial rule, the name Pan-gak became Fan-gak. The reason for changing the name was for convenience of the then rulers. All historical documents about the administration of the Central Nuer Region or District are under the name of Fan-gak. I suggest scholars should continue to use Fan-gak, otherwise, if researchers look for Pan-gak, they will easily miss some valuable archival data. The Nuer as a people have a common union based on covenantal principles. Each clan (clans may be referred to as states or provinces) has its own general system of governance within this union or commonwealth of all clans. Within each clan, or between the commonwealth and the clan administration, there are numerous local governments or autonomous units of limited jurisdiction such as neighborhoods (*pek dhoar*), village,

and cattle camp associations. Thus, the Nuer traditional society was a league of confederated clans (some call them "tribes") formed into the Nuer Commonwealth as an association of associations. During the 1940s, the British government in the Sudan used the Nuer Commonwealth as an instrument for their indirect rule. The appointed chiefs of the Nuer were brought together to participate in a governance of self-administration. The chiefs and other leaders of the Nuer codified the customary law and began a cycle of conferences to review and modify the customary law every five years at Fan-gak in the Central Nuer Region of what is now known as Pow State. These Fan-gak Conferences helped maintain the fabric of Nuer culture, provided correctives to the law, and were a stimulus to addressing new challenges to the culture. The Fan-gak Conference of 1963 was held, but the following one was ten years later. No Fan-gak Conference has been held since 1973.

[138] In March 1999, Dinka and Nuer chiefs, civil community leaders, elders, women, and youth met for a peace and reconciliation in Wunlit, Bahr el Ghazal, Sudan under the auspices of the New Sudan Council of Churches (NSCC). The Conference was initiated with the traditional sacrifice of a white bull, and the Covenant sealed with another traditional sacrifice. Christian worship was accompanied by an oath to the Deity to "see" or "watch over" the behavior of the ones who have sworn and to punish any violation of the Covenant by bringing into action the curses implied in the swearing of the oath. See NSCC: Wunlit Dinka-Nuer Peace Documents, Nairobi, Kenya.

[139] The Koran suggests that the varieties in humankind is one of the riches in God's world. The guiding verse is Chapter 49 Al Hujraat, verse 13 (Yusufali translation): "O mankind! We created you from a single (pair) of a male and a female, and made you into nations and tribes, that ye may know each other (not that ye may despise (each other). Verily the most honoured of you in the sight of Allah is (he who is) the most righteous of you. And Allah has full knowledge and is well acquainted (with all things)."

[140] "Islamic jurists saw jihad in the context of conflict in a world divided between the *Dar al-Islam* (territory under Islamic control) and the *Dar al-harb* (territory of war, which consisted of all lands not under Muslim rule). The inhabitants of the territory of war are divided between 'People of the Book' (mainly Jews and Christians) and polytheists. This requirement to continue jihad until all of the world is included in the territory of Islam does not imply that Muslims must wage nonstop warfare, however. Although there was no mechanism for recognizing a non-Muslim

government as legitimate, jurists allowed for the negotiation of truces and peace treaties of limited duration. Additionally, extending the territory of Islam does not mean the annihilation of all non-Muslims, nor even their necessary conversion: jihad cannot imply conversion by force, since the Qur'an (2:256) states that 'There is no compulsion in religion.' More than a religious aim, jihad really had a political one: the drive to establish a single, unified Muslim realm justified Islam's supercession of other faiths and allowed for the creation of a just political and social order." From *Parameters*, Spring 2003, pp. 82-94.

See: http://carlisle-www.army.mil/usawc/Parameters/03spring/knapp.htm (accessed 26 January 2005).

[141] The Koran was rendered into the form of Arabic expression so that human beings might understand from God (Taha 1987). God says in this respect: "We have rendered it into Arabic so that you may understand" (Koran 43:3). This verse and similar verses, according to Mahmoud Mohamed Taha, have misled many Muslim scholars into believing that the Koran itself is Arabic, in the sense that its meanings may be exhaustively understood only through the Arabic language. This is not so, as Taha points out in his discussion of Koranic chapters in *The Second Message of Islam* (1987).

[142] A belief in the equality of the sexes has been recognized by many religious faiths. It also is a tenet of the Nuer belief. See Chapter Four of this book, and Julia Duany (1996:19-39). In addition, social scientists and economists recognize that there is a relationship between human freedom and well-being. Women must be free to cater for their own welfare and development. Any well-being of women, observes economist Amartya Sen (1999:191-194), must draw on the agency of women themselves in bringing about such change that will rectify the inequalities that blight the well-being of women and subject them to unequal treatment. Understanding the agency role of women is thus central to recognizing all human beings as responsible persons: not only are we well or ill, but also we act or refuse to act, and choose to act one way rather than another. Thus both women and men must take responsibility for either doing things or not doing them. It is important to acknowledge the principle of the equality of the sexes, since the social repression of women is corollary to poverty, illiteracy, disease, and tyranny in the larger society.

[143] The new found faith through the prophets of the Meroitic people worshipping the God of Abraham, Isaac, and Jacob seems to have historical connections with the

Nuer religion. The Nuer believed in One True God. Nuer believed in the covenant with the God of Heaven.